THE BERLIN WALL

THE BERLIN WALL

13 AUGUST 1961–9 NOVEMBER 1989

Frederick Taylor

BLOOMSBURY

First published in Great Britain 2006

Copyright © Frederick Taylor 2006

Maps by John Gilkes

Die Jahre der Kommune I. Berlin 1967–1969 by Ulrich Enzensberger © 2004 by Verlag Kiepenheuer & Witsch, Köln

Excerpt from *Deutschland, Deutschland: Kurze Geschichte einer geteilten Nation* © Claus Christian Malzahn

Excerpt from *Driving the Soviets up the Wall* by Hope M. Harrison reprinted by permission of Princeton University Press

Bloomsbury Publishing Plc
36 Soho Square
London W1D 3QY

www.bloomsbury.com

Bloomsbury Publishing, London, New York and Berlin

A CIP catalogue record for this book is available from the British Library

Hardback ISBN 0747580154
Hardback ISBN-13 9780747580157

10 9 8 7 6 5 4 3 2 1

Trade Paperback ISBN 074758446X
Trade Paperback ISBN-13 9780747584469

10 9 8 7 6 5 4 3 2 1

Typeset by Hewer Text UK Ltd, Edinburgh
Printed in Great Britain by Clays Ltd, St Ives plc

The paper this book is printed on is certified by the © 1996 Forest Stewardship Council A.C. (FSC). It is ancient-forest friendly. The printer holds FSC chain of custody SGS-COC-2061

For my father
Thomas George Arthur Taylor, 1909–61

Through deceit, bribery, and blackmail, West German government bodies and military interests induce certain unstable elements in the German Democratic Republic to leave for West Germany . . . the Warsaw Pact member states must take necessary steps to guarantee their security and, primarily, the security of the GDR.

– Declaration of the Warsaw Pact, issued 1.11 a.m.,
Sunday 13 August 1961 as the first barbed
wire was being dragged into place along
the border between East and West Berlin

All autumn, the chafe and jar
of nuclear war;
we have talked our extinction to death.

Robert Lowell, 'Fall 1961'

The frequent result, said Austerlitz, of resorting to measures of fortification marked in general by a tendency towards paranoid elaboration was that you drew attention to your weakest point.

W.G. Sebald, *Austerlitz*

So . . . they built the Wall to stop people leaving, and now they're tearing it down to stop people leaving. There's logic for you.

– Unnamed drinker in East Berlin bar, just after
the fall of the Berlin Wall, November 1989

CONTENTS

CEMENT

MONEY

ACKNOWLEDGEMENTS

NO WRITER, AND ESPECIALLY no writer of history, can ever say that he or she takes full credit for the book that bears their name. The co-operation and help of many individuals and institutions in Britain, America and Germany was vital to the researching and writing of this book.

At the Bundesarchiv (Section SAPMO-DDR) in Berlin-Lichterfelde, all the staff were helpful beyond the call of duty, but I am especially grateful to Frau Beate Friedrich and Frau Petra Rauschenbach for their help with essential orientation in this huge collection, which was still in the process of re-organisation during my visit in the winter of 2004.

In the United States, the staff of the National Archives and Records Administration in College Park, Maryland enabled me to use my time there to the full. My special thanks to Wilbert Mahoney, to Marvin F. Russell, and finally to Steven Tiley, Chief of Special Access/FOIA, who provided crucial aid with accessing documents not yet fully declassified. It would in any case be hard to hate an institution set in a location of such astounding natural beauty – and where, moreover, lobster is routinely served for lunch in the cafeteria – but at the John. F. Kennedy Presidential Library in Boston, Ms Sharon Ann Kelly tirelessly and unflappably fielded all my requests and helped make my visit there even more delightful.

Lastly, staff everywhere proved friendly and helpful, and this was no less so at the National Archives of the United Kingdom (formerly the Public Record Office) at Kew, but in this case I would like to add an extra word of praise. Nowhere else have I seen so many ordinary citizens, as well as specialist researchers, making use of an archive's facilities with such naturalness and easy self-confidence. This is directly due to Kew's efficiency, unstuffiness and user-friendliness, which makes the National

Archives a truly public institution – and one we British can really be proud of.

Those who gave me the benefit of their memories of the Berlin Wall and the Cold War crisis surrounding it in face-to-face interviews are mentioned elsewhere, but I say my hearty thanks to them here. I should also like to give special acknowledgement to Götz and Regine Bergander, and to Joachim and Iwonna Trenkner, for their recollections and their hospitality during my stays in Berlin.

For help, advice, and calm but tireless facilitation of deadline-defying tasks, I am deeply grateful to Bill Swainson, my editor at Bloomsbury Publishing in London, and for continuing support to Tim Duggan, who took over the book at HarperCollins in New York when Dan Conaway moved on to even greater glory. And many thanks to Bill's assistant, Sarah Marcus, whose energetic and creative approach to the nuts and bolts of permissions, picture selection, and generally getting the manuscript to press lifted great weights from my shoulders. My agents, Jane Turnbull in London and Emma Parry in New York, proved themselves yet again to be this writer's best friends.

This book is dedicated to my father, for reasons which will become clear, but as ever was completed largely due to the astonishing patience and consideration that my wife, Alice Kavounas Taylor, unaccountably continues to show in the face of my writer's mood swings and long hours at the workface.

Frederick Taylor

Saint Keverne, Cornwall

3 July 2006

LIST OF ILLUSTRATIONS
AND PICTURE CREDITS

Victor and vanquished – Berlin, August 1945 (© *Hulton-Deutsch Collection/COR*)

The Blockade – coming in to land at Tempelhof, 1948 (*ullstein bild*)

Stones against tanks, 17 June 1953 (*ullstein bild*)

The Kurfürstendamm, West Berlin, 1960 (*ullstein bild*)

'No one intends to build a wall,' Walter Ulbricht, 15 June 1961 (*ullstein - dpa*)

Exhausted refugees, Marienfelde reception camp, July 1961 (*Landesarchiv Berlin/Schültz, Gert*)

The first hours – border troops on the Potsdamer Platz, 13 August 1961 (*ullstein - Alex Waidmann*)

Building the Wall, August 1961

East German Workers' Militiamen, 14 August 1961 (*ullstein - AKG Pressebild*)

Families divided, August 1961 (© *Bettmann/Corbis*)

Families Flee, Bernauer Strasse, August 1961 (*ullstein - AKG Pressebild*)

Conrad Schumann jumps the wire, 15 August 1961 (*ullstein - Leibing*)

A 77-year-old East Berliner caught in a tug of war between *Vopos* at the window and West Berliners below, Bernauer Strasse, 24 September 1961 (*ullstein - Alex Waidmann*)

General Clay (*left*), Vice-President Johnson (*centre*), and Mayor Brandt (*right*), 20 August 1961 (*ullstein - Jacoby*)

Berliners welcome US reinforcements, 20 August 1961 (*ullstein - Berlin-Bild*)

Götz Bergander, at the Reichstag, 1960

Bergander's fiancée, Regine, West Berlin, 1960

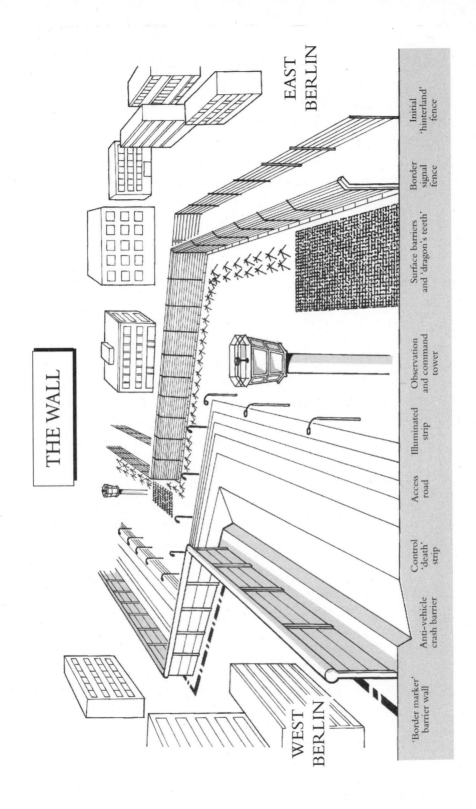

THE WALL

WEST BERLIN

EAST BERLIN

'Border marker' barrier wall

Anti-vehicle crash barrier

Control 'death' strip

Access road

Illuminated strip

Observation and command tower

Surface barriers and 'dragon's teeth'

Border signal fence

Initial 'hinterland' fence

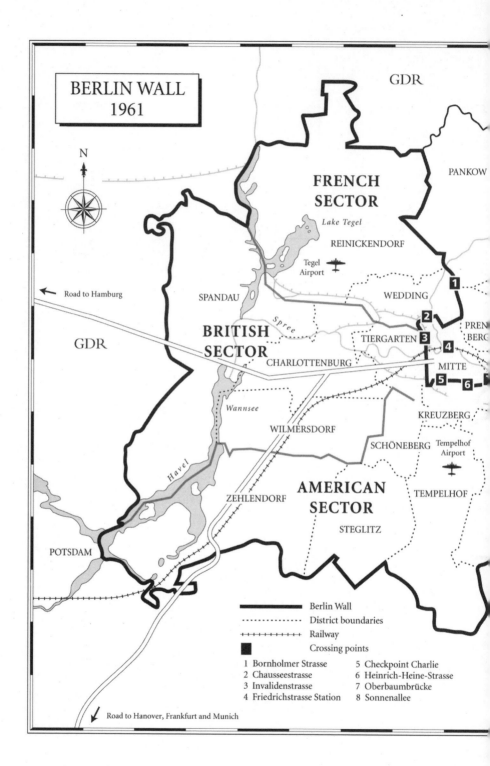

BERLIN WALL
1961

N

GDR

PANKOW

FRENCH
SECTOR

Lake Tegel

REINICKENDORF

Tegel
Airport

WEDDING

1

Road to Hamburg

SPANDAU

2

Spree

PREN
BERG

BRITISH
SECTOR

TIERGARTEN 3

GDR

4

CHARLOTTENBURG

MITTE

5   6

Wannsee

KREUZBERG

WILMERSDORF

SCHÖNEBERG   Tempelhof
Airport

Havel

ZEHLENDORF

AMERICAN
SECTOR

TEMPELHOF

POTSDAM

STEGLITZ

———————   Berlin Wall
·············   District boundaries
+++++++++++   Railway
▪   Crossing points

1 Bornholmer Strasse   5 Checkpoint Charlie
2 Chausseestrasse   6 Heinrich-Heine-Strasse
3 Invalidenstrasse   7 Oberbaumbrücke
4 Friedrichstrasse Station   8 Sonnenallee

Road to Hanover, Frankfurt and Munich

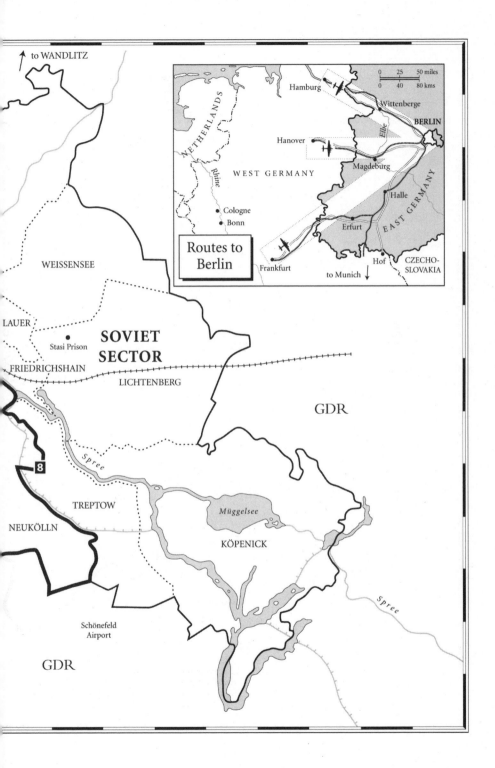

FOREWORD

WELCOME TO THE WALL

IT WAS A WEEKEND in August 1961. I had passed through a happy childhood and reached the age of thirteen, the threshold of adolescence, without too much untoward incident. Now, though, there was a cloud on our family horizon. My father was not well, really not well. Smoking, his only vice as far as I knew, had already cost him one of his lungs. He had seemed to recover after the operation eighteen months previously, but that summer he seemed weak and tired again, and often took to his bed. I used to go up and talk to him, keep him company. This is why I recall it was a weekend, because we had discussed an article in the Sunday newspaper. Important, somewhat ominous things were going on in the world.

Dad had a serious heart attack that same evening. Our neighbour, who was a nurse, hurried round and I glimpsed her through the half-open bedroom door, pushing at his chest to keep him going. Then we were gently persuaded to go downstairs. The doctor came. To keep us occupied, someone switched on the television. Flickering black-and-white pictures of a cityscape, with angry people and people with guns, and barbed wire. Maybe a scout car or two. The memory, like the pictures, is a little fuzzy. It's a long time ago.

I still don't know if it has anything to do with why I decided to write this book, but for me the Berlin Wall will always be associated, not just with the state of the world then or now, but with a strong sense of ending, of separation. The day of its creation would signal the end of one part of my life and the beginning of another, harder part, just as it did for so many millions of other human beings. The difference was, my difficulty on that day was neither economic, nor geographical, nor political – it had nothing, in fact, to do with Berlin as such.

My father stayed upstairs for some time. I think they were afraid to move him. I saw him just one more time, later that night, again through a half-open door, this time the entrance to my bedroom. The ambulance men – paramedics as they would be called now – were carrying him across the upstairs landing on a stretcher. He was conscious and looking around. He seemed serious but calm, almost curious about what was happening to him.

He suffered another coronary infarction after they got him to hospital, and this one killed him. The date was 14 August 1961. On the previous day, Sunday 13 August, the rough version of what would later be known as the 'Berlin Wall' had been constructed, dividing a great city and cutting off human from human, friend from friend, parent from child, brother and sister from brother and sister. It was also the day, of course, that I was cut off from Dad. The barrier that separated him from us was dark, mysterious, and above all permanent. The Berlin one was brutal, material, and not at all mysterious. It turned out, moreover, not to be permanent, though we could not know it at the time.

I first arrived in Berlin itself almost exactly four years later, in August 1965, when the Wall certainly felt as if it would be there for my lifetime. I was now seventeen, and a year away from taking my final school exams, my 'A' levels. I had started learning German the year before Dad's death, and now here I was, on a school trip to the city I had watched being torn apart as he died. I remembered the pictures from that night in 1961, though when I actually got there the cityscape was all in colour, and instead of having an overlit, looming quality, like a silent horror film – which was how I had somehow imagined it – it was not that different to London. London with a lot more shell- and bomb-inflicted holes where buildings should have been, and with what still looked like an improvised, ramshackle cement and barbed-wire barrier running through it.

The hotel we were being put up in – more a pub, I suppose – was in a corner of the once quite grand but by then largely ruined and not yet rebuilt Askanischer Platz, in the West Berlin district of Kreuzberg. Opposite us was the wrecked entrance façade of the Anhalter Bahnhof, all that was left of what had once been Berlin's largest railway terminus, destroyed in the big American air raid of 3 February 1945, which had levelled so much of that part of Berlin. A couple of hundred yards further on lay the Wall, and, within easy walking distance, the famous border crossing point for foreigners, known as Checkpoint Charlie.

Near the hotel, there was a wooden platform, served by steps, on to which one could climb for a view over into the 'East'. The view seemed at that time to consist mainly of battered and largely unoccupied government buildings in the Leipziger Strasse and the Wilhelmstrasse. I now know this was the 'government district' and that one of the most prominent of the buildings was Hermann Göring's famous Air Ministry building, dating from the 1930s. It looked a mess. All silent and empty, with weeds growing between the paving stones and concrete of the traffic-free streets.

I think there were about a dozen of us, led by our amiable German teacher, Mr Kitson, and that year's German language assistant, a jolly, neat young Austrian university student with a habit of humming tunes and breaking into short dance sequences as he walked, which once you got used to it was quite endearing. It was obviously, now I think back, some kind of sponsored political-education trip.

I recall being struck at first sight in West Berlin by how unlike any of the stereotyped 'Germans' (that is, war-film Germans) the people there seemed to be. Few uniforms, lots of casual clothes, a bit blonder and pinker-skinned than most Brits, but otherwise surprisingly, even disappointingly, normal. And from what I could understand with my still-limited command of German, they seemed to have a cheeky sense of humour, like cockneys. We were taken along to a genuine Berlin cabaret. There was one number where this trio of actresses did a 'three little maids from school' song, each clad in transparent raincoats and very high heels and supposedly working girls from the Augsburger Strasse. I even got some of the jokes, like the one about how their busiest time was when the West German parliament had sittings in Berlin. That one got the biggest laugh of all from the audience. Berliners are not noted for their respectfulness.

Before we took the inevitable first journey through the 'Iron Curtain' into East Berlin, we were treated to a coffee, cakes and Cold War information session on the Western side led by a young man who I thought at first must be American – crew cut, button-down shirt, horn-rimmed glasses – but who turned out, though he addressed us in highly Americanised English, to be a West Berliner. We were told what we had already realised within minutes of arriving at our accommodation and taking a stroll down the block – that the Berlin Wall was a monstrosity erected by people who considered freedom not just expendable but really very dangerous.

So when we finally did troop across the border one morning, I was feeling pretty grown-up and even at home here. I remembered that Dad, who had served in the North African desert during the war, had always liked and respected the Germans there, even though they were trying to kill him. Their commander, General Rommel, was definitely one he wished we'd had on our side. The Germans at El Alamein and points along the coast were the normal, average-Joe Germans of the Afrika Korps, not the ghastly Gestapo or the SS who had carried out the terrible atrocities on the Eastern Front and in the occupied countries. Most West Berliners looked like Dad's remembered average-Joe Germans to me.

The first shock, then, was the attitude, and the look, of the uniformed East Germans at the checkpoint. Stony-faced, curt, staring repeatedly down at the passport photograph, then back at me, and so on apparently *ad infinitum*. Orders were barked in a German I couldn't understand – I now realise they had probably been brought in from Saxony, like so many of the border guards, and the dialect takes some getting used to. Even when we tried unconvincingly to tailor our body language to a saunter as we walked past the last guards and entered the bare, billboard-free zone of East Berlin, I had to stop myself from turning round to see if they were still staring at us.

And the uniforms. Everywhere. And, actually, strongly reminiscent of what the Nazi bad guys in the war films wore. A little later, when we stopped to observe the neo-classical *Neue Wache* (New Guard House) on Unter den Linden, the East German soldiers on duty there were *goose-stepping*! Wearing jackboots! And strapped on their heads were weird hybrids of the Wehrmacht coal-scuttle headgear and the classic Red Army model-40 helmet.

We did the historical tour. The East Germans had started to restore some of the beautiful old neo-classical buildings with a respect that I naïvely wouldn't have expected from Communists. And as afternoon turned to evening, we all piled into a big new building on the Alexanderplatz, the heart of East Berlin. Covered in huge, sub-Picasso murals, it was called the *Haus des Lehrers* (House of the Teacher), which I suppose might have been some kind of in-joke by our own tour leader, Mr Kitson, or maybe he really did have some kind of professional arrangement there. The building actually contained a restaurant and an events hall of some kind. We ate supper there. I don't recall much about the meal, except that I managed to sneak a beer, despite being under eighteen.

What I do remember is that, as we came out and began to file down the stairs to leave the building, a man in his late thirties or early forties, dressed in full East German army fig, with big, ornately tooled epaulettes that signalled seniority from twenty yards away, and of course the obligatory jackboots, locked his steely, pale-eyed gaze on to me. He snarled. And he launched into a tirade, which my German was just about good enough to understand, to the effect that I was a decadent whippersnapper with too much hair (those were the days . . .) and not enough respect for a uniform. If I were in his country he'd know what to do with me, oh yes, he'd know how to make a man out of me.

The intimidating military effect was slightly marred by the fact that the man was obviously drunk, and that he had a pouting bottle-blonde hanging on to his arm who even to my inexperienced eye seemed unlikely to be his wife. All the same, it was a scary enough experience. Mistaking my tongue-tied silence for insolence, the East German military grandee continued in this vein for some minutes. By the time he had got on to the kind of hair cut he planned to give me, the Bardot look-alike at his side was tugging at his sleeve, but the message was clear enough.

East Germany, I realised, might pretend to be the workers' paradise, but when you came down to it, and put to one side the free nursery-school places and the cheap flats and the jobs for life, the place was about power. Unrestrained, unmitigated power. The kind of power that could build a wall to keep seventeen million people captive, seventeen million people in a place where characters like the military drunk in the *Haus des Lehrers* could tell them exactly what to do and they had to just stand there and take it. After 13 August 1961, there was nowhere those people could go, nothing they could do to stop him.

We got out of there in one piece. I think Mr Kitson had acquired a certain amount of diplomatic experience while serving with the army in Germany just after the war. Or maybe the blonde managed to persuade her companion that he had better things to do than intimidate skinny Brit kids who thought they were the fifth Beatle. Finally, towards midnight – always the witching hour in those days of the Wall, when the day-visit pass for foreigners expired – we emerged out of the border-control complex back into West Berlin, a few hundred yards from our hotel, and let out a collective sigh of relief. Rude things were said – shouted, in fact – about the regime we had just experienced and been glad to stop experiencing.

I made another couple of trips to Berlin, as a student studying German language and history. But in 1972/3, researching a dissertation about the far Right in Germany before the First World War, I came back to the East with more in mind than just a day trip. While a lot of post-1918 material was in West Germany, by the misfortunes of war, most of the pre-1918 stuff had ended up in East German archives. I had to go East, for several weeks or even months.

It was easy to make a casual day-trip to East Berlin, as so many foreign tourists did, but spending time beyond the boundaries of Berlin, treading the sacred soil of the GDR proper, was another matter. The bureaucracy involved in getting a residence permit that would allow me to visit these archives in the East was gruelling.

Staying with a German friend of a friend in West Berlin, I trekked, it seemed, endlessly – though it must have been just two or three times – through the border at Friedrichstrasse and then over to the police headquarters on the Alexanderplatz – just opposite the *Haus des Lehrers*, as it happened. There I stood in line and experienced the full force of the Workers' and Peasants' State's dislike and suspicion of the people who wanted to visit it. I recall standing behind a rangy, smiling South American who was innocently trying to get a permit to take his bike, yes his pedal bicycle, through the territory of the German Democratic Republic in order to get to Prague. Hah! This was impossible! Why did he want to do this? The look on the East German official's face said: spy, you must be a spy. Permission refused!

The bureaucratic gatekeeper was no more polite to me, but I had already done the official spadework. So I finally got my permit for a three-week stay at Potsdam, just to the west of West Berlin. This was contingent on my changing what was for a student an enormous wad of Western currency into otherwise worthless East marks, and also on my booking into a boarding house selected by the East German authorities. For this I also had to pay in advance, in Western money, at an exorbitant exchange rate.

Although Potsdam was just across the Havel river from the West Berlin district of Wannsee – literally a thirty-second walk across a bridge – I was not permitted to approach it that way. No, I had to cross via the Friedrichstrasse station, then embark on a two-hour trip, travelling to the eastern boundary of East Berlin by commuter railway. Then I had to change on to another train that took me on a long, slow journey around the perimeter of the entire city until I finally got to Potsdam, brandishing the permit that enabled me, as a Western foreigner, to be on GDR soil. The strange thing was that the archive too was within sight of West Berlin. At lunchtime, I would break off from my work on the files and stroll down into the beautiful waterside park just outside the building. An idyllic scene except for the warning signs, the armed border guards patrolling in their launches, and the barbed wire festooning the nearby Glienicke bridge, which had been closed ever since 13 August 1961 except, notoriously, for East–West spy exchanges. Even in the GDR, land of rules, there was always an exception.

But the fact of power on the hoof was always there. Another of my other lengthy visits to East Germany involved consulting a different spread of evidence. These documents were stored in the GDR's second major archive, at Merseburg, a suburb of Halle, a couple of hundred kilometres south of Berlin. There was a small band of other Western students also researching there that summer, and of course we spent a lot of time together. We would eat plain food in the dreary little local hostelries – outside the showcase of East Berlin, things deteriorated rapidly – drink a little too much cheap beer and chat to the locals. This was when I began to get a feel for the people, and liked what I found. Our co-drinkers were often workers from the huge Leuna chemicals works, the biggest local employer. They would openly tell you about the appalling pollution, the arrogance of the plant management, the lack of scruple in pursuit of quotas and norms, a scramble for results that was just as cut-throat as it was in capitalist business. Independent trade unions, or investigative journalism, or any of the counterbalances found in a pluralistic society, whatever its faults, were, of course, wholly absent from the GDR.

The other frequent question, especially from those under twenty-five, was: 'Do you know the Rolling Stones?' My answer: 'Yes, of course, I have several of their albums at home.' Pause. Sigh. 'No, I mean do you *know* them . . .'

With most East Germans, though, keen as they were to talk, one started to notice the slightly narrowed-down gaze into the middle distance that they seemed to affect most of the time. They would glance around to make sure no stranger was listening, then start to talk, usually complaining about the poor quality of everything they got in the stores because everything decent went for export to get hard currency. 'Big' politics was hardly ever mentioned. Then came that middle-distance look, a gaze belonging to people trapped in a small country with no way out, a country where to express discontent or even mild wanderlust was liable to be treated as treachery.

There were, of course, those for whom life in the GDR was good, very good indeed. I saw that on the Merseburg trip as well. We were supposed to stay in the district for which our visas had been issued, but like the insolent seventies capitalist brats we were, when the weekend came we ignored this. We piled into a train that took us on an illicit day-trip to the German cultural capital, Weimar, home of Goethe and Schiller. We were lucky. There were quite a few tourists in Weimar, so we didn't stand out. And thankfully, no one checked our visas. Before catching the train back to Merseburg that Sunday evening, we dropped, as Westerners thoughtlessly will, into the best hotel in town, the *zum Elefanten* (At the Sign of the Elephant) and went down into the basement to order some supper.

There we found the usual lackadaisical state-employed waiters, apparently specially trained not to catch your eye. We suffered a long delay for our drinks, an even longer one for the menu. Gradually, our attention was drawn to a group of not especially distinguished middle-aged men in the corner. A little loud, actually. Ties loosened, cheap suit jackets draped over the backs of their chairs. But the help responded like lightning to their every demand, every snap of the nicotine-stained fingers, smiled at every banal remark. Fawned over them, in fact. How could this be? Then I walked past the group to go to the cloakroom and realised why. I saw the little party badge displayed first on one jacket lapel, then on another. These were the local Communist (SED) bosses. Years later I would recognise that scene's similarities with the fictional one in Martin Scorsese's film *Goodfellas*, where the Mafia-connected hood turns up at the restaurant, they know he's a 'made guy', and suddenly he's a king . . .

Like most mafias, the Communist one, in East Germany as elsewhere, arose because at the beginning it seemed to offer hope and protection for the oppressed. In a way it did, though at a very high price in human freedom and pleasure. And like any mafia, once it had established its hold on the masses, it dared not allow choice. Who knows, perhaps in the bad old days in Sicily, even without the suffocatingly thorough exculpatory mechanisms of Marxism-Leninism to support their dominance, the Godfathers used to persuade themselves that the oppression they inflicted was all for the people's own good.

The combination of high moral tone with low oppression is certainly familiar.

Welcome to the Berlin Wall. This book hopes to explain something of how, through blood and sand, and then barbed wire and cement, this closed world came into being; how for half a human lifetime it enjoyed a foetid flourishing; and how in one unpredicted and unpredictable, exhilarating night it met its end.

SAND

1

MARSH TOWN

IN THE SUMMER OF 1961, sixteen years after the end of the Second World War, the world was faced for the first time with the realistic threat of nuclear annihilation.

The background cause was the development, during the 1950s, of massively destructive nuclear weapons by both East and West. The immediate reason was the construction of a wall, a wall dividing a city built on sand.

Berlin, where this ominous thing happened, had always been an improbable metropolis. A fishing and trading settlement, surviving on sandy, boggy soil, it then became capital of one of the poorest monarchies in Europe: Prussia, a state whose very weakness gradually became its strength, and whose habitual trade of military violence – forced on it by its meagreness of natural resources – made it powerful, and Berlin one of the great urban centres of the world.

So how and when did the city's rise begin?

Twentieth-century Berlin was divided. And at its very beginning it also consisted of two cities – or rather, large villages. One was called Berlin and the other Cölln, located on opposite sandy banks at a narrow point in the northward flow of the river Spree. Cölln on the western bank owed its name to the ancient western German Christian city founded by the Romans, Cologne (Köln in German); on the eastern side, the settlement of Berlin was probably not named after the noble bear – as sentimental natives still insist – but more prosaically after the old West Slavic word for marsh, *brl*. Marsh town.

Two heritages found expression in those two names. One was brought with them by the Germanic colonists from the West who flocked into the Slav lands between the Elbe and the Oder as these were conquered. The other expressed the lasting spirit of the non-German people who lived here until this time. These people were gradually Germanised but remained, in some mysterious way that would frustrate later theorists of racial purity, not pure 'Aryan' in the Nazi sense. This was the Berlin 'mix', reinforced by mass immigrations from the eastern and southern regions of Europe in the nineteenth and early twentieth centuries, when the capital of the united Germany became one of the great boom towns of the continent.

At the beginning the expansion of the twin settlement was gradual. There was no fertile hinterland, but Berlin-Cölln's location was sufficiently convenient that it grew steadily on the basis of the Baltic river-borne trade with landlocked central Europe. Local rye and oak timber were shipped north along the veins of the waterways that covered the North German Plain, and in exchange herring and dried cod came from Hamburg. Later, Thuringia supplied iron, Flanders fine cloth, and even oils and Mediterranean exotica such as figs and ginger found their way there. Walls were built. Soon a mill-dam straddled the Spree. In 1307, the towns merged.

Berlin-Cölln owed allegiance to a local magnate. Its overlord was the Margrave of Brandenburg, to whom annual taxes were paid. Though represented by a governor, the margrave left the town mostly to its own devices.

City magistrates and guilds, dominated by patrician families, regulated everyday economic and social life. Punishments were harsh. Crimes that warranted death or lethal torture included not just murder or treason but also poisoning, practising black magic or witchcraft, arson and adultery. Between 1391 and 1448, in a town with a consistent population of around 8,000 souls, 46 alleged miscreants were hanged, 20 burned at the stake, 22 beheaded, 11 broken on the wheel, 17 buried alive (a specially favoured fate for women), and 13 tortured to death.[1] Countless mutilations, including severing of hands, slicing of ears, and ripping out of tongues, were administered for lesser transgressions.

Nevertheless, town life even under such harsh conditions offered a certain security, and relative freedom. *Stadt Luft macht frei*, as the ancient German saying went – 'City air makes a man free'.

Of course, wars, plagues and fires tormented its inhabitants, just as they did other Europeans in the unlucky fourteenth century. The Ascanian dynasty that ruled Brandenburg for centuries eventually died out. Disease, war and famine stalked the land. The Holy Roman Emperor decided to name a new ruler for this neglected area, a scion of a Nuremberg family that had flourished as hereditary castellans of that powerful imperial free city. The family was called Hohenzollern. Its members would rule here through triumph and disaster for 500 years.

Frederick VI Hohenzollern officially became Frederick I of Branden-burg in 1415. Berlin's citizens were delighted. The patrician élite was pleased that this busy man from a distant province left them to rule as they had done for centuries. Berlin kept its privileges, and so did they.

In 1440, the first Hohenzollern ruler died. His successor, Frederick II, unpromisingly known as 'Irontooth', proved the city's nemesis. He played the citizens off against the patricans, then crushed the rebellion that followed. Henceforth the city was ruled by his nominees. The Margrave would deal with Berliners' property and levy taxes on them as he wished.

In 1486, the city became the lords of Brandenburg's official residence. From now until the second decade of the twentieth century, the monarch ruled there, in person and almost entirely absolutely.

In the 1530s, Brandenburg's ruler, Joachim II – now bearing the title of 'Elector', as one of the princes who chose the Holy Roman Emperor – adopted Protestantism. In February 1539, he attended the first Lutheran service to be held in Berlin. His subjects followed him – on the whole, willingly – into this new religious direction.

The states of the Holy Roman Empire agreed on a policy of mutual toleration. According to the neat Latin slogan, *cuius regio, eius religio* (whose region it is, his religion), it would be up to each German prince to determine whether Lutheranism or Catholicism would be the official religion in his particular area. The religious truce and Germany's prosperity lasted until the early 1600s.

At that time, the ageing Holy Roman Emperor Matthias appointed as his heir a nephew, Grand Duke Ferdinand. Ferdinand, a Catholic diehard, became king of Hungary and, in 1618, of Bohemia. He began persecuting Protestants within his lands, an ominous indication of what would happen when he gained supreme power in the 'Holy Roman Empire of the German Nation'.

As it happened, 1618 was also a landmark year for the Hohenzollerns of Brandenburg. The Duke of Prussia, descendant of Teutonic knights and a vassal of the Polish king, ruled over extensive territory bordering the Baltic Sea. Having only daughters, he bequeathed the dukedom to his son-in-law, the Elector of Brandenburg, who inherited it after the Duke's death that year. Henceforth the word 'Prussian' was one with which the family would be forever connected. This would transform a Slavic tribal designation (the *Prus*, original inhabitants of the land, had been Slavs) into an idea, a way of life, a world-view. For good or for ill.

Meanwhile, the religious and dynastic powder-keg of early seventeenth-century Europe was about to explode.

Bohemia was divided between Protestants and Catholics. Ferdinand's moves against the Protestants provoked an uprising by local nobles. The rebels proclaimed Ferdinand deposed and elected a Protestant prince as king. He and his wife, daughter of James I of England, were crowned in Prague.

In 1620, at the Battle of the White Mountain, imperial forces defeated the Bohemian Protestants, wiping out the flower of the native aristocracy. Emperor Ferdinand decided to continue the war into Germany and forcibly regain the Protestant northern states for the Holy Mother Church.

The hellish maelstrom that ensued was known as the Thirty Years War. It was the most terrible conflict since the Dark Ages, in proportion to the population of Europe at that time, killing more than the Second World War. Bloody battles and sieges scarred the landscape. A rapacious, often half-starved mercenary soldiery roamed Germany for year after year, raping and looting and killing, destroying crops and laying waste to towns that had once been the pride of Europe. Bubonic plague and typhus cut a lethal swathe through a population weakened by malnutrition. In 1648, the exhausted powers arrived at a peace settlement, but Germany and Central Europe were changed for ever.

Berlin escaped lightly at first, but after the city was sacked in 1627 by imperial troops, a long night of horror descended. A few years later, the Swedish King, Gustavus Adolphus 'rescued' the city, but his soldiers' depredations proved every bit as appalling as those of the emperor's desperadoes.

Berlin's civilians were routinely tortured by roasting, boiling, and mutilation, to force them to confess the whereabouts of 'treasure' or food hoards. One method favoured by Gustavus Adolphus's men was to pour raw sewage down the throats of victims; for many years afterwards this type of waste was known as the 'Swedish drink'. In 1631–2, starvation in Berlin grew so widespread that knackers' yards were raided for food. Even the city's gallows were plundered. One report described fresh human bones found in a pit with their marrow sucked dry.

The foraging demands of huge, wandering armies, and the combatants' determination to drain their conquests of every last gold piece and ear of corn, left Brandenburg, like the rest of Germany, impoverished, brutalised and stalked by famine. At the end of the war, only 845 dwellings still stood in the whole of Berlin. Cölln, on the western bank of the Spree, had been put to the torch in 1641 and all but destroyed. The population of Brandenburg had been reduced to 600,000.

Only with peace did Berlin's and Brandenburg-Prussia's luck begin to turn. Succeeding in 1640, Elector Frederick William I, turned out to be the first of a series of energetic and talented rulers who would turn their barren, devastated homeland into a European power of some consequence.

There had been no real winner in the Thirty Years War, no one strong enough to impose his own version of 'victor's morality'. The Treaty of Westphalia, which ended the war, declared that there should be no question of blame or war-guilt, or punishment for atrocities. The Latin phrase used was *Perpetua oblivio et amnestia* (eternal forgetting and amnesty – simply put, 'forgive and forget'). Europe had paid a terrible price for intolerance.

At the peace, young Frederick William I acquired more territory: Eastern Pomerania, filling in the gap between Prussia and Brandenburg; the former bishoprics of Magdeburg and Halberstadt; and some lands in the west of Germany.

He took away what traditional rights and liberties the populace still enjoyed, and his war-weary subjects did not resist. Brandenburg-Prussia embraced the form of efficient, measured and (for most people) benevolent despotism that became its hallmark.

The 'Great Elector', as Frederick William became known, also founded an institution that would have enormous significance: the Prussian army. When he succeeded to the throne, his army had been a small, rather ineffectual mercenary operation. He determined to build a permanent, professional fighting force that would gain Brandenburg, known contemptuously elsewhere in Germany as 'the sandbox', some respect among his peers. By 1648, the Elector commanded a professional army of 8,000 men, enough to turn him into a useful ally and to ensure a share in the spoils of peace.

Though authoritarian, the new, post-1648 Electorate emphasised religious tolerance. There were practical reasons for this. The Thirty Years War had caused a catastrophic reduction in the population. Ruined and deserted farm and manor houses dotted a neglected landscape. Brandenburg-Prussia desperately needed people, whatever their original nationality or personal creed.

Towards the end of Frederick William's reign, the Catholic French King Louis XIV began, in a fit of piety, to persecute his country's sizeable Protestant minority. In 1685, Louis officially banned Protestantism and began the destruction of its churches. The French Protestants, known as Huguenots, were skilled craftsmen and tradesmen, diligent and hard-working – exactly what Brandenburg-Prussia needed. Frederick William issued the Edict of Potsdam, in which he openly invited Huguenot refugees to come to Brandenburg.

More than 20,000 Huguenots settled in Brandenburg. By 1687, when the Elector died, they amounted to 20 per cent of Berlin's population. Berlin became an immigrant city, and would remain so until the twenty-first century.

Frederick William's successor reacted against his father's budgetary stringency. Government became lax. There was an air of indulgence around Berlin that would not be seen again until the 1920s. The new Elector's only political achievement came in 1701, when the Holy Roman Emperor awarded a royal crown for Prussia. Henceforth, he became also 'King in Prussia' (the word 'of' came into use only later in the century).

The palace's free-spending ways put a lot of money into circulation in Berlin. The city's population increased from 4,000 at the end of the

Thirty Years War to 55,000 in 1713. Unfortunately, Prussia went bankrupt in the process.

Ascending the throne as King Frederick William I, the new ruler was coarse and narrow-minded. Not in the slightest interested in the arts, science (except the military kind) or the usual royal pleasures, he nevertheless transformed his state in many ways for the good, reforming education and the state machinery and making the army even more formidable.

An impressive, even remarkable monarch. But the strangest thing was that, although he put up to 80 per cent of the budget into his army, and would go down in history as 'the soldier king', Frederick William was in practice a man of peace. Brandenburg Prussia's population increased to over two million, and massive strides were made in economic development.

The King's personal behaviour, however, was obsessive, neurotic, even sadistic. His officials scoured Europe for men over six feet tall, who were inducted into his army. When ill or depressed he would have these 'tall fellows' (*lange Kerle*) paraded for his delectation, even marching them through his bedchamber. Seeing the army as a model for society, and yearning for that society to be perfectly ordered, he inflicted brutal discipline.

In 1730, Frederick William also built the most comprehensive wall Berlin had so far seen. Its aim was not just to defend Berlin against enemies, but to act as an 'excise wall', enabling the King to tax travellers, commercial shipments, or any consumer goods being moved in and out of the city. The wall was also intended to prevent frequent desertions from the king's army. A sentry was posted every hundred metres, and if any unhappy soldier was seen escaping, a cannon shot would alert the nearby villagers. Captured deserters faced a brutal running of the gauntlet, while a second attempt meant death.[2] A similar wall was built at nearby Potsdam, to keep the garrison there in as well.

Frederick William sired ten children. In a continuation of the turn-and-turn-again tradition in the Hohenzollern family, his eldest son, Frederick, was a complete contrast to his father: a slightly-built, sensitive boy, interested in the arts and philosophy. Keen to toughen up his heir and ensure his fitness for the throne, Frederick William had him woken each morning by the firing of a cannon. At six years old, young 'Fritz' was given his own unit of child cadets to drill, and soon granted his own arsenal of real weaponry. The boy was beaten for letting himself be thrown by a bolting horse; and again for showing weakness by putting on gloves in cold weather.

At eighteen, the Crown Prince tried to flee the kingdom with an older aristocratic friend, Hans Hermann von Katte. They were caught. Fritz was kept under arrest at a fortress, and forced to watch from a window as his friend was beheaded on the parade ground below. Within a couple of years, the Crown Prince was married off to a pleasant, pious princess, Elisabeth Christine of Brunswick. The marriage proved childless. After his succession, they lived apart. Fritz kept no mistresses. His possible homosexuality has been the subject of keen historical gossip ever since.

When the 'soldier king' died, many of his subjects heaved a sigh of relief. However, in one of the great paradoxes of European history, where the 'soldier king' had brought peace, his son, the 'philosopher king', would inflict war and suffering.

Frederick had succeeded in May 1740. In October, the Holy Roman Emperor, Charles VI, died, leaving no male heir. Since the imperial throne, though technically subject to election, had, in fact, become the family property of the Austrian Habsburgs, a power vacuum threatened. Charles had changed the law so that he might be succeeded by his daughter, Maria Theresa. Most of royal Europe had accepted this. Prussia was one of the states that had not.

In an act of unscrupulous opportunism, the 'philosopher king' marched the powerful army his loathed father had created into the neighbouring Habsburg province of Silesia. This rich district, once part of Poland, would, if Frederick could hold on to it, immeasurably increase the wealth of Prussia-Brandenburg, supplying it with the agricultural, industrial and mineral resources that the state urgently needed. He justified this occupation in terms of an obscure sixteenth-century treaty that his lawyers dug out of the diplomatic cupboard.

Thanks to his excellent army, the young Prussian king won the so-called 'War of the Austrian Succession', and held onto Silesia's riches, but this was not the end of the story. The highly intelligent and astute Maria Theresa made the peace she had to make, but withdrew to plan her revenge. She began weaving a new web of alliances, combining the power of Austria, France and Russia against the upstart Prussia.

In the decade of peace that followed, Frederick ran a highbrow salon at the glass-and-stone pleasure palace, *Sans Souci* ('Without Care'), which he built just outside Berlin at the royal seat of Potsdam. He introduced many reforms, some of them genuinely humane. He abolished the torture of civilians and the death sentence except for murder. He extended religious tolerance, allowing the Catholics to build a cathedral in Berlin. Like his father, he was also an obsessive micro-manager. It was due to Frederick's efforts that the potato became Prussia's staple food.

In 1756, with war once more threatening, Frederick undertook a characteristically sly war of pre-emption, invading the rich but militarily weak state of Saxony. This he occupied for several years, exploiting its wealth and manpower to underpin his war-making. 'Saxony,' he quipped cynically, 'is like a sack of flour. Every time you beat it, something comes out.' Almost a hundred thousand out of two million Saxons (5 per cent of the population) died as a result of the Prussian invasion and occupation, including roughly the same proportion of the inhabitants of Dresden, Saxony's beautiful capital. A third of its built-up area was destroyed by Prussian cannon fire and petrol bombs in 1760. Despite having killed more Germans and destroyed more of Germany than any commander until the RAF's Sir Arthur Harris 200 years later, Frederick the Great remains a national hero.

None the less, by 1760 he had suffered several crushing defeats. Berlin was occupied by the Russians and the Austrians. Surrender seemed inevitable. Then the Empress of Russia, Elisabeth, died. The son who succeeded her, Tsar Peter III, was a fanatical fan of Prussian militarism. This unexpected *deus ex machina* restored Frederick's fortunes. The young man granted peace on highly favourable terms, ending the 'Seven Years War'.

Moreover, Prussia's main ally, Britain, had driven the French out of North America (where this conflict is known as the 'French and Indian War') and had also established itself as the dominant power in India. Britain became the first world superpower. The country's heroic friend, King Frederick, was wildly popular in Britain. Until Prussia's name was blackened by the First World War, there were inns in England named after him, and well into the nineteenth century the Anglo-Prussian alliance was taken for granted in both countries.

The final *coup* of Frederick's reign was the dismantling of the almost thousand-year-old kingdom of Poland. Paralysed by internal dissent, this once-mighty Eastern European power made tempting prey for its neighbours. In 1772 Frederick agreed with Austria and Russia to carve great slices off Poland. Within a little over two decades, Poland was wiped from the map and would not re-emerge as a properly independent country until 1918. Prussia, however, gained a solid, continuous block of territory and a much increased population.

In 1786, Frederick died at Sans Souci, alone except for his dogs and by all accounts world-weary and reclusive in old age. Berlin had recovered from the disastrous wars with remarkable speed. Its population stood at 150,000. Thirty thousand worked in industry and trade, while 3,500 were civil servants. The Berlin garrison numbered 25,000 men, and 20 per cent of Berliners were connected with the military.[3] The future of Frederick's system of government seemed assured for decades, even centuries to come.

Three years later, the French Revolution broke out and changed everything. The first eruption of popular democratic rebellion on the continent, it spread like a virus and threatened to destroy the whole system of hereditary privilege upon which Frederick, like all European monarchs, based his thinking. When that revolution turned sour, a new despot rose to power in the shape of Emperor Napoleon Bonaparte.

The greatest general and most successful conqueror the post-medieval world had seen, during two decades of dominance the Corsican upstart created a new Europe that remains recognisably his 200 years later.

Napoleon was old Prussia's nemesis. And, in the short term at least, Berlin's.

On 27 October 1806, Napoleon entered Berlin. Two weeks before, the Emperor had inflicted a massive double-blow on the Prussian forces. The French had prevailed first at Jena, near Weimar, south-west of Berlin, and then again at Auerstedt, a few hours' ride to the north. The victory, achieved against a Prussian army exceeding a hundred thousand men, was total. At Auerstedt, King Frederick III's forces outnumbered the enemy two to one, and still they turned tail and ran from the superbly disciplined French.

Napoleon marched his victorious army down the wide boulevard of Unter den Linden into the heart of the city, and paraded through the magnificent Brandenburg Gate.

The gate was a new, grander opening in the defence and customs wall, now totalling seventeen kilometres in length, and 4.2 metres high, that still surrounded central Berlin. It had been designed by the famous architect Carl Gotthard Langhans, and completed just a few years earlier. Atop its neo-classical columns the sculptor Johann Gottfried Schadow had created a huge stone quadriga or four-horsed chariot, the symbol of victory in the old Olympic Games. In this case the goddess Victory, who drove the chariot, carried the olive wreath of peace, which was a pleasant and perhaps over-optimistic touch.

Initially, those Berliners who wished for more freedom, especially the unenfranchised middle classes, had hopes of Napoleon. The Emperor promised reform of the laws, even a constitution. Elections were held for a Berlin city council.

The French dictator's real aims were, however, soon clear. He planned to use Berlin and Prussia as a money-pump and supplier of manpower, to turn it into another puppet regime in French-ruled Europe. Already impoverished and stripped of huge areas of territory, with her army reduced to just over 40,000 men (of which 16,000 were to be at Napoleon's disposal for new military adventures), Prussia was also forced to pay hundreds of millions of francs in reparation and occupation costs. The French set about stripping the Prussian capital of its treasures, including the quadriga from the Brandenburg Gate, which was carted off to Paris. And that was just the official looting. With 25,000 often rowdy French occupation troops quartered on its citizenry, Berlin stood at its lowest ebb for a hundred and fifty years.

Napoleon himself seemed amazed at how swiftly Prussia had been vanquished. Just before entering Berlin, he paid a visit to the grave of Frederick the Great, in the crypt of the Garrison Church at Potsdam. There he told his officers: 'Hats off, gentlemen! If he were still alive, we would not be here!'[4]

The people of Prussia were forced to take a hard look at the system under which they had been living. So was the state's ruling élite.

Some of the ensuing reforms were aimed at making Prussia better run. Others had to do with re-establishing its military power. The latter were necessarily covert, including General Scharnhorst's most cunning creation, the *Landwehr* (Home Guard), which by training a revolving, part-time citizen army circumvented the limitations placed on its size by Napoleon. Its official strength may never have exceeded these restrictions, but somehow by 1813 an army of 280,000 stood at the King's behest.

A passionate spirit of rebellion seethed beneath the relatively calm surface of occupied Berlin. The anti-French forces within Prussia, and in Germany as a whole, were merely awaiting their opportunity.

In June 1812, after massing an army of a million men from all over Europe, including Prussia, Napoleon invaded Russia. The Emperor won every major battle, but the campaign's outcome was catastrophic. In the fierce winter of 1812/13 Napoleon's *Grande Armée* left Moscow in flames and retreated through snow and ice towards the safety of Europe, harried by Cossacks, plagued by cold, hunger and disease. Only 18,000 troops crossed the river Niemen back into Poland.

The Prussian king, Frederick III, who had meekly supplied Napoleon with 20,000 soldiers for his disastrous march on Moscow, finally changed sides. The entire Prussian army was turned against Napoleon, and men who had been secretly training flocked to the colours. For them the architect Schinkel designed a special medal for bravery, to be awarded to any hero, irrespective of rank. It was called the Iron Cross.

Prussia, Germany, and the rest of Europe rose up against French domination in a wave of idealistic, romantic nationalism known as the 'War of Liberation'. Napoleon was defeated and exiled. Many in Berlin and elsewhere hoped that a new, better Germany would arise.

A brave new world for Berlin, Prussia and Germany? Not at all. The following years saw a concerted effort to put the stopper back in the reformist bottle. The victorious absolutist monarchs thought they could turn the clock back to the eighteenth century. For forty years they almost succeeded. All talk of national liberation and civic freedom was suppressed, in Prussia as elsewhere.

It was a hopeless task. Prussia was no longer a bleak 'sandbox', isolated in the far east of the German lands. It had gained large amounts of territory in western Germany, including the Rhineland and Westphalia. These were mostly Catholic, fertile agricultural districts – and most important of all for the state's future, rich in coal and mineral deposits.

Soon these newly Prussian western towns began to be transformed into industrial powerhouses. In the 1830s, railways were built. The last maintenance on Berlin's city wall was performed in 1840. Within twenty years the whole structure, seventeen kilometres long, would be knocked down, and Berlin could finally burst its boundaries. So, for around a hundred years, Berlin was without any internal wall.[5]

Industry expanded rapidly in the capital, but the late 1840s saw an economic downturn. In 1848, revolution broke out in France. The movement spread to Germany, Austria, Hungary and Italy. In Prussia, all the passions that had lain dormant since the defeat of Napoleon once more rose to the surface: the desire for German unification, for political representation and intellectual freedom.

An uprising in Berlin, involving the middle classes and the rapidly growing industrial proletariat, resulted in bloody clashes with the city's garrison. None the less, King Frederick William, a well-meaning reactionary, agreed to elections and the appointment of a liberal government.

The liberals formed a 'civil guard' that bore more than a passing resemblance to the old militia from the War of Liberation. They took the black, red and gold banner of the pre-revolutionary radicals (itself based on the uniform of a famous Prussian unit from the War of Liberation) as their flag instead of the black and white of the old regime. They promised themselves a new Prussia as part of a united Germany, with a democratic, free Berlin at its heart.

Again the optimists were fated to disappointment. The civil guard was used against workers demanding a social as well as a political revolution. For centuries now, the city had more or less willingly traded civic freedoms for security. There were signs that Berliners were already becoming wary of democratic experiments.

The reactionaries, who had been sulking on their estates and plotting revenge, saw their moment. In November 1848, the King called the army back to Berlin and dissolved the elected assembly. Faced with the royalist general Baron von Wrangel and his troops, the commander of the liberal militia defending the parliament building declared that he would 'only react to force'. The baron replied with brutal simplicity: 'Well, force is here.'

Force would, sadly, always 'be here' in Berlin from now on, whether from left or right.

Prussia retained a parliament of sorts, heavily rigged in favour of the aristocracy and the wealthier classes, and without control over ministerial appointments. Frederick William IV's new-found passion for a united Germany faded in the face of Habsburg opposition. For almost twenty years more, the Emperor in Vienna would still dictate what happened in Germany, even though the actual political and economic balance of power there had long tipped in Prussia's favour.

It would take another reactionary, the cleverest one in German history, to translate this fact into power-political reality. In 1861, Otto von Bismarck became prime minister of Prussia.

Soon the Germans got a united nation, but on very different terms to the ones the Berlin revolutionaries of 1848 had imagined, and certainly not at all what they would have wished.

In January 1861, Frederick William IV died. His brother, now King William I, faced constitutional deadlock. Despite elections' being loaded in favour of the propertied classes, since 1848 the liberals, or 'Progressives', had gained a majority. They were demanding powers that the Prussian establishment did not want to give them. To force the situation, they were blocking the annual budget, which included funding for a reorganisation of the army.

William's solution, instead of appointing a liberal prime minister, was to give the post to 46-year-old Otto von Bismarck, a bluff Pomeranian landowner and keen proponent of the divine right of kings.

As a former ambassador to Russia and France, Bismarck knew how to play the political game. He found ingenious ways around the budget issue. For eighteen months he hung on in office, generally hated but retaining the support of the King.

Bismarck's breakthrough came when the Danish King died. An

international disagreement emerged regarding the status of the duchies of Schleswig and Holstein, adjoining Denmark, which were held by the Danish crown but remained technically part of the German Confederation. The new Danish King proposed to annex the northern territory of Schleswig directly to his kingdom. The Germans objected. It was a complicated problem. As the British Foreign Secretary, Lord Palmerston, commented waggishly, there were only three men in Europe who understood the complexities of the Schleswig-Holstein question: Queen Victoria's consort, Prince Albert, who was dead; a German professor, who had gone mad; and Palmerston himself, who had forgotten.

In 1864 Prussia, acting for all the German states, occupied the two provinces in concert with Austria. The arrangement lasted for a year or so, until they disagreed over the province's ultimate fate. The result, in 1866, was a war in which most of the other German states supported Austria. The Prussian armies won easily, crushing the Austrians and their allies in seven weeks.

Immediately after this victory, Bismarck called elections. He rode a wave of patriotic enthusiasm. The Progressives were soundly beaten. A conservative prime minister now had a conservative parliament at his disposal.

The formal unification of Germany came in 1870, after the last of Bismarck's victorious wars, in this case against France. William I of Prussia became Emperor William I of Germany – and Bismarck his Reich Chancellor.

In 1862, Bismarck had grimly told the Berlin parliament: 'The great questions of the day will not be decided by speeches and the resolutions of majorities . . . but by iron and blood.' Tragically, he was all too right. Not just for the nineteenth but for the twentieth century too.

The stage was set for what some would call a 'revolution from above'. Bismarck would be the architect of this fascinating, ominous new development. In the course of the country's transformation, Berlin would spread out across what had seemed all those centuries ago to be such inhospitable and unpromising sands and lakes. It would become a great, darkly glittering world city.

2

REDS

ON THE EVE OF the first great war of the twentieth century, Berlin was the second-largest city in Europe. Since unification, massive industrial growth, a breakneck expansion in construction, and a huge increase in wealth, especially for the middle and upper classes, had transformed the German capital into a boom town comparable with San Francisco or Chicago.

Great tenement blocks, often built in gloomy grey stone, spread out from the heart of the city, especially in the east. Consisting of concentric courtyards like Chinese boxes, getting cheaper as the inner courtyards became darker and more airless and the apartments smaller, such blocks were known in Berlin as *Mietskasernen* (rental barracks). In the west, away from the historic centre, well-to-do suburbs ate into the agricultural land and swallowed up the lake landscape that surrounded the city. The newly rich middle and professional classes wanted space and greenery. Districts such as Grunewald, Wilmersdorf, and Zehlendorf rapidly filled with desirable residences in a variety of inauthentic but grandiose styles, be they colonnaded classical villas or turreted, mock-medieval fortresses.

Bismarck's long dominance as first chancellor of the German Empire (1871–90) saw the liberal flame that burned so brightly in the middle of the century all but die. Many liberals joined Bismarck's reactionary project, calling themselves 'National Liberals' to make their allegiance clear. Middle-class Germans were content to exchange truly representative government for the wealth, power and prestige that rapidly ensued.

After unification, a national parliament or Reichstag was established. Bismarck's trick was to make this body electable on the basis of universal male suffrage, thus superficially democratic. However, he gave its members no say over the formation of the Reich government, which remained wholly the Emperor's prerogative. Who won how many seats was therefore only marginally important. This hybrid form of authoritarian government was Bismarck's most problematical legacy.

The 'Prussianisation' of Germany continued apace. A large national army on the Prussian model, based on conscription, meant that all German males were influenced by military values. The new regime slyly transformed the liberal idea of the 'Home Guard' into a reinforcing element for the authoritarian status quo.

The officer in uniform became a figure of great prestige and privilege, not just in small garrison towns but even in the great, cosmopolitan city of Berlin. Officers might not beat soldiers in public any more, as they had in the eighteenth century, but they were assured of a place at the front of the queue in a store, and of a table in a restaurant. This unique attitude of arrogant invulnerability was much remarked on by visiting foreigners.

Berlin in 1914 was none the less not just a big military cantonment. It was also a great world capital and industrial centre. Especially important were dynamic new areas of manufacturing like the electrical and chemical industries. Germany quickly outstripped Britain in this 'second industrial revolution', and also in machine-tools and steel-making. The Reich was now the largest and most efficient industrial power in Europe and, after the United States of America, in the world. It enjoyed a literary and journalistic flowering the equal of anywhere in Europe.

So what was the problem? How did the twentieth century, which started, for Germany and for Europe, with such hope and dynamism, become the most catastrophic in history?

It is true that imperial Germany had its neuroses. So did Britain and France. Think of the Dreyfus Affair. It is true that imperial Germany was jingoistic and insecure. But anyone who looks at Britain and France at the same period will also see distasteful hyper-patriotism, and cities that were breeding-grounds for a host of verminous political movements and ominous social anxieties.[1] German society was militaristic, but then what else was the early Boy Scout movement in Britain (founded by a soldier-servant of the empire in 1907) but a system of military training for boys?

It was also true that, as a counterbalance to nationalist xenophobia, Marxist internationalism had grown into a hugely powerful political force in Germany. The Social Democratic Party (SPD), founded in 1875, became the defining mass movement of the quickly expanding German working class. When the British Labour Party was not even a twinkle in Keir Hardie's eye, the German socialist movement had a membership measured in millions, and scores of deputies in the Reichstag. Its myriad clubs, debating societies, self-help groups, trade unions, and welfare institutions amounted to an alternative society within society.

In 1881, Chancellor von Bismarck had created the world's first comprehensive state-directed social welfare system, in great part as a means of heading off the spread of socialism among the German workers. He persuaded the Emperor to sanction a contributory welfare scheme that would protect workers from the worst consequences of poverty due to ill health or old age. In this way he hoped to bind the masses to the authoritarian status quo.

But at the same time as he introduced this welfare system, which put Germany decades ahead of the rest of the world, Bismarck made one serious mistake, which the country would pay for not just during his chancellorship but in the decades to come. The Chancellor attempted not just to hinder but to suppress the expanding socialist movement, whose members he described as 'rats . . . who should be exterminated'.

After two assassination attempts against the Emperor in 1878, Bismarck seized his chance. Cynically equating the respectable Left with anarchist regicides, Bismarck enacted emergency legislation to shut down the SPD. Newspapers were banned, homes and offices searched, activists and editors thrown into jail or forced into exile (especially to America). However, it was not possible for Bismarck to stop socialists putting themselves forward for election, or to prevent the foundation of unions, so long as they were not technically affiliated to the illegal party.

The periodically renewable anti-socialist law lasted until 1890. By then thirty-five socialists, representatives of the illegal movement, sat defiantly in the Reichstag. Oppression had, in fact, only made the movement stronger, more defiant and self-reliant. Bismarck's twelve-year attempt to turn back the political tide failed disastrously.

Emperor William I died in Berlin in March 1888, a few days before his ninety-first birthday. His heir was an enthusiastic liberal, a tendency in which he was encouraged by his wife, the British Princess Victoria.

Tragically, Emperor Frederick III was already ill with throat cancer. He reigned for ninety-nine days. His son and successor, William II, would rule for thirty years and lead the prosperous, united, dynamic Germany he had inherited into unimaginable disaster. He was a believer in his divine right to kingship, and of Germany's equally divinely ordained position of world dominance, to which, in his eyes, her new strength entitled her.

At twenty-nine, when he became emperor or *Kaiser*, young William was quick-minded but intolerant, stubborn but mercurial, and possessed of a spectacular set of personal neuroses that reflected in important ways the insecurities of his country itself.

The new Emperor was determined not just to reign but to rule. Within two years, he had forced Bismarck out of office. He abandoned Bismarck's subtle system of alliances, which kept Austria and Russia close to Germany, while France, still smarting from her 1870 defeat, remained safely isolated. William decided that Germany must become a real world power, and she must therefore have a navy to rival Britain's.

William succeeded only in driving his rivals into each other's arms. In 1894, France and Russia signed a treaty of alliance. Within another few years, Europe's ancient enemies, Britain and France, ended hundreds of years of mutual hostility. The agreement they signed covered colonial disputes, but it led directly to a *de facto* alliance and eventually to a triple alliance of Britain, France and Russia. By 1914, this faced the Central European alliance formed by Germany and Austria-Hungary.

The Kaiser heaped fuel on the fire by wild rhetorical outbursts, for which he became internationally notorious. He never learned that being a great power involved great responsibilities. There were plenty of Germans who did understand this, but they were often out-shouted by a new and influential breed of ultra-nationalists. This group was particularly numerous in the prosperous suburbs of Berlin, among the officer corps, the academic élite, and the highly successful industrial salariat, especially those involved in what would later be called the 'military-industrial complex'.

The paradox within Germany was that, encouraged by the Kaiser, the nationalist Right came to dominate establishment politics, while among the masses socialist internationalism enjoyed ever greater support. In

January 1912, two years before the war, the SPD gained almost 35 per cent of the vote in the Reichstag elections and became the the largest single party. The electoral maps of highly urbanised areas such as Berlin, Hamburg, the Ruhr and Saxony were a sea of socialist red.

The success of the Left in 1912 had no moderating effect on the country's policies. In fact, it may have persuaded the Right that their anti-democratic ends would be best served by an even more aggressive military and foreign policy, one that would rally support for the ruling élite. Rightists muttered darkly about the 'encirclement' of Germany by envious rivals. They complained about the alleged role of Jews in 'undermining' traditional authority. They talked of the inevitability of war, and of war as the solution to Germany's internal divisions.

When the Reichstag met after the 1912 elections, the SPD's veteran leader August Bebel, who had faced off Bismarck during the period of illegality and sat for thirty years in a parliament where he was daily insulted and humiliated by the 'patriotic' establishment, made a chillingly prophetic speech about the dangerous international situation:

> There will be a catastrophe . . . sixteen to eighteen million men, the flower of different nations, will march against each other, equipped with lethal weapons. But I am convinced that this great march will be followed by the great collapse (*at this moment many in the chamber began to laugh*) – all right, you have laughed about this before; but it will come . . . What will be the result? After this war we shall have mass bankruptcy, mass misery, mass unemployment and great famine.[2]

The record states that his words were drowned out by mocking laughter. A right-wing deputy called out: 'Herr Bebel, things always get better after every war!'

The socialist patriarch would be dead within a year. Another year after that, booming, brilliant Berlin would be a city at war. A city of hunger. A city of despair.

When the guns fell silent on 11 November 1918, the Kaiser had been overthrown, and his people were no longer the envy of Europe. A ruthless blockade by the British navy had all but prevented the importing of food into Germany.

Rural areas managed to survive, but the cities starved. Berlin suffered worst of all. Its huge population and its remoteness from fertile growing land contributed to a food crisis that was already a fact as early as the first winter of the war. In February 1915, Berlin saw the introduction of bread rationing. In 1917, the potato crop, on which the city had depended since the time of Frederick the Great, failed. For the first time since the Thirty Years' War, rats became candidates for Berlin's dinner tables.

By 1918, meat consumption was down to 12 per cent of pre-war levels, that of eggs to 13 per cent, and of fish to 5 per cent. Thousands died from hunger and from diseases associated with malnutrition. The rampant black market created vast resentment. Although many of Berlin's large Jewish population served bravely at the front, Jews were perceived as complicit in increasing corruption.

In the end, even German technical know-how, discipline and courage could not overcome the numerical and industrial superiority of the Allies, especially after America joined the war in 1917. One last German thrust in the west during the spring of 1918 at first promised success, but the Allied line held and the advance petered out.

Though still fighting on enemy territory in France, Belgium, Italy and the Balkans, Germany had shot its bolt. In October 1918, a liberal ministry under Prince Max of Baden began to consider peace. By early November, there was open revolt in the streets of Berlin and other cities. The Kaiser went into exile in Holland. A republic was declared.

Peace on the battlefield brought no peace of mind. How could it be, asked those conditioned by the egoistic, ultra-nationalist assumptions of the pre-war years, that a nation with its armies still holding out on foreign soil, could suddenly collapse? Treachery, was their answer. The legend of the 'stab in the back' – invincible Germany betrayed by Jews and revolutionaries – became accepted by many as fact.

Berlin in 1920, expanded by reorganisation, had a population of around four million. The working class part of it – mainly in the east – was thoroughly Red.

The problem was, the labour vote had split. In 1914, the majority of the SPD experienced a similar fit of patriotism to the rest of German society. It voted for the war and joined the 'siege truce' (*Burgfrieden*) announced by the Kaiser. As the war dragged on, and the urban masses suffered, and the slaughter of Germany's young men reached intolerable levels, the SPD split between the still-loyal main party and the USPD or Independent Social Democratic Party, which took a pacifist and subversive stance. And then there was the far Left, which coalesced around an extreme anti-war, revolutionary grouping led by a vigorous Russian apostle of 'scientific' political violence, Vladimir Ilyich Ulyanov, known as Lenin.

When the monarchy fell, the Leninists, known as the Spartakist League (after the slave rebels in ancient Rome, followers of Spartacus), remained tiny in number. None the less, they enjoyed support in rebellious units of the army and navy. So risky was the situation in Berlin that the assembly set up to frame the new republic's constitution had to be held in the provincial town of Weimar. The new state was known as the 'Weimar Republic'.

The declaration of a republic did not satisfy the far Left. Lenin had seized power in Russia in November 1917, and his Soviet dictatorship was a beacon to idealists of all kinds. In January 1919, the Spartakists attempted a similar revolution in Berlin. To defeat them, the Social Democratic government had to find a strong arm, which it did not itself possess. It was forced to call on the former imperial army.

The Prussian army duly put down the rebellion. After its suppression, a group of officers abducted and murdered the Spartakist leaders, Karl Liebknecht and Rosa Luxemburg. Both had opposed the uprising but been overruled. Their bodies were found in the Landwehr Canal, between what would later be West and East Berlin. No one ever stood trial for the killings.

In 1920, a 27-year-old First World War veteran and member of the USPD joined a large chunk of his chosen party in peeling off to combine with the newly founded KPD (Communist Party of Germany), which had arisen from the ruins of the Spartakist movement. Many years later, he would claim that even while in the army he had been a firebrand Spartakist. In fact, Leipzig-born Walter Ulbricht had shown no previous sign of extremism. However, once he was in the new Leninist party he rose rapidly and showed himself to be a true believer with a gift for organisation.

In 1924/5, Ulbricht was one of the first young German Communists to undergo ideological training at the new Lenin School in Moscow, established by the Communist International (Comintern) to educate future leaders of the international revolution. His exceptional loyalty to Moscow and its political line would characterise his entire career. Possessed of a high-pitched voice, the result of a severe throat infection in his teens, and a strong Saxon accent (mercilessly mocked by his enemies), his humourlessness and general lack of likeability were also the stuff of legend.

A fellow young party official at that time, Ernst Wollweber, recalled:

> He was regarded as incredibly hard-working, always willing to take the initiative, extremely solid: he had no vices and no obvious weaknesses. He didn't smoke, he did not drink, and he had no personal associates. He was not friends with anyone in the Party.[3]

Another contemporary recalled returning by train from a conference with several comrades, including Ulbricht. The earnest young activist from Leipzig spent the whole journey talking politics, while the others, having had enough of such talk during the long speeches and discussions, just wanted to enjoy the passing countryside and unwind. Ulbricht had no sense of these simple human compensatory mechanisms.

While with the KPD delegation that attended the Fourth World Congress of the Comintern in Moscow in November 1922, Ulbricht was present at a meeting addressed by Lenin himself. Though only fifty-two, the great revolutionary suffered a stroke in May of that year, but had recovered sufficiently to speak at the congress. In December 1922, another, much worse, seizure laid him how. He withdrew from politics and died in January 1924. Walter Ulbricht never ceased to remind colleagues that he had breathed the same air as the founder of Marxism-Leninism, and discussed vital matters of world revolution in his sacred company.

At home, the KPD showed worrying signs of independence during the early 1920s, resisting 'Bolshevisation' (that is, Russification) of its organisational structure and electing to senior posts comrades the Soviet leadership didn't like. Ulbricht helped organise a counter-coup. Ernst Thälmann, a Hamburg-born transport worker and Moscow loyalist, became leader of the KPD. Henceforth, strict adherence to the Soviet line was enforced. In 1927, the General Secretary of the Communist Party of the Soviet Union (CPSU), Josef Stalin, made it official Comintern policy that any Communist, anywhere in the world, must hold the defence of the Soviet Union to be his or her unshakeable duty.

In 1926, Ulbricht was elected to the Saxon provincial parliament, and in 1928, he switched to Berlin as a KPD member of the Reichstag.

Ulbricht actually spent most of the next parliamentary session back in Moscow, representing the KPD at the Comintern. During his second sojourn in the Soviet Union, Ulbricht was admitted to membership of the CPSU as well as to the Executive Committee of the Communist International. Soon after his return to Germany, Ulbricht was elected to the Politburo of the KPD, the élite leadership. In November 1929, he became Party Secretary for Berlin and Brandenburg.

Ulbricht was now in charge of one of the real Communist strongholds. Recent elections for the Berlin city government had seen the KPD garner a quarter of the vote and become the second-largest party after the SPD. In some areas, its vote had exceeded 40 per cent. Ulbricht became one of Germany's most controversial politicians, making inflammatory speeches and going head-to-head with the Nazi *Gauleiter* of Berlin, Josef Goebbels.[4] The 'limited civil war' between Communists and Nazis in the streets of Berlin contributed powerfully to the collapse of the Weimar Republic. Ulbricht, a keen apostle of political violence, was as much responsible for this as Goebbels. The bruisers of the KPD's paramilitary 'Red Self Help' fought pitched battles with Goebbels' brown-shirted thugs.

Though still in his mid-thirties, Ulbricht was already a key member of the German Communist Party's leadership. He was linkman *par excellence* between Moscow and Berlin, as familiar with Red Square as with the Potsdamer Platz. To Walter Ulbricht, the sufferings or joys of the people of Berlin were then, and would be thirty years later, strictly subordinated to the needs of international Communism.

*

Germany had been knocked to the ground by defeat in 1918.

In the years immediately following, the horrors of hyperinflation devastated Germans' savings. In June 1920, the rate of exchange stood at 50 marks to the dollar, a year later 101 marks, and by July 1922 550 marks. Then the French invaded the Ruhr industrial area to enforce payment of reparations, and the whole German economy went crazy. In June 1923, the dollar stood at 75,000 marks and two months later at 10,000,000. By the autumn the rate of exchange reached that of one dollar = 4,200,000,000 marks. The far Right claimed the Jews were responsible; the far Left, including the KPD, blamed the militaristic Prussian aristocrats, known as Junkers, and the war-profiteering capitalists.

On 9 November 1923, an obscure ex-serviceman with the gift of the gab tried to talk the authorities in Munich into supporting his planned coup against the 'Reds' in Berlin. His name was Adolf Hitler. In Saxony, the Communists attempted their own putsch. Ulbricht was heavily involved.

Both rebellions failed. The right-wing seizure of power, however, was put down with kid gloves. Hitler received a couple of years' comfortable imprisonment, where he wrote a confused and toxic memoir called *Mein Kampf* (My Struggle). The Communist rebellion was suppressed much more brutally. It was clear which violent radicals the establishment considered the greater danger.

Something had to happen to stabilise Germany. A government enjoying wide support across the political spectrum came to power. The talented banker Dr Hjalmar Schacht organised a revaluation of the mark that gave domestic and foreign creditors some confidence again.

By the mid-1920s, with the currency stabilised, the economy buoyed by foreign loans, and the country enjoying relative political and social peace, Germany made a recovery. The arts and sciences flourished – Germany supplied more Nobel Prize winners in the 1920s than any other nation – and with the dead hand of the imperial censors removed, Berlin became the freest, frankest – some would say, most licentious – city in Europe. By May 1928, Hitler's National Socialists, who had briefly flourished in the middle of the decade, won only 2.5 per cent of the vote and were down to a mere dozen Reichstag deputies, less than the tiny Bavarian People's Party.

None of this brought back the property and the savings that millions of Germans had lost in the inflation, but at least there were jobs and money moving around the system. Germany had got back on his feet and was walking upright, albeit with a slight limp.

The 1929 American stock-market crash and the consequent economic depression hit Germany harder than any other European country. Foreign loans were called in, banks collapsed, and export markets (always a great source of German prosperity) shrank drastically. The country seemed to fall even lower than before. Hopelessness spread once more throughout Germany, like a cancer thought beaten that returns with new virulence.

The depression hit skilled working-class and white-collar workers especially hard. The political extremes began to recruit successfully. In September 1930, the Nazis won 107 seats to the KPD's 77; in July 1932, 230 to 89; in November 1932, 196 to 100. Almost half the deputies in the Reichstag represented parties that rejected parliamentary democracy. The situation was even worse in Berlin. Although in the capital, with its strong socialist and liberal traditions, the Nazi vote never reached 30 per cent, in July 1932 the Communists were not far behind them on almost 25 per cent. The once-dominant Social Democrats now ranked third. Berlin's streets were in constant uproar. Knives, knuckle-dusters, fire-arms, and even explosives were used in battles that really did resemble engagements between armies in a vicious little civil war.[5]

By the end of January 1933, the civil war was over. The Nazis had won.

According to one story, the 85-year-old Reich President, First World War hero Field Marshal Paul von Hindenburg, peered out of his palace window on the night Hitler became chancellor. A torchlit parade was sweeping down Unter den Linden. The first thing he saw was a regular-army unit, moving in perfect marching time. He smiled with senile pride. There followed a bunch of brown-uniformed Nazis. Street thugs, whose attempts at marching failed to conceal shambling, often drunken gaits. The President rubbed his ancient eyes and turned to one of his staff.

'Ah,' murmured the man who had routed the Tsar's armies at the battle of Tannenberg in 1914, 'I did not know we had taken so many Russian prisoners!'

New elections, held with Hitler controlling the levers of government, gave the Nazis a majority. The Communist Party was forbidden. Walter Ulbricht went into hiding, initially sheltered in their garage by a family of Social Democrats. He was one among a handful of prominent Communist leaders who managed to avoid arrest.

Absurdly, while individual Communists risked their lives to oppose the Nazis, a bitter power struggle broke out between the surviving leaders. The Comintern had no notion of the urgency of the situation. Hitler's rise to power was not a final situation but a temporary phase, Moscow insisted, just a predictable stage in capitalism's death-throes. The Social Democrats and other anti-Nazi parties were to be combated as savagely as before.

Meanwhile, the Gestapo was sweeping up remaining members of the anti-Nazi underground into concentration camps. While the Communists, an instinctively conspiratorial party, might survive a little longer, they too were doomed. Admitting defeat, Ulbricht travelled first to Moscow, then to Paris. There another prominent German Communist, Wilhelm Pieck, was setting up a Central Committee in Exile.

Ulbricht remained the ice-cold, loyal servant of Moscow, for whom the party could do no wrong. At the end of that catastrophic year, 1933, he glibly announced: 'Developments have confirmed the correctness of the KPD's strategy and tactics.'[6]

He and the other surviving Communists would return to Berlin under circumstances that before 1933 only a madman could have imagined. Berlin would lie in ruins. The red, hammer-and-sickle flag would flutter over what remained of the German Reichstag.

3

'IT MUST LOOK DEMOCRATIC, BUT WE MUST HAVE EVERYTHING IN OUR HANDS'

ON I MAY 1945, Walter Ulbricht set foot on German soil for the first time in twelve years.

Before dawn the previous day, Ulbricht had woken in his room at the Hotel Lux in Moscow. Since 1917, this splendid Tsarist-era building on Tver'skaya Street had provided comfortable accommodation for favoured foreign comrades. Ulbricht belonged to that privileged few. Otherwise, he would not have been there. He would have been dead, like Hermann Schubert and Fritz Schulte, also leaders of the underground KPD, or former Politburo member Heinz Neumann. All had sought refuge in the welcoming bosom of the Soviet Union, and had perished in the cellars of the NKVD or the cruel wastes of the Gulag.

For Stalin, all humans were suspect, but foreigners, even Communist foreigners, were most suspect of all. Many thousands of lesser fish, refugees from Fascism, were sacrificed, along with their families, to the Soviet leader's paranoia. In August 1939, Stalin made a pact with Hitler, opening the way for the rape of Poland. In a breathtakingly cynical gesture of goodwill to the Führer, during that autumn Stalin delivered hundreds of refugee German Communists back to the Reich. Those not immediately executed disappeared into Gestapo prisons and concentration camps.[1]

The exiled Ulbricht obeyed every bizarre twist and turn of Stalin's policies. He spent years travelling on Comintern business. Following Hitler's attack on the Soviet Union in 1941, he turned to political work with German troops captured by the Red Army on the Eastern Front. His job was to persuade POWs to turn against Hitler and support a Communist future for post-war Germany.

Now all that work, and all that subservience, was bearing fruit. By 1945, Ulbricht ranked second in the exiled German Communist hierarchy after the veteran Communist leader, 69-year-old Wilhelm Pieck. Spring was here, and the war against Hitler was now all but won. A new phase was beginning.

At six a.m. on 1 May, a bus arrived to collect him and nine other German exiles.

Courtesy of Lend-Lease, two American McDonnell Douglas transport planes were waiting on the tarmac at Moscow airport – one for Ulbricht's group and the other for members of the 'National Committee Free Germany', prominent German prisoners of war who had agreed to work against the Nazis. They were also flying home, but for presentation reasons would travel separately from the Communists.

Little was said during the flight. 'Under Stalin you didn't ask questions . . . Under Stalin you didn't talk much.'[2] The Communists' plane landed at a captured German *Luftwaffe* base seventy kilometres east of Frankfurt on the Oder.

They stayed overnight at an inn and carried out preliminary discussions with Soviet political officers before travelling by road to Bruchmühle, near Strausberg, thirty kilometres east of Berlin. The fires of the burning capital could be clearly seen from their new base, the headquarters of Soviet Colonel-General Berzarin. Berzarin had been appointed by Stalin as city commandant of Berlin on 24 April 1945, when Hitler still had nearly a week to live. Berzarin was currently visting the front line, but his staff had organised accommodation for the German Communists in a nearby villa.

Ulbricht headed for Berlin, while the others stayed at their new quarters. Their leader returned that evening. The tireless Ulbricht called a meeting, which Soviet political officers also attended. He told his comrades: 'It will be our task to build the structure for the organs of German self-government in Berlin.' They would gather any technicians, engineers and construction experts they could find, plus teachers and artistic leaders. This was what the Russians wanted. This was the correct next step.

His colleagues glanced at each other in astonishment. Everyone knew of the unspeakable chaos and destruction in Berlin. Hitler had killed himself twenty-four hours previously, but fighting was still going on. Ulbricht talked as if he had just been made mayor of a town that needed a few problems sorted out.

Berlin was the administrative, political and economic hub of the Reich. Its last census had recorded a population of four and a quarter million. Six hundred thousand of these worked in factories. One German industrial worker in thirteen lived in the Greater Berlin area. The city accounted for nearly a tenth of German production. After five years of relentless Allied bombing and two weeks of vicious street fighting, costing almost a hundred thousand Soviet army dead and twice as many German civilian lives, scarcely a building remained standing in the city centre. The population was roughly half the pre-war level. Forty per cent of buildings had been destroyed.[3] Berlin had no power, sewerage system, or functioning public transport.

As the 'Ulbricht Group' settled into their comfortable quarters at Bruchmühle, Berlin's citizens were in hiding in cellars, or crowded into the maze of subway tunnels that ran beneath their city. Especially Berlin's women. 'Frau, komm' (Woman, come), the Soviet soldier's pidgin-German command to females he encountered, became the words every woman in Berlin, from seventeen to seventy, knew and dreaded.

Perhaps Ulbricht was aware of the wave of murder, looting and vengeful sexual violence sweeping through Berlin in the wake of the Red Army's advance. If so, he did not admit it and never would. Colleagues who tried to bring it to his attention were simply frozen out. In his fantasy version of 'liberation', such horrors could not have happened. After twelve years in Stalin's USSR, Ulbricht knew that, above all when reinforced by fear, such political fantasy could constitute a stronger power than any reality, however universally known.

However, though their new Communist masters might force them to keep silent, the people of Berlin and eastern Germany knew what they knew. The post-war Soviet War Memorial in the Tiergarten was known, with typical dark Berlin wit, as the 'Tomb of the Unknown Rapist'. The two million abortions a year carried out in occupied Germany in the immediate post-war period, mostly in the Soviet Zone, witnessed unimaginable suffering, as did the rocketing incidence of venereal disease and the 150,000 to 200,000 'Russian babies' born as the result of the rapes.

Such problems were described in Soviet military literature as applying to 'women who have been visited several times by soldiers of the Red Army'.[4]

There were many Soviet soldiers who behaved kindly and honourably, who did their best to help civilians. Many educated Russian officers were more deeply acquainted with German artistic and musical life than their Anglo-American equivalents. None the less, the Soviets and their German allies would always struggle to gain support in post-war Berlin.

It was clear from the first day that Ulbricht and his band were tools of the occupiers. On his first evening in Germany, Ulbricht met with General Galadshev, head of the Main Political Administration (PUR) of the Red Army. The Germans would carry out Soviet orders, he was instructed. 'Those travelling [to Germany],' as Comintern boss Dimitrov told the titular head of the KPD, Wilhelm Pieck, in May 1945, 'stand not at the disposal of the Communist Party of Germany, but of the Red Army and its organs.'[5]

Ulbricht would take his day-to-day orders from Galadshev's titular deputy, General Ivan Serov. This corrosively corrupt figure, brutal veteran of numerous purges and forced deportations, was in fact more powerful than his nominal superior. It was he who would dictate Ulbricht's and East Germany's fate. Serov was the senior NKVD (predecessor to the KGB) officer in Germany, reporting directly to Stalin and his secret-police chief, Lavrenty Beria.

Serov's chief task was to dismantle vast areas of eastern German industry and ship it to the Soviet Union, as part of the reparations Moscow was determined to extract from the defeated Reich. This devastated a part of Germany that had previously contained much of the country's most advanced industry. By March 1947, 11,800 kilometres of railway track (almost half the 1938 total) had been removed, while 30 per cent of the Soviet Zone's industrial capacity had been stripped and shipped.[6] Serov was also authorised to seize any wealth or valuables that could be viewed as compensation. This provided opportunities that made him and his aides notorious.

On 2 May 1945, Ulbricht's group got their first look at conquered Berlin. Wolfgang Leonhard described that first journey through the eastern suburbs into unimaginable suffering:

Our cars made their way through Friedrichsfelde in the direction of
Lichtenberg. The scene was like a picture of hell – flaming ruins and
starving people shambling about in tattered clothing; dazed German
soldiers who seemed to have lost all idea of what was going on; Red Army
soldiers singing exultantly, and often drunk; groups of women clearing
the streets under the supervision of Red Army soldiers; long queues
standing patiently waiting to get a bucketful of water from the pumps;
and all of them looking terribly tired, hungry, tense and demoralised.[7]

Remarkably, the first weeks of occupation saw considerable progress.
The raping and looting continued for quite a while. None the less,
surprisingly few Berliners actually starved. General Berzarin remains a
controversial figure. He died in a – some say – mysterious motorcycle
accident in Berlin on 16 June 1945. However, he did organise basic
supplies for the German population, often from the Red Army's own
stores. He also showed a keen interest in reviving the cultural life of the
city.[8]

As early as 17 May 1945, exhibitions from Berlin's museum collections opened in temporary quarters. On 26 May the Berlin Philharmonic
gave its first post-war concert. The Soviets, accustomed to the harsh
exigencies of a command economy, immediately dragooned thousands of
Berliners into labour gangs, and so the streets soon started to be cleared.
Trams started running once more. The first stretch of subway was
reopened on 15 May. Before long, the Russians had rounded up enough
biddable journalists to publish a daily newspaper, the *Tägliche Rundschau*
(Daily Review). However, since it was mostly filled with Soviet propaganda, the paper was known as the *Klägliche Rundschau* (Pitiable Review).[9]

Meanwhile, on 19 May the city government was re-instituted. A
former Social Democratic trade-union leader, Josef Orlopp, was persuaded to join. The method used to legitimise his 'election' was a little
basic. The Russians scoured the surrounding buildings, rounded up a few
dozen men and women, herded them together and told them to 'vote'. A
pre-war Catholic politician, Dr Andreas Hermes, who had served as Food
Minister during the 1920s, was drafted in to take charge of feeding
Berlin. The famous surgeon and director of Berlin's Charité Hospital, Dr

Sauerbruch, was tracked down to his lakeside villa at Wannsee and invited to lead the municipal health department. The architect Hans Scharoun and the film and theatre star Heinz Rühmann became advisers on architectural and cultural matters.

This city authority of all the talents did something to restore confidence. No matter how much the Russians were distrusted, an appeal to the Prussian sense of duty could be surprisingly successful. Ulbricht played this card for all he was worth.

On 12 May, Ulbricht found his Lord Mayor (*Oberbürgermeister*) for Berlin. His choice was an unpolitical college principal by the name of Dr Arthur Werner. Werner was elderly and becoming somewhat vague. Leonhard recalled the group's futile attempts to raise this problem with their leader:

> 'I don't know, Walter,' said somebody. 'Dr Werner doesn't seem to me quite the right sort of man. Besides, he's too old.'
>
> 'I've heard it said sometimes that he's not quite right in the head', said one of the men we were intending to put in the city government.
>
> 'That doesn't matter,' said Ulbricht. 'His deputy will be one of our men.'[10]

As Dr Werner's deputy, Ulbricht brought in 42-year-old Kurt Maron, one of the hardcore Communist group. The directors of education and personnel were also trusted Communists. The latter was the son of KPD leader Wilhelm Pieck. Arthur Pieck had been serving, until discharged earlier that week, with the political department of the Red Army.

Either because Stalin wished to keep good relations with the West, or because he genuinely believed that the German people could be seduced over to the Soviet side, his initial policy appeared to encourage democratic diversity. Ulbricht expressed this in a directive:

> In working class districts the mayors should as a general rule be Social Democrats. In bourgeois quarters – Zehlendorf, Wilmersdorf, Charlottenburg and so on – we must appoint a bourgeois member of the Centre, the Democrats or the German People's Party. Best of all if he has a doctorate, but he must also be an anti-Fascist and a man we can work well with.[11]

He added an instruction belying the notion that Moscow's carpet-baggers had abandoned Leninist toughness in favour of wishy-washy bourgeois democracy:

> And now to our comrades. The first deputy burgomaster and the heads of the personnel and the education departments have to be our people. Then you have to find at least one absolutely reliable comrade in each district whom we can use for building up the local police.

This was the 'regime of deputies', of which Dr Werner's appointment was a fine example. The figurehead would be a non-Communist, but the deputies must be Ulbricht's men. Communists would also be in charge of the police, giving them a monopoly of institutional force. Last but by no means least, they controlled the hotline to the true power in the shattered land, the Soviet Military Administration (SMA).

Wolfgang Leonhard was twenty-four when he accompanied the party veterans back to Berlin. As an adolescent, he had left Germany for Moscow with his Communist mother and had studied at the Comintern Political School, learning ideology and conspirational tradecraft as if it were geography or maths. He spoke fluent Russian. Ulbricht's Russian was serviceable, but he preferred to use Leonhard as an interpreter during meetings with his Soviet masters. He also sent the young man out to rustle up an administration for the middle-class suburb of Wilmersdorf. A respectable member of the bourgeoisie was required as the usual 'front'. Leonhard solved the problem by approaching every male he saw wearing a necktie until he found someone who would do.

It was at this time that Ulbricht uttered to Leonhard the famous sentence that perfectly summed up Communist strategy in newly occupied Berlin: 'It has to look democratic, but we have to hold everything in our hands'.[12]

The Ulbricht group's agenda in Berlin was urgent. Within a little less than eight weeks, the three Western allies would enter 'their' sectors of the city. Meanwhile, the Communists' task was to establish as many 'facts on the ground' as possible.

The division of Berlin between the three wartime allies – Britain, the

USA and the Soviet Union – had been agreed by the inter-Allied European Advisory Commission (EAC). This was set up in January 1944 in London. Its task was to draw up plans for the temporary administration of the defeated country, pending its political rehabilitation and the establishment of a German government. The Allied Control Commission, which would meanwhile rule Germany, would be based in Berlin.

The capital itself was too far east for the occupation zones to abut each other there, so a mini-occupation regime was set up in the capital. Each ally was assigned a chunk of Berlin, known as a 'sector', reflecting the areas controlled by the allies in Germany as a whole.

So far, so good. There were, though, problems that were either ignored or unforeseen in the warm glow of allied unity and the euphoria of approaching victory.

First, the three-power government of the city increased to four when the French demanded and were given a bit of Germany (and Berlin). Government was to be conducted by a collective *Kommandatura*, whose decisions must be unanimous. This gave any one ally a veto over the government of Greater Berlin.

Second, no formal written arrangements were set down concerning the Western allies' access to Berlin, even though it lay 160 kilometres (100 miles) inside the Soviet Zone, entirely surrounded by territory under Stalin's control.

VE Day found the Americans often hundreds of kilometres east of the demarcation lines, occupying Leipzig, Magdeburg, Halle, Weimar, and other major German cities earmarked for the Soviets. The British had part-occupied Mecklenburg on the Baltic coast. Western forces had taken a third of the territory due to be Soviet-controlled. The question was, would America and Britain withdraw from those places before the Soviets allowed them to take over the proposed Western sectors of Berlin?

Churchill was aware of the importance of 'facts on the ground'. He had wanted to march on to Berlin during the final weeks of the war. He warned Washington of the 'Iron Curtain' that a Soviet presence in the heart of Europe would create. The British Prime Minister was in favour of retaining all conquered territories until 'we are satisfied about Poland and also about the temporary nature of the Russian occupation of Germany'.

Churchill was overruled by the new US President, Harry S. Truman, who succeeded Roosevelt after the wartime President's death on 12 April 1945. Truman, busy finding his feet, did not want to upset the Russians.[13]

To the distress of German civilians, the Anglo-Americans withdrew honourably and in orderly fashion to their side of the river Elbe early in June. The Soviets, including the NKVD, swept into the vacated areas, and did what they had done elsewhere.

The West faced the task of getting its forces into Berlin. This was not easy. The Russians claimed that 'mine-clearance operations were not yet complete' or that roads were blocked by 're-deployment of Soviet troops'. This went on for six weeks after peace had allegedly broken out.

Finally, on 23 June 1945, permission was given for an American 'Preliminary Reconnaissance Party' to go to Berlin. One hundred vehicles and 500 men set off, commanded by Colonel Frank L. Howley. The column was stopped when it reached the river Elbe at Dessau. Half the force was allowed into the Soviet Zone. It proceeded under close Red Army escort to Babelsberg, just short of Berlin. There it was again held up. Personnel were forbidden to leave their vehicles. Eventually, they had to turn around and go back west.

Stalin, whose men were hard at work dismantling factories, looking for gold and other valuables, and each day introducing more proxies and agents into positions of power, was in no hurry to hand over two-thirds of the Reich's largest, richest city to his erstwhile allies. What Stalin had, he held – at least until it was prised from his stubby grasp, from the fingers that the long-since liquidated Russian poet Osip Mandelstam had described as 'thick . . . fat like worms'.[14]

It took a flying visit to Berlin eight days later by General Eisenhower's deputy, General Clay, and the British Deputy Military Governor, Sir Ronald Weeks, before progress was made. The Soviet commander gave a verbal assurance that their people could travel to Berlin via one main highway, one railway line, and two air corridors. Later Clay would write:

We did not then fully realise that the requirement of unanimous consent would enable a Soviet veto in the Allied Control Council to block all our future efforts . . . I was mistaken in not at this time making free access to Berlin a condition of our withdrawal into the occupation zone.[15]

Colonel Howley tried again on 1 July. He manoeuvred through a series of obstreperous Soviet checkpoint squads into the American sector, to find the Russians *in situ* resentful at having to abandon districts they had won at such terrible cost two months earlier. When Howley posted proclamations of the Americans' arrival, the Soviets tore them down. He had to place the placards under armed guard.

The British experienced similar difficulties. Their advance group was stopped at the Magdeburg Bridge. It was 'closed'. Undaunted, His Majesty's Forces found an unguarded bridge elsewhere on the Berlin perimeter and sneaked in that way. Further Russian obstruction prevented sufficient Western troops from establishing themselves in Berlin in time for the parade the Americans had planned for 4 July.

Two weeks later, the conference of the victorious 'Big Three' opened, at Potsdam just outside Berlin. The city was festooned with huge posters of Stalin, Marx, Engels, Lenin and other heroes of socialism. Under these circumstances Truman, Churchill and Stalin met to decide the final shape of post-war Europe. A few days into the proceedings, Churchill was voted out of office and replaced by a new prime minister, Labour's Clement Attlee. With Roosevelt's death in April, and Churchill's election defeat in July, two of the wartime 'Big Three' were no longer on the scene. The third, Josef Stalin, seemed more powerful than ever.

In the kitsch splendour of the Cäcilienhof Lodge (built in 1913 for the German Crown Prince in English villa style), fine words were said about the 'five d's' – demilitarisation, de-Nazification, de-industralisation, decentralisation and democracy. Nothing was done about Poland, where borders were being redrawn at the point of a bayonet and a bloody purge of non-Communist elements was under way, or about the fates of other countries of Central and Eastern Europe, where the Red Army was likewise enforcing Stalin's will.

The Russians must have been delighted that America proposed to withdraw from Europe by 1947. There was still nothing in writing about access to Berlin.

Harry Truman announced that America had the atom bomb. The

Soviet dictator did not seem especially impressed. This was, as so often, misleading. Stalin knew about the bomb through a spy within the American atomic establishment. He had already ordered his scientists (and the German rocket experts the NKVD was busy kidnapping) to accelerate the Soviet nuclear programme.

Walter Ulbricht had undertaken visits to Moscow twice during June 1945. He was again instructed to resist attempts to initiate a dictatorship of the proletariat and the wholesale state seizure of industrial and financial companies.

Calls to this effect came especially from home-grown Communists. When the German Communist Party was re-founded on 10 June, of the sixteen signatories to its appeal, only three had spent the Nazi period as 'illegals' in Germany. The rest were Moscow-trained exiles, blooded in the savagely conformist cockpit of the Hotel Lux on Tver'skaya Street.

Slowly the British, the Americans and the French established themselves. The Berliners' welcome was complex, but on the warm side. One British officer wrote:

> Germans are by no means sullen or resentful . . . they gaze fixedly, but many smile and wave, a few almost cheer. It is indeed a more sober liberation welcome than a triumphant entry into a conquered city, and for that, without doubt, we have the Russians to thank. Who would ever have foretold this, the most amazing irony of all, that when we entered Berlin we would come as liberators, not as tyrants, for the Germans.[16]

George Clare had come to Britain in 1938 from Vienna as a young Jewish refugee, and now returned as a British soldier to work with the Control Commission. His route to Britain seven years previously had led via Berlin. He had become attached to the Kurfürstendamm:

> Its wide tree-lined pavements were always crowded with strollers . . . Wherever you looked, at people, at shop windows, at the dense traffic, you saw the signs of prosperity. In the early autumn of 1938 life in Germany – unless one was either a Jew or valued justice, liberty, individuality – was pleasant . . . I, however, was a Jew . . .[17]

He was shocked by the changes war had wrought. And yet life continued:

> Berlin was not a lifeless moonscape. It lived – albeit in something of a zombied trance – mirrored in the dazed looks of many of the people I passed, more often noticeable in men than in women. But then the men were mostly old or elderly, bowed and bitter-faced; the few youngish ones who were about – emaciated shadows of the soldiers who had almost conquered an entire continent – looked pathetic and downtrodden in the tattered remnants of their Wehrmacht uniforms.[18]

Sadly, one particular part of Berlin that no longer lived was the family of George Clare's mother's aunt, Frau Bartmann, with whom he and his parents had spent evenings while awaiting their visas in the autumn of 1938. The Bartmanns, also Jews, had never emigrated. Clare knew enough to guess what that probably meant.

One day, Clare found himself outside a familiar apartment block. Seven years before, this was where they had lived: sixty-year-old Frau Bartmann – Aunt Manya – and her daughter, Clare's cousin, the attractive, quick-witted Rosl, who had worked for Air France in Berlin, avoiding the Nazis' ban on employment of Jews in public bodies. He examined the door of the apartment, but found only names he didn't know. On careful examination he saw 'a small oblong space on the upper-left door panel where the name plate "M. and R. Bartmann" had kept it free of Berlin's grime'. As Clare wrote many years later: 'That little rectangle, a shade lighter than the rest of the door, was their only epitaph. The only one they would ever have.'[19]

During talks that eventually 'allowed' the three Western allies to take possession of their sectors, they made a serious misjudgement. Their negotiators agreed that all orders issued by the Soviet commandant since Berlin had been under 'Allied' (i.e. until July *de facto* Soviet) control, remained in force until further notice.

These Soviet orders were more than simple administrative provisions. They included the appointment throughout Berlin of block and street wardens. Just as in the Nazi period, these people reported on and disciplined anyone who did things of which the authorities (that is, the SMA and its agents) might not approve.

On 17 August, the British commander for Charlottenburg district stripped such persons of all powers, and forbade them from interfering in the private lives of local people. The American military authorities followed suit. Westerners realised that they would have to take concrete steps to ensure that genuine representative democracy, with its concomitant freedoms, would return to Berlin. It would not happen of its own volition.

It took some weeks until the extent of the French sector was agreed. The British were the main supporters of a French role, so their share of Berlin, comprising the districts of Reinickendorf and Wedding, was carved out of the northern part of the British sector. The difference between Paris and the other Western allies was that it wanted to keep the Germans as weak and disunited as possible.

The French opposed turning the Allied Control Commission into an Allied government for the whole of the country, and at first discouraged German self-government. France continued to lay claim to the German-speaking Saar industrial area, as well as to control of the Rhineland and the mighty Ruhr industrial basin. Fiercely opposed, for patriotic reasons, to Soviet interference in their sector, they were unprepared to join the Anglo-Americans in standing up for the rights of Berliners in the face of increasingly blatant power-plays by the East and its agents.[20]

For the meantime, anyway, many Westerners persuaded themselves that these excesses were oversights, the result of Soviet inexperience in running a modern city.

Political life began to revive in the Soviet Zone. Ulbricht hoped that the SPD's erstwhile supporters would flock to the KPD, attracted by its dynamism and its closeness to the Soviet occupiers.[21] He was wrong. The SPD re-formed very quickly and within weeks had branches all over the Soviet Zone. Many on the left of the SPD had become so excited by the heady atmosphere of liberation that they started campaigning for the 'reunification' of the German workers' movement. In the 1930s, it was the split on the Left that had handed power to the Nazis. Never again!

Ulbricht's team dutifully followed Stalin's orders and kept its distance. To retain an element of control, however, Ulbricht proposed joint policy committees in which they would discuss how best to rebuild Germany in a democratic, socialist fashion. The SPD agreed.

The middle-class parties were also encouraged to re-form. They would be invited to join the KPD in a post-war 'block'. In the case of the Liberal Party (LDPD), the 'bourgeois democrats' were slow to get going. 'Walter, what can I do?' complained Richard Gyptner, the *apparatchik* charged with co-ordinating this. 'They talk a lot, but don't seem that keen on founding a party.' 'Well, Richard, just give them a good talking to,' Ulbricht replied sternly. On 5 July 1945, the Liberal Democratic Party was founded in Berlin, following the establishment of the centre-right Christian Democrat Union (CDU) on 25 June.

On 14 July, the 'Unity Front of the Anti-Fascist Democratic Parties' was announced. It comprised five representatives each from KPD, CDU, SPD and LDPD. Ulbricht's pseudo-democratic edifice stood in place. Two years later, the finishing touch was added by the creation of the National Democratic Party (NDPD), a home for repentant small-fish ex-Nazis and ex-militarists who wanted their sins forgiven and a role in the 'building of socialism'.[22]

The trick was that, although the KPD would appear to be just one party among equals, it was in fact the only political group within the 'Unity Front' that had the ear of the all-powerful SMA. Ulbricht met with senior Soviet officials every day. Without these officials – and therefore without him – nothing happened in the Soviet Zone.

This was the situation the Western Allies faced: a 'block' of superficially independent parties, a Berlin city administration fronted by democratic and/or bourgeois figures, but with shadowy, Soviet-controlled groups in the background.

In November, elections were held in Hungary and Austria, where similar 'blocks' existed under Soviet auspices. Local Communists did badly and the bourgeois and moderate-left parties very well. The hope that Soviet nominees would sweep all before them as part of a natural historical process was seen to be mistaken. A worried Soviet official told Ulbricht that if they wanted to avoid the 'Austrian danger', they would need to take a more forceful attitude towards non-Communists.[23]

Soon came a policy change. In late January 1946, Ulbricht again flew to Moscow. Stalin now told him that a merger between KPD and SPD must be achieved at all costs. The process was to be completed by the symbolic date of 1 May 1946.

Leftist Social Democrats such as Otto Grotewohl were in favour, and carried some of the rank and file with them. Many other SPD activists resisted. Those in the East quickly found themselves banned from speaking by Soviet commanders, who held absolute power in their localities. Others were dismissed or arrested on spurious charges. Attempts to organise a free Berlin-wide ballot of SPD members were foiled by the Soviet authorities, sometimes at the point of a gun. Polling stations in the West that managed to stay open showed a substantial majority against the merger.

It didn't matter. In the German State Opera House in East Berlin on 21/2 April 1946, a thousand delegates formally voted to merge the parties. More than half the membership of the new 'Socialist Unity Party of Germany' (SED in German) was made up of Social Democrats. The fourteen seats on the party committee were distributed 50/50 between Social Democrats and Communists. Joint leaders were Wilhelm Pieck (KPD) and Otto Grotewohl (SPD), while their deputies were Walter Ulbricht (KPD) and Max Fechner (SPD). Grotewohl and Pieck shook hands to a storm of applause. A stylised version of the handshake became the SED's emblem, later reproduced on a million banners and badges and posters.

With the creation of the SED, the real power in the Soviet Zone rested with the man who was technically its joint deputy leader. Walter Ulbricht, the relentless Saxon, reigned supreme in the entity he had so industriously and ruthlessly constructed. It was now a year since his arrival in the ruins of the German capital.

And Ulbricht had not finished with Berlin yet.

With Germany at their feet, the victors were soon at each other's throats. The Western Allies found themselves overwhelmed by too little of some things and too much of others. They had too little shelter and food. They had too many helpless, unproductive human beings.

In May 1945, the population of Berlin was half what it had been a few months earlier. Much of the population had fled west to escape the Russians, and many who stayed died in the fighting for the capital.

At the Potsdam Conference, a fateful step was taken. The borders of Germany were moved hundreds of miles to the west. The Poles would get most of the territories east of that new line. Protocol XII stipulated that if long-established German populations were removed from these areas, this would be done 'in an orderly and humane manner'.

Sadly, humaneness had nothing to do with it. Countries that had suffered the cruelties of German occupation thirsted for revenge. Of the five million Germans in the Polish-occupied territories, almost all were also expelled, often suddenly and with great brutality. On 19 May 1945, the Czechoslovak government announced that their three million German-speaking compatriots, the so-called 'Sudeten Germans', would be forced to leave. Women were raped, families robbed by thugs who roamed the roads and preyed upon refugee trains. Murder was commonplace.

Many of the roads and railway lines led through Berlin. Robert Murphy, political adviser to the American commandant, described the parlous situation of the refugees in a message to the State Department on 12 October 1945:

> At the Lehrter Rail Station in Berlin alone, our medical authorities state an average of ten have been dying daily from exhaustion, malnutrition and illness. In viewing the distress and despair of these wretched people . . . the mind reverts instantly to Dachau and Buchenwald. Here is retribution on a large scale, but practised not on the *Parteibonzen* [Nazi Party bosses] but on women and children, the poor and infirm.[24]

Life magazine gave a figure of eight million refugees in Berlin. Perhaps a wild exaggeration, but the city was full to overflowing. The Allies had enough trouble feeding the 1.5 million Berliners under their care. At one point, up to 25,000 refugees were reaching the Berlin city boundary each day. Perhaps these desperate people hoped that something of pre-war, splendid Berlin, with all its possibilities, survived. They could not have realised how much of the city lay in ruins. Hundreds of thousands of dwellings had been reduced to rubble. In the British sector, forty-three out of forty-four hospitals had been destroyed or seriously damaged. Newcomers were pushed straight on to westbound trains, any westbound train.

At this point, the Soviets forbade the importation of food from the surrounding countryside. They also began, under administrative pretexts, to limit the number of trains that could travel to and from the Western zones. Since original Russian regulations remained in force, for a long time the Soviets retained control, by default, of most aspects of everyday life. They could increase the pain any time they chose.

Constant hunger became the Berliners' lot. Allied soldiers or officials had access to drink, food, nylons, and especially cigarettes (which became Berlin's unofficial currency). If they were not averse to bending the rules, they could live like kings. The going price for sex with a German woman was five cigarettes. The activity of *Kippensammler* (cigarette-butt collector) became a recognised calling. A waiter in places frequented by Allied troops made a tidy side-income in this way; those at the *Café Wien* could earn five dollars per hundred.[25] A black-market bazaar spread across the huge expanse of the Tiergarten park in the centre of Berlin, where East met West.

In August 1945, it was reported that each day between fifty and a hundred children who had lost both parents, or had been abandoned, were collected from Berlin's stations and taken to orphanages or foster-parents.[26] These were the lucky ones. Gangs of children roamed the streets, thieving where they could, looting abandoned buildings and hoarding scrap to sell.

By October 1945, the German civilian ration was 800 calories per day. In the British sector at New Year 1946, it had fallen to about 400. Fuel shortages were inevitable. Previously, most of Berlin's coal had come from Silesia, just a few hundred kilometres to the east. Now the Silesian mines were in Polish hands. All coal had to be imported, mostly from the Ruhr, far away in western Germany. It was required at the rate of 600 tons per day as winter came on. There was never enough.

Around 12,000 Berliners died during that first post-war year, of starvation or of illnesses associated with malnutrition. However, for the survivors there ensued a feverish cultural flowering – newspapers opened in the Western sectors, theatres and night-clubs and cabarets, and even film studios were open again for business. Berliners might have little to eat, and they might freeze in unheated cellars, but for the first time since 1933 they could do, say and write what they wanted. With grim humour, these were known as the 'golden hunger years'.[27]

In the Soviet Zone, SPD and KPD had merged to form the SED. This was not, however, the end of the old SPD. When allowed, most SPD members had voted against union with the Communists. Despite persecution in the Soviet sector, the oldest and largest working-class party continued to operate on a citywide basis.

Elections for provincial and municipal assemblies throughout the Soviet Zone (and in parts of the Western zones) took place in September/ October 1946. The Soviets and the Communists did their best to persuade – or intimidate – the electorate into voting for the SED. All the same, the results were, for Ulbricht and his Soviet masters, a disappointment. This was crushingly true in Berlin.

In the Berlin city elections, the SPD won almost 49 per cent of the votes. Second came the right-of-centre CDU with 22 per cent. Despite massive support from the Communist political machine and the Soviet Military Administration, the SED trailed at 19.8 per cent. The SPD beat the SED in every district – even 'Red' Wedding, where before Hitler came to power the Communists had regularly won 60 per cent of the vote.

Colonel Sergei Tiul'panov, director of propaganda for the Soviet Military Administration, was outraged. It would in future, he declared, be necessary 'to forbid categorically even the slightest degree of disrespect towards the Soviet Union and Soviet occupation authorities'.

In the winter of 1946/7, the Communists decided to pursue a 'hard' course. There was a wave of arrests, of real or imagined Nazis and 'subversives', including liberal and Social Democrat activists. In 1946, the Soviets set up the German Administration of the Interior (*Deutsche Verwaltung des Innern* = DVdI), made up entirely of trusted Communists, which would control a German auxiliary police force soon dubbed the 'People's Police'.

Ominously, 'special camps' were set up. Some of these, as an appalled world would later learn, were converted Nazi concentration camps such as Buchenwald, near Weimar, and Sachsenhausen, thirty-five kilometres from Berlin. At least 150,000 Germans and 35,000 non-Germans from the Soviet Zone disappeared into these brutal places between 1945 and 1949.

Whether these were death camps like those run by the Nazis remains a matter of controversy. There were many executions and beatings. Deaths through disease, malnutrition and maltreatment accounted for at least a third of those imprisoned, as they did in the Soviet Gulag system. Although the Soviets and their German allies claimed that many of those who died were Nazis and war criminals, the vast majority were, in fact, either relatively low-level Hitlerite fellow travellers or simply opponents of the Stalinist system.[28] The leaders of the rapidly growing DVdI would emerge openly in the 1950s as commanders of the internationally notorious *Stasi*.

It took one of the Communists' own to lead the fight-back. That figure was Ernst Reuter. In common with many who rose to prominence in Berlin (as in New York and London), Reuter was originally from somewhere else.

Born, like Hitler, in 1889, Reuter grew up as son of a sea captain in Friesland. In the First World War, he served on the Eastern Front. He was captured, became a prisoner of war in Russia, and after the revolution was drawn to Bolshevism. Reuter caught the attention of Lenin himself, who sent him back to Germany at the beginning of 1919. He became Berlin Secretary of the infant KPD.

Reuter underwent a meteoric rise to the top of the German Communist Party, but his career as a revolutionary was short-lived. Disillusioned by the KPD's violent methods, he found his way to the SPD.

Reuter was elected an SPD city councillor and became a successful member of Berlin's magistracy, responsible for transport policy. He originated the unitary ticket and pushed forward with building more subway lines, aware that the automobile could change the city in profound and probably undesirable ways. From 1931 to 1933, Reuter accepted the job of High Burgomaster of Magdeburg. During the economic crisis, he worked tirelessly on relief projects for the unemployed. After 1933, he was saved from a concentration camp by friends who got Reuter a job advising the Turkish government on transport. He spent the war years exiled in Ankara.

Reuter returned to Berlin in 1945. He was once more elected to the city council and awarded his old job in charge of transport. Then, in May 1947, the existing Mayor was forced to resign, and Reuter was offered the top post.

The Communists hated no one more than an apostate. The Soviet commandant refused to recognise Reuter's election. He had to stand down in favour of the SPD veteran Louise Schröder, but remained the key figure around whom Berlin's anti-Communists rallied. Reuter's understanding, as an ex-KPD insider, of the mentality of *apparatchiks* such as Ulbricht, proved invaluable.

Frustrated by their inability to run Berlin as they wished, the Communists started arresting their opponents, not just in the Soviet Zone but also in the West. Paul Markgraf, a former Wehrmacht captain, captured at Stalingrad and transformed into a keen Communist, was appointed Police President of Berlin by the Soviets in May 1945. More than 5,000 individuals thought undesirable by Markgraf's masters 'disappeared' from the streets of Berlin, including the Western sectors.[29]

George Clare described the routine, based on his own experience as a British employee of the Control Commission in Berlin:

> The Russians . . . began to 'take out' political and human-rights activists who opposed them. It was all over in seconds. A car screeched to a sudden halt, hefty men jumped out, grabbed their victim, bundled him into their vehicle and, before those who witnessed it could even begin to comprehend what had happened, they were racing off in the direction of the Soviet sector.[30]

After each abduction, the Western commandants lodged a protest at Red Army HQ in Berlin-Karlshorst. General Kotikov, their Soviet colleague, would deny involvement, sigh, and remind them that it was their job to prevent 'banditry' in their sectors, not his.

4

BLOCKADE

BY MID-1947, MUTUAL distrust marked relations between the Western powers and their former Russian ally. The so-called Truman Doctrine aimed at the 'containment' of Soviet power. In June 1947, after a harsh winter brought Europe to its knees, President Truman's new Secretary of State, General George C. Marshall, announced a comprehensive system of recovery aid for Europe. Its official title was the European Recovery Plan (ERP). History would call it the 'Marshall Plan'.

What Marshall proposed was a delay in the withdrawal of American forces from Europe and a programme of financial aid for receptive European countries. It was actually little more than pump-priming, but came at a time when a psychological boost was badly needed. Britain was struggling to cope with the economic and human aftermath of the terrible winter, as well as running its own zone in Germany, not to mention backing the monarchist Greek government against Communist rebels.

Britain found itself, in truth, at a low ebb. It could no longer provide the balancing factor in Europe that America had originally thought to rely on. Communists in France and Italy, buoyed by their role as heroes of the anti-Nazi struggle, seemed on the brink of power. There was still widespread hunger and unemployment, among the 'victorious' nations as well in defeated Germany. An opportunity for Stalin and his supporters. After the traumas of the Great Depression and the catastrophe of Hitlerism, capitalism and democracy were not automatically accepted as panaceas for the ills of civilisation. Communism – especially the shiny, sanitised anti-Fascist version put about by Stalin's propagandists – still held a wide appeal to many in the West, both workers and intellectuals.

Many non-Communist Germans also blamed Hitler's rise on the

capitalist system, the Nazi regime as an unholy marriage of big business and reaction. To avoid a new Thousand Year Reich, society must go beyond capitalism. Ulbricht and the Soviets played successfully on this antipathy to the past. They expropriated the big landowners within months of the war's end ('Junkers' lands into farmers' hands' went the slogan), and nationalised almost half the big-business concerns in the Soviet Zone as retribution for their complicity in the crimes of Nazism.

The land reform was popular with small farmers, as such redistributions generally are. The substantial majority that voted for it had not read their history. In 1917, Lenin drummed up support in the Russian countryside with the appeal 'All Land to the Peasants!'. In the 1930s, those peasants found their newly granted lands absorbed into state-run collectives. If they resisted, they and their families were condemned to starve. In Ulbricht's kingdom things would be little different, as the farmers would soon discover.

Nazi officials also seemed to be more swiftly expelled from their positions in the Soviet Zone. An aggressive anti-Fascist spirit was promoted. Some, especially intellectuals and left-wing idealists, looked disapprovingly at the Western zones, where the Anglo-Americans were willing to rely on ex-Nazi experts and officials to keep things going. Many Germans decided that, for all their faults, Ulbricht and Co. were the only true anti-Nazis. A pro-Soviet Germany seemed a sure guarantee that the far Right would never again plunge the world into war.

The struggle for German hearts and minds continued. Marshall's aid plan was strongly angled at the Western zones, though it was offered to the Soviet Zone as well, and to the fragile post-war democracy in Czechoslovakia and other Central and Eastern European states. No one in Washington expected Stalin to let the East Germans or any other of his new dependencies benefit, and he did not. The Soviets vetoed the Czechoslovaks' acceptance and initiated intrigues that would lead to the March 1948 Communist coup in Prague.

In the Soviet Zone, the SED responded with a barrage of political insults that showed the Cold War was already a reality:

The industrial West [of Germany] is being incorporated into a peace-threatening western bloc. The power of the German company bosses will be maintained. In place of a German economy tailored for peace, a new power-centre of reactionary and warlike elements is arising. In place of co-determination for the work force and economic growth, there will come wage slavery for the benefit of foreign and German monopoly capitalists.[1]

The temerity of Jakob Kaiser, chairman of the CDU in the Soviet Zone, who spoke in favour of the Marshall Plan's adoption there, led directly to his loss of office, and in short order to his forced flight to West Berlin. The supposedly independent 'block parties' were nothing of the sort.

In March 1947, Communist leader Wilhelm Pieck took ex-Social Democrat Otto Grotewohl, his co-chair in the SED, to visit Stalin. They asked permission to take their embryonic German state further towards fully fledged Communism.

The old fox in the Kremlin held back, perhaps hoping he could still achieve a unified Germany that was pro-Soviet, even Soviet-controlled. All the same, when the SED leaders bemoaned the continued presence of the Western Allies in Berlin, Stalin told them: 'Well, let's try with all our might, and maybe we'll drive them out'.[2]

There had been some economic progress in the Western zones in 1947/8. Mines had started to produce, factories to manufacture. Life remained hard, but few Germans were starving. The political situation (especially between the Anglo-Saxons and the French) was slowly improving. But industrial production had reached only 50 per cent of its pre-war level. Purchasing power remained dangerously low.

Besides, most of what should have been available was being withheld from the market. The old Reichsmark, still official currency throughout occupied Germany, was all but worthless. This was partly due to the fact that the Soviets had acquired the old Reich Bank's printing presses and had set to producing paper money as if it were going out of fashion. Which, due to rampant inflation, it soon was. There has been, so far as the world knows, no sophisticated industrial economy that ever de-pended on the cigarette as its basic monetary unit. Short of creating a gunpoint command economy, how did one persuade the producers of goods to sell and the consumers of goods to buy? The answer was, by creating a currency that was worth something.

In March/April 1948, following the collapse of inter-Allied talks, the Russians withdrew from the Allied Control Commission. This ensured paralysis in the administration of Germany and an end to hopes of a peace treaty. However, the Western allies could now in all (or almost all) honesty cease having to take into account the economic and political needs of the Soviet Zone when judging the requirements of their own. This they were pleased to do.

In April 1948, Secretary Marshall met American military governor General Lucius Clay in Berlin. Something had to happen if the occupation zones were to cease being a burden on the administering powers, become less vulnerable to Communist pressure, and develop their own (capitalist and parliamentary-democratic) social systems. Clay was instructed accordingly.

The British and Americans had already created 'Bizonia', a free-trade area in their two zones. France and the USSR had opposed this. The Russians supposedly supported unified German organs of government but in practice did not; while the French supposedly opposed such centralised organs, but in practice were gradually drawn by economic and political necessity into the Anglo-American orbit. On 1 June 1948, the French abandoned claims to the Ruhr and the Rhineland. 'Bizonia' eventually became 'Trizonia'.

On 18 June came a decisive step, not just in German economic history but in the development of the Cold War.

The British, the Americans, and the French withdrew the Reichsmark from circulation and issued everyone in their zones with 40 new Deutsche Marks (D-Marks), with another 20 due shortly, in exchange for 60 old marks. This was a week's pay for a working man. All payments thereafter would take place at a rate of 1:1. The new D-Marks were put into circulation elsewhere at the rate of between 10:1 and 15:1 to the Reichsmark depending on the type of currency or debt held. Notional savings were lost, but purchasing power was created overnight.

From an economic point of view, the gamble paid off. Goods appeared in the shops, as if by a miracle, almost from the first day. Industrial production would increase by 24 per cent in 1949 and 12 per cent in the first half of 1950. The average annual growth rate rose to 15 per cent per year.

The Russians were furious at this breach of the Potsdam Agreement, but they could do nothing. Then, on 23 June, the West announced plans to introduce the new D-Mark (overprinted with a 'B' for Berlin) into Berlin. To the Soviets, this was a step too far. It gave them the justification for drastic measures.

The Soviets had already been making things more difficult for Allied personnel and for Berliners who wished to travel. Russian aircraft had been buzzing Allied planes. Trains had been deliberately re-routed to pass by West Berlin. Civilian road traffic had been all but banned. Travellers were held up for long periods at the interzonal border. The Soviet-licensed press claimed a dramatic increase in banditry, theft and black-market activity. 'Starving thousands' from the West were allegedly endangering food supplies in the Soviet Zone, egged on by 'criminal elements including Fascist activists expelled from the Soviet Zone'.[3]

On the day after the currency reform, the Russians announced that rail links between the Western zones and the Western sectors of the city were closed until further notice because of 'technical difficulties'. The Elbe bridge over which the autobahn to Berlin passed was declared out of use due to repairs. Within a short time, all routes became unavailable. Claiming fuel shortages, Eastern power stations near enough simultaneously ceased to supply electricity to the Western sectors of Berlin.

Just after midnight on 24 June 1948, the Berlin Blockade had begun.

The Soviet/East German attempt to force the issue on Berlin started out as a potential catastrophe and ended as a political and moral triumph for the West.

The question was, could the two-and-a-half million West Berliners survive? The city had coal supplies sufficient for around forty-five days. There were reasonable stocks of diesel fuel and oil, less so for petrol. All raw materials for Berlin's factories had to be imported. Having been forced to feed their own sectors of the city since they arrived in 1945, the Western Allies were well aware of what it took to save their civilians from starvation: 641 tons a day of flour, 105 of cereals, 106 of meat and fish, 900 of potatoes, 51 of sugar, 10 of coffee, 20 of milk, 32 of fats, 3 of yeast.[4]

Before 24 June, most of Berlin's power had come from the Russian sector. Even after energy rationing, there was no prospect that the shortfall in the city's electricity supply could be made up from generating capacity in the Western sectors. The Berlin West power station, in the British sector, had once supplied a quarter of the city's electricity. It had been stripped by the Soviets in June 1945. Only in April 1948, after three years of fruitless four-power negotiations over reconstruction plans, did the British decide to go it alone. Work on the plant had not yet started. With all access by land and water cut off, how could steel, concrete and other raw materials and machinery be brought to Berlin?

At the time the Soviets enforced the blockade, the US army's Chief of Plans and Operations, General Albert Wedemeyer, was on a tour of inspection in Europe. Wedemeyer had commanded the China Theatre in 1944–5. He was familiar with one of the most famous supply operations in history: the Allied airlift from India across the Himalayas (the 'Hump') to Chinese troops fighting in southern China and Burma. Wedemeyer thought an airlift for Berlin could work, and suggested a suitable organiser – another veteran of the 'Hump', Lieutenant-General William H. Tunner.

The track record of airlifts was patchy at best. Notoriously, *Luftwaffe* commander Hermann Göring had boasted of his ability to supply the beleaguered Germany army in Stalingrad by air during the savage Russian winter of 1942/3. He had failed miserably, leading to one of the Third Reich's most humiliating defeats.

None the less, the Western Allies in 1948 had advantages over their wartime predecessors: two decently equipped airports to fly into (at Gatow in the British sector and Tempelhof in the American); a supportive population; and last but not least, the fact that, as things stood, no one shot at the aircraft as they went about their business.

The Russians, by contrast, seemed confident that the West could not supply Berlin by air, and their optimism was not irrational. Tempelhof in particular was not an ideal cargo port. It was hemmed in by suburbs, with seven-storey buildings looming either side of the landing-path. Gatow was way out on the periphery, with a long arm of the river Havel between it and the main part of the British sector.

There were basically only two alternatives to an airlift. Either an Allied military strike along the autobahn to open up the route through to Berlin – which would lead to war if the Soviets chose to oppose it. Or, on the other hand, surrender. The former was considered too risky and the latter would mean a humiliating defeat that might have repercussions throughout the world. This was why the airlift started quickly. Once war not an option, and surrender considered out of the question, there was no alternative to supplying Berlin by air.

The nearest equivalent operation was the RAF's effort to supply the starving German-held areas of Holland during the last days of the war. In 1945, 650 sorties by Lancaster bombers had been required to drop 1,560 tons of food in two days. This, however, occurred under wartime conditions of full mobilisation, with massive numbers of aircraft in service that could be diverted to such a mission at short notice. The operation also enjoyed unequivocal public support. By 1948, airforces had been run down to something like peacetime levels, military aircraft scrapped or converted to civilian use. A Berlin airlift would require a similar mobilisation on the part of countries that were struggling to feed their own people, let alone the inhabitants of a city that had recently symbolised all the evil in the world: Nazi Berlin.

Astonishingly, the Anglo-Americans pulled it off. The French were not actively involved, although they helped achieve the rapid construction of a new airfield in their sector, at Tegel. This was one of the few places in West Berlin where sufficient open space existed. However, an obstruction had to be removed: the radio tower used by the Soviets for 'Radio Berlin', their local broadcasting mouthpiece.

At first the French attempted to negotiate, but when the Soviets proved stubborn, the French commandant, General Jean Ganéval, had his men attach explosives to the tower's base and blow it up. General Kotikov stormed up to Ganéval and demanded to know how he could do such a thing. 'With the help of dynamite and French sappers, my friend!' Ganéval coolly replied.[5] Seventeen thousand civilian volunteers from the Western sectors of Berlin helped construct 5,500 feet of runway, built with over ten million bricks salvaged from wartime rubble. The first transport plane landed at Tegel Airfield on 5 November 1948.

The American supply operation was codenamed 'Operation Vittles', and the British 'Knicker' and then 'Carter Patterson' (a reference to a well-known British freight company). In July 1948, the airlift moved 69,000 tons per month.

Things were initially chaotic. On 13 August, in foggy conditions, a C-54 Skymaster overshot the runway at Tempelhof and caught fire. Others also suffered from misjudged landings and burst tyres, leading to incoming aircraft stacking up over the airfield. General Tunner later described such a scene in his memoirs:

> As their planes bucked around like grey monsters in the murk the pilots filled the air with chatter, calling in constantly in near panic to find out what was going on. On the ground a traffic jam was building as planes came off the unloading line to climb on the homeward-bound three minute conveyor belt, but were refused permission to take off for fear of collision with the planes milling around overhead.[6]

Tunner, the systems expert, gradually imposed order. By October, the monthly tonnage had risen to 147,581. In April 1949, 7,845 tons was achieved in a single day, almost a quarter of a million tons on a monthly basis. By Easter, a fully laden plane was landing in West Berlin every sixty-two seconds.

It was a feat of organisation, far beyond anything thought possible. It would never have happened without the thousands of Berliners who threw themselves into the tasks of unloading and distribution, and who tolerated the shortages and privations of the blockade with amazing good grace.

Western aircrew were mobbed by cheering, flower-presenting Berliners. British and American pilots became celebrities. Lieutenant Gail S. Halversen, who started out casually dropping candy wrapped in handkerchiefs to kids he saw watching his plane from the ground, became a popular hero, and started a trend for Allied pilots to drop sweets and chocolate bars on their landing approaches. In honour of the little luxuries they brought along with the basic necessities, and in a play on the fact that just a few years earlier the same aircraft had delivered a much deadlier wartime cargo, the aircraft were known as *Rosinenbomber* ('raisin-bombers').

The Soviets never actually attacked the Western aircraft. Stalin was not prepared to risk outright war. But their Yak fighters did everything short of inviting combat. They played 'chicken' with the incoming planes, buzzing them aggressively and performing dangerous acrobatics around the air corridors. The Soviets blinded Allied pilots with searchlights, jammed radio frequencies, and carried out 'exercises' with their anti-aircraft artillery that involved shooting perilously close to the corridors.

In those months, blockaded Berlin changed its character. The population felt for the first time that the West really cared about them. A wave of affection for the USA swept through Berlin. American slang, films and music became wildly popular.

To complement the morale-boosting drone of supply aircraft overhead, there were the newly powerful media that the West had established, especially RIAS (Radio in the American Sector). Founded in September 1946, after the Soviets refused to relinquish unilateral control of 'Radio-Berlin', RIAS was controlled by the United States Information Agency. However, the station featured an extraordinary cavalcade of German journalistic and artistic talent. Its 20,000-watt transmitter enabled it to broadcast twenty-four hours a day from new studios in the Kufsteiner Strasse in Schöneberg, with a good reach into the Soviet Zone. This was further aided by a booster transmitter at Hof, in northern Bavaria, which could reach into the key Soviet-controlled industrial areas of Thuringia and Saxony.

Apart from intrepid news journalists such as Peter Schulze, Richard Löwenthal, Jürgen Graf and Egon Bahr, RIAS also became popular for the quality of its entertainment shows. Most famous was the cabaret-style satirical show *Die Insulaner* (The Islanders), where the cast made fun of Berlin's position in the middle of the Soviet Zone and mocked the hardships this entailed. By 1948, 80 per cent of Berliners listened to RIAS. Despite Eastern jamming and interference from Radio Belgrade, it had a good audience in the Soviet Zone.

RIAS played a crucial role, since the drama within the city itself was almost as important to its survival as the external one symbolised by the airlift.

Since 1946, Berlin's city assembly or *Magistrat* met at the 'Red Town Hall'. This landmark, with its 230-feet high tower, stood near the Alexanderplatz in the Soviet sector. Its name had nothing to do with politics. It was due to the fact it had been built in 1870 of garish red brick.

When the D-Mark was introduced in June 1948, the SED organised protest demonstrations. There were altercations in the city assembly. The crisis came, however, a month later, when a majority of representatives demanded an end to the blockade. In response, the Soviets' tame press accused them of 'crimes against humanity'. The city treasury, also based in the East, froze the *Magistrat*'s bank accounts. City employees could not be paid. On 4 August, Police President Markgraf's deputy, Johannes Stumm, announced he was setting up a police authority in West Berlin. Stumm invited all Berlin policemen to join him. Three-quarters of them – 1,500 out of 2,000 – soon did so.

Markgraf and the Communists remained very much in control of the Eastern sector. When the *Magistrat* met on 26 August, a huge and intimidating crowd of SED supporters showed up, waving red flags and shouting slogans such as 'Down with the bankrupt *Magistrat*!', 'No Marshall Plan', and 'No more airfields'. The SED called for the *Magistrat* to resign. It would be replaced by a special commission, whose job would be to enact emergency measures and co-operate with the 'great Soviet Union'.[7]

That evening, 30,000 anti-Communist Berliners gathered on the parkland in front of the Reichstag to hear a speech from Ernst Reuter:

> We Berliners have said *No* to Communism and we will fight it with all our might as long as there is a breath in us . . . the *Magistrat* and the City Assembly together with the freedom-loving Berlin population will build a dam against which the red tide will break in vain.

The next day, another threatening crowd of SED supporters gathered outside the Red Town Hall. Markgraf's police were clearly on their side.

The acting Mayor, Dr Friedensburg, tried vainly to persuade the Soviets to guarantee the safety of the city assembly. The non-Communist councillors were divided. The Right wanted a safe place to meet in the West, while SPD members felt they should continue to work in the East until this became impossible. The SPD won. A new council meeting was announced for 6 September, ten days later.

By eleven a.m. on 6 September, 3,000 Communist demonstrators had gathered. They let the assembly members enter. Then they violently invaded the building. Western journalists were attacked, microphones ripped out. Some assembly members managed to break through the cordon around the building and escape. Others holed up in their offices. Markgraf's police did nothing.

The Communists roamed the town hall, discovering forty-six plain-clothes West sector ('Stumm') police that assembly members had brought for their protection. Other Westerners fled, or found refuge in the offices of the Allied liaison officers attached to the *Magistrat*. Things went quiet. Then, at around eleven p.m., Markgraf police demanded that Dr Friedensburg unlock his office. He refused. They marauded through the building, trying doors until they managed to break into the American liaison officer's room. They found a number of German civilians in there and carted them off in handcuffs.

From now on, all *Magistrat* members and employees, as well as the Western liaison officers, were hostages. A break-out attempt in the early evening foundered on the tightness of the ring around the town hall, now reinforced by Soviet troops. The British liaison officer had his answer: he sent out urgently for tea, milk and sugar. His French colleague, Captain Ziegelmeyer, also reacted admirably in accordance with his national stereotype. On returning at around nine p.m. from a visit to the theatre, he found his way blocked. Ziegelmeyer, not to be foiled by a handful of Germans, pushed past and sprang through the shattered glass doors, crying out, 'This is the French way in!' Other French colleagues, bearing champagne, followed him.

Finally, the Soviet commandant responded to Ganéval's plea to allow the remaining inmates of the Red Town Hall to leave in safety. At five a.m., Western-sector police officers who had spent the night in hiding inside were loaded into one French truck, and exhausted German and American journalists into another.

The hostages set off for the sector border, just ten minutes' drive away. They had scarcely gone a kilometre when a Russian jeep, full of armed soldiers, blocked their way. Some of the Stumm police were kept in custody and ended up spending months in the former Nazi concentration camp at Sachsenhausen.

When the American representative on the *Kommandatura* entered Kotikov's office to deliver a protest, he was told that 'peaceful workers' petitioning the city assembly had been assaulted by Western soldiers and 'black guards' from West Berlin (equating the Stumm police with the Nazi SS). It was he, Kotikov, who should be protesting, was it not?

It became clear that anything like a democratic government in the Eastern part of the city was impossible. The SMA moved into city halls in the Eastern districts and began to dismiss employees who were not SED members. Western city councillors, meeting at the Free University, agreed to hold new elections in November.

On 9 September, 250,000 Berliners thronged the *Platz der Republik* (Republic Square) in front of the Reichstag to hear their leaders urge them to hold out against the blockade and oppose attempts to topple their elected representatives.

Ensuing demonstrations began in the British sector, but spilled over into the Soviet sector just by the Brandenburg Gate. The reaction of the Eastern police was prompt. A dozen demonstrators ended up in hospital, ten with bullet wounds. A sixteen-year-old boy was shot in the stomach and bled to death. Five demonstrators were arrested by the East sector police and condemned to twenty-five years' hard labour by a Soviet military court. After international protests, the Soviets were forced to cut the sentences. In explanation for this unaccustomed clemency, they said that the impressionable young men had been fired up by 'Fascistic, provocative' speeches.

The Soviet blockade of Berlin still had eight months to run. However, from now until 1990, Berlin was divided, both politically and administratively. For three years the Allied Control Commission, based there, was supposed to have been the ruling body for the whole country, pending a peace treaty with a reunited Germany. The ACC was now a dead letter. And within a year there would be two German states.

Even now, with that decisive development still to come and relative freedom of movement remaining between Eastern and Western sectors, there was no longer any point in pretending that Berlin was still the capital of Germany. It wasn't even one city any more, though it wasn't yet clearly two.

BLOOD

5

'DISSOLVE THE PEOPLE AND ELECT ANOTHER'

FEW DRAWN-OUT HISTORICAL events or processes came to their ends on the conveniently precise dates cited in the history books. The Berlin Blockade was no exception.

A few seconds after midnight on 12 May 1949, a corporal of the British Royal Corps of Military Police opened the iron gate at the Helmstedt crossing point on the border between the British and the Soviet zones. For the first time in almost a year, a convoy of cars and trucks moved through, heading along the autobahn towards Berlin. At 1.23 a.m., a British military train, pulled by a German engine and driven by a German engineer, set off for Berlin. The first vehicle coming from Berlin arrived at Helmstedt around two that morning, a car driven by an American.

But all was not yet quite what it seemed. Within a very short time, it became obvious that the Soviets had replaced the blockade with a new set of hindrances and restrictions.

After lengthy negotiations about the lifting of the blockade, the SMA had sneaked in a last-minute stipulation that there should be only sixteen trains a day. These must be pulled by Eastern engines and manned by Eastern crews. Moroever, they changed timetables without notice, delayed military trains so that the journey between Helmstedt and Berlin took seven hours instead of two, and produced lists of forbidden exports from Berlin that left 90 per cent of the city's trade impossible. Trucks were forbidden to travel on the autobahn at night. All mail and postal traffic still had to come in by air, since the Soviets diverted mail trains to their sector and would not release their cargoes.

On 18 May, 400 food trucks were stuck at the border due to Russian demands for a stamp from the German Economic Commission, an organ of the occupation regime controlled by Soviet appointees. Barge traffic, a large proportion of the city's trade, was held up by Soviet demands for crew lists and transit permits.[1]

Bizarrely, within days of its apparent salvation, Berlin was paralysed from within by a transport strike. The dispute's cause was a political and economic powerplay. The S-Bahn (overground city railway) was part of the old German railways, the *Deutsche Reichsbahn*. The Directorate of the *Reichsbahn* (the RBD) was Soviet-controlled, and paid its railwaymen in East marks even after the D-Mark was introduced. The 15,000 of these who lived in West Berlin found themselves in real distress, unable to pay for goods and services. On 20 May, these employees refused to operate the rail network in Berlin and also the routes to western Germany. They occupied many stations and disabled the signals and the tracks.

The Soviet response was to send Eastern-sector police not only into Eastern stations but into Western ones, including the main Zoo station. There was shooting. Several strikers were wounded and one killed. For a state that claimed to represent the workers to behave in this fashion was, to say the least, interesting.

The British, in response, sent Stumm police into Charlottenburg, and then to Zoo. After three-sided scuffles between Eastern- and Western-sector police on the one hand and strikers on the other, the Easterners withdrew. It wasn't until 24 May that the Eastern police agreed to withdraw from all Western rail facilities. Days of negotiations stretched into weeks. The Easterners, whose own economy and distribution networks were starting to be affected, offered up to 60 per cent of the men's wages in West marks.

The offer was refused. The strikers were getting strike pay and unemployment benefit – all in hard D-Marks – which made them better off staying on strike than going back to work. Two further compromise packages were turned down. The Allies found themselves in a quandary. Was this not the democracy they were claiming to introduce? Were not workers within their rights to strike for the pay rate they desired?

In the end, on 26 June, the Western commandants made a final offer to the transport strikers. First the carrot: the Allied authorities would make up the men's wages to full D-Mark equivalents for three months, and the city government would find alternative work for anyone who was afraid to go back to work for the RBD. Then the stick: anyone who stayed out on strike got no more welfare payments.

On 1 July, the S-Bahn reopened. From the following day, trains to other destinations, most importantly western Germany, were running once more.

From now on, for four decades, the Allies and the West Berlin authorities would ensure there was always enough food and fuel for the city to keep going. A reserve of five months' supplies became standard, in case of a new blockade.

The Soviets and the German Communists continued with their obstructionism and carried on with aggressive attempts to undermine West Berliners' morale. A four-power conference in Paris about Berlin – called as part of the blockade settlement – broke up on 20 June after a month of pettifogging argument, with only the vaguest of 'gentlemen's agreements' regarding long-term access to Berlin from the West.

Meanwhile, an event of far more importance to the future of the city and of Germany had already occurred. On 23 May 1949, the Federal Republic of Germany came into being.

The expropriation of the big landowners in the Soviet Zone, plus widespread nationalisation of private companies and banks there, guaranteed well before the end of 1946 that the economies of the Soviet Zone and the other three had already dramatically diverged. Even then, Ulbricht's SED was fully in charge.

Stalin's policy of keeping his options open in the matter of German unity became all but untenable. He could instruct the few Communists in the West German constituent assembly not to sign the basic law that established the Federal Republic, and they obeyed. His propaganda machine could breathe fire and brimstone against the 'fascists', 'capitalists' and 'revanchists' in the West, and it did. But, short of invasion, Stalin could do little to stop the creation of a three-quarter-size version of Germany west of the Elbe.

In fact, the very name of the new West German state – the Federal Republic of Germany rather than 'German Federal Republic' – was a challenge. It implied that the state represented the whole German land and people. Its provisional seat of government was the modest Rhineland university city of Bonn, which obviously could not be taken seriously as a permanent capital. To have chosen a major city such as Frankfurt or Hamburg would have implied the permanent loss of East Germany and Berlin, which was unacceptable. Right from the start, the West German state viewed itself as the legitimate successor state to the pre-war German Reich.

Moscow was forced to make its move. In May 1949, elections were held in the Soviet Zone for a so-called 'People's Congress' (full name: 'People's Congress for Unity and a Just Peace'). In March, Stalin had sanctioned a purge in the SED and reluctantly allowed plans for an East German government and parliament to be drafted. All the same, nothing was done until the West acted. Stalin may have done a lot to cause the division of Germany, but he was determined not to be blamed for it.[2]

The elections took place for the first time on a basis that would become all too familiar: the single-list ballot. This offered a pre-decided list of candidates from the so-called 'block' parties that, whatever their official names, were controlled by the SED. Electors could vote either 'yes' or 'no' (since there were no alternative candidates, purely a protest vote). Under the circumstances, the 66 per cent 'yes' vote – 34 per cent daring to register fruitless dissent – was scarcely a ringing endorsement. At the next elections the 'yes' vote suddenly increased to 90 per cent plus, and stayed unwaveringly at that level throughout the history of East Germany.

The 2,000-member People's Congress met in the Russian sector of Berlin and selected a People's Council of 330 members. On 30 May, a constitution for the 'German Democratic Republic' was agreed. But even as a Marxist-Leninist state was being assembled, the rhetoric of German unity remained official usage in the Soviet Zone. Sometime between the elections to the West German federal parliament, the *Bundestag*, on 15 August 1949, and the emergence of the first West German government a month later, the balance tipped.

On 16 September 1949, the venerable Catholic politician, Konrad Adenauer, became chancellor in Bonn. That same day, an East German delegation in Moscow agreed on the foundation of a separate state in the Soviet Zone. The German Democratic Republic (GDR) was formally established on 7 October 1949. Pieck, the veteran KPD leader, became president, while Grotewohl, the former Social Democrat, became provisional prime minister, pending elections of whose outcome there could be no doubt. Ulbricht, First Secretary of the SED, remained the real power in the land.

The new government took over most functions of the SMA. The SED's security service became the Ministry for State Security (*Ministerium für Staatssicherheit* = *Stasi*). Its role was to persecute opponents of the Communist state and protect state and party apparatus against subversion. To this end it established a labyrinthine system of informers, agents and *provocateurs*. Like the Federal Republic, and the Weimar Republic before, the GDR took as its flag the black-red-gold banner of the 1848 revolutionaries. The flag remained indistinguishable from the West's until 1959, when the GDR symbol of a hammer (for the workers) and a compass (for the intellectuals) inside ears of grain (for the farmers) was placed at its centre to give it a clear identity.

So now there was a capitalist and a Communist Germany. The seat of the GDR government was declared to be Berlin. The people of the Western sectors, embarking on their first post-blockade winter, were surrounded not just by Russian occupiers but by a separate German state, with its capital in the eastern part of the Berliners' own city.

The Berlin blockade signalled the advent of the 'hard' Cold War. Relations between the West and the Soviet Union finally deteriorated from disillusioned and sporadically violent bickering to a kind of undeclared conflict.

Nineteen forty-nine also saw the establishment of the Communist People's Republic of China under the brilliant and ruthless Mao Tse-tung. The American-backed former Chinese leader, Chiang Kai-shek, was driven from the mainland. He took his government, army, and even his parliament to the offshore island of Formosa (Taiwan). There, for the rest of his long life, he fulminated against the theft of his country. Nationalist or Kuomintang parliamentarians, still officially representing Shanghai, Chungking or Canton, based on the elections of November 1947, sat for decades in a ghostly assembly, the *Yuan*, in the Taiwanese capital, Taipei, and tried to behave as if China was still theirs.

The German situation was different. Two Germanys had arisen because of disagreements among the victorious anti-Hitler coalition. Both sides knew that Germany, even in its weakened and truncated post-1945 condition, was the key to Central Europe, and perhaps even of the entire continent.

America would have liked to bring the whole of Germany over to the Western, capitalist camp, but had decided, when it became clear this was unlikely to happen, to settle for less; similarly, Stalin would have loved to get a united Germany under his influence, but would, as it turned out, be prepared to keep just the bit that he held.[3] By contrast, the remaining two Allies – France, especially, but also Britain – were not at all displeased by a disunited Germany. They could, of course, never admit this to the Germans for fear of hurting their feelings.

Only the Germans wholeheartedly wanted their entire country back, and at this juncture they had little say in the matter.

Adenauer was chosen as chancellor of the Federal Republic of Germany by its newly elected parliament. He won by just one vote. Born in January 1876 (two days after Communist leader Wilhelm Pieck) to a pious middle-class Catholic family in the Rhine Province of Prussia, Adenauer studied law and served his native city of Cologne as a legal official. Later he went into politics for the Catholic Centre Party, first elected as a city councillor, then assistant burgomaster, and finally (from 1917) High Burgomaster of the city.

Adenauer became a prominent figure in the Weimar Republic. From 1921 to 1933, he was president of the Prussian State Council, the second chamber of the state's parliament, made up of representatives of the city and provincial assemblies. Afer 1945, he helped found the Christian Democratic Party, which hoped to unite Catholic and Protestant Christians in creating a socially aware but broadly conservative post-war German state.

As a leading member of the CDU in the British Zone, Adenauer was asked to chair the constituent council that drew up the constitution for the Trizonia state. Like the venerable George Washington, who in 1776 had occupied a similar position in the Continental Congress, Adenauer, at the age of seventy-three, would now occupy the highest position in the state over whose creation he had presided.

Extremes were utterly foreign to him. He had little time for the absolutist Right. On the other hand, he was also a firm Catholic anti-Communist. He looked at central and eastern Germany and saw an 'unreliable' electorate that was not only predominantly Protestant but had tended to support radicalism, of the brown-shirted or red-flagged persuasion. Adenauer was a patriot, but was not prepared to sacrifice his vision of a Western-orientated, Christian Germany on the altar of unity.

It was the firebrand Social Democrat leader Kurt Schumacher who, though also fiercely anti-Communist, yearned to restore German unity. Schumacher was a Prussian from the east, born in what had become Poland. His savage attacks against Adenauer, and his tireless campaigning for German reunification (despite a war wound that would send him to an early grave), established the courageous Schumacher as a legend in the SPD. However, they did nothing to unseat the wily Adenauer, or to attain the goal of unity that Schumacher so passionately sought.

Nine months after Adenauer became leader of the new West German state, something happened that would change the Western powers' attitude towards the German situation even more drastically than the Berlin Blockade.

At around four a.m. on 25 June 1950, a rainy Sunday morning, North Korean artillery opened fire on South Korean army positions south of the 38th parallel, the line then serving as the border between the two Korean states. The barrage was followed by armoured and infantry attacks all along the parallel. Only at eleven a.m. did North Korea formally declare war.

The Korean War resulted from a situation similar to that in Germany: a country divided according to the positions of Allied forces at the end of the Second World War. A Soviet protégé (Kim Il-sung) had quickly been installed in the north, where Russian troops had the power, as leader of the People's Democratic Republic of Korea; and an American-supported counterpart (a conservative representative of the Korean *ancien régime*, Syngman Rhee) in the south, where US forces held sway and the country was known as the Republic of Korea. Now the Communist side had directly attacked the other.

The rapid advance of the Communist forces terrified everyone in the West. US President Harry S. Truman returned from his home in Independence, Missouri, to Washington, DC, arriving in the early afternoon of that June day in 1950. The UN Security Council passed a resolution calling for the immediate cessation of hostilities and the withdrawal of North Korean forces. Instead, the North Koreans advanced and took the South Korean capital, Seoul, at enormous human cost. The war would see-saw back and forth. It would last almost three years and millions of innocent Korean civilians and hundreds of thousands of soldiers would die – including some tens of thousands from the largely Western-supplied United Nations force that was sent to stiffen South Korean resistance.

Stalin's support for the invasion of North Korea, which extended beyond propaganda to military aid and the use of Soviet pilots to fly combat aircraft, was one of the his last and worst mistakes. Inevitably, many in the West drew the conclusion that Korea was just rehearsal for a similar violent coup in Europe.

The first Soviet atomic bomb had been tested on 29 August 1949. There was rising anxiety in the West. Either Stalin didn't see this, or he misjudged it. The same might be said for Ulbricht, who immediately made boastful claims that, after South Korea, West Germany would be the next makeshift capitalist state to fall.[4]

So, what if something similar had happened in Germany? The balance was less equal. West Germany had 50 million people, and the East only around 18.5 million. But there were 300,000 Soviet troops stationed in the Soviet Zone, and in 1946 the East Germans had started to build up paramilitary People's Police units, initially classified as *Grenzpolizei* (border police) or *Bereitschaftspolizei* (public-order police) but soon organised on a proper military basis and given the title of *Kasernierte Volkspolizei* (People's Police in Barracks = KVP).

The KVP uniform bore a disturbing similarity to the old *Wehrmacht* garb, as did the jackboots. Only the helmet, an adaptation of the Red Army's, differed radically from what a Second World War German soldier would have worn. Drill and discipline were tough. Former *Wehrmacht* generals were appointed to regional commanders' roles. Officers who had been Nazis and in some cases judges in the notorious military tribunals set up towards the end of the war, were also given prominent positions.[5]

So, perhaps the means existed in the East to attack. But the will? It seems unlikely. Ulbricht and his Soviet sponsors wished to subvert the West German state. Their propaganda power was channelled ferociously and persistently to this end. Although East German society was at this point further down the road to remilitarisation than West Germany, talk of 'revanchism' in Bonn and of a reborn SS had become standard in Communist circles. But a direct military attack on West Germany seems unlikely to have been seriously considered.

The West did not know this. Due to the Korean War, few Americans thought any more of cutting, let alone withdrawing, US forces from Germany.

Earlier that year, Truman had received National Security Council Memorandum No. 68 (NSC-68) in which experts at Defense and State broadly recommended rearmament as a response to Communist ambition and the testing of the Soviet bomb. Then came Korea. Resistance to the recommendations dissolved in the face of clear Communist aggression. The armed-forces budget almost quintupled from $15.5 billion in August 1950 to $70 billion at the end of 1951. By 1952–3, defence expenditure took up 17.8 per cent of American gross national product, versus only 4.7 per cent in 1949. Military expenditure increased in all Western European victor states.[6]

In shattering what remained of post-war complacency in America, Stalin and Kim Il-sung had awoken a giant who may not have been sleeping, but who had been hoping to get some rest. Throughout the half-decade following the Second World War, there was talk, especially from diplomats, of 'not upsetting' the Russians. Now that talk dwindled. Many of these same diplomats were under heavy attack from Republican Senator Joseph Raymond McCarthy and his Permanent Investigations Sub-Committee, which was reaching the zenith of its inquisitorial power.

For the people of the Western sectors of Berlin, the intensified Cold War had paradoxical effects. On the one hand, the dangers for the capitalist-democratic boat bobbing in the dark sea of Stalinist rule appeared more threatening than ever. On the other, the solidarity of the NATO powers and the USA in the face of Communist ambition meant that the West was much less likely to quietly abandon Berlin.

The blockade had turned West Berliners from washed-up Nazis into anti-Communist heroes. The retention of Allied military rule in Berlin had become a prestige matter. The city was a military and political asset, a valuable listening station and irritant inside the belly of the Red beast. The experience of the blockade had showed that Western rule in Berlin would not succumb to any action short of outright military conquest – which would mean full-scale European, even world war.

Living in West Berlin had been an unpredictable business since 1945, and it remained so. But by 1950 it was also, strangely enough, more secure.

The Basic Law of the Federal Republic did not apply in West Berlin, where the writ of the Allied commandants remained the ultimate power. The grandly titled 'governing mayor' (*Regierender Bürgermeister*) of the Western sectors – from November 1948, Ernst Reuter – was responsible to the Western military, who also controlled the West Berlin police and regulated such events as political rallies and demonstrations. In Bonn, West Berlin's representatives were mere observers.

The partially unfree status of the half-city was a bargain struck for perilous times. In the loss of some rights for West Berliners lay the guarantee of more important ones.

There were now two Berlin city administrations. One in the West and the other in the East. At the same time as Reuter was elected in the Western sectors, in the East a prominent SED man named Friedrich Ebert had been made mayor.

Berlin still functioned, in many ways, as one city. There were signs showing sector borders, occasional checkpoints and restrictions, temporary or permanent, but for a dozen years after the end of the Berlin Blockade, citizens moved freely around the former German capital. Telephone lines, sewage, transport were all shared.

This was all the odder in view of the fact that the long border between the two German states, running 1,381 kilometres (858 miles) from the Baltic coast in the north to the Bavarian forest in the south, where

Czechoslovakia, East and West Germany met, would soon become a fortified and all but impassable barrier.

In the summer of 1945, the victorious Allies established buffer areas and checkpoints on routes that passed between their areas of rule. The initial object was to catch diehard Nazis and war criminals if they tried to cross zonal borders. Then came the problem of smuggling, the movement of money and goods in defiance of the strict Eastern customs regime. None the less, borders remained relatively porous.

In March 1952, the Cold War still seemed frozen solid. Then Stalin surprised the world by sending a note to each of the other three occupying powers – France, Britain and the USA – in which he offered a peace treaty and free elections in a unified Germany. A draft of such a treaty was helpfully included. This was at first sight an amazingly attractive proposal, especially for the Germans; designed, in the words of a recent German writer, echoing Mario Puzo's *Godfather*, as 'an offer they couldn't refuse'.[7] The main stipulation was that a reunited Germany, while permitted to rearm for its own defence, must not join any alliance directed against any of its former opponents in the Second World War.

Adenauer dismissed the offer almost immediately. It was argued that the East German government (which would, while negotiations were going on, have constituted an equal partner to West Germany) was not freely elected. This 'no' to the Stalin note has since been criticised by historians, including Germans East and West, for ruining a serious chance of painless German reunification without war and thereby condemning the country to almost forty more years of division. To them it is a big black mark against Adenauer's record.

The West German Chancellor was convinced that only a Germany anchored to the West could survive, at least in a form he found tolerable. 'Only an economically and spiritually healthy Western Europe under the leadership of England and France,' Adenauer wrote in 1946, 'a Western Europe of which the area of Germany not occupied by the Russians forms an essential component part, can halt the spiritual and power-political advance of Asia'. By 'Asia' the old Rhinelander clearly meant Stalin's Russia.

There were, of course, the usual stings in the small print of Stalin's suggestion. For example, part of his proposal involved the recognition of the eastern Oder-Neisse boundary for a reunited Germany. This meant the permanent abandonment of the ancient Prussian heartlands of East Prussia, Silesia and Pomerania, only a handful of years after their populations had been violently expelled. This concession alone would have wrecked Adenauer's party, in which the vocal refugee organisations representing these millions of expellees played a powerful and uncompromising role. An opinion poll threatened catastrophe for any party that abandoned the 'eastern territories': two-thirds of ordinary Germans were against attaining reunification at that price.[8]

It would be another forty years before a bold German leader, empowered by post-Cold War euphoria, would be able to officially recognise the new boundaries.

After his proposals were turned down by the West, Stalin received the East German leadership in Moscow. He told Ulbricht and his colleagues that he was resigned to a divided Germany and instructed them to 'organise your own state'. As for the porous border between the former Soviet Zone and the West, it had become a danger. The East Germans must therefore 'strengthen the protection of this frontier'.[9]

The GDR leaders didn't waste time, or scruples, in carrying out this command. The zone border was closed, and its transformation into a fortified international boundary began. The project carried the startlingly brutal title of 'Operation Vermin' (*Aktion Ungeziefer*).

A no man's land five kilometres wide was cleared. In 'night and fog' actions planned by the *Stasi*, thousands of people living near the border were removed at short notice from their homes. The authorities concentrated on 'unreliable' types such as known anti-Communists, those with close Western contacts, or farmers known to oppose collectivised agriculture. Towns and villages were split in two, families often divided. Barbed wire was laid down along its entire length, and secondary and local roads leading to the border were ripped up in order to prevent access.

Special permits were needed for non-residents to enter the border area. There were further graduations within this: between 'five kilometre' permits, the more select band allowed within 500 metres, and the élite permitted to approach the 'ten metre' zone without being fired upon (in practice, only officials and border guards).

By no coincidence at all, the day of the border closure, 26 May 1952, was also the day the 'Germany Treaty' was signed in Bonn, confirming West Germany's sovereignty and preparing the way for it to join the anti-Soviet alliance system.

Meanwhile, the Communist regime was tightening its hold on society and economy within the Soviet Zone/GDR. Further purges in the SED were accompanied by a campaign against the churches.

In the past two or three years, the number of people in Eastern Germany who decided to leave everything behind and head westward had increased dramatically. In 1947, around 165,000 people had been detained for 'illegal' crossing of the zone border in Thuringia alone, though many of these did not intend to leave, but were merely exercising a casual freedom of movement that before 1945 was taken for granted.[10] Three years later, permanent resettlement had become the aim of many 'illegal' border-crossers. In 1950, 197,788 headed for the West. The following year saw a slight drop to 165,648. The number of those who chose exile in 1952, including those who left after the border was fortified, increased again to 182,393.

Unlike Poles, Bulgarians, or Czechs, when East Germans crossed the border they did not leave their culture behind. They did not have to learn another language or adjust to a different way of life. In the Federal Republic they could still feel at home – and enjoy not just more political freedom but, especially as the 1950s went on, better conditions and wages than all but a tiny minority enjoyed in the GDR.

If someone wanted to leave East Germany, but did not want to brave the long and now-defended border, they had only to get to Berlin. In Berlin they could cross to the Western sectors. Thence the refugee could fly to West Germany proper without worrying about being arrested by a GDR border patrol and thrown into jail.

There was one more factor that encouraged many to take the step to the West. In July 1952, the SED announced that East Germany was entering the phase of 'building socialism', signalling its development into a fully fledged Stalinist-Communist state. Pressure on farmers to join collectivised units increased. Discriminatory measures against churches, intellectuals, business people and so-called 'border-crossers' (who lived in East Berlin but worked in the Western sectors) were stepped up. The

West beckoned ever more urgently for those who valued the fruits of their own enterprise.

Ulbricht was quite aware of this. In January 1953, he succeeded in gaining Stalin's approval for a scheme that would allow the East Germans to station their own guards along the border between the Eastern and Western sectors of Berlin so as 'to end uncontrolled access to East Berlin from the Western sectors' – and, more to the point, vice versa. It was essentially the charter for a fortified border in Berlin.[11]

But this was eight years before anything of the sort happened. Just when Ulbricht had his nod from the Soviet dictator, a train of events began that would rock the world to its foundations. It would also bring Ulbricht's own domination of his new fiefdom into urgent question and test his survival skills to their limit.

In the small hours of the night between 28 February and 1 March 1953, after a lengthy drinking party at his *dacha* outside Moscow, Josef Stalin took to his bedchamber. He remained there well into the next day, which was not unusual. However, when by the evening Stalin had still not emerged, guards hesitantly entered the dictator's room. They found him motionless by his bed, sprawled in a pool of his own urine. He had suffered a stroke, lost control of his faculties, and never again regained consciousness.

Stalin remained in a coma until his death at the age of seventy-four on 5 March. His passing unleashed a wave of grief among many Russians. To this surprisingly large group, the *vodzh* (leader) was a harsh but protective father figure, who had saved their homeland from Hitler's hordes and brought about a spectacular increase in its power and prestige. To others, including his closest colleagues in the Communist leadership, he was a homicidal monster, at whose demise they felt little else but profound relief.

At the same time as approving Ulbricht's plan to seal off Berlin, Stalin also announced the arrest of a group of prominent doctors, whom he accused of poisoning members of the leadership. The physicians were Jewish, allegedly agents of 'world Zionism' and the West. There were rumours of a major pogrom. The old man had started to get completely out of control. Some still suspect he was murdered.

Within two weeks of Stalin's funeral, the new Soviet leadership abandoned the plan to enforce tough border restrictions within Berlin. This would 'lead to the violation of the established order of city life' in Berlin, as Foreign Minister Molotov put it. The new leaders wished to embark on a conciliatory course, to pull back from Stalin's paranoid brinkmanship.

Accordingly, Marshal Chuikov, chairman of the Soviet Control Commission, which liaised with the German Communists, was given clear instructions. Ulbricht had missed the chance to seal his infant republic tight. Worse was to come.

In his advice to Chuikov, Molotov (on behalf of the new leadership in Moscow) made the revolutionary – or perhaps under the circumstances counter-revolutionary – suggestion that the problem of population loss from the GDR should be solved not by shutting the people in but by making their life better. The political system should be less harsh and the economy tailored more towards consumers. Light industry should be given priority over heavy industry. Between 1951 and 1953, 60 per cent of growth in the capital stock of state industry had occurred in the areas of iron, steel, mining and energy. Only 2 per cent had been devoted to the production of consumer goods.

The East German economy was in trouble. In 1952, the budget showed a deficit of 700 million marks. The negative trade balance with other Communist countries was almost 600 million (more than it sounds – these are 1952 prices).

Big brother in Moscow no longer wanted to subsidise Ulbricht's experiment. The Soviets made some concessions to the East Germans to soften the blow but, as Moscow made clear, the Soviet Union needed to make expensive changes of its own in order to improve the lot of its own people. The GDR leadership's answer to their problem should be wide-ranging liberalisation.

All this was anathema to Ulbricht. In his grim way, he was an idealist whose quasi-religious belief in a rigorous command economy constituted a lifelong article of faith. If the masses disliked such a policy, this could not be because it was wrong, but because they lacked the proper political consciousness.

Not all his colleagues shared his unbending views. Rudolf Herrnstadt, editor of the SED newspaper, *Neues Deutschland* ('New Germany') and the head of the secret police, Wilhelm Zaisser, openly supported a more flexible, liberal course and told Ulbricht so. They began talking to Soviet representatives along these lines.

Meanwhile, Ulbricht carried stubbornly on with 'building socialism'. Farms were sequestered – after their owners had been bankrupted by the machinations of uncooperative state officials. Citizens trying to get round the shortages with a little private trading were prosecuted under a catch-all 'law for the protection of the people's property'. This law was also used to persecute the owners of hotels and boarding houses, who represented a reservoir of 'reactionary' elements. Thousands had their businesses confiscated or fled to the West (even better for the state, since it made the paperwork easier).[12]

By 1952, the standard of living of ordinary East Germans had actually declined compared with 1947.[13] Production targets were not being met. This was blamed on 'subversion' and the corrupting effect of capitalist remnants. Ration cards were withdrawn from 'bourgeois' elements such as the self-employed and the owners of rental property. This meant they had to turn to state-owned shops, which were dearer and offered a less wide choice of goods.[14]

Nearing his sixtieth birthday, Ulbricht celebrated in advance by using the 13th plenum of the Central Committee of the SED on 13–14 May to oust his most likely rival, Franz Dahlem, from the leadership. He piled on more misery by announcing the raising of 'work norms' by 10 per cent (making workers do 10 per cent more work for the same wage).

The Moscow leadership was not clear what it wanted. These mixed feelings were revealed in mixed recommendations. For example, the Foreign Ministry's report on the GDR called, on the one hand, for leniency and liberalisation, while on the other suggesting that GDR citizens visiting East Berlin from the provinces be forced to apply for a special permit. The state gives with one hand, and snatches back with the other. Such mutually contradictory ideas typified an authoritarian system in crisis, feeling its way towards a 'safe' level of liberalisation that would leave its power intact, but constantly forced to pull back where it saw danger – which, given the all-embracing and constantly overlapping mechanisms of the system, ended up lurking almost everywhere. Post-Stalinism was already revealing itself as 'Stalinism Lite'.

This ambivalence was reflected in the discussions among the new Soviet leaders. Khrushchev and Molotov later claimed that Beria, the black eminence of Stalin's security empire, had wanted to abandon the GDR in favour of a 'bourgeois, neutral and peaceful' Germany. According to Foreign Minister Andrei Gromyko, Beria declared contemptuously: 'The GDR? What does it amount to, this GDR? It's not even a real state. It's only kept in being by Soviet troops.'[15]

The package presented by the Soviets to Ulbricht in Moscow between 2 and 4 June 1953 was a compromise. It was nevertheless a bitter pill for him to swallow. The Soviets' list involved halting forced collectivisation of agriculture, encouraging small and middle-sized enterprises, ensuring universal and fair distribution of ration cards, and switching the emphasis of industrial development from Stalinist-style heavy industry to light and consumer industry. The anti-church campaign was to be reined back, civil rights to be more widely respected, and the finance system reorganised. The aim was not just to staunch the flow of population from the GDR but if possible to tempt the exiles back.[16]

On their return to East Berlin, the SED Politburo was in almost continuous session from 5 to 9 June, under the supervision of Soviet High Commissioner Semenov. Finally it signalled willingness to enact the reforms. The liberal Herrnstadt was in charge of drafting the announcement. When he suggested to Semenov that they delay its release for two weeks to prepare the people for such radical changes, Semenov replied cuttingly: 'In two weeks you may not have a state any more.'[17]

The Politburo communiqué was issued on 11 June. The leadership even admitted that 'in the past a series of mistakes has been made'. This degree of frankness was unheard of. Secret police reports on the public's reaction described surprise and pleasure, but also suspicion of the ruling party's motives.

The one thing missing, however, was any move to rescind the onerous new work norms, which particularly affected workers in manufacturing and construction. In fact, on 11 June, Herrnstadt's *Neues Deutschland* actually praised the workers for fulfilling the new, more arduous work norms so assiduously.

There was a confusing contradiction even in the pronouncements of the SED's mouthpiece newspaper. Three days later, Herrnstadt wrote in the same newspaper, expressing doubt about the new norms and arguing that they should not be imposed 'dictatorially' but only after consultation with the workers. The article was passed from hand to hand in factories and construction sites.

Rumours were circulating in East Berlin that Moscow had heavily criticised Ulbricht, his 'mistaken line' and the 'cult of personality' surrounding him. The Russians were seriously wondering what do about Comrade Ulbricht and his stubbornly unpopular programme of 'building socialism'. These rumours were true. Ulbricht, a short, superficially unimpressive leader with a strong Saxon accent, had now lost his great protector – a short, superficially unimpressive leader with a strong Georgian accent by the name of Josef Stalin.

It was also said that the Soviets had asked Herrnstadt to submit a new Politburo list that would not include Ulbricht.[18] After eight years as Moscow's loyal though far from tractable instrument, at sixty Walter Ulbricht seemed to be heading for compulsory retirement, to be replaced by someone more in tune with the times.

What saved him was, as Ulbricht had always hoped, the East German working class – though not in any way that, no matter how keenly he searched the dark recesses of his ageing Marxist-Leninist heart, he could ever have imagined.

The party should have been forewarned. Trouble was already rife elsewhere in the Soviet imperium.

In early June 1953, as East Germany's Politburo wrestled with the 'new course', there were strikes and riots in industrial areas of Czechoslovakia, affecting 129 factories. On 6 June, there were mass demonstrations in the key manufacturing and brewing city of Plzn (German, Pilsen). Workers stormed the city hall and occupied the Skoda armaments factories. Portraits of Stalin and Gottwald were burned. Demonstrators hoisted the American flag. The government sent in the army. There were deaths. Thousands were imprisoned.

In the GDR the problems began on 16 June 1953. In the Stalinallee (formerly Frankfurter Allee) a huge, high-rise residential building project was emerging from bombed-out ruins. Designed in 1930s Stalinist 'wedding cake' style, with neo-classical touches that quoted the Prussian master Schinkel, on a scale that hinted at Albert Speer, the building process began with a huge propaganda fanfare.

The Stalinallee – no accident that the name of the *vodzh* had been lent to the project – was to show what the new, Communist Germany was capable of. The buildings would stretch, like a great windowed wall, along a wide, tree-lined boulevard. And the 'first socialist street of the German capital, Berlin' was to be built very quickly.

On 16 June 1953, the construction workers decided that the pace demanded of them was too much. They held a meeting at which they voted to deliver a petition directly to Otto Grotewohl, protesting against raised work norms. As they marched through the streets they found other construction and factory workers joining them. In time the demonstrators reached the huge 1930s building in the Leipziger Strasse that had once housed Hermann Göring's Air Ministry but was now the home of the GDR's Council of Ministers. They were now 10,000-strong.

The cream of the working class assembled outside the headquarters of their alleged representatives. They started shouting insults aimed at the SED leadership, such as '*Spitzbart, Bauch und Brille sind nicht des Volkes Wille!*' (Pointy beard – Ulbricht – Belly – the corpulent Pieck – and Glasses – bespectacled Grotewohl – are not the people's will!). A construction worker named Horst Schlaffke sprang on to a table and demanded that Grotewohl and Ulbricht address them in person. 'If they don't come out, we'll call a general strike!' he declared to huge applause.

None of the big names showed themselves. The relatively junior Heavy-Industry Minister, Fritz Selbmann, was sent out to placate the workers. He tried a routine appeal to their political solidarity ('My dear colleagues, I, too, am only a worker'), but got boos and whistles. Selbmann re-consulted and then reappeared. He announced changes in the work-norm ordinance that would make compliance voluntary.

The workers, who knew how little the concept of 'voluntary' meant in the SED state, became increasingly angry. A general strike was declared for the next day. The workers marched back via Police Headquarters in Alexanderplatz. Windows were broken, SED banners and posters destroyed or defaced. They seized a government loudspeaker van and used it to spread their message as they headed back towards the Stalinallee. There the crowd broke up, parts of it heading towards Lichtenberg and other eastern suburbs, where many lived. Touchingly, the government-property loudspeaker van was parked where the authorities could find it.[19]

In Berlin, two night shifts refused to work: first some track-maintenance crews of the transportation authority and then the workers at the ball-bearing factory in Berlin-Lichtenberg.[20] When the workers arrived at the huge Upper Spree Cable Works in Berlin at 6.30 a.m., they also refused to work.

Meanwhile, police units had been bused in from Potsdam, Leipzig and Magdeburg in preparation for more trouble. The authorities had closed the Strausberger Platz subway station, at the western extremity of the Stalinallee. At yet more factories, the morning shift did no work but engaged in discussion of the situation. Soon dozens of other workplaces in East Berlin, including large-scale enterprises such as the Borsig locomotive works, were also paralysed by strikes. When the party sent in agitators or (state-employed) union officials to persuade the strikers to return to work, they were howled down.

West Berliners streamed over the Oberbaumbrücke from the American sector to join the demonstrations around the Ostbahnhof. At Friedrichstrasse station and the nearby House of Ministries, state-owned shops – blamed for high prices – were set on fire. SED banners were torn down, piled up and also torched.

At the same time, between the Strausberger Platz and the Alexanderplatz, Soviet army all-terrain vehicles were seen for the first time rumbling into position, though as yet taking no action.

By ten o'clock, demonstrators were seen carrying banners that declared: 'We demand free elections!' A euphoric crowd surged towards the Brandenburg Gate, singing the Social Democratic workers' song, 'Brothers to the Sun, to Freedom!', and later the third verse of the old German national anthem, 'Deutschland über Alles', which called for 'unity, law and freedom' and had recently been adopted as the official anthem of the Federal Republic.

At the modernistic Columbushaus, on the Potsdamer Platz, where a police station shared the space with a state-owned retail store, the police were overpowered and forced to strip. Windows were broken, furniture and police documents tossed from on high to crash into the Potsdamer

Platz below. A white flag was hung from the building. It was said that several of the captured *Vopos* (*Volkspolizei*) were delivered to the Western police, who stood just over the border in the Tiergarten. A group of youths clambered up the Brandenburg Gate and tore down the Soviet flag that flew there, chanting: 'We want freedom, we want bread, we will beat all Russians dead!'

Something close to a full-scale uprising was taking shape, involving tens, even hundreds of thousands of ordinary Berliners. They were calling for freedom, elections and, increasingly, a reunited Germany. The Communist authorities were preparing to give them their answer.

Noon came and went. After trying unsuccessfully to break into the Economics Ministry, a large crowd veered off towards the Potsdamer Platz to be confronted by the power of the Red Army. Dozens of Soviet T-34 tanks had moved into Berlin. The official order had been given by the Russian city commandant, Major-General Dibrova, but behind the decision lay the Soviet leadership, which had been informed the previous day of the gathering unrest.

Lavrenty Beria, Stalin's executioner, had flown to Berlin during the night and was now personally supervising the counter-attack.

The first shots were fired on the Marx-Engels-Platz, where a group of young East Berliners tried to clamber atop a tank. Demonstrators fought back with bricks, paving stones, and chunks of metal, but they could make little impression on the might of the Red Army. The Russians fired into the crowd. Their guns swept the border areas to prevent demonstrators escaping into West Berlin.[21]

At 13.00, a state of emergency was declared by the SMA. Public gatherings of more than three people were banned. Anyone contravening these instructions could be shot. Once the Soviet tanks had broken the momentum of the uprising and sealed the sector border in the centre of Berlin, a mass of KVP squads, including the reinforcements summoned during the night from other cities, moved in to clear up. Many were as brutal as the Russians – beating up protesters and bystanders alike and firing into crowds – even shooting some from behind as they tried to run away.

Among those shot was Rudi Schwander, a fourteen-year-old schoolboy from East Berlin, son of a bakery worker. He had been fleeing the scene when a *Vopo*'s bullet hit him in the back of the head. Young Rudi collapsed. The unconscious boy was picked up by fellow demonstrators and carried over the nearby border into the French sector, where he died. By late afternoon, the resistance in Berlin was broken.

The seventeenth of June, the day of the GDR workers' uprising, gave its name to a long, wide boulevard in West Berlin. Formerly the Charlottenburger Chaussee, the 'Street of the 17 June' (Strasse des 17. Juni) runs four kilometres from the Ernst-Reuter-Platz, past the 'Victory Column' to the Reichstag and then the Brandenburg Gate. Its name makes many think of the uprising as a Berlin event, but in fact it was a phenomenon that spread across the length and breath of the GDR.

According to official records discovered after the fall of the East German regime, around half a million employees throughout the country went on strike on 17 June 1953. Four hundred and eighteen thousand were estimated to have taken part in demonstrations. Strikes and demonstrations were even more widespread in the southern industrial area of Halle/Merseburg than in the capital. The number of strikers in the light- and precision-industrial city of Dresden actually equalled those in Berlin. In Leipzig and Magdeburg, historic strongholds of the Left and the trade-union movement, there were violent clashes between workers and security forces.

In rural areas, there was violent unrest. Party officials and collective-farm managers were attacked. There were protest meetings and mass withdrawals from agricultural collectives. In eastern Saxony, Soviet troops intervened when a farmers' demonstration attracted hundreds of sympathisers from local factories, a junction of resistance forces that amounted to a nightmare for the authorities.[22]

As in Berlin, the actual outbreaks of disorder were dealt with by martial law and curfews, but so deep-seated were the resentments that protests rumbled on into July in individual factories and farming collectives.

The demonstrators called for Ulbricht to discuss their grievances, but where was the all-powerful First Secretary of the SED? The answer was a humiliating one. Ulbricht spent 17 and 18 June under Soviet protection at Red Army headquarters in Berlin-Karlshorst, with Grotewohl, Herrnstadt, and Zaisser, while the Soviets and the police dealt with the trouble.

Semenov, Moscow's representative, was also at Karlshorst, and reportedly showed only contempt for the East German leaders. At the height of
the crisis, he told them: 'RIAS says that there is no longer any
government in the GDR'. Semenov then turned to his senior Red Army
colleagues. 'Well,' he remarked acidly in Russian, 'that is just about
true.'[23]

When the Central Committee of the SED met again on 21 June, its
members were seriously shaken. 'If masses of workers do not understand
the party,' someone said, 'then the party is guilty, not the workers'. Only
slowly did a counter-version emerge: the uprising had been the product
of Fascist *agents provocateurs*, operating at the behest of Eisenhower, John
Foster Dulles, and their puppets in Bonn, with the hyenas of RIAS
screaming encouragement over the air waves.

All the same, in the cold light of the post-uprising dawn, Ulbricht was
not in a strong position. Beria was said to have called him an 'idiot'.[24]

Ulbricht's support in East Berlin was even shakier. Only the arch-
Stalinist Herman Matern, and the youth-movement leader Erich Honecker (a relative stripling at forty but a hardliner just the same) still
supported Ulbricht. A couple of others were undecided. It seemed that
Ulbricht was doomed.

The problem was that his enemies lacked killer instinct. In late June,
Herrnstadt proposed that the single-person party secretariat be modified,
the Politburo expanded, and a committee formed that would oversee the
'new course'. This would turn the SED over to a collective leadership.
The Soviets seemed supportive. Greeting Ulbricht on his sixtieth birthday, they addressed him not as 'General Secretary' but as 'one of the most
well-known organisers and leaders of the SED'.

They had underestimated him. On 2 July, after a week of intrigue, the
Politburo met again. This time, the veteran leader fought back, his tactic
clearly to hold on at all costs. When Zaisser proposed replacing Ulbricht
with Herrnstadt, the result was a heated debate but no resolution. In the
end, Semenov's deputy, Miroshinchenko, who presided over the meeting,
insisted that they postpone any decision until his boss returned from
Moscow.

Zaisser, the *Stasi* chief, tried again on 7 July, the day before Ulbricht
and Grotewohl were due to fly to Moscow on a brief, apparently routine

visit. After a meeting lasting several hours, it remained obvious that the SED boss had little support. However, Ulbricht was a master of detail and procedure. He knew how to delay things while he planned his counter-attack. Again, the matter remained undecided. Then he and Grotewohl left for the airport.[25]

The embattled East German leader arrived to find Moscow full of other heads of satellite governments, who had also been summoned to the Kremlin to be briefed on the latest developments. And these were dramatic in the extreme.

Beria had been arrested almost two weeks previously for alleged 'criminal anti-party and anti-governmental activities'. He was, the charge went, 'an agent of imperialism'. His colleagues, terrified of what the Security Minister would do to them when he got the chance, had struck first; and, unlike Ulbricht's enemies, their aim was swift and true. Beria had been seized at a Kremlin meeting, where his professional killers and special troops could not protect him. He was now languishing in jail and would be executed the following year. Ulbricht's most active enemy in Moscow was no more. Had Beria remained the most powerful man in Russia, Ulbricht would undoubtedly have been deposed (and worse).

Ulbricht and Grotewohl returned to Berlin twenty-four hours later to attend an evening session of the Politburo. They reported the news of Beria's arrest. Again Ulbricht's opponents did not go in for the kill, assuming that the end of the autocratic Beria would inevitably mean the end of the autocratic Ulbricht.

Not so. Ulbricht used the time to gather his forces. Faced with renewed criticism, he announced that Zaisser's and Herrnstadt's behaviour amounted to an 'anti-party' attitude. They must be investigated by the party's control commission, which happened to be headed by his ally, Matern. Using his still-extant powers, Ulbricht announced that the monthly plenum meeting of the SED Central Committee would take place on 24–6 July. He prorogued the Politburo session until then.

It soon became obvious that it was not Ulbricht but his opponents who were finished. Semenov had performed a 180-degree turn and now supported him, on instructions from his superiors in Moscow. The plenum later that month was graced with the presence not just of Semenov but of I. Kabin, the shadowy but powerful figure responsible to the Soviet Central Committee for relations with Germany.

When Ulbricht took to the podium to address the SED plenum, it was already plain he had the Kremlin's approval. He launched a blistering attack on his enemies, asserting that Zaisser had conspired with the disgraced Beria to betray the GDR, and that Herrnstadt had been part of the plot. The plenum voted to dismiss Zaisser and Herrnstadt as a 'party-hostile faction with a defeatist line' from their jobs and from all party posts.[26]

Ulbricht had triumphed. They might dislike him, but the Soviets had decided that to let him fall would be a sign of weakness. And weakness, it was clear from the turmoil in the satellite countries that had followed Stalin's death, was one thing they could not afford.

So the workers, by rebelling against Ulbricht's regime, paradoxically saved their tormentor's political life. Ulbricht would allow the 'new course' to continue for a time while he re-established his grip on power, purging reformists and weak links. Thousands of those who had participated in or expressed approval of the 17 June uprising were tracked down, arrested and imprisoned. Two hundred and sixty-seven East Germans had been killed during the disturbances. A further 200 were executed, 1,400 imprisoned for life.

From now on, no one could pretend that the SED government was based on popular approval. It was, as anyone could see, a regime imposed by Soviet tanks.

Berthold Brecht, the world-famous radical poet, playwright and darling of the international Left, had returned from America to East Berlin after the war, supplying vital cultural credibility to the SED. On 17 June, he supported Soviet intervention against the strikers, but before his death three years later, he was sufficiently conscience-stricken – or cunning – to show that he too understood what had happened on that day. The SED state, while ever more loudly protesting its democratic credentials, had shamelessly abandoned the last remnants of them.

In his poem, 'The Solution', Brecht satirised 17 June 1953 with supreme irony:

After the uprising of 17 June
The Secretary of the Writers Union
Had leaflets distributed in the Stalinallee
Stating that the people
Had forfeited the confidence of the government
And could win it back only
By redoubled efforts. Would it not be easier
In that case for the government
To dissolve the people
And elect another?

6

THE CROWN PRINCES

DURING THE 1950S IN Berlin, two Germans of roughly the same age, both humbly born, both men of the Left and resisters of the Nazis in their youth, faced each other across the Cold War political divide.

Neither of these rivals were Berliners. In fact, both came from the outermost edges of Germany. Erich Honecker, SED official and later East German leader, was born on 25 August 1912 in Wiebelskirchen, a mining town in the Saarland, in the far west of Germany. Willy Brandt, future mayor of West Berlin, came into the world sixteen months later, in December 1913, in the country's far north. He was a son of the ancient Baltic sea port of Lübeck, from where the next landfall is Denmark.

The first would be the creator of the Berlin Wall, the second would ensure the survival of the isolated island city that the Wall created. They would both spend a long time as leaders-in-waiting, only to gain power within a year of each other. And one would destroy the other; although it would be, in the end, a hollow victory.

Communism was in Erich Honecker's blood. Honecker senior, a coal-miner, had been a member of the KPD since 1919. His son was politically active from the age of ten.

At eighteen, pursuing an apprenticeship as a roofer, young Erich also graduated to membership of the paramilitary 'Red Front Fighter League'. He was picked to join the élite youth intake at the International Lenin School in Moscow. On his return to the Saarland (which by the Treaty of Versailles lay under League of Nations administration and French economic control) he became an official of the Communist youth movement, abandoning his apprenticeship. In 1933, he was elected to its central committee.

After Hitler came to power, Honecker ducked in and out of the underground, before turning up in Berlin under a false identity. In December 1935, after three months of clandestine activity, he was arrested by the Gestapo.

In June 1937, 24-year-old Erich Honecker was convicted by the Nazi People's Court for 'conspiracy to commit high treason'. He was sentenced to ten years' hard labour, served in the notorious prison at Brandenburg-Görden, west of Berlin.

During the Second World War, Görden became a transit camp for the concentration-camp system and also the site of a judicial death house, where between 1939 and 1945 almost 2,000 inmates, including gypsies, Jews and political prisoners, were executed. Honecker spent the time between 1940 and 1943 working in a toy-soldier factory. After that, because of his training as a roofer, he was assigned to external construction squads, repairing bombed buildings in Berlin.

On 27 April 1945, the Red Army arrived at Brandenburg-Görden. Quickly released because of his political credentials, Honecker reported to the Soviet city commandant's headquarters at Berlin-Friedrichsfelde. He acquainted the Russians with his curriculum vitae and was referred to the Ulbricht group as a possible recruit.[1]

Honecker was assigned the task of recruiting young people to the resurgent Communist party. Within a year, he was made national chairman of the SED's youth organisation, the Free German Youth (Freie Deutsche Jugend = FDJ). An obedient and tireless worker and conspirator, he would retain this key post for nine years. He joined the central committee of the SED and the GDR parliament. Still in his mid-thirties, Honecker advanced into the party's leadership alongside men and women fifteen, twenty, or (in Pieck's case) thirty-five years older than himself.

In 1958, now a full member of the SED's innermost circle, the Politburo, Honecker was appointed Secretary for Security Questions. This was a big job – overseer of the police and army – and brought Honecker closer to the position of leader-in-waiting to Ulbricht. Honecker was efficient and absolutely committed. The party was his life. One of the underestimated attractions of Communist states lay in the steep career paths they offered to the energetic and ruthless offspring of simple workers. Honecker was a fine example of this principle.

So, a long way from the Saarland? Geographically, certainly. By now Honecker was only in the most notional fashion still living in the country where he was born. But one of the strange things about the man, who appeared so much the perfect, almost robotic *apparatchik*, who subordinated everything to ideology, was his fondness for the remote industrial district where he had spent his early years.

A cellmate of Honecker's at Brandenburg-Görden would claim, many years later, that he could furnish the listener with a plausible tour of Wiebelskirchen, based simply on what Honecker had repeatedly recounted to him during those long days of imprisonment at the hands of the Gestapo. Honecker, by all accounts, was often homesick.[2] This remained true even after he reached the heights of Communist power, but by then his perspective was confined to the area between the Elbe and the Oder, hundreds of kilometres from where he had been born.

Willy Brandt also grew up with a distinctive accent, that of Lübeck. The ancient Baltic port's most famous son was the writer Thomas Mann. Unlike Mann, who came from wealthy patrician stock, Brandt – born neither Willy nor Brandt but Herbert Karl Frahm – grew up 'across the tracks' in the humble suburb of St Lorenz. His mother, Martha Frahm, was a single parent who worked in a grocery store.

The most important single figure of the boy's childhood was his grandfather, Ludwig Frahm, a former labourer-turned-truck-driver, originally from poverty-stricken rural Mecklenburg, whom he called 'Papa'. The boy often did not see his working mother for days on end, and was never quite sure where he should call home.

Later, Brandt and his biographers would speculate on the effects of such a childhood on his character: a certain distance that endured beneath the mask of friendship; a tendency towards self-reliance and independence; and paradoxically, a constant reaching-out for company, especially of the female kind, which expressed itself in numerous love affairs.[3]

Only in his teens did Herbert move into a broader world beyond Lübeck's working-class subculture. He was very bright, and at fourteen was awarded a city scholarship that enabled him to go to the Johanneum, a fee-paying *Gymnasium* or high school. There Herbert studied the classics, history, languages and high-level science with the sons of Lübeck's prosperous middle class.

None the less, young Herbert Frahm did not lose his loyalty to the people he had grown up with. Nor did pride in his new school, and his eagerness to learn, stop him from becoming absorbed in politics. At fifteen he was elected chair of his local socialist youth group and was soon writing pieces for the local SPD newspaper.

The problem was that, as democracy came under ever greater threat, Frahm became more of a firebrand leftist. The SPD establishment tolerated the semi-authoritarian rule of the Catholic conservative chancellor, Brüning, who governed through presidential decree after the slump hit Germany in 1930. The far Left of the SPD, especially its youth, preached revolution and militancy as answers to the economic crisis and the rise of the Nazis. They drifted closer to the KPD than to their own party.

Herbert acted on his disillusionment in 1931 by deserting to an idealistic splinter group, the Socialist Workers' Party (SAP). The SAP's founders hoped to attract support from both SPD and KPD and form a common front against the Nazis. For young Herbert, there was considerable personal sacrifice involved in his desertion to the SAP. As a promising young SPD organiser, he could have expected the party to support his university studies. Now that was out of the question. When he left school in February 1932, he became a trainee clerk with a shipping brokerage company. Meanwhile, he devoted almost every hour of his free time to politics.

Needless to say, however, the SAP had no mass support. The membership reached no more than 12,000. There were two elections to the Reichstag in the crisis year of 1932, in which the party gained 0.2 per cent and 0.1 per cent of the national vote. Despite the tireless agitation of young Frahm, who was proving a fine public speaker, it did little better in Lübeck. When the Nazi tide washed over Germany, the not yet twenty-year-old was becoming well known. This did not bode well for his future safety.

After Hitler came to power, several members of the SAP's central committee were immediately picked up by the Gestapo. One was detained while travelling to Oslo, in Norway, to set up an SAP base in exile. The leadership asked Frahm to take his place – either presciently confident of his abilities or simply desperate. In April 1933, he was smuggled across the Baltic in a fishing boat and made his way to Oslo.

So Herbert Frahm left Germany. At the same time, he ceased being Herbert Frahm. After Hitler came to power, the SAP central committee formally dissolved the party, but many of its members refused to accept defeat. A secret meeting was called at a location near Dresden. Representative of the diehard comrades from Lübeck was Frahm. In the process, he used for the first time the *nom de guerre* that would make him famous: Willy Brandt.

From the moment he set foot in Norway, and for the rest of his life, Herbert Frahm became Willy Brandt. Charming, intelligent and articulate, he had a gift for languages, learning Norwegian so quickly that within a year he could give lectures in his adopted tongue.

In 1936, Willy Brandt visited Berlin on an intelligence mission for the SAP. He used a borrowed Norwegian passport under the name Gunnar Gaasland – profession, student – and, helped by the fact that the Olympic Games had filled the city with foreign tourists, survived to tell the tale. In Berlin (codenamed 'Metro' among SAP exiles), he experienced a shocking realisation. Nazism was not, as Marxist-Leninists insisted, a shaky, temporary phenomenon foisted on the country by an élite. The fact was, Hitler had Germany – and most of its people's allegiance – firmly in his grip.[4]

During these years, Brandt's gifts as a writer blossomed. He published articles in Norwegian, Dutch, Swiss and Swedish publications, as well as a successful book, *Why Did Hitler Win in Germany?*

The young revolutionary Brandt, meanwhile, moved slowly but steadily away from extremism. The murderous chaos of the Spanish Civil War, which he experienced during a visit in 1937, the bloody purges in the Soviet Union, and finally the Hitler-Stalin pact, convinced him that collaboration with the Communists was fraught with problems. Though still a Marxist, he set out on the road to the moderate, democratic socialist stance of which he became a leading post-war exponent.

In September 1938, Brandt was one of many exiles to lose his German nationality by Gestapo decree. He married Anna Carlota Thorkildsen, a

Norwegian citizen, and applied for citizenship himself. Norway had become 'home'.

It was a home, sadly, that he would have to give up before long. When the Germans invaded Norway in April 1940, Brandt could have been tracked down and arrested as a traitor, had not a friend lent him a Norwegian army uniform. Brandt was treated briefly as a prisoner of war by his unwitting fellow countrymen and then released. But he could not be sure of his personal safety in occupied Norway. Within weeks, he escaped across the border into neutral Sweden.

Brandt was granted Norwegian citizenship by the country's government in exile and then a licence to practise as a journalist. He opened a Swedish-Norwegian news agency with two local colleagues, reporting on the situation in Sweden and in occupied Norway, and acting as stringers for agencies in America and the United Kingdom. Brandt was undoubtedly also involved with Allied intelligence.

The end of the war brought a brief moment of euphoria, followed by some difficult decisions. Brandt returned to Oslo with his wife and family. But now, of course, with Hitler's Germany defeated, there was another decision looming. Which country should he live in?

Many exiled German politicians – some technically stateless – had to wait years for permission to return to their own country. But Brandt was now a Norwegian citizen. In November 1945, a Norwegian Labour Party newspaper sent him to report on the Nuremberg war-crimes trials.

After observing the war-crimes trials, Brandt wrote a book entitled *Criminals and Other Germans*. He pleaded against the idea of collective national guilt. Brandt acknowledged the trials as legitimate and necessary, but felt passionately that the judges should have included a German – to speak and condemn on behalf of those who had opposed the Nazi regime, but had none the less also suffered for its crimes.

Brandt's views were not shared in Allied countries, including Norway, where some said he was an apologist for Germany. He found his thoughts becoming bound up with the future of his native land. The collapse of his marriage was also a factor.

Brandt returned to Germany in 1947 as a press officer working for the Norwegian Military Mission in Berlin. He wore a Norwegian army uniform and drew the pay of a major (necessary under the rules attached to the presence of the military mission). In years to come, opponents would accuse him of exploiting his privileges as a 'Norwegian officer' while his compatriots starved. His Norwegian companion in Berlin and future wife, Rut, would write:

> We lived in requisitioned houses with requisitioned furniture and slept in requisitioned beds. The provisions were imported from outside: we ate in allied restaurants, shopped in allied stores, paid with allied military money – British BASF pounds or American SCRIPT-dollars – and went to allied cinemas and clubs. It was an unnatural colonial life and in fact from a human point of view just as degrading for those who lived in relative plenty as for those forced to stand outside and suffer . . .[5]

The smell of death that still hung over Berlin, its legacy from the wartime bombing and fighting, affected Brandt deeply. As did the fact of German suffering. Finally, after almost a year, he decided that he must choose, and accepted a job as Berlin representative of the SPD. It meant giving up his Norwegian nationality and becoming German again – citizen of a country that did not, at this point, technically even exist. He had burned his boats.

It was a new beginning that would take the one-time young revolutionary from Communist sympathiser to determined enemy of the SED, from firebrand journalist to international statesman. Willy Brandt's journey was an adventure of the mind and the heart. His experiences had changed him profoundly. Unlike those of Erich Honecker.

Honecker had shown courage and commitment in fighting National Socialism, but nothing about his views, or his feelings, changed as a result of his experiences. Despite his harsh experiences at the hands of the Gestapo, the SED's post-war persecution of its opponents did not seem to cause him any concern. The end justified the means.

Honecker assisted loyally and uncritically in the creation of the SED, helped build its minute control over society in the Soviet Zone/GDR. He climbed that society's ladder through hard work, organisational skill, and, above all, conformity.

Brandt did not always find conformity easy. By 1949, he had joined the group of young Social Democratic high-flyers surrounding the newly appointed West Berlin mayor, Ernst Reuter. They were the generation-in-waiting.

Many post-war democratic leaders were former Weimar-era politicians, in their fifties, sixties or even seventies. Some had been imprisoned by the Nazis. To young men like Brandt, the former Weimar politicians – 'the beards and bellies' as he once irreverently described them – were to be respected for their courage, but ever so slightly despised for their failure to stop Hitler.

Brandt was, of course, unusual in other ways. Most of his contemporaries had either been convinced Nazis or had been swept up in the mass mobilisation of war. In 1947/8, many were still prisoners. All who had lived through the Third Reich between adolescence and adulthood remained a generation in recovery, getting by from day to day. Brandt, the successful returned exile, belonged to a small group of young people untainted by involvement with the Nazis and undamaged by the experience of fighting on Hitler's behalf.

As early as the SPD/KPD 'marriage' that created the SED, Brandt had observed that this was a shot-gun wedding. Nevertheless, he had hoped that a peace treaty might create a democratic German central government based in Berlin. Final disillusionment came with the Soviet blockade of West Berlin in the summer of 1948.

Though Brandt still supported the then SPD policy of state ownership and control, he gained a reputation as a determined anti-Communist. He learned much from Ernst Reuter, the former Bolshevik, who believed that a democratic Germany and a democratic Berlin needed to be supported by a strong Western anchor. Reuter was the last in a series of men, a generation older than Brandt, who could have been the father he never knew and were crucial mentors at various times in his life.

In 1949, Brandt was offered Reuter's old job running the city's transport system. He turned it down. Instead, he went to Bonn as a part of the Berlin delegation of deputies, who because of the city's special status were not directly elected but nominated by the city assembly. He commuted between Berlin and the Rhineland, until 1957, when he was elected as governing mayor.

This was in future. Though some regarded him as Reuter's heir apparent, when the hugely respected High Burgomaster died suddenly in September 1953, aged sixty-four, Brandt, who had just celebrated his fortieth birthday, did not succeed him. In the 1950 Berlin elections, the CDU and its allies had won an equal number of seats to the SPD. The CDU's candidate withdrew in favour of the popular Reuter, but when the latter died, the CDU declared its intent to govern. Berlin had its first non-SPD mayor since the war, and Brandt was in opposition.

In December 1954, the SPD won back some seats and was returned to power. Brandt, however, was passed over in favour of the veteran Otto Suhr, a hero of the blockade. As president of the Berlin house of assembly, Suhr had bravely resisted the Communist crowds that tried to intimidate the city's elected representatives. Brandt was awarded Suhr's old post, the second-most important job in the city.

Only when Suhr died, in August 1957, did Brandt attain the heights of power in the divided city. The handsome young governing mayor and his attractive, fashionably dressed Norwegian wife, Rut, became popular favourites, a Berlin pre-echo of Jack and Jackie Kennedy. Opponents sneered at his 'American' style and the superficiality of the press coverage, but with television sets now appearing in Berliners' homes, with rock 'n'roll and the headlong worship of youth starting to take over every branch of the media, the sceptics made little headway.

Erich Honecker, by contrast, had officially given up youth in 1955, just when it was coming into fashion. That was when, aged forty-three, he stopped being chair of the SED's junior section, the Free German Youth, which he had built up into a millions-strong apparatus for controlling the post-war generation in the GDR. Honecker was sent to attend the Soviet Central Committee's training college in Moscow. Successful graduates of this school were headed for the very top of their party organisations. For an ambitious young Communist, this was heady stuff.

Sure enough, shortly after his return from Moscow, Honecker became secretary to the Central Committee for security questions and a permanent member of the Politburo. Since the fiasco of 17 June 1953, Ulbricht had insisted on exercising this vital role himself. His willingness to hand these functions over to Honecker was a special expression of trust.

At the same time as Brandt became mayor – by free election – so Honecker reached a key position in the GDR, though not by any election process considered valid in the West. In 1953, when Ulbricht was threatened with overthrow, Honecker had been one of the few East German leaders who supported him. 'Pointy beard' Walter did not forgive a traitor, but neither did he forget a favour.

After the 1953 uprising, and the trauma of the Polish and Hungarian revolts in 1956, security went from being one key aspect of government policy in East Germany to becoming arguably the most important. The economy had to be improved, it was true, but the main priority was to keep the SED in power until a rise in the masses' standard of living could be secured and the regime made more popular. Meanwhile, subversion and dissent must be suppressed. For the good of the people, of course.

The record year for population loss was, for obvious reasons, 1953, year of revolt and repression. During those traumatic twelve months, almost 400,000 left for the West. The figure dropped in 1954 to less than 200,000 before starting to climb again, staying at around a quarter of a million annually for the next three years. Since the foundation of the GDR in 1949 and the end of Honecker's first full year as Secretary for Security in 1958, 2.1 million East Germans had fled the country that Ulbricht built. Almost a million would leave during the next three years. In the first twelve years of its existence East Germany lost around a sixth of its population.

The 'new course' of 1953–4 had been intended to make life more tolerable for all those tempted to leave, especially small-business men, scientists, doctors and dentists, and skilled craftsmen, who made up a disproportionate percentage of those who were classified in tellingly military terms as 'deserters from the Republic' (*Republikflüchtige*). Even though Ulbricht had managed to hold on to power, it seemed that reform of the system was inevitable, a hope further fuelled by CPSU Secretary Nikita Khrushchev's denunciation of Stalin in February 1956.

Ulbricht faced challenges from liberals within the Politburo, including *Stasi* Minister Ernst Wollweber and Karl Schirdewan, Secretary to the Central Committee with responsibility for Cadre Questions (party membership). Unsure of Moscow's support, Ulbricht could not deal with these challenges as summarily as he might have wished. None the less, these two Politburo members formed a latent threat to his power that he could not ignore. And, being Walter Ulbricht, did not.[6]

In June 1956, widespread rioting in Poland led Khrushchev to appoint the relatively liberal Wladyslaw Gomulka, who had been imprisoned under Stalin, as leader of the Polish Communist Party. Gomulka was permitted to carry out market and economic reforms (including a stop to agricultural collectivisation) so long as he continued to toe the Soviet line internationally. This looked like good news for reformers everywhere.

Unknown to the liberals in the GDR, however, the high tide of reform was already about to turn. At the end of 1956, the Soviets were forced to use the Red Army to suppress a revolt in Hungary – led, moreover, by a reformist Communist prime minister, Imre Nagy. This bloody business shocked the world. In Moscow it presaged a turning-away from the post-Stalinist liberalising process and a revival of belief in brute strength.

Ulbricht did not rush things. Using Honecker, who had now slotted his old FDJ trusties into key parts of the security and party apparatus, and marshalling his old Stalinist cronies, the First Secretary gradually isolated the liberalisers. In December 1956, the new Security Secretary, Honecker, accused Wollweber of neglecting the pursuit of the state's enemies. He demanded regular reports on this problem, keeping the *Stasi* chief on the defensive for the next months and aiding the construction of a portfolio of alleged failures that could be used against him. At the end of 1957, the reformist economic planner and close Schirdewan ally, Gerhart Ziller, who had been brutally criticised by Ulbricht at a Politburo meeting, gave way under the pressure and took his own life.

Ziller's suicide was the signal for the hardliners to go in for the kill. In February 1958, Wollweber, Schirdewan and Fred Oelssner, deputy chair of the Council of Ministers and a moderate, were accused of 'factionalism' and sacked from the Central Committee.

From now on, Honecker exercised a key overseer role. He stood in charge of security, the army, and the party organisation. In short, every process that was key to the regime's hold on power passed through his office. The slogan Honecker adopted and issued to the comrades whose political life he now controlled gave a clear message: 'He who attacks Walter Ulbricht, attacks the party!' This would remain Honecker's motto until the day, more than a decade later, when he decided to overthrow Ulbricht himself.

At the Fifth Party Congress of the SED in July 1958, Ulbricht reigned supreme. The economic and political policies he announced to the cowed comrades represented a virtual return to the old 'building socialism' programme he had so disastrously pursued until the summer of 1953: more restrictions on the dwindling numbers of private businesses and craft workshops, a resumption of enforced collectivisation of agriculture. Ulbricht made a further astonishing declaration: soon the GDR would overtake West Germany in the production of foodstuffs and consumer goods.

A few weeks later, this claim became daringly specific. The two Germanys would, Ulbricht predicted, achieve parity as soon as 1961. This was clearly a risky fantasy. Even by the somewhat optimistic official figures, industrial and agricultural productivity in the east was 25–30 per cent lower than in the West. The GDR's reserve of skilled workers was draining away through the open border with West Berlin.

Ulbricht's trump card was that he could now rely on the support of Khrushchev. The pressing reason for their alliance was that the new Soviet leader, having finally, like Ulbricht, asserted himself against all possible opponents, had decided to reopen the 'Berlin Question'.

With a bang.

On 27 October 1958, Ulbricht addressed a mass meeting at the *Friedrichstadt-Palast* theatre in the heart of East Berlin. He launched a blistering attack, not just on the West in general but on West Berlin's very right to exist. During the summer, Ulbricht had been ratcheting up his rhetoric, calling for the West to recognise the GDR and to sign a peace treaty that would ratify the post-war settlement in Europe. This time he went even further. He described the whole of Berlin, including the Western sectors, as 'part of the territory of the GDR'.

The newly-elected Mayor Brandt responded by mocking Ulbricht as a 'Saxon Lenin-Imitation', but something sinister was in the wind. A month later that something became apparent – at last a move by Moscow, and not one that any West Berliner would have wanted.

Nikita Khrushchev was puffed up by the USSR's success in putting the first satellite into orbit in the shape of *Sputnik*, and by the advances in rocket science that made this possible – successes that, as anyone could see, could launch not just a capsule into space but a nuclear warhead on to New York or Philadelphia. The West had lost its nuclear monopoly in 1955, when the Soviets exploded their first hydrogen bomb. Now, with Russian development of long-range missiles, America itself was no longer protected by distance.

At the same time, in another direct challenge to America, Khrushchev declared the Soviet Union's intention to overtake the West in prosperity and productivity in just a few years. It was a boast that probably influenced Ulbricht's equally foolhardy statement of intent at the SED's Fifth Party Congress.

Before he died, Stalin liked to humiliate his henchmen by telling them that once he had gone the capitalists would 'strangle them like blind kittens'.[7] Khrushchev felt these contemptuous remarks acutely. He wreaked revenge in his 1956 posthumous denunciation of Stalin to the Central Committee. Then, at the beginning of 1958, Khrushchev defeated the 'anti-party' group within the CPSU (again, see the resemblance to Ulbricht's 'factionalists') and stood alone at the helm of the Soviet Union. He assumed new powers as head of government. Thus equipped, Khrushchev determined to show the shade of the old Georgian murderer what he could do.

In foreign policy, Khrushchev decided to start applying pressure where the West was most vulnerable – in Berlin. He would describe Berlin as 'the testicles of the West. Every time I want to make the West scream, I squeeze on Berlin.' Publicly, he referred more delicately to a 'bone in his throat' which had to be removed.

Two weeks after Ulbricht's notably aggressive speech on the subject of Allied rights in Berlin, the Soviet leader made a forceful statement calling for the signatories of the 1945 Potsdam Agreement to 'create a normal situation in the capital of the German Democratic Republic'. The Soviet Union would, he said, soon hand over all functions in Berlin to the East Germans. If they wished to settle the Berlin question, the Allies would have to negotiate with the GDR. Khrushchev ended with an affirmation-cum-threat: the USSR would 'sacredly honour our obligations as an ally of the German Democratic Republic'.

Eisenhower was initially outraged, and told acting US Secretary of State Christian Archibald Herter, 'if the Russians want war over the

Berlin issue, they can have it'. However, in the end the administration decided to ignore Khrushchev's challenge and wait and see.[8]

They waited. They saw. At four in the afternoon on Thursday 27 November 1958, Khrushchev marched into the impressive, mahogany-panelled oval room that housed the Soviet Council of Ministers. It was the first formal Kremlin press conference he had ever held, and had been called at such short notice that American journalists were forced to desert their Thanksgiving Day dinners in order to attend.

The stocky First Secretary, bronzed from a late vacation in the Crimea, announced that he had decided to do some surgery, to remove the 'malignant tumour' of Berlin. He assured the assembled scribes that he had sent a 28-page note to Western ambassadors that very morning. This note contained a dramatic ultimatum. The West must agree to sign a German peace treaty within six months. It must also 'liquidate the occupation regime' and turn West Berlin into a demilitarised 'free city'. If the West did not agree to this, Khrushchev would unilaterally sign a treaty with the GDR and turn over all control of access to Berlin to the East Germans.

On receiving the news, Eisenhower – spending the Thanksgiving weekend with his family in Georgia – made aggressive noises. Within a few days, he again backtracked. Nevertheless, the maintenance of the occupation regime and of access rights to the Western sectors of Berlin remained central to American policy. This was made clear to Moscow. As was America's commitment to West Germany and her readiness to use nuclear weapons, if necessary, to defend it.

It was difficult to work out exactly what Khrushchev hoped to achieve by the 27 November press conference. Once the West had refused to budge, if he went ahead and turned over control of access to Berlin to Ulbricht, then in practice the self-willed East German leader would be given the power to determine peace or war. And the Russians, because of their 'sacred alliance' with the GDR, would be committed to supporting him. Meanwhile, the West started carrying out manoeuvres and issuing statements of military solidarity that further heated up the situation.

There was a disconcerting sense in Khrushchev's unleashing of the Berlin Crisis, as on other occasions, of a gambler tossing all the dice into the air to see where they landed.

His son, Sergei, was then twenty-three. He asked his father what would happen once the ultimatum ran out. Would it mean war? Of course not! No one would want a war over Berlin, Khrushchev assured him. Before that time came, his threat would scare the West into negotiations. And if the negotiations failed? Sergei persisted. Khrushchev replied irritably, 'Then we'll try something else. Something will always turn up.'[9]

It was, in fact, the British Prime Minister who turned up. In January 1959, Harold Macmillan came on an official visit, at which an offer of top-level discussions was made. His Soviet counterpart withdrew the time limit on the ultimatum.

The West had agreed to a conference on a German peace treaty. Khrushchev solved the problem of saving face with a breathtaking distortion of the truth. He simply pretended that there had never been an ultimatum. The West had misunderstood him, he insisted.

Nothing actually came of the resulting talks, but the immediate crisis was over. The zigzagging over Berlin went on for more than two more years, until the end of the Eisenhower administration and into the next. Sometimes it was a live issue, sometimes not, but it was always there.

In the words of the post-Communist Russian historian, Vladislav M. Zubok:

> Khrushchev must have believed he was killing many birds with one stone. He was pressing hard on an 'acorn' of the west to deter the United States in the Far East and to pre-empt *Drang Nach Osten* (drive toward the east) from West Germany. He also gave decisive support to Ulbricht's regime in the GDR. And all that was couched in the language of a peace settlement designed to sound irresistible to world public opinion.[10]

Berlin was still the West's most sensitive part. All Khrushchev had to do was squeeze.

Khrushchev seemed to be on the GDR side. But the security of their regime was not the only source of anxiety for the leaders of the GDR. What about their own personal security? Who guards the guards?

As they tightened their grip on the Soviet Zone in the post-war period, the SED bosses settled into a group of requisitioned villas in the north-east Berlin suburb of Pankow. Ulbricht, Pieck, Grotewohl and the other Politburo members lived within a few hundred metres of each other, in a leafy area surrounding the Majakowskiring, close by the castle of Schönhausen (Pieck's official residence). This 'VIP quarter' was sealed off by a security fence and by guard units.

Even before 17 June 1953, there were signs that this location might prove insufficient for future needs.[11] Then came the Hungarian revolt. The swiftness of the revolutionaries' seizure of Budapest, and the violent, often lethal, summary punishment they inflicted on the Communist officials and secret policemen they rounded up, were a warning to the SED leadership of what might happen to them in case of another, this time more successful, uprising in Berlin.

At a Politburo meeting two months before the Hungarian revolt, on 28 August 1956, security measures for the élite were discussed. The minutes conclude: 'Measures are to be prepared for a new residential settlement'. There is little question, however, that the experiences of October 1956 gave added impulse for the Politburo to move out of Berlin.

But to where? Ulbricht, a fitness fanatic, was keen to live in the fresh air, near water and trees. Various possibilities were discussed. Then someone suggested the area near the appealing small town of Wandlitz, north of Berlin, as a possible solution to the Politburo's very special housing needs.

Wandlitz lay amid state forest near the town of Bernau, thirty-five kilometres north of Berlin. It was wooded country threaded through with attractive lakes, far enough from Berlin to provide a good quality of life, yet close enough that a minister's or Politburo member's limousine could be circling the Alexanderplatz within half an hour of leaving home. 'Deep in nature – at the gates of Berlin!' as the town declares in its tourist literature. Moreover, the summer residence of the Soviet ambassador lay on one of the nearby local lakes, the Liepnitzsee, within easy reach.

In the spring of 1958, a group of bureaucrats suddenly appeared from East Berlin and started inspecting the terrain, under the bewildered and slightly nervous gaze of forestry workers. Word spread that local land was being earmarked for 'a special purpose'.

By the summer the town of Bernau had been informed that initially 60 hectares (approx. 145 acres) would be required, which was later expanded to 101 hectares (approx. 240 acres) which would finally become 357 hectares (approx. 860 acres). A connecting road would be built to link up with the north–south autobahn. Existing and new woodland and shrub-planting would make the area invisible from outside, and provide visual, personal and weather protection for the individuals who lived and worked there.

The basic building work on the soon-to-be-notorious 'forest settle-ment' (*Waldsiedlung*) was finished by February 1960. There were no street names, and never would be. The houses, comfortable and roomy but not especially grand by most standards, were simply numbered from 1 to 23. They were mostly built of pre-fabricated materials and not considered especially modern even at the time. They enjoyed pleasant gardens.

Years later, the actor and director Vera Oelschlegel married a Polit-buro member and came to live here. She hated it and wrote of the place they called 'the bosses' paradise':

> The houses were situated as nice and symmetrical as matchboxes. They
> were soulless, and seemed alien in the landscape with its beech and pine
> trees . . . It was a ghetto, and while I was there I felt about as at home as an
> emigrant. When in the mornings the same dark Volvos stopped in front of
> the garden gates, and when from each house an old man emerged, escorted
> by a younger man, who carried his bag and opened the door for him . . .[12]

This referred to a later period, when the official car for the East German party boss had become a specially lengthened and reinforced Volvo. Earlier, the limo would have been a Soviet-built Chaika, which was standard transport for GDR ministers and party bosses between the 1950s and 1970s. The party leaders were provided with a so-called 'A-Certificate', which rendered them exempt from normal traffic rules, especially speed limits (which for normal mortals were strictly en-forced).[13]

The gentlemen of the Politburo moved into their plain but roomy homes in the early winter of 1960. There was a private clinic not far away. In summer, the bosses could follow a private lane down to their own part of the lake shore, where there were bathing huts and boat houses. For less pleasant contingencies, there was even a system of bomb-proof bunkers a few hundred metres from the VIP residences. Here the SED bosses' families could take refuge if the Cold War ever turned hot, while the men of the house would be spirited away to an underground governmental complex elsewhere in the area, from which they would direct the GDR's fight for survival.[14]

They had at their disposal the large and roomy Functionaries' Club-house complex (known as the 'F-Club'). This contained a cinema and a swimming pool. In the F-Club's restaurant the SED functionaries and their families could also eat extremely modestly priced meals (four marks for roast venison!), cooked by a team of gourmet chefs who followed their every culinary or dietary whim. The Politburo members could drink a beer in the bar after their car dropped them back from a long day at the ministry or the party office.

There was also a general store where fresh food and (usually imported) household necessities were available, though, given the astonishingly reasonably priced menu, functionaries and their families tended to eat at the club restaurant. The store, like the club's restaurant, was guaranteed the best produce at all times, including foreign and Western goods accessed through *Stasi* channels.[15]

According to one account, when Lotte Ulbricht, the First Secretary's wife, conceived a passion for 'Jonathan' apples, couriers were despatched to Bulgaria to get some.[16] Ulbricht himself rose at six a.m. every morning, regularly worked out, took long walks, rowed on the lake, often appeared on television swinging Indian clubs or leading enthusiastic GDR citizens in mass callisthenics sessions. Well into old age, he remained a ferociously competent table-tennis player. He often ate meals confined to raw vegetables and eggs.

As the years went on, up to thirty gardeners were employed, and a series of large greenhouses produced a constant supply of fresh vegetables and flowers for the settlement dwellers. Grotewohl's successor as prime minister, Willi Stoph, was a keen vegetable gardener and would even press his *Stasi* security detail into work on his produce beds if he felt they had nothing better to do. Stoph, considered cold and inhumane, was reportedly the least popular of the high-ups the staff had to deal with.[17]

The area where the bosses and their families lived was known as the 'Inner Ring'. Of the 600 or so servants, officials and security staff who serviced the Politburo settlement, many lived near by in much more modest homes in the 'Outer Ring'. They were all, even the cooks and housekeepers and gardeners, responsible to the 'Main Department for Personal Protection' of the *Stasi* and were paid according to *Stasi* graduations of rank. For some reason, cooks were not allowed to rise above the rank of lieutenant.

The employment conditions of the settlement staff were very demanding. A circular to the domestic help from *Stasi* minister Erich Mielke admonished them that 'by showing an amenable and professional attitude, and by sensitively carrying out of their duties, [they] should constantly foster the subjective well-being of our leading representatives'. This was wryly referred to by staff as the 'Love-Me-Directive'.[18]

For all the egalitarian rhetoric, the atmosphere was not unlike a traditional feudal estate. The gamekeeper upon whose shoulder the ageing Honecker rested his gun when he took aim and fired at the wildlife, went deaf in his right ear.[19] All the same, jobs at the forest settlement were much sought after. Nearness to power brings reflected prestige even to the humblest drudge. And there were all those imported goodies, which tended to trickle down.

During the 1960s, the high officials would also be allowed access to the hunting reserves that lay twenty or thirty kilometres to the north, straying over into the huge area that once been the preserve of Hitler's old crony and Reich Master of the Hunt, Field Marshal Göring. Göring had built a great house that he called, in memory of his Swedish first wife, Karin, 'Karinhall'. The house was demolished after the war, but Göring's hunting lodges and the houses belonging to his huntsmen still existed and were reserved for the exclusive use of Politburo members at peppercorn rents. Foreign visitors, especially Soviet grandees such as Khrushchev's successor Leonid Brezhnev, were treated to lavish hunting parties in the wild-animal reserve adjoining the 'forest settlement'. The hunting lodge on the Döllnsee was also used for high-level weekend conferences of the GDR élite.

The settlement sometimes seemed like a kind of leafy political reservation. Every night the system gathered its rulers in, as if to leave them wandering about outside might be dangerous, both for them and for the people at large. Despite the luxury of life there compared with elsewhere in the GDR, few if any of the élite seem to have lived there out of preference or desire. Many of the settlement dwellers confessed later to a distinct sense of claustrophobia.[20]

Günter Schabowski, who moved there in the 1980s when he joined the Politburo, said that there were was no place for real friendships, no truly authentic social life. Anyone who socialised too often with specific fellow Wandlitz-dwellers would be suspected of conducting intrigues, of 'forming a faction'. Walter and Lotte Ulbricht never socialised with other residents. The only outsider to enter their home except on official business was their daughter, who would come up from Berlin at the weekend. When she did so, the staff were sent out of the house. The Ulbrichts wanted to keep their private life private.[21]

The consequence of such anxiety-inducing rules of interaction was that people either stayed at home alone with their families, or they went to the F-Club, where they were safely visible and part of the 'collective'.[22] Ulbricht, who had spent the entire 1950s fighting off leadership challenges of one kind or another, liked having the rest of the party's leaders at Wandlitz, where he could keep an eye on them. His under-lings, powerful men in the outside world, were in a real sense under surveillance once they passed through the settlement gate.

Not for nothing, though somewhat tastelessly given recent German history, did Wandlitz become known among the general population of the GDR as the 'Ghetto of the Gods', or simply, 'the Ghetto'. The imprisoners became the imprisoned. The 'forest settlement' was the GDR élite's golden cage.

Surrounding the forest settlement at Wandlitz from the time of its construction in 1960 was a wall. This wall was eight kilometres long and two metres high, with manned guard towers at regular intervals. The entire, magnificently paranoid structure was screened by trees and newly planted, quick-growing giant shrubs such as juniper, mahonia and rhododendron. The casual viewer would never know it was there.

'Five kilometres on from the Wandlitz autobahn exit, one took a left turn,' as one account has it:

There stood two glass sentry boxes with uniformed guards . . . and a traffic light. Well before you got to this, of course, there were 'halt' notices, and warning signs that forbade 'unauthorised vehicles' from turning off the main road. Even after passing through this electronically regulated entrance, you had to look very carefully to make out, amidst the thick growth of the forest, a two-metre-high wall.[23]

Erich Honecker, as Secretary for Security, had directed the privacy and safety aspects of the forest settlement's construction with great success. The next year, he would face his greatest challenge yet. Having sealed themselves off so carefully from the threat of a hostile outer world, the men of the East German leadership now had to see about doing the same for their fellow citizens.

All seventeen million of them.

7

WAG THE DOG

ON 20 JANUARY 1961, in front of a host of invited dignitaries and 20,000 citizens willing to brave (in the words of the *New York Times*) 'a Siberian wind knifing down Pennsylvania Avenue', bringing outdoor temperatures of minus seven degrees centigrade, John Fitzgerald Kennedy was sworn in as thirty-fifth president of the United States.

He gave a stirring inauguration speech that raised hopes of a new era in American politics. It made him a liberal icon. This was to a great extent justified, though much of the change that the Kennedy White House seemed to represent was more cosmetic than real – Jack and Jackie replacing Dwight and Mamie, elegant, Eastern culture-vulture socialites replacing plain-vanilla Midwestern mom and dad. The truth about the politics of the President and his family was, of course, more complicated.

Jack Kennedy and his brother, confidant and campaign organiser, Robert, were the sons of Joseph Kennedy. Joe Kennedy, an anti-Semitic, Communist-hating multimillionaire whose wealth, it is said, was of dubious provenance (bootlegging has been mentioned) had been an enthusiastic supporter of Senator McCarthy. This last aspect of the Kennedy patriarch's world-view found an echo in the career paths of his clever, ambitious surviving sons (his eldest, Joe Jr, having been killed on active service in 1944).

As a junior congressman, Jack publicly praised McCarthy for his anti-Communist vigilance. Robert actually worked as a counsel on the Wisconsin senator's then all-powerful Permanent Sub-Committee on Investigations. A senator since 1952, Jack was the only Democrat to abstain in the Senate's vote of condemnation against McCarthy, passed by a majority of 67 to 22, which broke the demagogue's power in December 1954.[1]

Moreover, Senator Kennedy, was not above playing the 'Red scare' card. Looking to place himself for a presidential run in 1960, he began loudly complaining that the Soviets were pulling ahead of the United States in the arms race. In a way that, for all its anti-Communist thrust, oddly colluded with Khrushchev's self-serving post-*Sputnik* braggadocio, Kennedy made the alleged 'missile gap' one of the main themes in his presidential campaign.

So the young, handsome President who made such a brilliant inauguration speech that freezing January day, was something of a puzzling mixture. He was not really considered by the liberal wing of his party to be 'one of them'.[2] It was not the sophisticated, Harvard-educated Kennedy but a conservative military man, the retiring President Eisenhower, who warned the American people in his valedictory television broadcast about the dangers of the 'military-industrial complex'.

Kennedy appeared the picture of the civilised liberal yet had no clear record of supporting liberal causes. He talked of peace and yet railed in aggressively anxious terms against the 'missile gap'. He certainly seemed to have nothing much against the military-industrial complex. As another Massachusetts-Irish politician said of him:

> There's something about Jack – and I don't know quite what it is – that makes people want to believe in him. Conservatives and liberals both tell you that he's with them because they want to believe that he is, and they want to be with him.[3]

In the weeks after Kennedy's election, the Eastern Bloc's leaders had a similar problem. How to handle the new man in the White House?

In September 1960, the former KPD chief and President of the GDR Wilhelm Pieck died at the age of eighty-five. Within weeks, the post of president was abolished and a 'State Council' set up to replace it. The council's chairman was, of course, Walter Ulbricht. The First Secretary of the SED became also *de facto* head of state. It was thus an even more powerful Ulbricht who entered the crucial new year of 1961. In effect, a dictator.

The omnipotent one had much to do, many decisions to make. Detailed official briefings for Ulbricht broke down the new American

President's support in conventional Marxist-Leninist terms, outlining Kennedy's ties to Wall Street and the major corporations.[4]

Fair enough. Kennedy came from money, and no politician got that far without corporate support. JFK's appointment of the Californian-born president of the Ford Motor Company, Robert S. (for Strange) McNamara as Secretary of Defense fitted perfectly into this Marxist paradigm. The GDR officials did not fail to remind their boss, with some relish, that Ford had provided financial support for Hitler. Equally predictable for the East Berlin analysts was the presence of an 'unrepentant Republican' in the form of C. Douglas Dillon, Secretary of the Treasury. Dillon was a holdover from the Eisenhower administration. As a leading investment banker, he provided the new Democratic administration with a touch of non-partisan appeal and the much-needed *gravitas* of an establishment figure who could, as Kennedy recognised, 'call a few of those people on Wall Street by their first names'.[5]

The tendency in general among Kennedy's advisers (his so-called 'brains trust') was, however, more biased towards academics, including such Ivy League luminaries as J.K. Galbraith, Arthur Schlesinger and Seymour Harris (all Harvard), and the economic historian and expert on 'overcoming backwardness', Walt Rostow (MIT). Kennedy's administration was the first one in which 'think tanks' – especially the RAND Corporation – came to the fore, and memoranda on every subject from just about every conceivable angle started to flood into the White House's in-tray.

Even Kennedy's Secretary of State was no toughie Cold War warrior in the mode of the late John Foster Dulles but a conscientious, not especially combative Georgian liberal, Dean Rusk. The President in any case planned to make his own foreign policy. In this he was advised by his younger brother, Robert, whom he had daringly brought into the administration as attorney-general, defying inevitable accusations of nepotism.[6]

The advice to Ulbricht from his advisers was that, while the new administration would still stand strongly on Western rights in West Berlin, Kennedy would be more flexible than Eisenhower when it came to the city's overall status. Here was a faultline in the edifice of Western solidarity that might be exploited.

This view was shared by Ulbricht's ultimate master, the mercurial Nikita Khrushchev, who by all accounts saw Kennedy as potentially weak, a rich man's son whose daddy's money had bought him a high position which might prove beyond his powers. And the new American President, at forty-three, still lacked experience at the highest level – he was, as Khrushchev pointed out, 'younger than my own son'.[7]

But would this enable the shrewd, aggressive Soviet leader to bully Kennedy into making significant concessions? Or might it mean, on the contrary, that the younger leader, with his plutocratic background, would prove an obedient tool of the Wall Street capitalists, who were sworn to destroy the USSR at any price?

Khrushchev wobbled between these two possible scenarios, even confiding to US Ambassador Thompson before the elections that he wished Nixon would win 'because I'd know how to cope with him. Kennedy is an unknown quantity.'

Scarcely had Kennedy settled into the White House than the Bay of Pigs fiasco in April 1961 – a disastrous, American-supported attempt to overthrow the regime of Fidel Castro in Cuba – ensured that hopes of a bright new morning were dashed. The Bay of Pigs made fools of Kennedy and his advisers, and damaged hopes of impressing developing nations with America's new, progressive foreign policy. On the other hand, it strengthened Khrushchev, who could posture as the true friend of the Third World and its protector against the interfering, imperialistic Americans.

A few days before the Bay of Pigs disaster, the Soviets managed to put into space, for a little more than an hour and a half, and then bring back to earth, Lieutenant Yuri Gagarin (he was promoted to major in the middle of his flight, which he was not expected to survive). The world was treated to a glorious and peaceful technological achievement of the USSR, contrasted just a few days later with naked American aggression against Cuba. It was, especially for those who failed to recognise the underlying and deeply frightening violence that underpinned the Soviet sphere of influence, a telling comparison. That comparison did not favour the United States.

The Gagarin flight, notwithstanding its apparently innocent public-relations benefits, also underlined the military potential of Soviet rocketry. Khrushchev himself had, by this point, become drawn into a passionate, quite strange love affair with missile-delivered nuclear weaponry, and the success of his country's cosmonauts was intimately associated with this. It involved the same powerful technology. The fact that it delivered Gagarin, a winningly handsome, though compact, five-foot-two metallurgist and father of two from a small town near Smolensk for a 108-minute flight above the atmosphere, rather than a nuclear warhead against Pittsburgh, did nothing to diminish its intimidating effect.

Khrushchev spoke publicly of turning out long-range missiles 'like sausages on an assembly line'. At the end of 1959, he had created the imposing-sounding 'Rocket Strategic Forces'. A few weeks later, he announced huge cuts in conventional military manpower (throwing up to a quarter of a million Red Army officers out of work), making it clear that he could afford to do this because the USSR's thermonuclear strength was now unmatchable.

Hence Kennedy's campaign talk of the threatening 'missile gap' between the US and the USSR. The bright young senator from Massachusetts genuinely believed the Russians were pulling ahead. In fact, Khrushchev's 'missile' talk was mostly bluff. His impressive-sounding 'Rocket Strategic Forces' consisted of 'four unwiedly R-7s on a launching pad near Plesetsk in Northern Russia'.[8]

In one matter, however, Kennedy and his advisers were right to be concerned. Far from making Khrushchev more cautious, the Soviet leader's grasp of the importance of thermonuclear equality made him more, not less, bold in his foreign-policy calculations. As Khrushchev later boasted to colleagues, he had realised as early as the mid-1950s, when the Soviets still possessed only conventional aircraftborne nuclear bombs, that Secretary of State Dulles's threats of massive retaliation were also bluff – brinkmanship based on the fact that both sides knew where the brink was and would act accordingly.[9]

Now that the Soviet Union had ended this monopoly, it could rely on the resulting assurance of mutual destruction to keep the peace while Moscow 'protected' the independence of Third World countries and supported 'national liberation movements'. These movements would chip away at capitalism's power and draw most of the world into the socialist camp within the foreseeable future without the need for a decisive war.

Meanwhile, the West would have to 'respect' Russia. The short, egotistical Khrushchev, mocked by Stalin as a clown and secretly despised by colleagues for his unsophisticated peasant ways, was keen on 'respect'. This made him unpredictable. Humiliate Khrushchev, and there was no clear limit to what he might do.

The Russian leader's public pronouncements did not help. 'We shall bury you!' Khrushchev famously declared – meaning not that the Soviets planned to exterminate the other side, but that the East would preside over the last rites of capitalism when the latter finally collapsed in the face of socialism's unstoppable success. However, the remark could be interpreted in a more worrying way. And Khrushchev was not above crude threats. At official receptions, the normally genial Soviet leader would suddenly cut the small talk, turn on Western diplomats, and remind them exactly how many missiles it would take to destroy their major cities.

Khrushchev was 'on a roll'. Not only was the East starting to prove its superiority in space and weapons technology, but soon, Moscow assured the world, it would show its economic superiority as well.

There were, of course, flaws in this optimistic view, some more obvious than others. The situation in the GDR was one. All the talk in East German official documents of the 'crisis of capitalism' that was supposedly wrecking the USA could not conceal the regime's increasing concern about its own economic difficulties – and especially the persistent haemorrhaging of its population to the West.

Something had to be done.

Ulbricht was sure he knew what it was. Khrushchev, who had staked a great deal on the inherently superior nature of the socialist system over the capitalist one, and hoped to convince the rest of the world of this, still remained to be convinced.

Two years had now passed since Khrushchev's original 'ultimatum' on Berlin.

The irritatingly persistent Ulbricht kept reminding his protector that in the interim nothing had actually happened. Khrushchev protested that this was not true, that the West had been 'shaken up' by Moscow's pressure, and so on. He continued to stall, but Ulbricht did not give up. In late January 1961, an East German delegation passed through Moscow. Not unusual, except Khrushchev was only now told that they were on their way to talks with the Chinese in Peking. This was the first he had heard of it.[10]

Khrushchev's relations with Chairman Mao Tse-tung had been deteriorating for years, in part due to the Russian's denunciation of Stalin, who was still officially worshipped in China. Mao had also started dropping none-too-subtle hints that Khrushchev's talk of coexistence with the West amounted to capitulation. What was the point, the Chinese argued, of all this bragging about the Soviet Union's nuclear capacity, if Khrushchev did not use it to spread revolution and overthrow capitalism?

In early 1960, Russia had pulled its advisers out of China and scrapped a host of joint projects. A Sino-Soviet truce was patched together in November, but for high-level East German officals to be visiting Peking just two months later was a signal that they were prepared to pursue an independent line. Ulbricht remained on better terms with 'the great helmsman' in Peking than was strictly comfortable to Moscow.

What was happening in early 1961 was quite simple. The tail was practising how to wag the dog, and finding that it wasn't so hard a thing to master. The paradoxical position of the GDR as the Eastern Bloc's politically weakest but at the same time most strategically crucial element had, back in 1953, led to Ulbricht's unexpected survival. The 17 June uprising had been mostly due to Ulbricht's rigidity and stubbornness. This was a fact of which Moscow was fully aware. But it could not afford to get rid of him, for fear of admitting weakness, and thus further destabilising an already unstable situation. Over and over, Khrushchev would continue to assure Ulbricht of his support, and of the GDR's importance to the Eastern Bloc.

Seven years later, Ulbricht was more firmly than ever in the saddle in the GDR, but the state itself was in increasing trouble. What to do?

Attempts at economic reform, imposed by Moscow during the post-Stalin liberalisation, had been half-heartedly implemented for a while and then slowly reversed.

The results of what amounted to a re-Stalinisation of the economy were predictably poor. The collectivisation of agriculture, which was once more aggressively pursued during the late 1950s, led to food shortfalls and a flight from the countryside (often to the West).[11] The radical restructuring of industry, involving further attacks on privately owned concerns, meant that productivity and living standards remained low, despite continual raising of 'work norms'.

By early 1960, the GDR was suffering from serious shortages of raw materials and quality industrial products as well as food. It was heavily in debt both to the USSR and the West. Far from overtaking West Germany, the GDR was falling farther behind. If such a word were permitted in the Communist economic lexicon – which it was not – then the situation in East Germany could only be described as a recession.[12]

The exodus from East to West Germany had continued. It had averaged around a quarter of a million a year from 1955, took a dip in 1959 to 143,000, then rose again in 1960 to a little over 199,000. The deterioration of the situation in 1960 itself was a sharp one, with numbers more than doubling from just under 10,000 in February to 20,285 in May. Again it was the skilled workers, the doctors (of whom 20 per cent fled westwards between 1954 and 1961) and nurses and teachers and engineers, who were choosing to go west.

With the propaganda offensive against West Germany increasing in virulence, and the gradual tightening of restrictions on movement between East and West Berlin, a sense was spreading throughout the GDR that can only be expressed by a German word: *Torschlusspanik* – literally, panic that the door will be closed.

Because of these population losses, the GDR was also suffering from a labour shortage. This led Ulbricht at one point, during a private conversation with Khrushchev, to suggest that 'guest workers' be brought from the Soviet Union to do the jobs that East Germans were either unavailable for or unwilling to perform. Khrushchev was furious. 'Imagine how a Soviet worker would feel,' he snapped back. 'He won the war and now he has to clean your toilets!'[13]

The two men had known each other for about twenty years. Khrushchev, a member of Stalin's inner circle, was senior commissar on the Stalingrad Front in 1942. Ulbricht and other German Communist exiles were sent there to encourage members of the *Wehrmacht* to surrender, and if possible to join one of the Soviet prisoner-of-war organisations such as the 'National Committee Free Germany'.

The wartime relationship was an uneasy one. The stocky commissar wasted few opportunities to make jokes at his dour German comrade's expense. As the staff sat down to enjoy their evening rations after a day's work in the front line, a grinning Khrushchev would frequently chide him: 'Oh, Comrade Ulbricht, it doesn't look as if you have earned your supper today. No Germans have surrendered!'[14]

Well, if Ulbricht hadn't brought any Germans to Khrushchev on those dark wartime days, in peacetime he had brought, and kept, many millions of them.

The view of most Russians, including Khrushchev, was that they had fought and vanquished Germany and were entitled to the spoils.

But there were also sound military aspects to the Soviets' attachment to East Germany. To have that forward position, pointing at the heart of NATO, had always been important, and became harder to give up as weaponry became more advanced. Even more so since April 1959, when the first Soviet medium-range SS3 nuclear missiles were stationed in East Germany, apparently without the knowledge of the GDR government. These were the first nuclear-armed missiles that Khrushchev stationed outside the Soviet Union.[15]

The Americans quickly suspected, from their own intelligence, that missiles had been introduced to East Germany. Had the CIA but known it, the original deployment had contained a distinct element of dark farce, familiar to armed forces everywhere but to the Russian ones in particular. Not only did the liquid oxygen in the missiles evaporate within thirty days – a common problem with the Soviet rockets of the time[16] – but it was found that soldiers had been literally drinking the rocket fuel. 'Some . . . replaced the blue-coloured 92 percent ethanol, which was coveted by the troops under the name "the Blue Danube", with a typical yellow methanol.'[17] With potentially disastrous results.

In early 1961, Khrushchev was pursuing a risky twin-track policy. On the one hand, he was presiding over a propaganda campaign to give the impression of overwhelming nuclear force, and backing it up with nuclear braggadocio.[18] On the other, he was concerned to set up a summit with the new American President at which he could reach some peaceful understanding on world problems.

President Theodore Roosevelt had advised statesmen to 'speak softly and carry a big stick'. Khrushchev carried a big stick (or pretended to) but did not speak softly. The result was that the West – and Washington in particular – became genuinely concerned that he might use his weapons of mass destruction. In short, Khrushchev made Kennedy and his people nervous. And distrustful of his intentions.

Nor was Walter Ulbricht any help. For a while he had been turning the screw on the rights of West German citizens to enter East Berlin, and on West Berliners to travel there with West German passports. But on 23 September 1960, on his own initiative, Ulbricht suddenly announced that all Western diplomats accredited to the West German government would have to obtain permission from the GDR Foreign Ministry in East Berlin before entering either the Eastern sector of Berlin or the territory of the GDR proper.

Free movement between West Germany and Berlin by Allied diplomats had been a routine matter for fifteen years. When Walter Dowling, US ambassador in Bonn, heard of this new outrage, he flew direct to West Berlin. There he sat himself in an official car with diplomatic number plates, flying the American flag, and presented himself at the border with East Berlin. The East German guard refused to let him pass. Dowling insisted on his rights. Despite the official paraphernalia festooning the car, the guard demanded identification. Dowling did then show his ID, thus conceding the guard's right to demand it and surrendering his own right to unimpeded access to the Eastern sector.[19] The Allies argued that the *Grepo* (border policeman) was simply a local agent of the Soviet authorities and therefore basic four-power rights were unaffected. All the same, Ulbricht had won a victory of sorts in his war of attrition.

But his Soviet superiors were displeased. He had not consulted them. For a satellite country to conduct policy independently in this way was unheard of.[20]

As the long-suffering Soviet ambassador in East Berlin, Mikhail Pervukhin, told Moscow with weary understatement, there was 'a certain inflexibility of the GDR leaders in practical activity concerning West Berlin'.

Exasperated, Khrushchev demanded that Ulbricht desist from further provocations until they next met at the end of November. Ulbricht backed down for the moment. Their point made, the East Germans no longer insisted on prior applications from Western diplomats.

Khrushchev and Ulbricht met in Moscow on 30 November 1960. The encounter took place just after the end of an almost three-week-long conference of eighty-one Communist and workers' parties, during which the headline subject had been the difficulties between the USSR and the People's Republic of China.

At this mini-summit with Khrushchev, Ulbricht bemoaned the GDR's continuing economic difficulties, for which he blamed not his rigid command economy, but dependency on Western imports (particularly machinery and spare parts from the Federal Republic). Plus, of course, there was West German political interference and the poaching of his qualified work-force, attracted by higher salaries, resettlement grants, and the more ready availability of consumer goods in the West. 'We shall,' Ulbricht concluded, 'try to protect ourselves from these unpleasant things, and the number of conflicts in Berlin will increase . . .'

The Soviet leader reminded Ulbricht that he, Khrushchev, had an agreement with the Americans. There would be no basic change in the status quo over Berlin until he had a chance to discuss the world situation with the new American President at the forthcoming summit, projected for summer 1961. The West must never be able to accuse Nikita Khrushchev of bad faith. Under no circumstances, it was made clear to Ulbricht, would Soviet forces move into West Berlin. Instead, Khrushchev suggested, 'we will work out with you a tactic of gradually crowding out the Western powers from West Berlin, but without war'.[21] Ulbricht was to behave like a good, obedient satellite leader.

Not for the first time, Khrushchev's hopes proved illusory. Ulbricht was a master of pinprick politics, of creating facts on the ground by changes so small that only the keenest observer could realise his ultimate aim. He kept to the letter but not to the spirit of his agreement with Khrushchev.

Throughout the winter of 1960–1, the East Germans continued to harass border-crossers and German trans-sector visitors. There were temporary closures of crossing points, spot checks, swoops on public transport at the sector borders at which East Berliners who worked in West Berlin were turned back, and threatened with future punishment if they persisted. But all this was done within existing practice.

Planning for the superpower summit was meanwhile still in its earliest stages, but that did nothing to deter Ulbricht. He raised the subject of a full Berlin border closure again in January 1961 and pressed for it to be on the agenda at the Warsaw Pact meeting in late March.

The East German leader had it all worked out. He just needed Khrushchev to say the word.

Ulbricht's amazingly stubborn and persistent *modus operandi* was largely what had brought him to supreme power in the GDR. It was almost a pity that his outstanding (though by no means attractive) qualities were confined to such a small stage as that of the sickly, synthetic, seventeen-million-strong client state over which he ruled.

Ulbricht was also bolstered by a bizarre personality cult within the GDR, comparable with that of Stalin and certainly more conspicuous than the relatively modest status accorded to Khrushchev in contemporary Marxist-Leninist hagiolatry.

The young East German writer Brigitte Reimann noted in her diary that year:

> The personality cult never flourished before as it does today. Our writers are not ashamed to write slimy abominations in which they compare him with the great, truly great, Lenin. There are 'Ulbricht shrines', the whole thing reeks of religious nonsense.[22]

Reimann was a convinced Marxist who hoped that eventually the regime would come good. Others were not so idealistic, nor so patient. They continued to flood into West Berlin, especially as the months passed and Ulbricht's 'pinprick' policy continued.

Once across the border, such 'deserters' would identify themselves as refugees from the GDR. They would then be directed to Marienfelde reception camp.

Marienfelde lay in the far south of West Berlin's Schöneberg district, part of the American sector. An enclosed, somewhat depressing complex

of barracks-like accommodation blocks and processing halls. The camp
had been built to cope with West Berlin's new status as the 'escape hatch'
from the GDR after Ulbricht sealed off the main German/German border
in the summer of 1952. It had been opened in 1953, shortly before the 17
June uprising. The frantic exodus that followed the uprising flooded its
facilities to overflow. Marienfelde became internationally famous.

Emigrants would be interviewed on arrival, to ascertain their wishes
and filter out possible East German spies. They would stay at Marienfelde
until flown out to West Germany proper, where accommodation and jobs
would be arranged.

Those who wanted to remain in West Berlin faced difficulties. The
half-city was better off than the East, but it was not booming in the way
of the Federal Republic. Refugees were automatically sent to West
Germany, where there was a need for skilled labour of all kinds, or where,
if qualified, they could study.

Joachim Trenkner, a doctor's son from a provincial town in Thuringia,
arrived in West Berlin 'with a twenty-pfennig one-way train ticket'
towards the end of 1959. Twenty-four years old, he had decided to escape
what he described as 'the stink of petit-bourgeois GDR provincial life'.
Joachim had studied engineering at Leipzig University, frequently
visited Berlin, and liked what he saw there. He could have continued
to study any subject he liked in West Germany. The trouble was, he
loved Berlin and wanted to stay in the divided city.

At Marienfelde, Joachim endured questioning by all three Allied
intelligence services, then made the wearying progress from office to
office, bureaucrat to bureaucrat, before gaining the precious Western
identity card that entitled him to live and work in the Federal Republic.
Successfully delaying attempts to put him on a plane to West Germany,
he found that there were, in fact, certain categories of person permitted to
stay in West Berlin. One was industrial fitters, of which there was a
shortage there. Joachim had actually taken a factory-based practical
course before going on to study in Leipzig. So, this somewhat bookish
young man, flourishing his East German certificate, went to work in a
West Berlin factory, situated just on the other side of the street from the
East but a whole universe away.

There were adjustment problems, of course. On the factory floor,

Joachim's mid-German accent led at first to his being referred to by his rough-edged Berlin-born colleagues as 'Saxon shit' (*Sachsenscheisse*). Ulbricht was conspicuously from Saxony, as were many other leading East German Communists. The presence of so many carpet-bagging Saxon careerists in East Berlin caused Berliners to describe them disparagingly as 'the fifth occupying power'. Unsurprisingly, Joachim quickly modified his native burr into an approximation of the local argot.

Joachim eventually moved from the 'hopelessly over crowded' refugee camp to a small furnished room near his new workplace. He was earning West marks, and found that he could cross the street into East Berlin and 'suddenly I was Croesus'.

> For a Westerner, a beer in the pub on the eastern side of the street cost just a quarter or a third of the price of what you had to pay in the West – according to the rate of exchange. We Westerners could visit a hairdresser for a few pfennigs, for a handful of change we could spend an evening at the State Opera in East Berlin, or the Berliner Ensemble theatre. For a few marks, we could go into state-owned stores and buy records or books. East Berlin was a shopping paradise, a kind of duty-free port. The only thing was, you mustn't let yourself be caught with this low-priced booty on your way back into West Berlin. Of course, at that time we did not know how long the East German state could go on permitting this 'fire sale' situation, or how long, with the refugees still pouring over the border into the West, it would be able to cope with the loss of its human life blood. But by the beginning of 1961, at the latest, we were discussing this subject every day. There were heated debates among friends and workmates, and everyone sensed that something dramatic was going to happen. But a wall right through the city, as was occasionally suggested? No, our imaginations didn't stretch that far . . .[23]

Here was just one more son of the GDR who slipped westwards in the final months when Berlin was still an open city. Joachim owed the workers' and peasants' state his education, or so its leaders insisted. While the decision to cross the border had been his alone – he simply wanted more than the East could give – it was not surprising that Ulbricht and co. blamed wicked Western machinations for the loss of such precious human assets. They were, after all, hardly going to blame themselves.

During the early months of 1961, the East began to ratchet up its propaganda machine. There was talk of 'people-trafficking', of innocent East German citizens being lured west by bribes, even kidnapped off the streets. There was nothing to prevent the capitalists from infiltrating the GDR to do their evil work. The GDR was left defenceless against the West's tricks and wiles.

So Ulbricht claimed at the Warsaw Pact meeting in March 1961, when he brought up the subject of Berlin once more:

> In this political and economic struggle against our republic [he told the Moscow conference], West Berlin plays the role of the channel with whose help this trade in people is practised, and through which also food and other materials flow out of our republic. West Berlin is therefore a big hole in the middle of our republic, which costs us more than a billion marks each year.[24]

There is no written proof from the actual records of the meeting that he made any material suggestions as to how this 'hole' night be plugged, but Jan Sejna, a senior aide to the then Czechoslovak Defence Minister, who later defected to the West, testified that during another session Ulbricht actually did talk about counter-measures. He suggested, so Sejna claimed, plugging it with 'guard units from our border organs, with barriers, even with barbed wire fences'. The others rejected this as too provocative.[25] However, Khrushchev allowed Ulbricht to start exploring military options to stop the refugee flow, including the closing of the sector border.[26]

Two months later, in May, the East Germans (coyly referred to as 'our friends') were reported by Ambassador Pervukhin to be pushing the same line, and to blazes with the global priorities of Soviet foreign policy:

> Our friends would like to establish now such control on the sector border between democratic and West Berlin which would allow them to, as they say, 'close the door to the West' and reduce the exodus of the population from the Republic and weaken the influence of economic conspiracy against the GDR, which is carried out directly from West Berlin.[27]

*

Khrushchev's options were narrowing down. Ulbricht knew it. Perhaps the Soviet leader did too, but he was determined to change nothing in Berlin until he could sound out Kennedy. The long-awaited Soviet-American summit had now been fixed for the first week of June in Vienna.

Khrushchev wanted to look Kennedy in the eye and see if he looked as though he would start a war over Berlin. He knew that among the President's entourage were some who favoured a variation of the 'free city' solution for West Berlin. Ever an optimist and a gambler, perhaps Khrushchev hoped against reason that Ulbricht's embarrassingly repressive solution to the problem could be avoided after all.

It goes against most received wisdom in the West, even now, that Khrushchev and his fellow Soviet leaders actually acted rationally in their attempt to deal with the disastrous situation of the GDR and the (to Moscow) equally important fact of an economically and increasingly militarily powerful West Germany.

The Russians suspected Adenauer's West Germany of biding its time, waiting for the GDR to fall apart, and furthering this in various subtle and not so subtle ways. Khrushchev could justifiably worry that reunification would become inevitable simply because the GDR was no longer viable. This was why he tried to force the West's hand from 1958 onwards, in the hope that the capitalists would decide to buy peace by making an acceptable deal. The Soviet leader did not want war. In fact, he wanted (and needed) *détente* so that the Soviet Union could tackle its own economic problems.

Khrushchev faced a dilemma. If he was not aggressive enough, the West would sit tight and wait for the GDR (and possibly the East Bloc in general) to fall apart. If he pushed too hard, however, he might provoke a counter-reaction, in the shape of Western military and economic sanctions against the East. Such sanctions would seriously harm the economies of the Warsaw Pact countries in general and East Germany in particular. Khrushchev was on a tightrope. This highly intelligent but naturally aggressive man was not really built for such a delicate operation – especially when he had Ulbricht constantly shaking the rope from below . . .

In the end, the much-heralded meeting with Kennedy from 3 to 4 June in Vienna was a clear disappointment. The US embassy hosted the leaders for the first day's talks. They met in its spacious music room, elegantly decorated in grey and red. Later they attended a big dinner on neutral ground, at the Austrian government's Schönbrunn Palace. On the second day, they moved to the Soviet embassy.

The summit turned into a tense, scrappy affair. It was not quite as bad for Soviet-American relations as the abandoned Paris summit the previous year, but it did not lead to anything like the hoped-for improvements, or get either Khrushchev or Kennedy far in their immediate aims.

Personal diplomacy in the age of the ICBM proved altogether problematical. Kennedy seemed somewhat dazed by Khrushchev's sheer brutal energy. However, if Khrushchev hoped to bully the younger, less experienced man into concessions, he was proved wrong. His attempts to browbeat the American backfired.

By the same token, if Kennedy hoped to use his famously potent charm, that too failed. For Khrushchev, hardened in the triumph-or-die Stalinist school, an opponent's reliance on emollient personality traits indicated just one thing: weakness.

It must be said in mitigation that the President made no concessions worth mentioning, either on Berlin or on the idea of an immediate German peace treaty. Khrushchev blustered and threatened as usual. He would end all occupation rights in Berlin, he kept reminding Kennedy, including Western access to the city, and sign a peace treaty with Ulbricht alone.

'Khrushchev repeated this pledge no fewer than ten times that day,' the Soviet leader's biographer tells us, 'as if trying to convince himself as well as Kennedy.'

The last time Khrushchev did this, just as they were about to part after the second and final day of the summit, Kennedy made his famously cool reply: 'If that's true,' he said, 'it's going to be a cold winter.'[28]

In an *aide-mémoire* that was handed to the Americans at the summit – a kind of slow-release poisoned pellet in text form – Moscow restored its six-month ultimatum on the signing of a German peace treaty. Deadlines had come and gone, starting in November 1958, but now Khrushchev insisted his ultimatum was final. If no agreement was made by the end of 1961, he would sign a separate peace treaty with East Germany. Yes, he would.

'Roughest thing in my life,' Kennedy confessed to an American journalist after the Vienna summit:

> I think he did it because of the Bay of Pigs. I think he thought that anyone who was so young and inexperienced as to get into that mess could be taken. . . . I've got a terrible problem. If he thinks I'm inexperienced and have no guts, until we remove those ideas we won't get anywhere with him. So we have to act.[29]

Prime Minister Macmillan of Britain saw Kennedy in London after the summit, and commented on how exhausted he seemed. The President told Macmillan that he had been 'concerned and even surprised by the almost brutal frankness and confidence' of the Russian leader. The summit, Kennedy admitted, had led to 'no progress on any issue'.[30]

At Vienna, Khrushchev, most commentators agreed, had 'won' the actual encounter between the two men. Khrushchev also thought this, and believed that he could run rings around Kennedy in future too. This belief in his own superiority would dictate an aggressive foreign policy over the next year and a half or so.

The misunderstandings that marked and then followed the Vienna meeting brought great danger for the world. It was not until the Cuban Crisis of October 1962 that the leaders really got each other's measure, and when that happened it was Khrushchev who came out the loser.

On the ground in Berlin everything was moving in Ulbricht's direction. The East German leader had successfully parlayed his weakness into strength. He had the superpowers at each other's throats, which was just where he wanted them.

The day after the Vienna summit, Ulbricht's Interior Minister, Karl Maron, ordered a so-called 'special security unit' of 1,500 *Vopos* to be established in Berlin. In addition, the strength of East Berlin's specialised 'Readiness Police Brigade' (responsible for crowd and riot control) was to be increased to almost 4,000. This was to be done by transferring one company per battalion from throughout the GDR to Berlin, stripping the élite security police in the provincial GDR of around 30 per cent of its total strength. These reinforcement operations were to be carried out before 30 June 1961. Such radical and expensive measures could only point to an imminent major security operation in Berlin.[31]

Walter Ulbricht's great hour was finally approaching. The hour of the Wall.

8

OPERATION 'ROSE'

ON 25 JULY 1961, President John Kennedy appeared on television to address the nation.

Six weeks earlier, immediately following his return from Vienna, the President had given a sober appraisal of the progress (or lack of it) towards understanding with the Soviets, but had made few suggestions about how this might be remedied. The reaction from both press and public was less than favourable. The President had not performed as he should have in his big encounter with the Communist enemy.

Kennedy was in many ways a particularly self-aware individual, especially for a politician, and not one normally swayed by short-term praise or blame. All the same, he was rattled by growing public impatience with his presidency. 'There are limits to the number of defeats I can defend in one twelve-month period,' he told the economist J.K. Galbraith. 'I've had the Bay of Pigs, and pulling out of Laos, and I can't accept a third.'[1]

The most likely arena for a third defeat was, of course, Berlin.

The question ultimately being begged was, what would constitute a 'defeat' for America in Berlin? One of the things the President tried to do, in his broadcast on 25 July, was to define the Berlin problem in the way he wanted Americans to understand it. In the past month, East and West had been leaking information to show their last-ditch readiness for war. One wrong move, and the world could face the most serious threat to peace since the Korean crisis.

Kennedy was acutely aware of this danger. He wanted to avoid the risks inherent both in hardline nuclear missile-rattling on the one hand and a weak-seeming negotiations-at-all-costs stance on the other. This opened him up to criticism from all sides. Former Truman-era Secretary of State and the administration's unofficial foreign-policy *éminence grise*, Dean Acheson, who was more of the missile-rattling party, had tried to push Kennedy in a more aggressive direction. While Kennedy indulged in seemingly endless consultations and discussions, Acheson grumbled privately that 'the nation is without leadership'[2].

In the end, Kennedy's television speech on 25 July was a skilled example of the President's ability to give something to both parties. He spoke from the Oval Office. The mass of klieg lights and cameras crowding the room on what was already an uncomfortably hot summer night, and Kennedy's knowledge that the whole world was anxiously watching, lent the occasion an air of tension and unease.

Like Khrushchev, though for different reasons, the President was walking a tightrope. And he also had someone disturbing him while he was trying to do so. Kennedy had his own German protégé in the shape of Adenauer's West Germany.

Unlike the GDR, the Federal Republic was by no means a basket case. It was prosperous, socially stable and a growing military power. However, it aggressively resented both the Polish and Soviet absorption of Germany territory at the end of the Second World War, and the creation of an East German state. Maps in West German offices, atlases and school classrooms showed Germany 'within the borders of 1937', and vocal refugee organisations representing the millions of Germans expelled from their ancestral homes in the post-war period ensured that no West German government (especially of the Right) could afford to relax this policy. The strongly anti-Communist bent of the West Germans, further intensified by a natural sympathy with the sufferings of their seventeen million compatriots east of the Elbe, led to a militant attitude towards the GDR and the Berlin problem. This militancy did not always match the Washington administration's sense of world priorities.

Therefore, in his speech President Kennedy was talking not just to his own people, or to the Soviet Union and its allies, but also to West Germany and its government. He promised America to strengthen its armed forces, with a $3.25 billion increase in the military budget and an increase in total army strength from 825,000 to one million men. He promised, in the case of West Berlin, to 'make good on our commitment to the two million free people of that city'. Illustrating the situation with a map, just to be on the safe side, he showed Americans the facts of Berlin's geography but also warned the Communists against thinking that this meant the West would not risk a fight to protect it. Berlin had

> now become – as never before – the great testing place of Western courage and will, a focal point where our solemn commitments stretching back over the years since 1945, and Soviet ambitions now meet in basic confrontation.
>
> It would be a mistake for others to look upon Berlin, because of its location, as a tempting target. The United States is there; the United Kingdom and France are there; the pledge of NATO is there – and the people of Berlin are there. It is as secure, in that sense, as the rest of us – for we cannot separate its safety from our own.

But at the same time he became very specific about the nature of that commitment. The President added:

> So long as the Communists insist that they are preparing to end by themselves unilaterally our rights in West Berlin and our commitments to its people, we must be prepared to defend those rights and those commitments. We will at all times be ready to talk, if talk will help. But we must also be ready to resist with force, if force is used upon us. Either alone would fail. Together, they can serve the cause of freedom and peace.

The words 'West Berlin' in this part of the speech were crucial. They meant that America was not committing itself to preserving the status of the whole of Berlin as four-power territory. The message to the East was: try to restrict access to West Berlin, or to take over the Western sectors, and we shall fight. About the rest of Berlin – the part the East Germans now claimed as their own – Kennedy said not a word.

It was not the first time Kennedy had made this distinction, but it came at a defining moment. To German-born State Department analyst Karl Mautner, this was the '"Oh, my God" feeling of a government undercutting its own position'.[3]

But Mautner, along with his wife, Martha – also a State Department adviser – was one of the group known as the 'Berlin Mafia'. This was the name given to CIA officials, State Department hands and journalists who either lived in or had served in Berlin. They tended to feel strongly about Berlin's freedom, and to emphasise firmness in the face of Communist aggression. Members of this group were respected in Washington for their knowledge of the city and the intricacies of its position, but the administration tended to take their opinions with a pinch of salt. They were perceived to have 'gone native' – than which there can be no greater put-down of any diplomat, foreign correspondent or spy.

Khrushchev's reaction to Kennedy's television address concentrated almost exclusively on the stick part of the business and ignored the (admittedly disguised) carrot. The President had come up with a tougher response to his ultimatum than the Soviet leader had expected.

Khrushchev responded with his habitual bluster. The British prima ballerina Dame Margot Fonteyn was performing with the Bolshoi. On the night that Khrushchev went to see her, British ambassador Sir Frank Roberts was in the audience. In the interval, Khrushchev summoned Roberts to his box and subjected him to a lengthy harangue. Soviet forces outnumbered Western forces 'a hundredfold' he told the normally unflappable diplomat, and reminded him that 'six hydrogen bombs would do for Britain, and nine for France'.[4]

A few days later, Khrushchev retreated to his vacation *dacha* at Pitsunda on the Black Sea. There he was visited, at his request, by John J. McCloy, the US administration's chief disarmament negotiator. A former Assistant Secretary of Defense and military governor of the American Zone of Germany, McCloy was a doyen of the East Coast establishment. He had also served as chairman of Chase Manhattan Bank and was still chairman of the Ford Foundation. To Khrushchev and his advisers, who saw the American government and its president as puppets of Wall Street, McCloy represented the puppet masters.

McCloy stayed over night at the *dacha*. Khrushchev was on friendly form the first day, clowning around, challenging McCloy to a game of badminton, taking him for a swim, and so on. Then, overnight, Khrushchev got round to reading the full Russian translation of Kennedy's speech. Next day, he switched in that Jekyll-and-Hyde way of his from genial host into angry warlord. He was, McCloy said, 'really mad'.

Yet again, Khrushchev spelled out his ultimatum and pointed out that the war Kennedy seemed to want would be a thermonuclear one, perhaps leaving some of the USA and USSR standing but wiping Europe from the map. Civilisation would be destroyed. Kennedy would be 'the last President of the United States'.

It was clear by now that Ulbricht's campaign to seal off West Berlin from the East was reaching its climax. Moscow would have to make a decision regarding the possible measures involved, which could easily lead to physical confrontation with the Western forces in Berlin.

The SED's strong man had been further encouraged in his sense of invulnerability by the visit of Soviet Deputy Premier Anastas Mikoyan, two days after the Vienna summit, to discuss future economic co-operation. Mikoyan, an old Bolshevik of pre-revolutionary vintage, forcefully underlined the Kremlin's support for the GDR, which was, he said

> the western-most outpost of the socialist camp. Therefore, many, very many look at the GDR. Our Marxist-Leninist theory must prove itself in the GDR. It must be demonstrated in the GDR that what the capitalists and renegades say is wrong . . . Marxism was born in Germany and it must prove its correctness and value here in a highly developed industrial state. We must do everything so that your development constantly and steadily goes forward. You cannot do this alone. The Soviet Union must and will help with this . . .[5]

Secure in this support, the East German leadership began to tighten the screw.

A few days before Kennedy's speech, SED propaganda chief Horst Sindermann sent out a circular instructing media to no longer use the term 'desertion of the Republic' (*Republikflucht*) to describe flight to the West. This term gave an unfortunate (if truthful) impression that people were leaving of their own volition, and therefore implied, if only indirectly, that the system in the GDR itself might be at fault for their decision. Henceforth, those who went West were to be described as victims of Western 'trade in human beings' or of 'head-hunting' (*Kopfjagd*), implying that they had been dishonestly seduced, bribed, or even kidnapped into leaving the socialist state.[6]

The hard thing to work out was whether this extreme rhetoric primarily reflected or fed the refugee exodus. Each month, it increased. In May 1961, 17,791 fled through West Berlin, 19,198 in June, and then 12,578 in the first two weeks of July alone. Entire factories and offices were emptied of their staff as more East Germans left while they still had the chance. Even with increasing patrols on the sector borders, plus random checks at crossing points and on public transport, only a tiny minority of attempted 'illegal' crossings into West Berlin were being foiled – according to *Stasi* estimates, between 1 April and 13 August 1961 only 15 per cent. People who had come from the provincial GDR were generally sent back to their place of residence. It was, however, an indication of the helplessness of the authorities – and the high level of determination among would-be refugees – that many never returned home, indicating that within a short time of being released they simply tried the border again, and this time crossed successfully.[7]

No one was entirely certain what the GDR regime was going to do, but it was becoming increasingly likely that they would – must – do something.

In early June, according to Soviet records published since the end of the Cold War, Russian diplomats were hearing senior SED officials openly connect the imminent signing of the Soviet-East German peace treaty with the closure of the sector border in Berlin. Later that month, a report to Moscow from the Soviet embassy in East Berlin spoke of the GDR population's fears that 'this question will be resolved in the near future and that all paths for their exit to West Germany will be closed. Therefore some try to go to West Germany before it's too late.'[8]

Almost everything the regime did in these months seemed calculated to increase people's fears, and thereby to exacerbate the refugee problem. On 15 June, Ulbricht appeared at a press conference in East Berlin. Exceptionally, his aides had gone out of their way to invite the Western press corps. Ulbricht used the opportunity to make it clear that once the peace treaty had been signed, and the four-power status of Berlin nullified, the SED regime would assume control over all air as well as land routes to and from Berlin. This step would in itself, if carried through successfully, close down the escape route for the thousands of refugees being flown out of West Berlin to West Germany using the Allied air corridors.

Annmarie Doherr of the *Frankfurter Rundschau*, a West German newspaper, asked the East German leader: 'Does the formation of a Free City in your opinion mean that the state boundary will be erected at the Brandenburg Gate?'

> I understand by your question [Ulbricht declared] that there are men in West Germany who wish that we would mobilise the construction workers of the GDR in order to build a wall. I don't know of any such intention. The construction workers of our country are principally occupied with home-building and their strength is completely consumed by this task. No one has the intention of building a wall.

The problem was, no one at the press conference had suggested that any such intention existed. The person who reveals their guilt by denying culpability for a crime not yet discovered is a staple figure of detective fiction.

There is no evidence that Khrushchev had yet assented to a physical barrier being erected between East and West Berlin. So, was this a mistake on Ulbricht's part? Unlikely. The former Berlin correspondent of NBC, Norman Gelb, pointed out:

> Ulbricht could not act against the wishes of the Kremlin. But he could influence events and attitudes. His presence at the press conference and his comments implying that West Berlin would soon be his do with as he pleased were calculated to raise the level of tension already building in the city, and they did.[9]

For Ulbricht such pronouncements always served a dual purpose: to influence his own side (be it the East German public or the big men in Moscow), and also to undermine confidence inside the Western sectors. He was fond of reminding West Berliners of the fragility of their position; it weakened their morale and also helped encourage the capital flight from the city that would in the long term make it economically unviable, whether the West kept its troops there or not.

But what was the leader's message to his own people? The Western press did not make a big issue out of his curious remarks. But on the day after their leader's surprisingly frank press conference, the number of refugees entering West Berlin rose sharply. Easterners knew how to read the runes.

Was Ulbricht now deliberately encouraging people to leave the GDR? Was he attempting to ensure that the Soviets would have no choice but to support the measures – any measures – needed to stem the life blood pouring from the open wound in their enfeebled German client state? There is no proof of this, but neither is there much doubt, for anyone who observed the trajectory of Ulbricht's career over more than thirty years, that he was quite capable of such Machiavellian doublethink.

Almost immediately after the press conference, Ulbricht opened a campaign to call the Warsaw Pact members together. His suggestion was that they discuss the coming peace treaty and the practical measures (including the 'solution' of the Berlin problem) this would entail. He discussed this with Pervukhin, the Soviet ambassador, and formally wrote to Khrushchev on 24 June, suggesting a meeting in Moscow on 20–1 July. He also mentioned measures against 'border-crossers', workers who lived in East Berlin but worked for hard West marks in West Berlin. Such actions, he insisted, would be necessary *before* the peace treaty. In this small way, Ulbricht explicitly detached the treaty question from the security question. An interesting development. Prescient, as it turned out.

The Soviet Presidium met on 29 June and considered their German ally's request. They set the meeting for 3 August in Moscow. The 'border-crosser' question could also be considered then, the Russian comrades insisted.

With the Vienna summit a failure – no longer could Khrushchev counsel waiting on the meeting with Kennedy – and the GDR's refugee problem spiralling out of control, it was obvious the Moscow meeting would not be just a talking-shop.

*

At the moment, East German refugees who got to West Berlin could not travel by road or rail to West Germany without the risk of being arrested for 'desertion'. But they could safely be flown to West Germany from Tegel or Tempelhof.

As Soviet Ambassador Pervukhin saw it, once a peace treaty had been signed and control of access had been handed over to the East Germans, the goal would be to have all external air traffic from West Berlin channelled through the East Berlin airport at Schönefeld, effectively giving the East control of who was permitted to leave by air. Refugees from the GDR would be marooned in West Berlin, since to leave West Berlin by any means, now including air as well, they would have to cross GDR territory and be subject to arrest. Few East Germans would want to be stuck in West Berlin indefinitely, and neither would the half-city be able to cope with such a long-term influx. Refugee problem solved, and possibly West Berlin so weakened that it would fall into the East's lap.

This ambitious plan was Pervukhin's preference. It involved the successful signing of a peace treaty between the USSR and the GDR, very much his business as a diplomat, so perhaps it was natural that he would prefer it. The physical sealing of the sector borders, though it would be swift and decisive and so could not be ruled out, in his opinion presented vast problems from a technical point of view alone as well as risks of military conflict.

Pervukhin was under intense pressure, and whichever plan he might personally prefer, it was this pressure that he was passing on to Khrushchev. Ulbricht had warned him that 'the situation in the GDR was growing visibly worse. The growing flood of refugees was increasingly disorganising the entire life of the Republic. Soon it must lead to an explosion.' If something was not done, then East Germany's collapse was 'inevitable'.[10]

Ulbricht's Cassandra-like predictions were passed on to Khrushchev, who had evidently realised the matter was now urgent. According to his son, Sergei, in early July, while at his *dacha* in the Crimea, Khrushchev asked his commander-in-chief in Germany, General Ivan Yakubovski, to do a feasibility study on the closing of the border between the Western and Eastern sectors. Khrushchev studied a map of Berlin specially sent from Moscow. He also consulted with Foreign Minister Gromyko and his deputy, Vladimir Semenov, an old Germany hand.

Some time during those few days, the most powerful man in the Soviet imperium made up his mind. He had, perhaps, himself continued to hope that his insistent promotion of a separate peace treaty, accompanied by the usual measure of bluster, would persuade or intimidate the West into agreeing to changes in the status of West Berlin, such that the island half-city would no longer act as a magnet for East German refugees. Now Khrushchev saw that, if this happened at all, it would probably be the result of a long-term process, and time was of the essence. If the GDR was to be saved, something had to happen quickly.

According to Soviet diplomat Yuli Kvitsinsky (later ambassador to West Germany and Deputy Foreign Minister under Gorbachev), then a junior official at the embassy of the USSR in East Berlin, on 6 July he was called to Pervukhin's office.

The ambassador informed Kvitsinsky crisply: 'We have a yes from Moscow'.

Young Kvitsinsky was charged with finding Ulbricht. He tracked his quarry down to the People's Chamber, the GDR parliament. The ambassador and his assistant raced over to the nearby Luisenstrasse, where they were shown into Ulbricht's presence. Pervukhin told the SED boss the news. The Kremlin had plumped for the quick, labour-intensive solution: the sealing-off of the sector border in Berlin. Ulbricht simply nodded and asked the ambassador to thank Khrushchev.[11]

As the ambassador stood opposite him in the People's Chamber building, Ulbricht then launched into an explanation of exactly how the border closure could be achieved: with barbed wire and fencing, which would have to be brought into Berlin in secret. And the main border-crossing rail stations like the Friedrichstrasse would have to be instantly walled off – in the case of the Friedrichstrasse, with glass. Oh, and a Sunday would be best, a summer Sunday when Berliners would be picnicking in the forests or at the lake. By the time they returned home in the evening, it would all be over . . .

The ambassador was surprised at the unnerving depth of detail in Ulbricht's description of the proposed operation. He was, after all, personally pessimistic about the feasibility of sealing off the Berlin border. Khrushchev had not followed Pervukhin's alternative suggestion – possibly because he saw the plan as too long-term and dependent on international developments, certainly because he felt it was dangerous to give Ulbricht total control over access to Berlin – but there was no question the ambassador's dispatches had played a vital role in directing him towards the drastic action that the East was soon to take.

'If anything goes wrong,' Pervukhin warned Ulbricht, 'they'll have both our heads.'

The East German leader insisted that nothing could possibly go awry. At first, he told the Russians that he would oversee everything personally. Then, a few days later, he told them that he had appointed Security Secretary Erich Honecker to handle the practical details.

It would be the biggest job of Honecker's life, and the one that would finally make – or break – his career.

Honecker would co-ordinate a huge operation in which surprise would be all-important. Surprise used against the Western powers, of course, but also against the GDR's own people.

The numbers allowed into the secret of the planned border closure would be small. Honecker set up his headquarters in an inconspicuous suite of four rooms on the second floor of an East Berlin Police Department building in the Keibelstrasse, behind the Alexanderplatz. Members of the planning group, chosen on a strict need-to-know basis, were: Paul Verner, First Secretary of the Berlin SED; Deputy Prime Minister Willi Stoph; Minister of State Security Erich Mielke; Minister of the Interior Karl Maron and his deputy, Major-General Seifert; Defence Minister Heinz Hoffmann; Transport Minister Erwin Kramer; the East Berlin police chief General Fritz Eikemeier and his aide, Colonel Horst Ende. Honecker's own operational staff was limited to eight, including army lieutenant-colonel Hübner, his military adviser, and police colonel and Defence Council official Gerhard Exner. Exner would play a key role. He must ensure that, inasmuch as it was visible to outsiders, the whole thing must look like a large but routine police operation.

Handwritten reports on the progress of the project – given the codename 'Rose' – would be passed to Kvitsinsky and Ambassador Pervukhin by a single designated courier – Ulbricht's personal bodyguard. From the embassy, the documents, detailing matters such as the closing off of the East-West transport system or the shutting-down of the power connections between the sectors, would be forwarded to Moscow likewise by courier. No telephone or radio transmission would be permitted, for security reasons.[12]

On 7 July, a meeting took place at *Stasi* headquarters, led by the State Security Minister, Erich Mielke.

Mielke, then fifty-three, was a stocky, thickset Berliner. He had belonged to the KPD's paramilitary wing from his teens onward, and had been forced to flee Germany for Moscow in 1931, even before Hitler came to power, because of his involvement in the politically motivated murder of two Berlin policemen.[13] After training at the Lenin School in Moscow as an agitator and undercover agent, Mielke was sent to serve in Spain under the command of NKVD general Alexander Orlov. He became accustomed to using assumed names and ranks. His job seems to have consisted mostly of purging the Spanish Republican ranks of Trotskyites and other perceived 'traitors'. Physically strong and personally ruthless, he was a perfect 'enforcer'.

After a period of internment in Southern France following the collapse of Republican Spain, Mielke's trail goes cold for a while. He later claimed to have worked with the illegal French Communist Party during the war. It seems equally likely that he managed to return to the Soviet Union, where he continued his career as a collaborator with the NKVD.

All that's known for sure is that Mielke resurfaced in July 1945 in Berlin, when he walked into the offices of the newly re-established German Communist Party. He seemed already to enjoy close contacts in the Soviet Military Administration, implying that he had returned at their behest as one of 'their' men.

Put in command of a police district, Mielke climbed both the SED greasy pole and the post-war internal-security ladder with an extraordinary speed that confirms the suspicion that he was the Soviets' chosen creature. By the end of 1946, Mielke was leader of the Police and Security Department of the SED Central Committee and a vice-president of the DVdI (predecessor to the *Stasi*). From 1950, he acted as Deputy Minister of State Security.

In 1957, Mielke finally became head of the *Stasi*. He would remain in office for thirty years, a Communist J. Edgar Hoover, immovable and all-knowing, quietly feared even by his nominal superiors.[14]

The motto of the *Stasi* betrayed its true nature. It called itself the 'Sword and Shield of the Party' – not of 'the people' or 'the state'. Just as Mielke was a lifelong conspirator, so the *Stasi* itself was not a police force in any conventional sense but a conspiratorial organisation, created in order to sustain the rule (or 'leading role' in Leninist jargon) of a revolutionary party, the SED.

The *Stasi* was proud of this fact. To celebrate its twenty-fifth anniversary, posters were printed for internal display, telling the story of the organisation's antecedents not as a pillar of state but as the internal intelligence arm first of the old SPD (created during its years of illegality under Bismarck) and then of the KPD. The *Stasi* retained the mentality of an organ of opposition, and therefore necessarily of deceit. In power, given the SED's persistent unpopularity, the *Stasi* was a weapon directed against the overwhelming majority of the country's own people.

At the 7 July meeting, Mielke set in motion initial measures to strengthen security on the main West German-East German border and in the so-called 'ring around Berlin'. The latter had been created after the 1953 uprising, enabling joint GDR/Soviet forces to close off all movement between East Berlin and East Germany proper in the event of a political crisis.[15]

No one below Mielke had an overall view of what all this was for. The new level of activity was generally explained as 'preparations for the signing of a peace treaty with the Soviet Union'. Police patrols on the transport routes and at crossover points into West Berlin were stepped up. Colonel Gerhard Harnisch, ex-principal of the *Stasi*'s training school, was made chair of a commission that would supposedly study how to tighten things up further. Mielke would by this point have been totally aware of existing plans to tighten things further by sealing off the sector borders, so Harnisch's commission may have been a deception measure, to further conceal the purpose of the mobilisation from rank-and-file *Stasi* members.

The strengthening of the Readiness Police and Special Security Police ordered at the beginning of June was now complete, but this was only part of the preparations for 'Rose'. Honecker and Stoph, a former Minister of Defence, put together an overview of what internal resources the regime could rely on. Apart from 8,200 ordinary police, almost 4,000 Readiness Police and 1,500 Special Security Police, they decided that they could call on 12,000 members of East Berlin's factory militias, the so-called *Betriebskampfgruppen*.

These paramilitary units of loyalist workers had been established after the 1953 uprising as a backup for the state in case of emergency. The factory militias were armed with automatic weapons (often of antique Soviet provenance), light machine guns and even flak artillery, plus the kind of crude anti-tank weapons that had been issued to Hitler's *Volkssturm* in the dying days of World War Two.

To this total could be further added 4,500 armed *Stasi* operatives, and 10,000 regular East German army troops stationed in or around Berlin. If things got badly out of hand, more units could be transferred from Saxony, which was seen as relatively loyal to the regime.[16]

The Soviets had spent the first months of the year reinforcing and re-equipping their forces in the GDR in anticipation of a showdown over Berlin. Now the Soviets moved to take strategic charge of the affair. Moscow had no intention of letting its self-willed East German satellite leader call the entire tune.

On 15 July, the commander-in-chief of the Warsaw Pact's forces, Marshal Andrei Grechko, put the East German People's Army on a state of heightened alert, at the same time placing it under the command of the Commander of Soviet Forces in Germany. Ten days later, on the day of Kennedy's TV address, a secret meeting took place at the GDR's Ministry of Defence in Strausberg, outside Berlin. Present was Grechko's chief of staff, Lieutenant-General Grigori Ariko, and his East German opposite number, General Sigfried Redel.

The agenda of the 25 July meeting was the 'securing of the sector borders within Berlin and of the ring around Berlin'. The actual sealing of the border would involve only East German border police. Both the Red Army units (armour belonging to the 1st Motorised Division of the 20th Army) and the East German NVA units (tanks and armoured vehicles including gun-carriers) would hold back, remaining one or two kilometres behind the sector border. The actual use of such units was envisaged only if the East German Ministry of the Interior proved unable to secure the 'ring' – that is, the outer perimeter of East Berlin, where it met the GDR proper. The exact plans for such an eventuality would be developed over the next ten to fourteen days.[17]

What the Soviets planned to do in case of an uprising or of military conflict is only partially known. The military archives in Moscow remain closed. What the Soviets certainly took upon themselves was the creation of a deterrent effect that would inhibit the West, and especially the Americans, from aggressively opposing the sealing of the Berlin sector borders.

Throughout the summer, a stream of Soviet reinforcements, especially tank units and aerial reconnaissance forces, headed for the GDR. Facilities and armaments were upgraded. On 16 July, a massive exercise took place near Archangelsk, on the Arctic Circle, involving the USSR's strategic-missile forces. Two long-range ICBMs of type R-7A were launched – the only ones the Soviets possessed that were capable of reaching American territory carrying a nuclear payload (in this case five megatons). The Soviets knew that the West was capable of monitoring all such exercises in thorough detail. The point would not be lost on Washington.

Meanwhile, a high-profile appointment was made that would also send a message to the West. The World War Two hero and former Soviet Deputy Defence Minister Marshal Ivan Konev was recalled from retirement at sixty-three to take over as Commander of Soviet Forces in Germany. Konev was an acknowledged urban-warfare specialist who shared with Marshal Zhukov the laurels for the capture of Berlin in 1945 and also – notoriously – had commanded the forces that eleven years later crushed the Hungarian resistance in Budapest. His appointment was a typically brash Khrushchev public-relations stunt.

Did Khrushchev's psychological plan have any effect? Perhaps. Kennedy's television address had made it clear that, while America was boosting its defence capacity, this was explicitly for the protection of West Berlin. No mention was made of Berlin as a whole. Five days later, on 30 July, the powerful chairman of the Senate Foreign Relations Committee, Arkansas Democratic senator J. William Fulbright, went much further. He did not understand, he said, why the East Germans had not closed their border, which they had 'a perfect right to do'. The Soviets definitely took notice of that. It was practically an invitation.[18]

President Kennedy himself was privately aware of the limits of what could be done without risking a major, possibly cataclysmic war. He told his aide Walt Rostow during a private conversation a few days after his 25 July speech:

> Khrushchev is losing East Germany. He cannot let that happen. If he loses East Germany, then he loses Poland and the rest of Eastern Europe as well. He cannot let that happen . . . He will have to do something to stop the flow of refugees – perhaps a wall. And we won't be able to prevent it. I can hold the [Western] alliance together to defend West Berlin, but I cannot act to keep East Berlin open.[19]

The poker game was not, of course, a one-sided affair. Khrushchev held a strong hand because of West Berlin's geographical vulnerability and the seeming unwillingness of America to go to war over the question of four-power control of the city. As early as 20 July, he did, however, have a warning from the Chairman of the KGB, Alexander Shelepin. Shelepin told him that NATO was preparing for conflict and that, if the promised peace treaty with the GDR were to involve the closing-off of the transit routes to West Berlin, then the West was prepared to use force to restore access. *Raise you*, so to speak.

Khrushchev's calibration of the border closure was therefore crucial. To intimidate without provoking, to go as far as he could without going too far. These were fine judgements.

Moscow planned to keep Ulbricht on a short leash. Hence dominant Soviet participation in the planning process – though the idea had originated and been promoted by Ulbricht. And hence the trimming of excessively ambitious, not to say dangerous, East German suggestions. These included Ulbricht's hair-raising proposal to close West Berlin's airports by blocking the corridors with East German and Soviet aircraft, floating giant barrage balloons over the airports, and systematically jamming the airwaves, so that all civil air traffic would have to be redirected via East Berlin–Schönefeld. Such plans were firmly nipped in the bud.[20]

By 27 July, a map produced jointly by Soviet and East German staff officers showed the route of a barrier running through the heart of Berlin.

On the last day of July, Interior Minister Karl Maron issued an order to the Commander of Border Police. The commander was instructed 'under maintenance of the strictest secrecy and in the shortest possible time, to plan and prepare the strengthened military-architectural extension of the state border between the GDR and West Berlin'.[21]

On 1 August, border-police units, in co-operation with the Transport Ministry, began putting together the materials that would be needed for this initial phase of the operation. These included 18,200 concrete posts, 150 tons of barbed wire (a very precious commodity in the East Bloc), five tons of binding wire, and two tons of staples. Aside from this, materials were also scraped together to create a temporary barrier all around the 'Berlin ring', totalling 146.3 kilometres. The plan was not just to seal off West Berlin from East Berlin but to create a less formidable but none the less effective barrier to insulate East Berlin from its provincial hinterland. The barbed wire required for this entire extended project was more than 300 tons.

The Communist command economy may not have been able to provide a decent standard of living for its people, or to adequately maintain the country's once-proud architectural and industrial fabric, but for such a project as the border closure it was the perfect instrument. The apparatus for the border-sealing operation was largely in place by the beginning of August. This massive undertaking was being achieved at a breakneck speed, made even more remarkable by the fact that most of those involved had no precise conception of where their labours were leading.[22]

One more matter remained to be settled before the final order was given. The border closure must be presented as a defensive action on the part of the entire Warsaw Pact. This would show the West that the entire Communist world was behind the operation.

On 3 August 1961, Ulbricht and his team travelled to Moscow for a key meeting of the Warsaw Pact's Political Advisory Committee. Technically, the other satellite countries were to be consulted, but it seems probable that the border-closure operation was already a done deal before the plenary meetings began.

Ulbricht's handwritten notes of his preparatory tête-à-tête with

Khrushchev indicate this, as does the fact that the main features of the dramatic move in Berlin – and a text of the Warsaw Pact declaration that would accompany it – had already been approved by the Soviet Presidium on the morning of 3 August, before the actual Warsaw Pact meeting began. The same applied to the date set for the operation: 13 August 1961. Khrushchev had already formally approved the border closure, but he re-emphasised that it remained a defensive measure. As he told Ulbricht at this private meeting, the East Germans were 'not to go a millimetre further'. There was to be no encroaching on West Berlin territory.[23]

Khrushchev's opening speech later that day called for unity on all matters, including the economic ones that would arise from a separate peace treaty with the GDR and from 'practical measures which must be taken in the near future' (by which he meant the Berlin border closure). He also referred specifically to Kennedy's 25 July speech and the American's threat to go to war if the East tried to liquidate the occupation regime in West Berlin. It was both an assurance that he would not go too far, and a warning to the likes of Ulbricht, who showed a tendency to do so.

Leaders of other Warsaw Pact states had opposed the notion of a Berlin border closure back in March, when Ulbricht first brought it up. Now they more or less nodded the operation through. Gomulka, the Polish Communist leader, claimed that he especially had pushed for it all along. The exodus through Berlin had already led to political disruption and economic problems in the GDR's eastern neighbour.[24]

So far, so good. But no one could be sure what sanctions, besides military ones, the West would impose in response to the closing-off of East Berlin. East Germany, with its dependence on Western spare parts and close informal economic links with West Germany, was especially vulnerable to a total Western economic boycott. Thus the second important point on the agenda of the Warsaw Pact meeting. Ulbricht needed to be sure that the other Warsaw Pact countries would lend economic support to the GDR if such a crisis occurred.

However, at this point, despite Khrushchev's appeal for solidarity, the satellite leaders' reaction turned cool, even hostile. Most pleaded that they could not help the GDR economically because of their own problems. This was particularly true of states such as Poland and Hungary, whose relatively liberal governments had become reliant on food and grain imports from the West. In Hungary's case, 30 per cent of the country's trade was with the capitalist world, and 25 per cent of that with West Germany.

Ulbricht had been coming to Moscow and the Warsaw Pact states cap in hand for years, blaming East Germany's problems on West German 'militarists' and 'revanchists' rather than his regime's neo-Stalinist ineptitude. The August meeting was the point at which, we know, the other satellites tried to dig their heels in and say 'enough'. Even Khrushchev was awakening to this reality. The embassy in East Berlin had already told him that 'material facts alone' were not enough to explain the exodus from the country. His own international department, under future KGB boss Yuri Andropov, would soon express scepticism about the effectiveness of repeated 'pump-priming' aid to the GDR.[25] But Khrushchev was stubborn. The prestige of the USSR – and therefore his own – was at stake, and such considerations were more important than mere economics.[26]

The USSR had already sold fifty-three tons of gold on the world market to help the GDR through the coming crisis with credits and special supply deals, as well as to reinforce and re-equip its forces in East Germany.[27] Khrushchev could do little to persuade the satellite leaders to tighten their own people's belts to help the East Germans. None of this, however, changed his decision on Berlin. All the more reason, in fact, to seal off the GDR, integrate it more fully into the Communist COMECON system, and thus systematically reduce its dependency on the West.

Ulbricht had pointed out to Khrushchev that the open border, and the higher standard of living available in West Germany, forced the East German regime to 'artificially' increase the standard of living of its people. This Canute-like attempt to keep East Germans happy with their lot and thus slow the westward tide meant that the GDR had to import much more from the West than was desirable. Ulbricht's implication was clear: once East Germans were sealed into their country, unable to leave for the West, the regime could concentrate on austerity policies and consumer cut-backs with less heed for popular discontent.

Ulbricht made the arguments for the border closure starkly clear in his lengthy speech to the Warsaw Pact leaders on Friday 4 August, then concluded:

> This situation necessitates the introduction of a regulation stipulating that at a certain time the government border of the GDR (going through Berlin) *be closed and* may be crossed by citizens of the GDR only in the presence of the corresponding permission for exit or, in so far as it concerns visits to West Berlin by citizens of the capital of the GDR, with a special pass[28] [emphasis added].

The emphasised words, which made the drastic nature of the plan perfectly clear, were included in Ulbricht's original speech, but disappeared from the official Russian translation and from printed reports, presumably for security reasons.

So Ulbricht got his way, though not the enthusiastic offers of economic support he had hoped for.

The East German leader flew home on 5 August. On Monday 7 August, he finally informed the entire Politburo of the Moscow discussions and of the plan to close the border on Sunday 13 August 1961.

On the ground in Berlin, the American diplomatic and intelligence officials responsible for assessing the situation had no real idea what was about to happen.

There was much discussion of the refugee problem, and of how far they could push without endangering both the West's intelligence-gathering activities in the GDR and its military-political status within Berlin itself. Both sides in the Cold War saw Berlin as a vital listening-post, cockpit of a silent struggle for knowledge and control. Both sides actively spied on each other and worked to destabilise each other's spheres of influence in Germany – although, of course, Communists only ever referred to the West's covert activities, never their own. The West was also, it must be said, keen on 'deniability'.

There was a lot of bluff and counter-bluff going on. Each side, in its own way, overestimated its own power. For instance, at the end of June, the American President's National Security Adviser, McGeorge Bundy, issued an action memorandum. This requested the State Department's and the CIA's advice on 'preparations . . . for inciting progressively increasing instability in East Germany and Eastern Europe, at such a time after 15 October as it may be ordered'. Tellingly, he also asked how this 'capability' to undermine the East Bloc might be brought to the attention of the Soviets before they made their decision on Berlin.[29]

Bundy wanted to 'send a signal' to Khrushchev. The fifteenth of October would see the opening of the XXII. Congress of the CPSU in Moscow. There, before the assembled Communist parties of the world, Khrushchev was expected to announce a separate peace treaty with East Germany and the associated measures that might unleash a world crisis. Clearly Washington thought that the crisis would not come to a head before that date.

In June 1961, former head of the Berlin Operations Bureau (essentially the CIA station, which reported directly to Washington) Bill Harvey had already given a brutally frank assessment of what was and was not possible:

> It is unrealistic to believe that we could infiltrate into the East Zone a sleeper net of sufficient size, reliability, and skill to . . . play a part in organising resistance groups . . . Our abilities are not equal to this task when balanced against the defensive capability of the [East German] Ministry of State Security.

There was a mis-match between the dreams of Washington officialdom and appraisals by those on the spot. Where Bundy talked blithely of destabilising East Germany and of taking action to 'increase the refugee flow', the Berlin hands were much more cautious. After all, what could be more perfectly calculated to justify the Soviets' and East Germans' constant accusations of Western sabotage, espionage and subversion? The CIA even suggested, in late June 1961, that active subversion and attempts to encourage the refugee problem in East Germany 'might very well precipitate a Berlin crisis by forcing the East to blockade the city'.[30]

In other words, the effect of Bundy's 'signal' might be the exact opposite of what he intended. Instead of discouraging the Soviets, it would make them even more determined to cleanse the 'Augean stables' of West Berlin by turning it into a neutralised free city under strong Communist influence. It might even provoke them to seize it by force.

Kennedy's 25 July television address was a turning-point. The speech reflected a coldly realistic reappraisal on his part, a kind of cost/benefit analysis. Hitherto the policy had been to keep undermining the GDR and hope it would collapse into the arms of the West. Now, with the Russians unwilling to let this happen, Kennedy decided to pull back to a more defensible position. If the Soviets took measures to shore up East Germany, so be it. The alternative was nuclear war, and who wanted to risk nuclear war over the (by now largely notional) four-power status of Berlin?

However, the West, including the US, was still making calculations based on a crisis in late autumn/early winter, with a Soviet-East German peace treaty following the XXII. Communist Party Congress and precipitating possible conflict over the status of Berlin. The West thought, wrongly, that it had time to work out a strategy.

Four-power talks between Foreign Ministers of Britain, France, the USA and West Germany took place from 4 to 9 August 1961, in Paris. The meeting in Paris took a leisurely view. It agreed that preparations might be made to discuss Berlin with the Russians in October or November. No date was set for announcing this Western willingness to talk.

These discussions overlapped with the Warsaw Pact meeting at which, unknown to the West, the 13 August Berlin border closure was agreed.

One jarring note of urgency among the complacent Foreign Ministers in Paris came in a message from Mayor Brandt of West Berlin. He warned them of the painful effects of growing East German repression and expressed his fear that the population's situation could worsen 'if the Berlin door were to close'. Secretary of State Rusk was stirred to suggest that 'an attempt to seal off the refugees . . . might lead to an explosion and precipitate the problems under consideration sooner than expected'.[31] But no practical remedy was suggested. Perhaps none was possible.

That repression was increasing inside the GDR, there could be no doubt. On 2 August, a new campaign of intimidation against 'border-crossers' began – even though the closure of the border, which would make such choices irrelevant, was only ten days away.[32]

The 'border-crossers' had already been subjected to harassment in their homes. The tenancy agreements of people known to work in West Berlin were queried, in some cases cancelled, rendering them homeless. Now came more swoops on Easterners crossing into West Berlin, particularly at the beginning of the working day. Those who worked in West Berlin or were suspected of doing so were arrested and questioned. Others were summoned to government employment offices, where they were instructed to leave their employment in the West and seek work in the 'capital of the workers' and peasants' state'.

Many decided it was time to get out.

In June 1961, 19,198 refugees (approx. 630 per day) registered at Marienfelde reception centre. By July the total had leapt to 30,444, (a thousand per day), the highest since 1953. On 2–3 August, 1,322 refugees were registered at Marienfelde; on 3–4 August, 1,100; on 4–5 August, 1,155; and on 5–6 August, 1,283. Over the weekend of 6–7 August, 3,268 left East Germany for West Berlin. The figure for the next day was 1,741.

The total population loss for the GDR for those previous seven days amounted to 9,869. If this were kept up over a year, it would amount to around half a million 'deserters', dwarfing even the figure for the *annus horribilis* of 1953.

On Monday 7 August, Ulbricht had told the Politburo members of the coming border-closure operation At the same meeting, it was agreed that the GDR parliament, the People's Chamber, would assemble on 11 August, where it would approve any measures necessary. The 'anticipated measures for control' (i.e. the sealing of the border) would occur during the night between next Saturday to Sunday, on the basis of an order by the Council of Ministers.

So the official decision was revealed to the highest élite of the GDR, and duly rubber-stamped.[33]

Meanwhile, some Western intelligence sources inside the GDR had started to hint that the decisive moment might come sooner than expected. On 6 August, a CIA source, a doctor quite prominent in his district SED, reported being told at a committee meeting that 'drastic measures' to close off West Berlin were planned for the following weekend. Several Soviet and East German army divisions stood in readiness. A dentist passed on to his French intelligence handler details of a conversation with a patient who held a senior position in the SED. The man had told him that 'they intended to build barriers through Berlin'.[34]

Although Willy Brandt's SPD was now illegal in East Germany, it maintained a clandestine network there. Through this, on 4 August, came another report, from an official in the GDR Health Ministry, that West Berlin was to be sealed off. It gave details. In the Potsdam District alone, 14,000 troops of the East German army had been mobilised, and all police units in the district put under army control, along with the factory paramilitary groups. All leave for police and army units had been cancelled. Moreover, these measures applied not just to the border between West Berlin and the GDR (i.e. the Potsdam area) but also to that between East and West Berlin.

This last, astonishingly accurate report reached Brandt himself on either 6 or 7 August 1961. It was marked with the Mayor's personal green pencil for the attention of his chief of staff. Later, Brandt would say that no intelligence organisation had predicted the date of the border closure. This may have been true, but only in the very narrowest sense.[35]

The German intelligence service, the BND, also picked up this and that. As early as mid-July, one of their agents in the East told them that 'the refugee movement within the population of the Soviet Zone will soon force the SED to take rigorous measures', and a few days later another source claimed to have heard a 'top SED functionary' talking about plans for the sealing-off of West Berlin. The details were being worked out, but as yet the Soviets had not yet given formal permission. This was all true except the last point. Khrushchev had, in fact, finally approved Ulbricht's plan just a few days earlier.

As late as the first week in August, while Ulbricht and his aides were in Moscow, dotting the final i's and crossing the last t's of 'Operation Rose', the West German intelligence establishment at its headquarters in Pullach, near Munich, was still mired in speculation about when precisely the East German leader would get the Soviet go-ahead for his alleged Berlin plan.[36]

The big difficulty was one of imagination. How to divide a modern city of almost four million, to cut streets and railway lines and infra-structure networks that had been functioning, pulsating nerves and

arteries for a huge, lively centre of population – a living urban organism –
for many decades, even hundreds of years?

A West Berliner, then a student, toured Israel in the autumn of 1960.
He was given a tour of Jerusalem, and was shocked to see a city then
divided between an Israeli West and a Jordanian/Palestinian East. Their
hosts showed them a wooden wall just by the Catholic Cathedral of Notre
Dame. This, it was explained, had been built to stop clashes between
young Jews and Arabs, who had a habit of throwing stones at each other
across the border.

> For a few minutes, we West Berlin students discussed whether something
> like this would be possible at home. We rejected the thought immedi-
> ately. The four-sector city of Berlin was in our opinion far too large for a
> strict division like that in Jerusalem – it couldn't happen in Berlin, a
> metropolis that had arisen over centuries of technical progress, with
> extensive bodies of water and forest, with an intricate pattern of sewers,
> with a network of subterranean underground and city railway tunnels,
> inhabited by children who had no inclination to throw stones at each
> other, as if they were members of two hostile population groups.[37]

In early August, Erich Mende, chair of the West German Free Democratic Party, was tipped off about the BND's suspicions. He broke off from
campaigning for the elections due on 17 September and went to Bonn to see
the Minister for All-German Questions, Ernst Lemmer. The two politicians discussed the possibility. Lemmer, himself a prominent member of
the Eastern CDU who had been forced to flee to the West, produced a large
map of Berlin and unfolded it out on to the table in his office. He indicated
the border around West Berlin. All 164 kilometres of it.

'We discussed how hard it would be to seal off a great city in such a
hermetic fashion,' Mende wrote later, 'so that there wasn't even a mouse
hole in it. And Ernst Lemmer said, it just wasn't possible.'[38]

Meanwhile, Honecker and his fellow plotters were preparing to do
exactly what the Christian Democrat minister had defined as impossible.
Every day now, from 9 August, he was in his office, drafting, telephon-
ing, planning.

The omnipresence of the state and its officials in the days before 'Operation Rose', the rising wave of stop-and-search actions and spot checks, was already making life difficult for would-be 'deserters of the Republic', like 25-year-old Gerhard Diekmann. He left the ancient Baltic port of Wismar on 9 August.

On 9.8.61 just before 4 a.m., I left Wismar by train, travelling in the direction of Schwerin, in order to get to Berlin. During the journey I made the following observations: our train stood for around 15 minutes at the control point of Schönfliess, and we were guarded and had our papers checked by the *Trapos* [transport police]. When I got out of the train to smoke a cigarette, there were tanks and guns of the Red Army standing in a field about 50 metres distant. I saw exactly four, which were well camouflaged.

As the journey continued, I realised that a great part of the young people who had been with us in the train were no longer aboard.

When I arrived at Berlin-Lichtenberg, there were *Trapos* at the barrier again – four or five of them – and they were demanding that passengers submit their luggage for examination. Around six passengers were taken into custody by the *Trapos*. All passengers complained about the constant document checks. Anyone who did not submit to the orders of the *Trapos* had their German identity card confiscated.[39]

The situation was escalating. But where exactly was it escalating *to*? In the West, even the intelligence insiders seemed unable to distinguish rumour from fact.

On 9 August, the 'Berlin Watch Committee' met. This important body, which co-ordinated American intelligence organisations in Berlin and pooled their information, discussed the measures the GDR might be considering to stem the exodus. Some participants reported strong indications from sources inside East Germany that a border-sealing operation was on the cards. These sources were not, admittedly, considered wholly reliable. In the end, the majority opinion still held a total closure of the Berlin border to be technically unfeasible.

Like the Foreign Ministers in Paris, the spooks on the spot concluded that any drastic action by the East would occur in the autumn, when a separate peace treaty was signed, not before.[40] And like the Foreign Ministers, they were wrong.

The huge amount of materials and men required for the border closure was being moved around the GDR in some 400 trucks, deliberately dispersed and taking long routes so that no one would realise that they were all ultimately headed for Berlin.[41] Work parties and police teams were also kept away from the sector border until the last moment. These ploys seem to have worked.

All that remained now was to maintain internal secrecy as far as possible. As the clock ticked towards the weekend of 12/13 August, more people on the East German side had to be indoctrinated in 'Operation Rose'. By 9 August, some sixty GDR functionaries and military commanders of various kinds had been let into the secret of the imminent border closure. A critical moment was approaching when – as the information already starting to dribble through to NATO intelligence services indicated – the West would have more than just vague suspicions. All the more reason for Honecker to keep to his schedule, and to maintain what secrecy and/or external confusion he could muster.

Meanwhile, the Soviets were playing their own game of hide-the-border-closure. On Thursday 10 August, at 4.30 in the afternoon, the three senior liaison officers of the Western military missions based in Potsdam appeared by invitation at the Soviet military headquarters complex near Wünsdorf, south-east of Berlin. They were scheduled to meet with the Soviet commander-in-chief, Germany. In itself, a fairly routine event. Expecting to see the familiar figure of Colonel-General Yakubovski, they were astonished instead to be greeted by a balding, slightly portly figure in his sixties, resplendent in a Soviet marshal's uniform. 'Gentlemen, my name is Konev,' he announced with a stagy twinkle in his eye.

Later they exchanged social chit-chat with the legendary marshal – it was, as the American liaison officer, Colonel von Pawel later remarked, like having General Eisenhower suddenly emerging from retirement. Then one of the Westerners remarked: 'We are hearing about substantial military transport activity in your command'. They knew that the Soviets were claiming a routine army exercise, but there was no harm in raising the subject – and if Konev was here, surely something big was going on, or was about to.

The marshal merely smiled and told them in avuncular fashion: 'Gentlemen, you can rest easy. Whatever may occur in the foreseeable future, your rights will remain untouched and nothing will be directed against West Berlin'.[42] It was the all but final act of a classic piece of Khrushchev power-political theatre, and Konev played it perfectly.

On Friday 11 August, prominent East German journalists and regional SED chiefs assembled at the imposing Central Committee building on the Werderscher Markt, a block south of Unter den Linden. They were given a basic run-down of what was about to happen. The newspapers would have to print the formal announcements and also begin the propaganda counter-blast that would justify the action and help to keep the GDR population as calm, or at least as passive, as possible.

That evening, *Stasi* Minister Mielke gathered his senior officials in the officers' restaurant at the ministry's headquarters in Hohenschön-hausen and explained the situation. Although the organisation itself would play little direct part in the border closure, its job was just as vital. There must be no repeat of the 1953 uprising. This was the *Stasi*'s task.

'This new chapter demands the mobilisation of each individual member of the State Security,' Mielke told them, adding an appropriately Orwellian note: 'In this period we are entering, it will be shown whether we know everything and whether we are firmly anchored everywhere.' The aim would be to prevent 'all negative phenomena'.

Mielke didn't entirely trust the East German army and police either. *Stasi* operatives would also be charged with ensuring the 'reliability and combat readiness' of the armed forces during the border closure. In 1953, some soldiers and *Vopos* had sided with the rioters. This must not happen now. In the other main area of danger, the big factory complexes in Berlin and elsewhere, strikes had spread eight years previously like brushfires. 'Anyone who comes forward with hostile slogans is to be arrested,' the minister concluded brusquely.

Then Mielke vouchsafed the final secret: 'The overall operation has been given the codename: "Rose".'[43]

And so the *Stasi* set to work, covering Honecker's back while he put his final plans into practice.

Between Wednesday 9 August and Saturday 12 August 1961, 5,167 refugees were registered. During the following twenty-four hours, it would be about 2,400. Under drastically changed circumstances.

The last day of Berlin's open border dawned. The weather proved only sporadically summery, reaching only 20°C (68°F), with just three hours' sunshine in the afternoon. Otherwise conditions stayed grey and, in the crucial hours of darkness, under clear skies, the temperature would fall to 8.6°C (47°F).[44]

Changeable weather did not stop Berliners in East and West heading off to their favourite summer haunts among the woods and lakes. Joachim Trenkner recalls spending the entire day at the beach on the Wannsee, in the south-western corner of West Berlin, bordering Communist-ruled Potsdam. He and his friends took in what sun was available, discussed everything from approaching girls to approaching political crises in the beer gardens that gird the lake.[45] Millions did likewise.

As we now know, not everyone in divided Berlin was taking their ease that summer Saturday. At noon on 12 August, under heavy guard, government printers began to run off thousands of copies of a declaration by the GDR's rubber-stamp Council of Ministers (which had not yet even met), announcing the border closure. Thousands of troops and police had been placed on alert. Honecker and his staff moved into the Keibelstrasse office suite for the final push. They would stay there until the operation was over.

By contrast, the true begetter of the border closure, Walter Ulbricht, was chauffeured out to the Grosser Döllnsee, beyond Wandlitz, to the government guest house. This facility, the *Haus zu den Birken* (House among the Birches) was originally a large, hip-roofed hunting lodge belonging to Field Marshal Hermann Göring's personal huntsman.

This Saturday afternoon, Ulbricht seemed relaxed, almost jolly. He was throwing a garden party, to which almost everyone who was anyone in the GDR's government had been invited. He called it a 'get-together' (*Beisammensein*).[46]

It was not unusual for Politburo members and ministers to meet at

Döllnsee for occasional weekends to brainstorm problems or to finalise major decisions. Cooks and other staff from Wandlitz would be present during the daytime, then usually return at night to their homes some miles away. But this weekend things were different, as Ulbricht's personal chef, who helped prepare the meals, vividly recalled. The domestic staff were commanded to stay overnight in temporary accommodation near by. Only on Sunday morning would they be allowed to leave.[47]

Invitations had been extended to one or two Politburo members, but mainly to ministers and their state secretaries and leaders of the 'block parties'. These were the pseudo-independent organisations of the 'National Front', including the National Democratic Party, the East-CDU, and Liberal Democratic Party.

The guests were, in short, largely the kind of people that Ulbricht used rather than consulted: people with impressive titles but unimpressive real powers. After coffee that afternoon, they wandered through the birch trees to the tranquil lake. Back at the house afterwards, the leader had ordered up a Soviet comedy film, *Every Man for Himself!*, but few of the guests were interested. Music played in the garden. They stood around, making somewhat awkward small talk, swapping jokes. Some of them noticed that the woods surrounding the guest house were full of soldiers and military vehicles. None of this made for an easy atmosphere.

The president of the tame parliament, Liberal Democratic Party leader Johannes Dieckmann, asked Alfred Neumann, veteran Communist and Secretary to the Central Committee, why they had been summoned here. The extremely tall and impressive-looking Neumann, a decathlon competitor in his youth and an unrepentant crypto-Stalinist throughout his long life, told him he didn't know. This was a lie. As a Politburo member, Neumann had known for some days about the border closure, but it wasn't his job to inform the likes of Dieckmann before 'the boss' saw fit.

After supper, Ulbricht finally called his guests together. The staff had already cleared away the meal. It was now around ten p.m.

'We're going to have a little meeting now,' he announced in his high-pitched bark of a voice. Ulbricht informed the members of the Ministerial Council of 'their' decision to close the sector border between East and West Berlin – a decision which had already been printed up and distributed. 'Everyone agreed?' he asked. Unsurprisingly, no one demurred.

Once they had rubber-stamped the Polituro's plan, the members of the Ministerial Council had served their purpose. Like the domestic staff, they were also not permitted to leave until the big border-closure operation was under way.

Shortly before the blatantly stage-managed 'vote' at Döllnsee, Honecker's staff put the finishing touches to the complex patchwork that was 'Operation Rose'.

The final operational orders for 'Rose' and a copy of the planned official announcement left Honecker's office and were couriered a few blocks to the white-stone fastness of the Soviet embassy in Unter den Linden, within whose mazelike complex of offices the texts could be quickly translated into Russian for Moscow's benefit. The 'big brother' had to be paid his due.[48]

All day, thousands of police units and 'factory fighting groups' had been on stand-by in barracks and training grounds. At eight that evening, the sealed orders for 'Rose' were opened. Senior officers were initiated into the plan, the police in Berlin and the army people at the commander-in-chief's headquarters, Schloss Wilkendorf, just north of Strausberg. Then middle-ranking and battalion commanders were summoned by telephone. At nine they too were briefed on their role in the operation. By ten, Honecker knew that the huge machine was ready to move.

At midnight, Honecker rang army HQ and gave the crucial order: 'You know the assignment! March!'[49]

General Heinz Hoffmann, commander-in-chief of the Nationale Volksarmee (NVA), immediately put his forces on a state of 'heightened combat readiness'.

Three thousand one hundred and fifty soldiers of the 8th Motorised Artillery Division, based in Schwerin, rumbled towards the capital. Their 100 battle tanks and 120 armoured personnel carriers would take up position in the leanstock yards at Friedrichsfelde, just outside the centre of East Berlin. Four thousand two hundred more troops of the 1st

Motorised Division, in 140 tanks and 200 personnel carriers, left their barracks in Potsdam to cover the outer ring around West Berlin. Both sets of troops were positioned at least a thousand metres back from the sector borders; their task was to prevent any mass attempts to break through into the border area with West Berlin, so that the border police and the constructions gangs could carry out the border-closure operation undisturbed.

All units of the East Berlin People's Police were placed on combat-alert level II, and the 1st Brigade of Readiness (Riot) Police and the Berlin Security Command – 10,000 men in all – were given their orders. These were to seal off to pedestrian and vehicle traffic all streets that gave access to the Western sectors, with the exception of the thirteen designated crossing places.

A changeable day had turned into an exceptionally cool night. The temperature was very low for August. All the better when there was work to be done.

At one a.m., the actual border-sealing operation began.

Sentries were placed at two-metre intervals along the entire Berlin sector border to prevent escapes, while border troops, factory paramilitaries and construction units barricaded the streets by means of barbed wire, tank traps and improvised concrete bolsters. Street lights were turned off, masking the nature of the operation. Only at the Brandenburg Gate did searchlights bathe the terrain in a cold, pale-blue light as soldiers laboured with hydraulic drills to tear up the surface of the great East-West boulevard on which the gate stood.[50]

Sixty-eight of 81 crossing points were to be barricaded. All 193 streets that straddled the border would be closed. And then there were the transport systems. Twelve underground (U-Bahn) and surface (S-Bahn) city railway lines were to be blocked off at the sector borders. Dozens of stations on or near the border were to be closed and sealed. The police, including *Trapos*, had charge of that. The most challenging task was at the busy Friedrichstrasse station complex, favoured route for refugees, where U-Bahn, S-Bahn and international passenger trains all stopped on the east bank of the Landwehr Canal, just metres from West Berlin. The *Vopos* were even ordered to regularly check the entry shafts to the sewer systems that connected East and West.

Honecker, the bespectacled organisation man who had spent so many years as Communist youth leader, ensuring that festivals, camps and demonstrations ran smoothly, was in his element. Overcome by restlessness once the work began, Honecker had himself driven around the various parts of the border to check that all was in order, to talk with the commanders, praise the troops and fine-tune the operation where necessary.

By four a.m., Honecker was back in his office. The tireless Security Secretary continued for two more hours to rasp orders, make and take phone calls. Then, at six, he was told that the provisional sealing of the border between East and West Berlin was complete.

With dawn creeping across the sky outside, Honecker turned to his staff. 'Now we can go home,' he announced with weary satisfaction.

Wolfgang Leonhard, who as a 24-year-old in 1945 had accompanied Ulbricht's group from Moscow, and who in 1949 had decamped to the West, knew Honecker well. Of the devastating achievement that was the first phase of 'Operation Rose', Leonhard wrote later that it was 'strange, even terrifying' that Honecker seemed not to have experienced

> even the slightest twinge of doubt . . . [at] dividing a city with a wall and with barbed wire and fortifications, so preventing human beings from exercising their full natural freedom – something that did not just contradict the general principles of humanity, but also the original concepts of socialism.[51]

Honecker's greatest organisational triumph was now a fact. The Security Secretary's official car was waiting to take him back to Wandlitz, the tranquil, fortified Communist VIP settlement in the forest.

Soon Erich Honecker would be snatching a little sleep, secure behind his own wall. The difference was, of course, that the Wandlitz wall was designed to keep the millions out, not in.

WIRE

9

BARBED-WIRE SUNDAY

WITH MOST OF BERLIN asleep, it was the round-the-clock workers, the professional night owls, who first realised that the East-West border was being closed: transport workers, police officers, journalists.

Robert H. Lochner was probably the first American to know.

Born in New York in 1918, at five years old Lochner moved with his family to Berlin, where his journalist father was for many years correspondent for Associated Press. Lochner was educated there, and spoke German like a native by the time the family returned to the US in 1936. After wartime military service (which included interrogating Nazi war criminals), he went into radio. Having worked for many years in Washington for Voice of America, by March 1961 he was back in Berlin as newly appointed director of the US-sponsored German-language station, Radio in the American Sector (RIAS), a post that lay in the State Department's gift.

At one minute past midnight on Sunday 13 August 1961, Lochner was woken by a call from his station's monitoring section. East Berlin had announced that traffic from East to West Berlin would be halted until further notice.

This was 'the big one'. Lochner and the senior members of his broadcasting team gathered quickly at RIAS headquarters on the Hans-Rosenthal-Platz in West Berlin, not far from Schöneberg Town Hall. They turned the station over to solemn music and a fifteen-minute cycle of news bulletins. RIAS possessed the most powerful transmitter in Europe; everyone was aware that whatever it announced could be heard in almost every corner of the GDR. All the more reason to ensure that their information was accurate and first-hand.

Twice during the small hours Lochner drove alone over to East Berlin.

The *Vopos* might have blocked the border for East Germans, and West Berliners also had been forbidden access (allegedly temporarily), but as an American citizen with a diplomatic passport the RIAS director could travel without hindrance. He wore a coat to conceal the portable tape recorder he carried on his lap. As he drove, he murmured his thoughts into its microphone. In consequence, the first direct, on-the-spot radio reports of barbed wire being laid across Berlin's streets came from Robert Lochner.

A third trip, after dawn, took him to the Friedrichstrasse station, normally the last stop on both the main railway and S-Bahn lines before they trundled over the river Spree and into the West. A few hours earlier, the East German transport police had suddenly closed the ticket halls and barred all access to trains scheduled for the West.

In the tunnels and halls below the embarkation area, Lochner found hundreds of East Germans milling around in bewilderment and growing desperation. As yet unaware of the border closure, they still hoped to catch trains for the West. Most would-be refugees carried suitcases or, in a pathetic attempt to disguise their intentions, parcels and boxes tied up with string. Access to the trains was blocked by lines of black-clad transport police (*Trapos*), who stood shoulder-to-shoulder blocking the 'up' steps to the platforms, semi-automatic weapons slung ready for use. Lochner found himself irresistibly reminded, by their uniforms and their arrogance, of Hitler's SS, whose unattractive qualities he knew well from pre-war days.

As Lochner stood by, watching the miserable scene, he saw an elderly lady gather up her courage and slowly climb the steps until she reached the line of *Trapos*.

'When,' she asked nervously, 'is the next train to West Berlin?'

The sneer with which the young representative of the regime greeted her request would stay burned in Lochner's memory.

'None of that any more, grandma,' he told her. 'You're all sat in a mousetrap now.'[1]

By the time dawn broke at around five o'clock on the morning of 13 August 1961, the East German construction brigades and their armed escorts were already at work.

They had achieved complete surprise, and consequently a trouble-free start to their task. Comrade Erich Honecker's triumph in 'Operation Rose' was clear for all to see. To those who were awake, that is. Götz Bergander was then thirty-three years old, a political journalist with another West Berlin broadcasting station, Radio Free Berlin (Sender Freies Berlin = SFB). Between two and three a.m., he was wrenched from his slumber by the ringing of his bedside phone. He picked it up, recognised the voice of his night news editor.

'Götz,' the man growled, 'they're sealing the border. Get yourself over here.'[2]

Bergander eased his lanky frame out of bed and hastily dressed. Within minutes he was at the wheel of his pale-blue Volkswagen Beetle, nosing through the streets of suburban Zehlendorf. He arrived at the Avus highway, and from there sped north-eastwards towards the heart of Berlin. At this early hour, it was all but empty. The almost dead-straight high-speed route had been built in the early 1920s, to connect the suburbs directly with the city. It was also used for car races. Bergander made it to the SFB building in Charlottenburg in fifteen minutes, an all-time record. Other bleary-eyed colleagues were gathering in the boss's office. No one could say for certain what was really going on. They decided there was only one thing to do: each reporter would choose an area to scout, and so they would build up a picture.

Bergander hurried back to his car and drove over to the Invaliden-strasse, a frequently used East-West crossing point in the French sector. He arrived there as the sun rose, expecting to find a scene of drama. He was disappointed.

'It was a glorious Sunday morning, the birds were singing. So, anything but an atmosphere of crisis in the air. No cars around, no one about.'

By the time he had parked, he could see a few journalists hanging around, and some West Berlin policemen. He asked what was going on. A cop shrugged. 'They're not letting anyone over the border.'

On the far side, besides the familiar green uniforms of the *Vopos*, there were also members of the Factory Fighting Groups, dressed in their drab khaki paramilitary fatigues and distinctive peaked baseball-type caps.

Bergander waited there for a while, but nothing much seemed to be happening. He got back in his car and headed for the famous Brandenburg Gate, a few blocks distant in the British sector. There he found a lot more to see. More Factory Fighting Group members on the Eastern side, this time drawn up in large numbers and in military formation, automatic weapons slung across their bellies. A human barrier. Behind them were no armoured vehicles but a handful of water cannon. One thing, however, was the same. The eerie silence.

'Nothing was actually happening yet, at that early hour. It was like the quiet before the artillery barrage. You know, when you feel, "Any moment now it'll start".'

Bergander again found a cop and asked what was happening. All the policemen knew was that the border was closed. No one going in, no one coming out.

Such things had happened before. Temporary closures of parts of the border, usually for spot checks on border-crossers and possible refugees. But this was bigger. Bergander asked the cop where the British army was. The man didn't know. By contrast with the heavily armed East Germans, the scattering of Western policemen carried only service pistols. They were outnumbered and outgunned.

A half-hour passed. An hour. After a while, trucks arrived on the Eastern side. Slowly, barbed wire was rolled out across the area in front of the Brandenburg Gate.

'I must say,' Bergander recalled, 'that I have seldom felt so abandoned as at that moment. I thought, the Western Allies have to show themselves here. If only as a presence. A psychological measure.'

He rang his girlfriend (later wife), Regine, who lived with her parents in Steglitz, in the American sector. She quickly dressed and joined him. Of Western forces there was still no sign. They watched the East Germans' purposeful, disciplined activity for a while. A silent, gloomy crowd of local civilians gathered.

Two hours after Bergander's arrival, the representatives of British military might finally showed themselves. A jeep appeared. From it clambered two uniformed men wearing the distinctive red caps of the British Military Police. The Brits stood at a safe distance from the sector border, gazing impassively at the activity on the Soviet-East German side. After a while they turned smartly on their heels, got back into their vehicle and drove off again.

That was the last Bergander saw of the British that morning. He had not expected a fully armed battle group, but the minimal nature of the response shocked him.

'If only they had stayed there, you know? Maybe a jeep with four men. For everyone to see. That would show they cared. As it stood, the message was absolutely clear right from the outset: "Not our business",' Bergander recalled with a rueful laugh, repeating the last three words in English. 'Not our business.'

Bergander drove back to the radio station and compared notes with the other journalists. They filed their reports, trying not to sound as pessimistic as they felt.

To a man, they all believed that the Americans especially would have been in a position, with their powerful tanks and their armoured bulldozers, to simply roll forward and sweep the temporary barriers out of the way. Would the *Vopos* and lightly armed worker-militia members have been able to resist the power of an American armoured unit? Perhaps once Washington understood what was going on, the necessary orders would be given.

Another Berlin journalist, Lothar Löwe, had been posted to Washington as correspondent of the West German Public Broadcasting Service (ARD). The young high-flyer had settled eagerly into the glamorous social life of Kennedy-era Washington, but naturally kept closely in touch with colleagues, friends and family back in West Berlin. He had been attending a starry dinner party in Georgetown that Saturday evening. Those present included a number of young women who were reputedly, shall we say, on friendly terms with the President.

Towards midnight Eastern Standard Time (six a.m. in Berlin), the famous columnist Joseph Alsop dropped by. The young German reporter was introduced to the great man.

'Where are you from?' Alsop asked.

'Berlin.'

'My God! What are you doing in Washington? Berlin is exactly where you should be.'

'How so?'

'They've just sealed off the Brandenburg Gate. They've got guards there. Looks like the East Germans are closing the border.'[3]

Löwe got home to his apartment in Arlington in time to catch an NBC radio news bulletin. The first live transatlantic television pictures would not be beamed across the Atlantic for another year, after AT&T's 'Telstar' communications satellite was launched on 10 July 1962. In the meantime cinefilm or magnetic tape still had to be couriered by air to the US in order to be shown on American TV. The nature of the events in Berlin was thus not entirely clear, but Löwe knew better than most what all this meant. He was genuinely surprised. He had always thought that, if the East took action, it would be to close the border between East Berlin and the GDR rather than between East and West Berlin. The Russians, he believed, had too much to lose from such a drastic step as dividing a city.

Anyway, knowing that it was early morning in Germany, Löwe made some transatlantic calls. First he called his mother in Berlin and assured her that he was certain the Allies would not let the Communists take over. Then to business. He dialled the number of Al Hemsing, press officer for the American military government in West Berlin, whom he knew well from his days as a newspaper reporter. Hemsing was already in his office. He had just received a summary of overnight reports from the German police, and he willingly gave Löwe a thorough 'rundown of the border situation', from Spandau in the north to Rüdow in the south.

Löwe took notes as the American spoke. The German reporter had lived in Berlin almost all his life, and had the local's advantage of being able to picture what was happening where it was happening, and what this meant. This operation, he knew immediately, was a huge event, not just a temporary border closure but something of world importance. After speaking with Hemsing, he double-checked everything with an old friend from West Berlin police headquarters, who confirmed Hemsing's impressions.

Finally Löwe called the State Department analyst Martha Mautner. She was a respected expert on Central and Eastern Europe, and her husband, Austrian-born Karl Mautner, advised the Berlin Task Force. Surely the Mautners would know something. To his surprise, he found that his call woke Martha up. Literally and metaphorically, Washington was still half asleep.

She reacted with genuine astonishment to the news. Martha too had expected action from the East, but the kind of action that did not threaten the Allied position in Berlin and thus risk war. In any case, how could one divide a modern city and all its complex, delicate systems without destroying the basis of civilised life? She told Löwe that she and Karl were going into the office, and he should join her there.

Half an hour later, Löwe drove through the gates of the State Department. In 1961 a simple press pass was enough to enter the inner sanctum of American foreign policy. He made his way up to the Berlin Crisis Desk on the fifteenth floor and found himself alone with the night security man. A short while later, Mautner appeared. Soon other members of the Task Force began to trickle in. Löwe quickly realised that he knew more about what was happening in Berlin than did the highest representatives of the most powerful nation on earth.

This was not a good sign.

Even Mayor Willy Brandt was caught away from his post.

On the evening of Saturday 12 August, Brandt gave an election campaign speech in Nuremberg. In it he changed his usual script and specifically mentioned the ever-growing East German refugee problem. That day, aides told him the flood of emigrants from the East was reaching a new intensity. For the first time the number arriving in West Berlin in the past twenty-four hours had exceeded 2,500. If this rate continued, the population of Ulbricht's proletarian paradise could be expected to diminish at the rate of about a million a year. It was clear something had to give – and even clearer, for those knowledgeable about who held power in the GDR, that the 'something' was unlikely to be Walter Ulbricht. But what would the East German dictator do next?

Brandt was running as candidate for the West German chancellorship against the veteran Konrad Adenauer, almost forty years his senior. The theme of the Berlin Mayor's campaign was in many ways that of energetic, Kennedyesque youth (he was forty-eight) against tired age. But that night the challenger decided it was time to move his campaign on to a larger stage, literally and metaphorically. These refugees, he told his audience, were fleeing East Germany for a good reason.

They are afraid that the mesh of the iron curtain will be cemented closed.
Because they fear being shut into an enormous prison. Because they have a
burning anxiety that they could be forgotten, written off, sacrificed on the
altar of indifference and missed opportunities . . .[4]

The West Berlin Mayor all but accused both the West German
government and the Western Allies of dragging their feet on the
questions of German unity and the status of Berlin, thus encouraging
Khrushchev and Ulbricht's aggression. It was a spine-tingling speech,
thick with emotion and somehow lent extra weight by the hoarseness of
his delivery. A heavy smoker, Brandt was half-way through a demanding
campaign, and it was starting to show. But the effect that night was to
enhance rather than diminish the effect of his oration.

It was as if he had foreknowledge of the catastrophe to come. Late that
night, Brandt boarded a sleeper train for Kiel, far up by the Danish
border, where he was due to speak the next night. Time to snatch some
sleep. But at five a.m., as the train rolled northward, the candidate was
woken by determined knocking on the door of his wagon-lit compartment. It was the conductor. He bore an urgent message from Brandt's
chief of staff, Heinrich Albertz, in Berlin. The East was closing the
border. The governing Mayor must disembark as soon as possible and
return to his city.

Brandt got out at Hanover. A car whisked him to the airport. From
there his aircraft made the short hop to Berlin, around 170 miles to the
east.

Angry crowds of West Berliners were already on the streets, demanding action, but still there was no word from the Western commandants.
Brandt arrived in his office at breakfast time. He toyed with the wild idea
of putting himself at the head of his people and calling for the East to rise
up, then thought better of it.[5] He had to exercise his powers of
persuasion, to substitute the strength of his own conviction for the
firmness he suspected the Allies could not or would not supply. These
native emotional and intellectual weapons were all he had, and therefore
all the true defence that West Berliners possessed.

Willy Brandt's great testing-time had begun.

*

In fact, one of the Americans' lingering expectations had been precisely that the East would rise up. For a while, some in the administration even half-welcomed the idea.

Now, it was not a hope but a nightmare scenario for the West. The developing situation on 13 August had the potential to turn very dangerous. The East had now gone on the offensive within Berlin, challenging four-power rule. If the blowback consequences of this brought about unrest in the GDR, the Allies would be faced with a new 17 June 1953, this time in the middle of a huge diplomatic and military crisis where anything could happen, up to and including nuclear confrontation. Moreover, what if the hotheads among the West Berliners, especially the young men in their jeans and DA haircuts who were already assembling at the main potential flashpoints along the East-West sector border, including the Brandenburg Gate, were to 'rush' the half-built East German border barriers? America's priority was not to stir anything at all. Calm things down, rather.

Alan Lightner's initial telegrams to Washington were cool and objective. Relying on reports from an officer of the US Military Mission, who had crossed over into the East during the night, Lightner was able to assure the State Department that the situation there was fairly calm. This was in large measure due to massive numbers of police and soldiers being shipped into the border area by the Communists.

> Between 5:00 and 6:00 a.m., security control activity throughout East Berlin was rapidly accelerated. Security units appearing on streets at this time included customs police performing normal police duty, *Vopos*, Bereitschaft Polizei, Kampfgruppen units and East German Army Units. Kampfgruppen units entered almost all buildings on streets adjacent to East/West Berlin sector lines and inspected stairwells, upper floors, and roofs. *Vopos* took up assigned beats of streets, assisted by customs police. Security alert police opened schools, other public buildings and factories to house large numbers of police arriving in motorized columns. Major unit consisting of approximately 80 truck-loads police, accompanied by armoured cars, machine gun carriers and other vehicles, arrived at large industrial site near Rummelsburg S-Bahn station.[6]

In the same cable, Lightner noted that the Soviets, though holding back their military hardware from the city itself, were monitoring events closely. Many Soviet military-licensed cars, he said, had been noticed making observation tours of East Berlin. These indications of Soviet restraint were a positive sign. Lightner judged that the East Germans' *coup d'état* against their own people had been carried out cleverly and might well avoid the kind of extreme reactions feared in Washington:

> Most noteworthy feature is that almost all security control measures were completed before most East Berliners were awake from Sunday sleep. Although crowds began to gather at approximately 8:30 a.m. on streets leading to crossing points, most people kept considerable distance from police and appeared to be resigned to passive observation of events . . .[7]

No one wanted to risk war. The question was, how to stop things from boiling over without seeming to condone the East German actions? How to continue to oppose the East German regime without destabilising it – with unforeseeable consequences? And finally, how to make a credible protest without driving the Communists into even more extreme measures?

The Allied military commanders finally met at the *Kommandatura* building on the leafy Kaiserswerther Strasse in Dahlem, in the American sector. They had still not decided how to deal with the situation on the border when Brandt arrived.

This was the first time the West Berlin mayor had ever entered the *Kommandatura* building. He routinely met the Allied sector commanders at his offices in Schöneberg Town Hall or at official receptions and social events. Brandt was kept waiting for half an hour, and on being admitted to the mahogany-panelled conference room, was shocked to see that a portrait still hung there of General Kotikov, Soviet commandant at the time of the Berlin Blockade and the last Russian representative to attend the *Kommandatura*. An empty chair at the table indicated that the Soviets could rejoin the body at any time, should they so choose. Berlin was, after all, still technically under the same four-power occupation established at the Potsdam Conference in 1945, and the Western Allies wanted everyone to know it.

This was a pointed indication that the Allied commanders, while sympathetic to the Berliners' plight, did not necessarily share their perspectives and loyalties. Brandt had been perturbed to see no increased Allied military presence on the streets on his drive from the airport. Once he had their attention, he addressed the commanders and their civilian advisers not in his usual quiet, wry manner, but with a naked passion born of desperation.

Brandt was quite frank. The East German National People's Army had marched into East Berlin like a conquering power, he said. He compared this annexation of the other half of his city to Hitler's occupation of the Rhineland in 1936. If, he argued, they accepted this *fait accompli*, then they would be guilty of appeasement, as Britain and France had been a quarter of a century earlier. Moreover, at the same time as he had closed the border, the GDR's Minister of the Interior, Karl Maron, had also confined Allied military and government personnel visiting East Berlin to three crossing points. Were the Allies going to tolerate this?

Under the 1945 Potsdam Agreement, Allied access to the East was supposedly an untrammelled right. For the past sixteen years, servicemen and officials from Britain, France, and America had simply walked the streets anywhere in Berlin, crossing from sector to sector, West to East and back, as and when they wished. Now, Brandt reminded them, they were to be forced to obey orders from a puppet East German administration whose legitimacy they did not recognise. Like foreign tourists and German civilians, their troops would face border checks by East German officials. The West would risk humiliation before the watching world.

When Brandt emerged grim-faced from his encounter with the Allied representatives, his aides asked him nervously how the meeting had gone.

'At least those shits are now going to send some patrols to the border,' their boss growled. 'So the Berliners won't think they're all alone.'[8]

The Politburo's decision to mount the operation during Saturday night/ Sunday morning, at the height of the summer vacation period, had been triumphantly vindicated. The East German people woke up, for the most part, to a *fait accompli*.

However, by mid-morning the West Berlin side of the sector border had filled up with angry crowds, especially at the Brandenburg Gate. The deceptive peace of dawn, when Götz Bergander had first arrived, was a thing of the past. At the front of the throng were young Westerners. Many of them had ridden into the centre on their light motorbikes.

'There were ten or fifteen of us, all friends from the same neighbourhood in Charlottenburg,' recalled Wolfgang Baldin, then a nineteen-year-old bakery worker. 'With our Mambo portable radios and our motorbikes. We'd heard about it on the radio news. We got together and just headed straight for the Brandenburg Gate.'

When Wolfgang and his friends arrived, the limited space on the Western side of the gate was packed. There were many West Berlin police, keeping their own people back from the actual border, on the other side of which the Factory Fighting Groups and the *Vopos* were guarding the construction work. East German armoured cars had arrived. They were visible behind the troops and the workers, blocking the way into the Pariser Platz and the boulevard of Unter den Linden beyond.

Frustrated at their inability to get close to the action, the boys ducked around the corner, where the Ebertstrasse ran south along the sector border several hundred metres down to the Potsdamer Platz. Barbed wire had already been laid here, several densely spiralled layers thick. It looked formidable, but there were spots where it could be pulled aside by groups of determined Westerners, and where East Berliners waiting on the other side could dart through the gaps. Several escaped. The boys gave a hand. But then more Eastern armoured cars appeared, and more labour teams laid more barbed wire.

The boys moved southwards, with the open spaces of the Tiergarten – in the West – on their right, and the barbed wire of the newly imprisoned East to their left. Towards the Potsdamer Platz, instead of wire there stood lines of East German troops with fixed bayonets. Some shouting and abuse went on, but faced with armed guards there was little the Westerners could do. Their own police tried to move them back from the border, but initially had little success.

Soon the protesters had spotted new quarry over on the other side.

We saw some types over the on the Eastern side, inspecting things. They must have been from the SED. You know, they had their party badges on. Well, we started to chuck stones at them. Quite a hail of them.[9]

To the resentment and disappointment of the demonstrators, reinforcements of West Berlin police appeared and forced them further back into the Tiergarten, away from the sector border. The message was: no provocations.

Over in East Berlin, as Lightner noted in a later cable to Washington, 'crowds of curious and sullen onlookers' had gathered. A few risked rushing the nascent barrier, like the escapers in the Ebertstrasse, but the vast majority held back from the border. The now-trapped East Berliners were, however, often close enough to gesture towards the West, or to gaze over at the scenes on the Western side and harbour whatever thoughts they might behind their practised mask of impassivity.

It was not just soldiers, police and construction workers who were busy behind the new border. The East German government sent groups of professional party agitators among the crowds, and to East Berlin's S-Bahn and U-Bahn stations. Their job was to 'work' gatherings of civilians, promoting the official view of the 'protective barrier'. As early as 5.30 a.m., individual teams were busy at nearly thirty locations, with reinforcements planned for large S-Bahn stations such as Alexanderplatz, Ostbahnhof and, of course, Friedrichstrasse.[10]

In a bizarrely human touch, the internal SED report was also forced to note that even in a well-ordered, disciplined Communist state there were, in fact, drawbacks to staging such a major operation under conditions of high secrecy and on a Saturday night:

Most leading functionaries of the Berlin Transport Company (BVG) were attending a party, which meant that the necessary measures were delayed. The Director of the BVG, Comrade Paschau, declared, 'Well, you have picked a very unfavourable time.' Despite repeated demands, the active service units of the Transport Police did not arrive until close to six a.m.

Nor were all the East Berliners as reticent as Lightner reported from his vantage point on the Western side. The regime's agents were everywhere, keeping an eye on the situation at street level and observing large groups of East German citizens that might be accumulating at potential flashpoints. The agents' reports to party headquarters were not entirely encouraging.

Just as Western youths like Wolfgang Baldin and his friends reacted passionately to the outrage, in the East it was also the young who threatened trouble. As the day wore on, gatherings of young people caused real concern to the Communist authorities. Some confined themselves to complaining about how the closing of the border would affect their shopping and movie-going habits. Others presented a greater challenge. A hundred-strong crowd assembled in front of SED district headquarters for Berlin-Mitte, close to the Brandenburg Gate. The party's agents reported 'provocative speeches'. Members of the district leadership appeared and engaged the young people in discussion. After a while the crowd dispersed.

However, the trouble had merely moved on. At the corner of Friedrichstrasse and Unter den Linden, a couple of blocks away, larger crowds soon assembled. The participants' statements, reported to the party that same day, ran along the lines of 'Over there in West Berlin they do things right. Why do we have tanks on the streets?' and 'Arm yourselves! The West Berliners are freer than we are. At least now you can see who's responsible for the tension in this city!'

Worryingly from the point of view of the authorities, there was also talk of a mass attempt at a breakthrough into the West, maybe the next day.[11]

There was constant, hour-by-hour feedback to the Central Committee on the public mood in the East. The party's spies throughout East Berlin reported that the banning of 'border-crossers' was on the whole popular – they were perceived as gaining an unfair advantage by working in the West for hard currency and then buying cheap in the soft-currency East, where they continued to live. All the same, the average citizen was well aware what the closing of the border meant for their own personal freedom, and didn't like it.[12] The chief problem, the same report added, was that young people especially were inclined to listen to, and trust, Western radio and television broadcasts.

The influence of 'West-TV' was to be a constant problem. As the saying went, many Easterners 'spent their days in the East and their nights in the West'. With the exception of the area around Dresden, where the topography of the Elbe valley made it impossible to receive Western broadcasts (for which reason Dresden was known mockingly in the rest of the GDR as *Tal der Ahnunglosen* or 'Valley of the Clueless'), any East German could tune his TV or radio to the West.

Listening to Western radio was certainly the order of the day. Even in the country cottage of a certain ultra-loyal East German comrade, on the rural far-eastern edge of Berlin, nestled within a remote arm of the Müggelsee lake.

This person, an actor of leftist convictions, had moved from West to East in 1949 in order to 'help, as a cultural worker, with the construction of Socialism in the GDR'. Since then, he had laboured with success in the East Berlin theatre, as well as in the state-owned DEFA film studios in Potsdam-Babelsberg that had once been the famous UFA dream factory. In its 1920s heyday, classics such as *The Blue Angel*, *Nosferatu* and *Metropolis* had been filmed at Babelsberg, and in the 1930s, under the tutelage of Propaganda Minister Goebbels, such notorious films as *Jew Süss* and the pro-euthanasia *Ich Klage An* ('I Accuse').

The actor's problem was that this weekend, he had invited his teenage nephew, Till Meyer, to stay. Till's war-widowed mother, with whom the boy lived the rest of the time, was still resident in West Berlin.[13]

Breakfast time found Till's Communist uncle more subdued than usual. 'Is there going to be a war?' Till asked. The older man had no clear answer. Both of them were wondering how young Till was going to get back to his mother.

The uncle switched frantically between RIAS and East German radio, trying to make sense of what had happened at the sector border during the night. The Politburo and its servants rarely, in their public pronouncements, referred to a 'wall' or anything similar. The preferred euphemism was the bland phrase 'Measures for carrying out the decision of the council of ministers of 12.8.1961'. It made interpreting what was actually going on a little hard.

'Yes, it's certainly a serious situation,' he announced, finally hitting on an appropriately grave tone. 'Obviously, our state is no longer prepared to allow the West to keep plundering the GDR.'

He had now figured out the political aspect to his own satisfaction. But what to do? He told his nephew to pack his things. In the meantime, he would call his party friends in Berlin to see how things really stood.

To ring Berlin entailed an hour's trek to the nearest phone and back. While his uncle was away, Till packed his red-checked duffle bag, then sat down and listened to the radio. There were crowds assembling on the Potsdamer Platz and in front of the Brandenburg Gate, tanks in the back streets, and barriers being erected on the rail tracks in the north of Berlin. Waiting anxiously for his uncle's return, Till stepped outside into the lakeside greenery, but heard only the distant quack of ducks, the wind in the trees, the twitter of the birds. The dramatic scenario outlined on the radio seemed to belong in another world.

Around one that afternoon his uncle reappeared, looking far from happy. He had no idea, he said, what was going to happen next. The best thing would be if Till got going as soon as possible and just went back home as he had come — by a combination of ferry, bus and S-Bahn. And no dilly-dallying.

So the teenager began his journey back (he hoped) to the West. The route was quite lengthy. Over on the ferry to the far shore, then a fifteen-minute walk, carrying his stuff, to the bus station in Ransdorf; followed by twenty minutes on a bus to the S-Bahn station. Already, on the platform of this usually quiet suburban stop, Till noticed a lot of people waiting apprehensively for the westbound train. Many, like him, were Westerners, caught here while on weekend visits to families or friends.

Once the train arrived, it was eighteen stops on the east-west line to the Ostkreuz junction. Here Till changed on to a line that usually took him straight over the border into West Berlin. There were many worried, bad-tempered people on this train; a grumpy old man, a blonde woman with children who kept bursting into tears and wondering if the kids would ever see their grandparents again.

At Treptower Park, last stop before West Berlin, instead of a loudspeaker warning the passengers: 'Achtung! You are now leaving the Democratic Sector of Berlin!', the train stopped with a peculiarly final clunk. Then came an announcement that no one had heard before: 'End of the Line! End of the Line! The train ends here!'

The passengers emerged warily on to the platform. Black-uniformed *Trapos* bawled at the Easterners to go about their business, the Westerners to proceed to the crossing point at Harzer Strasse, where if their papers were in order they would be permitted to enter West Berlin.

Everyone stumbled in that direction with their luggage, as instructed. The old man from the train, obviously a Westerner, was among those who made their way, sweating in the August heat, several blocks to the designated crossing point. As they came within sight of the new barbed-wire barrier, the old man extracted from his bag a couple of East German sausages, which he tossed furtively into the front garden of a nearby apartment block.

'Don't want to give them an excuse to arrest me for smuggling,' he muttered.

Crowds of East Berliners milled at a safe distance from the armed border guards and the barbed wire, discussing the situation. The Westerners kept their heads down. They could see people leaning out of the windows of apartment blocks in the East, some out on their balconies, many calling over to the Western side – just a couple of hundred yards away – or waving handkerchiefs.

Approaching the crossing point, Till spotted tanks of the East German People's Army parked discreetly to the left and right of the border approaches, their turret guns pointed westwards. In the actual area of the border stood heavily armed men in steel helmets, who looked as if they meant business. Construction workers were already busy at the sector border, drilling holes for concrete posts to be inserted into the cobbled street.

On arrival at the barbed wire, the Westerners showed their identity cards to the armed border police. It was a tense moment. The young guards were just as nervous as they were. However, once their ID was accepted the crude barrier was eased apart and they were let through into West Berlin.

It still felt somewhat primitive, the whole new control arrangement. A clumsy, uncertain beginning to something that would one day be far more malevolently sophisticated and permanent. What they were creating here would become a symbol for the world of division and cruelty, but not yet.

On the Western side, in the Harzer Strasse, groups of youths had gathered. They worked off their frustration by bawling insults at the Eastern guards, and chanting slogans: 'Down with the pointy beard! Ulbricht, Murderer! Budapest! Budapest! Budapest!'

Eastern guards and Western demonstrators were roughly the same age.

Till did not turn around. He kept walking until he got to the next S-Bahn station in the West Berlin borough of Kreuzberg. From there he took a train to Friedenau, where his mother was waiting anxiously for him.

Also on the green edge of East Berlin, a young man a couple of years Till's senior was likewise holed up in a country cottage. Unlike Till, he was an East Berliner, though one of a rather complicated sort. And also unlike Till, he was in the full glorious flower of his first grown-up love affair.

Klaus Schulz-Ladegast was nineteen years old and thinking about his future: that is, his planned studies, which he hoped to commence this coming winter, and besides that the life he had in mind with his new girlfriend, with whom he was spending the weekend *à deux*. They too had listened to the radio and realised something big was happening. But, being in love and feeling that nothing could hurt them, they joked about it. Oh no, he said. I won't be able to get the Roth-Händle (strong West German cigarettes) that I like to smoke. Even worse, she countered, this is the end of my supply of decent stockings from West Berlin.

Klaus's background was unusual. His father, a former army officer, was also a leading lay official in the Lutheran Church in East Germany – just about to take up an important post as vice-chair of the Church Community in Brandenburg. Klaus himself, though brought up in East Berlin, had attended high school in West Berlin until he passed his leaving examination a few months previously. Then he had come back. It had been tempting to stay in the West, but at this point he didn't want to. West Berlin to him was bourgeois. The East was the old heart of Berlin. The best theatres and pubs were there. Klaus liked the Bohemian life, and East Berlin at the turn of the 1960s seemed much more interesting, full of rebels and writers, actors and artists, exotic foreign students from the Third World studying in the city with the help of generous scholarships provided by the Communist authorities. Many of his East German friends were privileged children of the GDR's élite, including, for instance, Brigitte, the writer daughter of Interior Minister Karl Maron.

And after all, the way to the West was just a matter of crossing the street! One could live in the East and enjoy the best of both worlds. This young man was looking forward to studying and living a full, exciting metropolitan life.

Klaus didn't know three things. First, that from now on, in the new closed-off East Germany, anyone who had chosen to study in the West would be suspect and thereby severely disadvantaged. Second, that the *Stasi* was already fully aware of the man whom Klaus had introduced to his father a few months before; the man from West German intelligence who was interested in having occasional talks with Herr Schulz-Ladegast senior about relations between the Lutheran Church and the Communist state.

Within a few days, Klaus Schulz-Ladegast would realise both these things.

The third realisation would take much, much longer to sink in: it was that thirty long years would pass before he set eyes again on the woman with whom he had spent that last, idyllic August weekend before the Wall went up.[14]

10

PRISONERS

THERE WERE TWO STRIKING sets of images that the world found itself focusing on, in print or in flickering black and white, during the days that followed the building of the barrier that would become the Berlin Wall.

The first set showed ordered ranks of armed East German soldiers, police and paramilitaries, and barbed wire being rolled out to sever the nerve networks of a great modern city, posts being driven like nails into Berlin's prostrate body: Erich Honecker's 'Operation Rose' in all its totalitarian, machine-like efficiency. The second set was the terrible, messy human side. People fleeing, or trying to flee, as the barrier closed; making dashes towards the Western side, encouraged by watching crowds. Human beings waving, calling, holding up children and pets, making final, vain attempts to get close to people they were beginning to realise they might not see again for years, perhaps for ever. Worst of all, most heart-rending, were the scenes in and around the Bernauer Strasse.

The Bernauer Strasse was in the borough of Wedding, in the French sector. Just. This soon-to-be notorious street began at the Nordbahnhof S-Bahn station and ran north-east from there for about a kilometre and a half until it hit the corner of Eberswalder and Schwedler Strasse, where the Wall turned north along the eastern edge of what for many years had been a busy marshalling yard and was now essentially no man's land between East and West. It formed the near-straight advanced edge of a three or four city-block square area that jutted into the East.

Those who lived in that the area were surrounded on three sides by Communist territory. By a quirk of the settlement that established the district boundaries of Greater Berlin in 1920, the Bernauer Strasse itself was divided between the districts of Wedding and Mitte (Berlin Centre).

Wedding lay in the West, in the French sector, while Mitte was in the East.

For the first three or four hundred metres of the street, coming up from the Nordbahnhof, the border ran along the edge of the cemetery belonging to the Sophienkirche congregation. This was followed by another cemetery, belonging to the Elisabeth-Himmelfahrt (Ascension of Elisabeth) congregation. These two sets of permanent inhabitants might reasonably be expected to have gone beyond caring whether they were Communist or capitalist. But when blocks of nineteenth-century apartments began to line the street on both sides, filled with live human beings, the situation changed. Many, understandably, cared a great deal. The border ran along the southern (in the strictly geographical context, but in the political context 'Eastern') side of the Bernauer Strasse, leaving the buildings on the northern side and the entire roadway as part of West Berlin, but, starting from the thresholds of the buildings on the south side, placing the actual apartment blocks in East Berlin.

Those who lived in West Berlin, directly on the sector border, found their daily routine suddenly devastated. They were used to shopping in the East, the children to going roller-skating after school at the rink in the Gartenstrasse or on Sundays picnicking at the Märchenbrunnen (Fairytale Fountain) in the nearby Friedrichshain Public Park. Even their church, the nineteenth-century Church of the Reconciliation (Versöhnungskirche), was situated in the East, though its front porch opened out on to the West. Until its demolition, the church was doomed to a pathetic non-existence in no man's land.[1]

Elke Kielberg, then thirteen, lived on the corner of Hussiten Strasse and Bernauer Strasse (and still does). Her closest playmate – since Elke remained an only child, almost a sister to her – was her cousin, who lived across the street. The closely related families were, of course, constantly in and out of each other's flats.[2]

The first inkling of catastrophe came at eight o'clock on the morning of Sunday 13 August, when Elke's mother went out to buy a newspaper. She returned to their apartment distraught and outraged: the streets that ran at right-angles to the Bernauer Strasse in the direction of Berlin-Mitte – Ackerstrasse, Gartenstrasse and Strelitzer Strasse – had all been closed off with barbed wire. There were Eastern police with guns blocking access. Already paramilitary workers seemed busy constructing a more permanent barrier.

The Kielbergs had been planning to drop over to their relatives for coffee later that day, but now those on the southern side of the street, including Elke's cousin and her family, were immured in East Berlin. 'Barbed-Wire Sunday', as Berliners called it, would mark the greatest change in most of these people's lives. Ordinary streets became traps, sometimes death-traps.

This was why, within hours of waking to the new reality of a divided Berlin, many of those trapped in the East made frantic last-minute attempts to make the journey that just hours before would have involved a simple crossing of the street.

The Bernauer Strasse was the scene of people jumping from the windows of apartment blocks, which were part of the East, down into the street, all of which belonged to the West. The *Vopos* and *Grepos*, realising the potential for escapes, had begun entering these buildings. Their ultimate aim was to clear the immediate sector-border area of 'unreliable' elements, but this would take time.

The escapes in the Bernauer Strasse soon turned into a human drama watched by an entire world, which, through the cameras of the press and the recently established television stations, enjoyed a grandstand seat. Crowds, police and fire fighters arrived on the Western side. They shouted encouragement as Easterners hesitated at upstairs windows. Fire fighters extended jumping sheets to break escapers' falls. In one case, as a man slid from a first-floor window, he found himself seized by *Vopos* from inside the room he had just left. Westerners in the street below managed to grab his ankles and pull him down. A tug-of-war ensued. In this case, with gravity on their side, the escaper and his Western helpers won.

Others were not so lucky. A number of would-be escapers died in the hours and days before the buildings were cleared. Ida Siekmann, fifty-nine years old, fell into the West from an upper floor and died,[3] as did Rudolf Urban, forty-seven, who suffered terrible damage after a fall from his apartment window. He lingered almost a month in a West Berlin hospital before succumbing to his injuries.[4] Even after the windows were bricked up, people tried to escape over the apartment-block roofs.

One of the last victims in the Bernauer Strasse was Bernd Lunser, a

Berliner who on 4 October was spotted by *Grepos* as he prepared to abseil from the roof of 44 Bernauer Strasse to the West, using a washing line. East German police rapidly appeared in the building. Lunser was forced to move elsewhere, pursued across the rooftops by the representatives of the Communist state. All the while, he called out for help from the West.

Below, on the street, the fire brigade set up a jump sheet. Several hundred Western onlookers assembled. As the police closed in, Lunser sprang from the roof. He missed the sheet and died on the ground minutes later. He was thirty years old.[5]

There was as yet no 'wall' in place, as it would later be understood, but even the improvised barrier erected during the night of 12/13 August proved surprisingly effective.

The Marienfelde reception centre in West Berlin remained full of refugees, but mostly ones who had arrived before Sunday and were awaiting processing. On Monday, when registration began, several thousand fugitives presented themselves, but they were mostly East Germans who had been visiting West Berlin for the weekend and decided to stay after the border was closed. The same applied to the few hundred who registered on Tuesday.

Twenty-eight escapers, according to official figures, managed to make it over during Sunday night, and forty-one the next. Some swam the Teltow Canal; another, a fifty-year-old railway worker, Alfons Dubinski, managed to sneak through the no man's land covering the remains of Hitler's Reich Chancellery and find his way through the barbed-wire fence of the Ebertstrasse into the Tiergarten and the safety of West Berlin. On Monday night, shots were fired at a couple swimming the as yet sparsely fortified Teltow Canal towards the American sector. No one was hurt, and they had made it safely to the West, but it was a grim warning of what might happen to future would-be escapers.[6]

Again, the East German regime's leaders could congratulate themselves on their success in carrying out their mission with minimum cost. And they did.

The party's official mouthpiece, *Neues Deutschland*, crowed over the triumph that the 'anti-Fascist protection barrier' represented. This was 'a black day for the warmongers . . . the track-switch has been set to peace

. . . the workers' response: production records'. A front page editorial was headlined 'Clear Conditions!' and said of the West Berlin authorities: 'With one stroke it becomes evident how bankrupt is their policy, how hopeless their position.' A crestfallen Brandt, according to a report of his rallying speech to the people of West Berlin, had 'held a funeral oration for the traders in human beings'.[7]

To a young journalist on the paper and convinced Communist, Günter Schabowski, this feeling of triumph was genuine. The regime he supported had won a wonderful victory. It had outwitted the capitalists, and for him and his colleagues this was a 'great day'.[8]

Beneath the façade of self-congratulation, though, the SED state was as insecure and paranoid as ever. The party was never satisfied. It was not enough that the GDR's citizens were quiescent. They had to love the party and everything it did.

Those who could be regarded as not loving the party were both obvious and less obvious. Obvious were the tens of thousands who had previously chosen to work in the West. They were the so-called border-crossers, and the regime had been persecuting them for years with every measure short of an outright ban. Equally obvious were those young East Berliners who had chosen (or their parents had chosen for them) to be educated in the West. Less obvious were those who put on a positive face in the workplace or at compulsory political meetings, but in private complained.

Now that the party had all these people in its clutches, unable to leave via the escape hatch of the open Berlin border, its policy towards all of them could, and would, change.

The former 'border-crossers' were easily dealt with. They were directed to labour exchanges to be found work in East German factories. But their status as doubtful elements would still cost them dear. They were subjected to a policy of discrimination. 'Concentrations' of such people in workplaces were to be avoided. They were not to be employed 'in key positions and especially crucial areas of production'[9]. By the middle of September, the *Stasi* reported that of 32,000 registered former 'border-crossers', 24,000 had accepted new employment 'within democratic [i.e. East] Berlin'.[10]

Significantly, and given the regime's preoccupations unsurprisingly, all qualified teachers who were resident in the East but had taught in the West were to be barred from the GDR's education system for life.

As for so-called *Weststudenten* ('West-students'), who had chosen to study in West Berlin or West Germany during the time of the open border, they were also to be punished. An element of 'class war' was clearly present in handling those who might be seen as privileged traitors to the 'workers' and peasants' state'. Such college or university students were 'categorically' not to be permitted to finish their studies in the East. Those studying technical subjects were to be directed into jobs in socialist industry where their knowledge might be exploited. They might after a while, with the agreement of their managers, be allowed to return to higher education in the GDR.

Those who had studied what might be called liberal arts subjects were to be treated with special vindictiveness. As the order put it: 'West-students who have been studying a social science subject in West Berlin – including those in their final semester – are to be placed without exception into the production process.'[11] In other words, anyone who had studied political subject matter in the West was to be put straight into unskilled factory work.

A thornier problem was that of children and young people from the East who had attended schools in the West before 13 August, and would now have to finish their studies in the GDR. Here, fear of 'contamination' was a major determining factor. If there were concerns about politically tainted border-crossers undermining innocent socialist factories, there were equal worries about these corrupted young people poisoning pure socialist schools. A concentration of 'former West-pupils' in individual classes or schools was 'absolutely to be avoided'. Questions of convenience or proximity to a particular school should not mitigate this policy.

At least most of the younger pupils were to be allowed to continue studying. Things got tougher as the subjects of the rule got older. In the case of 'West-pupils' from the 11th and 12th classes (the last-but-two and penultimate year of high school) they would not be allowed to finish school but would be assigned apprenticeships. No access to university, except in cases where this was considered 'appropriate in the interests of society as a whole' – which would decisively depend on 'the attitude of parents with regard to our government's measures and their willingness to help educate their children in accordance with our educational laws'.

The price for (possible) educational reprieve for their children was therefore the total, abject conformity of the parents.

West-pupils in the 13th (pre-university) year were, like the errant social-science students, to be tossed straight into the work-force with no chance of higher education.

Although, or perhaps because, the East German regime distrusted the educated middle classes so strongly, the attitude of the intelligentsia, of whatever age, was a matter of intense concern to the authorities.

Papers submitted to the Central Committee included surveys, based on informants' reports, detailing the educated class's concerns. There were doctors complaining about the sudden shortage of Western medicines, and fears that they would no longer be able to treat some private patients along with the state-supported ones. There were actors who considered themselves cut off from their German heritage. There were self-employed members of the middle classes who feared that the government would now clamp down on their independence. 'Why do they ask us now?' one complaint went. 'This business [i.e. the building of the Wall] was a foregone conclusion. There should be consultation and discussion first, to see if we agree. That is democracy.' This view was reported to be 'widespread' in educated circles.[12]

Occasionally criticism went public. At a chemical works in Halle, open dissent was expressed at a meeting to 'discuss' the 13 August border closure. Workers declared that 'the measures were a crime'. The report curtly described the consequences of such frankness: 'Two bandits were consequently arrested'.[13]

Elsewhere, a certain 'colleague Richter' announced that he did not agree with the 'measures', which he said would harm the GDR. His own life, he declared, was in any case already 'ruined' (*verpfuscht*). In this case, the government informant confined himself to enclosing photographs of the 'ruined' man's pleasant apartment and penning a few sarcastic remarks. 'Richter also possesses a Trabant De Luxe automobile,' the report noted, 'a refrigerator, a television set, new furniture for his apartment, and two fat pigs'.[14]

The choice of a weekend for the sealing of the border was calculated to catch the West asleep; but it also aimed at managing the response among the domestic work-force.

In June 1953, during the uprising, workers had downed tools to discuss their grievances, then streamed out of factories and construction sites on to the streets. It had taken Soviet tanks to quell their resistance. The party had learned a bitter lesson. On an August Sunday, it was calculated, those same workers would be with their families, relaxing at home, perhaps visiting their traditional German weekend allotments (*Gartenlauben*), or even off on vacation in the countryside. Much less likelihood of mass meetings and strikes.

By Monday, the East German authorities reasoned, the *fait accompli* would be unassailable. They were right.

Unlike 1953, the government arranged for meetings to be addressed by party officials and agitators, and for discussion to be tolerated. Iron glove in velvet fist. Only critics who went too far, like the fearless workers in Halle, were classified as 'bandits' or 'negative elements'. They were scooped up by the security forces.

There were thousands who did come into that category. Around 1,500 East Germans were arrested for political offences in the first half of 1961. That number increased almost fivefold in the second half to 7,200.[15] As reigns of terror go, it was not comparable to 1953, when the jails had brimmed over, but it was bad enough. Those swept up by this purge entered a world that was little known to outsiders or even most GDR citizens, but that they would, if they survived it, never forget.

The East German gulag.

At the end of that weekend, nineteen-year-old Klaus Schulz-Ladegast returned to the city from his romantic rural interlude. He settled back into the comfortable family home in the inner-city East Berlin district of Mitte.

In the meantime, of course, 'Barbed-Wire Sunday' had intervened and the great world had changed. So had Schulz-Ladegast's smaller personal world, though he did not yet know this. Because he had no over-whelming feelings about the new 'border measures' – the woman he was in love with also lived east of the new barrier – he assumed his life would continue along much the same course. Considering where to study, meeting his lover and his friends, hanging out in the cafés and bars of the city's historic centre.

It was not to be. Five days later, on Thursday 17 August, they came for him.

A car slid in alongside the kerb as he walked down a quiet suburban street in the August sunshine. Two men got out and he found his way blocked. They asked him to accompany them to 'clear up a matter'. Their polite language belied the firmness with which they took him by the arms and bundled him into the waiting Wartburg. A third man had kept the engine idling while the arrest took place. He now pumped the accelerator and the car took off quickly, rumbling over the cobbled street to God knew where.

Schulz-Ladegast's destination was a place that since the 1950s had been known as the 'forbidden area'. Catching the ordinary tram that started at the Alexanderplatz and trundled eastwards five or so kilometres along the broad boulevard of the Leninallee, the casual traveller would get out at the Gensler Strasse stop. Only when one tried to enter the small maze of streets north of the Leninallee did orientation difficulties begin.

The area was one of mixed residential and light-industrial use in the Hohenschönhausen sub-district of Lichtenberg. This was a busy outer district of East Berlin, yet a substantial part of it appeared on no city guide. Nearby streets were marked, but, on maps printed in East Berlin throughout the GDR's existence, they simply stopped and a blank area was shown. Even on Western maps, there were only vague outlines of buildings, plus a small goods station that had been there since before the war.

On the ground, had our traveller persisted in trying to find his or her way north from the Gensler Strasse tram stop, they would have reached a high wall festooned with warning signs. Had they turned into the Freienwalder Strasse, they would have seen a 'stop' sign, a checkpoint manned by armed guards in the uniform of the East German Ministry of State Security, and a set of high, panelled-steel barriers, blocking further progress along the street. This was the main entrance to the forbidden area.

A section of this industrial area, covering half a square kilometre, had been Jewish-owned before 1933 and was expropriated under the Nazis.

This benefited the expansion of one local 'Aryan' business, a large-scale button factory that flourished on contracts for the *Wehrmacht*. Other favoured companies included the Heikle plant, which manufactured meat-processing machinery, and Asid, a pharmaceutical factory producing vaccination materials. The Nazi welfare organisation, the NSV, built a modern canteen kitchen (*Grossküche*) on the site, capable of providing thousands of meals for the local population under the aegis of the 'Winter Aid Fund'.

These facilities were extensively damaged by Allied air raids. Also affected by bombing were a small punishment camp run by the Gestapo on the Gensler Strasse, where Jews and conscripted workers from Eastern Europe were sent if they failed to fulfil their norms, and a *Wehrmacht*-owned warehouse used to store looted goods from occupied Europe.

On 22 April, the 5th Army of the White Russian Front, under the command of General Bezarin, overran Hohenschönhausen. Huge amounts of warehoused materials, plus most of the equipment from the canteen kitchen, went missing. So far, an average fate for a typical suburban industrial development of that time and place.

The peculiarity of this district, however, was that the Soviet 'People's Commissariat for Interior Affairs' (NKVD), predecessor of the notorious KGB, chose to set up its headquarters precisely here. With the aid of local Communists and other variously motivated informers, the Soviets began to round up those in the locality who had been guilty of supporting Hitler. Especially the bourgeoisie.

On 23 April 1945, eighty-year-old Richard Heikle, owner of the meat-processing machinery factory, was identified to a Soviet patrol and shot dead on the spot, on the corner of Freienwalder Strasse and Gensler Strasse, along with his housekeeper and a family friend.[16] It was the kind of impromptu revenge killing common all over Eastern Germany in those tumultuous weeks, but soon such casual executions would be succeeded by a systematic purge. Richard Heikle junior, son of the dead meat-processing magnate, was arrested and disappeared for ever to a labour camp in the Soviet Union. Several other managers were imprisoned. Soon the NKVD requisitioned what remained of the Gestapo camp and the canteen kitchen. This area was in mid-May 1945 officially designated 'Special Camp No. 3'. One Major Smaroda of the NKVD was made its commandant.

Many thousands, prominent and obscure, suffered similar fates to Heikle junior. The most famous was the actor, Heinrich George. Star of the 1920s film classics *Metropolis* and *Berlin Alexanderplatz*, he had once been an opponent of the Nazis, but had allowed himself to be seduced by Goebbels and became a leading figure in the Third Reich's film culture. George was imprisoned here in June/July 1945 before being transferred to the former Nazi concentration camp at Sachsenhausen just outside Berlin. There he died a year later.

In the spring of 1951, 'Special Camp No. 3', now expanded to include almost all the half-square-kilometre industrial area, was handed over by the Soviets to the new East German Ministry of State Security. The area of the canteen kitchen and the former Gestapo punishment camp became the *Stasi*'s main interrogation prison.

The area was peculiarly suited to this use. It was relatively isolated and easily closed off, the buildings were conveniently configured, and (last but not least) into the midst of the location ran a branch railway line. The 'goods' transported could just as well be human beings as machines or consumer durables.

On Thursday 17 August 1961, scooped up off the street by *Stasi* operatives, Klaus Schulz-Ladegast came to Hohenschönhausen by car. He had been blindfolded shortly after his journey began, so all he experienced of his arrival was the end of the cobbled street and the sound of a gate opening. Then he heard the car crossed a flagstoned area, and pass through another metal gate. Schulz-Ladegast now realised from the echo that they were inside a contained space. The gate clanged shut.

The blindfold was removed. The lights were dazzling. As Schulz-Ladegast was dragged out of the car a terrifying chorus of shouting came from unseen voices. He was hauled through this din towards a door. The calculated psychological nightmare of *Stasi* 'interrogation-custody' had begun.[17]

The interrogation prison at Hohenschönhausen, as it existed in 1961, was part of a wider complex. It was not just a prison but also a *Stasi* administrative centre and a specialist labour camp. Elsewhere within the complex, long-term prisoners made false Western number plates that were used by *Stasi* employees operating in the 'capitalist abroad', plus there was a print shop for documents, forms and ID papers, legitimate and otherwise. In the 1950s, tools of the spying trade such as miniature cameras and recorders had also been manufactured here, but the department ('special camp X') had been closed down after information was leaked to the Western press.[18]

The interrogation prison was different. It concentrated solely on getting out of suspects what the state needed to justify the usually pre-ordained verdicts that secret courts would inflict on them. Klaus was one among many hundreds, and the way he was dealt with by his jailers – Department XIV of the *Stasi*, responsible for the running of political prisons – was fairly typical.

On arrival, after the routine ordeal of reception, he was stripped and put into rough prison fatigues. Then he was marched to an isolation cell. Moving around the interrogation prison was a strict, carefully monitored procedure. Especially in the early stages of incarceration, no prisoner was permitted to converse or even see another. A system of 'traffic lights' at corners in the maze of gloomy corridors warned if another detainee and his escort were approaching. If this was the case, the original prisoner would be pushed into a man-sized niche specially dug into the wall, where he would have to stand, face pressed against the dark brickwork, until the other prisoner and his escort had safely passed.

The cell itself, when the prisoner reached it, consisted of just a bed and a latrine. A frosted glass window let in a little natural light, but allowed no view of the outside. The entire place was desperately lonely, eerily silent. The prisoner, especially one, like Klaus, who had just arrived from the freedom and fresh air of the outside world, would soon feel as if he was being slowly buried alive.

Klaus's experiences at Hohenschönhausen, and later at the notorious 'Yellow Misery', as the Bautzen prison in Saxony was known – four years in all – would mark him for life. He was sentenced for knowingly having introduced to his father a man from West German intelligence who wanted to discuss the affairs of the Brandenburg Church Community. His father had resisted at first, then agreed.

The West German agent had been very firm. Neither father or son should ever mention their meetings with him to anyone, anyone at all. Klaus's father thought this could not apply in the case of his best friend and colleague at the Church Council, with whom – certain that they shared similar political sympathies – he discussed the meetings. How-ever, this apparent soulmate was in fact a *Stasi* agent, specifically assigned to him as a 'minder'. Hence the arrest of Klaus and, unknown to him, also his father on that Thursday five days after the Wall went up.

Both father and son underwent the same torment of isolation and interrogation. The methods used on each were similar. A mild threat of violence at times, though none actually used. *Stasi* methods in the 1950s had frequently been brutally similar to those of the NKVD and KGB, but paradoxically, after the outrage of 'Barbed-Wire Sunday', East Germany began to seek international respectability, which encouraged the *Stasi* to switch mostly to psychological methods.

The classic scenario was the 'corner-to-corner' interrogation room. The room was on the second floor and overlooked the edge of the prison, allowing a tantalising glimpse of the outside world. The interrogator's chair and desk were situated at an angle to this window corner, facing into the room. When the prisoner was brought in, he was placed on an uncomfortable small stool in the far, interior corner of the room, so that he crouched there facing the interrogator, who was a good ten feet away. The psychological effect, which had been thoroughly researched, was to make the prisoner instantly uncomfortable and apprehensive, subject to an animal unease, which the interrogator could increase by simply staring at him, and saying things like 'I have plenty of time. I have nothing but time'. It was clear to the prisoner that, just out of his line of vision, a window revealed the world he had left weeks or months previously for a lonely, silent cell. Often the prisoner felt an overwhelming sense to talk, to make something happen that would get him off that stool and out of there. Many gave in to this compulsion.

Klaus talked. But he did not tell his interrogators what they wanted. He instinctively denied everything about the West German spies, though he fed his jailers a lot about his life as a gadfly in the East Berlin social scene and his regular visits to places like the fashionable 'Press Café' in the Friedrichstrasse. Luckily, he had never taken money from the West Germans, so they could prove nothing in that regard.

This game of drip-feeding important-sounding but actually trivial information helped keep Klaus sane. Two other things also helped. First, within a month of arriving, he found himself afflicted with violent

stomach pains and had to be taken into hospital. There, though kept in
an enclosed wing, he got two weeks of better food, relatively normal
treatment, including the attentions of pleasant young nurses, and a
breathing space.

Schulz-Ladegast returned to the prison, after recovering from the
(probably psychosomatic) illness, much strengthened. Then he was
moved into a cell with another prisoner, an older man who had served
in the *Wehrmacht*. His cellmate taught him a few survival tricks. How to
handle interrogators, and above all how to keep that vital element of self-
respect while remaining within the rules. He told Klaus never to obey a
guard's order immediately. They discussed how to judge that split-
second pause when ordered to do something by a guard; the split-second
pause that allowed the prisoner to make the guard wait, while at the same
time avoiding punishment for disobedience. On such fine behavioural
detail depended a prisoner's sense of his own dignity and therefore his
emotional survival.

The original sentence intended for Klaus had been eight years, as he
later found out from viewing his *Stasi* file. Through his skill at the
interrogation game, he had managed, Klaus noted with grim satisfaction,
to get that down to four.

Klaus survived Hohenschönhausen. He survived a further three years
at Bautzen. It would be almost ten years before he once more set foot on
Western soil, a changed man and in a different country. While the Wall
existed, he never again set eyes on the woman he had fallen in love with
that summer.

Ironically, his father had had his freedom 'purchased' by West German
benefactors years earlier. He was one of the first East German political
prisoners released by this route. It was a sign that the East German gulag
would, unique among the prison systems of the Eastern Bloc, become a
trading organisation, exchanging human beings for hard currency.

The sealing of the border had been a sudden coup, crude but effective in
execution. Once the wire and the guards were in place, the fortifications
would be intensified and the more durable structure that would be
known as the Wall put into place.

Meanwhile, the dissidents and the amateur spies such as Klaus could be scooped up and dealt with. And, behind the new barrier, other inconvenient details could be tidied up.

In the Bernauer Strasse and the neighbouring streets, as autumn 1961 turned into winter, the regime finished removing residents from the houses and apartment blocks adjoining the new border, especially in the Mitte district. Of the total of 497 households that made up the Bernauer Strasse, reckoned to total 826 individuals, in the five weeks until 19 September 143 families (276 individuals) were removed to other accommodation; it was planned that by 21 October the other 354 families (530) would also be gone. This would leave the area safe from escape attempts on the part of its residents, by dint of the simple fact that there would no longer be any residents.[19]

The same went for border areas in Treptow. On 13 August Till Meyer had seen East Berliners waving and shouting from their apartments in the Harzer Strasse to their Western friends and relatives on the other side of the barbed wire. This was no longer possible after 15 October. By then, 42 families (108 persons) were removed from those very same apartment blocks in the Harzer Strasse. Elsewhere in that small complex of streets adjoining the West Berlin borough of Kreuzberg, a further 134 households were also due for deportation.

The cold numbers cited in the official reports fail to express the angry, desperate reality of human beings forced from homes they had occupied for years, perhaps even for their whole lives. These were famously close Berlin neighbourhoods. All the worse for their inhabitants to be torn from everything that was familiar and dumped into the company of strangers, often in the soulless new high-rise concrete-slab housing developments that the regime was busily building on the eastern edge of the city.

This happened in many streets close to the border. Some of the inhabitants had to be ejected by force. One resident whose home lay on the border with West Berlin at Spandau, having initially left peacefully enough, later 'returned to his flat and, being in a drunken condition, smashed to pieces several window panes and a stove'. Another family tried to ignore the *Vopos* knocking on their door and calling out at six a.m, 'so that the apartment had to be opened up by force'. Another young woman was arrested for protesting – 'acting in a provocative manner' as the official description had it.[20]

Eventually, the buildings on the Bernauer Strasse, as elsewhere on the East Berlin/West Berlin border, were entirely demolished. No more dramatic escapes from windows. No more abseiling from the roof. No more desperate fugitives plummeting to their deaths on the cobbled street below.

Nothing was to get in the way of the new, impregnable Wall. It would keep the state's citizens trapped inside the GDR until, like the detainees in the interrogation prison, they resigned themselves to their fate and simply stopped resisting.

11

'THAT BASTARD FROM BERLIN'

WHEN JOE ALSOP DROPPED by that high-octane Georgetown dinner party late on the evening of Saturday 12 August 1961, and told young Berlin journalist Lothar Löwe of the dramatic events in his native city, the veteran Washington communicator had taken his information from the American broadcast media. News was trickling out about the new Communist challenge in Berlin, even though, in the untidy way of information-gathering, few people, even on the spot, were sure exactly what that challenge consisted of.

A little later that same Saturday night, John C. Ausland, duty officer for the Berlin Task Force at the State Department, was woken by his bedside phone at his home in Washington. On the line was the night officer from the department's recently established operations centre. The man informed Ausland that garbled news about some kind of Communist move in Berlin was starting to come over the wire services' teletype network. There was talk of sector border crossings' being 'blocked', but it was not clear what this entailed. Temporary restrictions by the East of cross-sector traffic within Greater Berlin had happened before, of course. Ausland told his caller to stay in touch and went back to sleep.

Around four a.m. Washington time on Sunday – already ten in the morning in West Berlin – the night-duty man called Ausland back. Military channels had confirmed that this was a total blockade between East and West Berlin. So, astonishingly, a full ten hours after 'Operation Rose' had begun, Washington started to get the message. Ausland called several different people, including Frank Cash, a former senior official at the embassy in Bonn, who was running the Berlin Task Force while German expert Martin Hillebrand was on summer leave. Cash said he had to take his family to the airport in a couple of hours, but promised he would be in later.

Ausland was soon joined by Colonel Showalter, the Pentagon's liaison officer at the State Department, and more calls to Europe were made. However, the one thing they really wanted to do, they could not: call the American Mission in Berlin. This was because the phone line in question went right through East German territory. Any conversation would have been totally *en clair* and would assuredly have been tapped by East German intelligence. At six, with dawn breaking over Washington, Ausland picked up the telephone and found the White House duty officer on the line. Word had finally got through about events in Berlin, but the man expressed reluctance to wake the President, who was staying out at Cape Cod for the weekend. The White House official assured Ausland that he would start taking steps to alert Kennedy at the more civilised hour of eight a.m. EST.[1]

It was by now noon on Sunday in Berlin. 'Operation Rose' was twelve hours old, and still the American President knew nothing of it.

This hesitance to bother Kennedy may not have represented just the traditional reluctance of servants to displease their master. The President was in poor shape. As became known after his death, Kennedy's public image as a young paragon of masculine power, glowing with health, was largely a sham. He had suffered since young adulthood from Addison's Disease, a debilitating affliction of the auto-immune system, which among other unpleasant symptoms caused stomach problems, exhaustion and depression, and severe joint and back pain. For more than a quarter of a century, Kennedy had been on constant medication. In the summer of 1961, his health problems were especially severe. At that time, his personal physician was injecting him with procaine, a serious narcotic, two to three times a day to allay the pain. Cortisone shots were, moreover, a routine treatment for Addison's, and the President was also regularly on drugs for colitis, weight loss (testosterone), and insomnia (Ritalin). On 9 August 1961 Kennedy had complained of 'gut problems', 'cramps', and 'loose stool'; he had woken at five on the morning of Friday 11 August with severe abdominal discomfort. JFK was, as a doctor who later reviewed his medical records commented, 'tired because he was being doped up'.[2]

That fateful Sunday, as the wires hummed with the news from Berlin, America's most powerful elected official was indeed fast asleep. He was staying at the Kennedy family compound in Hyannis Port, where he and a small staff had joined the extended first family for the weekend, as the President liked to do in the dog days of summer. It was beautiful weather. A family trip on the Kennedys' cabin cruiser, the *Marlin*, was planned for later that morning.

At this time of the year, the President usually left for the Cape on a Friday afternoon, travelling by helicopter to Andrews Air Force Base and from there to Cape Cod by plane. As usual, on that last morning in Washington he would have been presented by his senior military aide, Major-General Chester Clifton, with a folder containing CIA reports on developments in various parts of the world that day. The folder was known as the President's 'check-list'. Looking through this was part of Kennedy's daily routine. Update folders would be flown to Hyannis Port on Saturday and then again on Sunday, along with any other material thought significant, so that the President could continue to keep up with current events. Urgent messages could be routed via a telex loop from the White House to the basement of the Yachtsman's Motel in Hyannis Port, where a unit of the US Signal Corps was installed for the summer.[3]

On Sunday 13 August, the President finally awoke to blue skies and sunshine, a glorious Cape Cod morning. Despite the White House official's promise, it seems that no clear message had arrived about the situation in Berlin. There was still no word when Kennedy set off to attend mass with the rest of the family at St François Xavier Church in Hyannis Port. The Kennedys returned a little less than an hour later and almost immediately embarked on the *Marlin*. They were heading for Great Island, where they had been invited to lunch with the director of Washington's National Gallery of Art and his wife.

A short while later, a radio message came from General Clifton, who had remained behind at the Kennedy compound. A cable had been delivered from Washington. Berlin was being sealed off. Clifton re-commended that the President return to shore.

The *Marlin* turned back. Kennedy was dropped off at the compound's jetty, where Clifton met him in a motorised golf cart. At the President's insistence, the first family continued with their cruise and their lunch.

Clifton immediately showed Kennedy the cable, then drove him back across the dunes to the family's holiday cottage. There the President put in a call to the State Department. Within a few minutes he was discussing the Berlin situation with Secretary Rusk.

The Secretary of State, in the calm, inscrutable tones that had earned him the nickname of 'Buddha', explained that he thought it was important to negotiatate, to 'talk the fever out of this thing'. The President wanted to know what the Russians were up to. Rusk said it appeared they were taking military measures all right, but only defensive ones. Nothing indicated that Khrushchev was out to gobble up West Berlin.

That was the main thing. Now, a world war over access to and from East Berlin? Forget it.

The instinctive impulse of Rusk and his aides, and of everyone around the President was to play down the news – at least for public consumption. Phone calls from Kennedy to McNamara, Bundy and Attorney-General Robert Kennedy confirmed that this low-key approach reflected a general consensus. No one wanted to appear weak or unresponsive; on the other hand, they didn't want to make it look as if the Soviet/East German measures were a *casus belli* or, anything like it.

None the less, some kind of official reaction had to occur. Walt Rostow, who was in Washington and had helped set up a 'Situation Room', joined Ausland in drafting a press release. This was cabled through to the President's press secretary, Pierre Salinger, at Hyannis Port, so that Salinger could field the media's enquires and make whatever statements were considered necessary.

There was no talk of a 'Wall' or anything similar in the press release, only of 'measures designed to halt the flow of refugees to West Berlin'. The East German moves were seen as a continuation of intimidatory actions undertaken earlier that weekend against travellers from Potsdam and East Berlin, thought to be aimed at 'border-crossers'. The main tack would be to deny that the West had done anything to 'induce' the flood of refugees, which was due to 'economic conditions in East Germany and the Soviet campaign against West Berlin'. From there Salinger went on to the offensive, pointing out that the restrictions were in 'direct contravention' of the four-power agreement and represented a 'damning admission by the Soviets of the inability of communist society to compete with a free society'.[4]

The official State Department response – discussed and approved by the President – eschewed even such anodyne rhetoric. It declared merely that the action did not affect the 'Allied position in West Berlin or access thereto', though it violated existing agreements and would be subject to 'vigorous protests through appropriate channels'.[5]

Soviet tanks might lurk on the outskirts of Berlin; machine-gun-wielding Communist goons might defy humanity and the world; Western crowds might come close to rioting at the sector border; the malevolent agents of the *Stasi* might be busy forcibly crushing resistance among recalcitrant East Berliners; but in Washington the State Department reacted with polite bromides.

Kennedy was not alone in confronting the undoubted ugliness of 'Operation Rose' with extreme caution. Other major Western leaders were even less eager to confront the Communist machinations in Berlin head-on.

The crisis found Harold Macmillan, Prime Minister of Great Britain since 1957, hundreds of miles north of London, at Bolton Abbey, in Yorkshire. There he was celebrating, as he did every summer, the opening of the grouse-shooting season. Macmillan spent Saturday 12 August in the company of his nephew, the Duke of Devonshire – owner of Bolton Abbey and of much else besides – engaged in appropriate use of firearms against indigenous bird life. Even after hearing the news from Berlin, the Premier saw no reason why he should not continue to do so on 13 August also.

Meanwhile, 71-year-old General Charles André Joseph Marie de Gaulle, last active Allied leader of the Second World War and since 1958 once more President of France, was resting at his country home in Colombey-les-Deux-Églises, south-east (in fact, rather a long way south-east) of Paris. So relaxed did de Gaulle seem about the Berlin affair that he failed to return to Paris until the following Thursday, 17 August.[6]

This caution was not due to mere indifference on the part of either leader. Each had problems of his own quite independent of Khrushchev's and Ulbricht's ploys.

Britain's military and economic decline had lately accelerated to a point where even the traditionally imperialistic Conservatives realised they had to cut their cloth to suit new circumstances. A certain testy obsession with cost had crept into discussions about Britain's military commitments. Even before this latest twist in the Berlin Crisis, plans had been put in motion by Defence Minister Harold Watkinson, not to increase Britain's military presence in West Germany and Berlin, but to drastically reduce it.

Conscription for the British armed services was due to be abandoned in the early part of 1962. The strength of the British Army of the Rhine (BAOR) would accordingly fall from 52,000 to 44,000 by the end of that year. It seemed likely that even the 3,500 troops London maintained in the British sector of Berlin might be subjected to a quiet culling operation. Despite occasional sabre-rattling from America and the USSR, and the manifest failure of the Vienna summit in June, until 13 August the attitude in London was pretty low-key. Macmillan, in his wry way, expressed the general feeling among London's élite in June 1961: 'I still think we are more likely to be bankrupted than blown up'.[7]

Moreover, Britain had problems elsewhere in the world. In the Middle East the British faced confrontation with the newly radicalised republic of Iraq under its fiery strongman, Brigadier Abd al-Karim Qassem. Qassem had laid claim to the small, British-protected (and oil-rich) sheikhdom of Kuwait, and had spent most of June massing his army in the arid border zone. London had hastily withdrawn substantial forces from Germany, Cyprus and the Home Command to defend the Kuwait flashpoint. The cost of such a major, if temporary, movement of personnel and equipment, including ships and aircraft, was extremely painful for the British treasury.

Macmillan's diplomats were still frantically occupied with arranging for peacekeeping forces from the Arab League to take over the long-term protection of Kuwait, while British conscripts sweated in temperatures of 50 degrees centigrade (120 Fahrenheit) opposite Iraq's putative military might in the desert south of Basra.

Before 13 August, Berlin was therefore not high on London's priorities list. This seemed, in any case, to be dictated by financial considerations rather than global strategy. For the past several years, Britain had been locked in a wrangle with West Germany. London wanted Bonn to share more of the cost of the British presence there, formerly an army of occupation but now part of the first line of defence against attack from the East. This had become a touchy point. In mid-July, during discussions about contingency plans in case of another Soviet blockade of Berlin, Macmillan had declared rather sourly that Britain 'should make it clear that we will pay *nothing*' toward the expenses of any new airlift.[8]

So trouble in Berlin was the last thing the British wanted. Even in the aftermath of the Wall, another personal communication to Macmillan from his Minister of Defence stated that

> from our own domestic point of view, I am now convinced that we can no longer afford either from a military or from a foreign exchange point of view to keep anything like the present level of forces in Europe. A measure of disengagement or détente would, therefore, serve not only the cause of peace but our own special and urgent needs.

A scribbled comment on the memo by Macmillan declared 'agreement with your thesis' and added, 'I think For Sec [presumably Foreign Secretary] is also in sympathy.'[9]

As for that other overstretched former imperial power, France still had several hundred thousand troops, mostly young conscripts, tied up in a vicious guerrilla war in Algeria. Talks to end the bloody Algerian struggle for independence from France had just begun in the spa town of Evian – a concession by de Gaullle that had already brought sections of his army and the Algerian white settlers out in open rebellion. It would be late the following spring before a cease-fire resulted. With France's largest 'overseas province' in bloody uproar, diverting serious reinforcements to join the 45,000 French troops already in Germany (of which 3,000 were based at the Quartier Napoléon military complex in Berlin) was out of the question.

Although, unlike Macmillan's hard-headed (and hard-up) Britain, de Gaulle's France was prepared to make considerable sacrifices for 'greatness', this readiness did not apply, as would soon become clear, when it came to the unity of Berlin. When the American President passed through Paris on his way to meet Khrushchev in May 1961, General de

Gaulle, playing the experienced father-figure, told Kennedy to 'remain firm on Berlin' and not let Khrushchev hoodwink him. De Gaulle tended to advocate a tough line over Berlin, both because he wanted to court the West Germans and because this was, in his experience, how one best dealt with the Russians and their puppets (he had a particular contempt for the East German regime). None the less, the French Defence Minister, Pierre Messmer, informed his British counterpart just weeks later that Frenchmen were not prepared to 'die for Berlin'.[10]

Privately, the French élite still found the existing division of Berlin, and of Germany, perfectly satisfactory, although (in the delicate words of a recent French official publication) de Gaulle thought that 'it was important to avoid dashing the hopes of the Germans'.[11] Another great Frenchman, the Nobel Prize-winning author and biographer of de Gaulle, François Mauriac, would later make the classic quip that 'I like Germany so much, I want two of her'.[12] Only an attempt to encroach on existing Allied, and especially French, occupation rights would therefore provoke de Gaulle into unsheathing his sword.

Guarded remarks over the telephone line to and from Hyannis Port that August Sunday were therefore not just an expression of timidity on the part of Kennedy and his aides. The administration was walking a diplomatic tightrope-act. Its caution reflected the complexity not just of dealing with the Soviet Union and its puppets, but also, and simultaneously, with the Western Allies, whose needs, capabilities and national ambitions varied. Unlike Khrushchev's satellites, the European democracies could not simply be browbeaten into place to suit their dominant superpower's needs. They had to be persuaded into unanimity, and were not yet so convinced.

The administration and its advisers had sensed these problems in the period before the building of the Wall. Walt Rostow summed it up in a memorandum to the President on 22 July, which may have influenced the carefully calculated toughness of Kennedy's television broadcast about Berlin three days later. The advice, self-consciously entitled 'A *High Noon* Stance on Berlin', argued that while the US should carry its allies with it into a firm position if possible (especially the Germans and the French – the British are not mentioned), it must be prepared, if necessary, to go the distance alone. Hence the *High Noon* stance. As

Rostow added dryly: 'You recall Gary Cooper dealt with the bandits alone'.

While understanding why the Europeans, after two costly wars, would be less willing to risk conflict, Rostow also declared the unquestionable but unpalatable truth that '. . . it is on the United States – its will and its power – that the Russians will ultimately focus . . . the final formula will be heavily determined by what we will take or not take'. He continued:

> I may be quite wrong. It may be that the importance of Atlantic unity and the inescapable moral commitment to the West Berliners will see us all together, right down to the final test. (And, of course, the crisis may abort at a relatively early stage.) But I do believe we must be prepared in our minds for the possibility of a relatively lonely stage; and we should accept it without throwing our sheriff's badge in the dust when the crisis subsides.[13]

And it wasn't just the big Western Allies that America had to deal with. Washington also had to consider smaller NATO members such as Italy, Belgium, Holland, Norway, and so on down to tiny Luxembourg, who had no military presence in Berlin or West Germany, but who voted in the alliance's councils.

The smaller NATO powers could reasonably argue that, in a war waged over Berlin with atomic weapons, they would suffer as much as those who were directly involved. Therefore they should have a say in America's and NATO's response to the Communist provocation of 13 August. The White House was acutely aware of this fact. It also was forced to ask a related question: having relied throughout the 1950s on the deterrent effect of America's atomic arsenal to keep the Soviets from launching an all-out invasion of Western Europe, what role did the atomic arsenal have in handling the more insidious salami-slicing tactics that Khrushchev and his minions now tended to adopt?

Kennedy's Secretary of Defense, Robert McNamara, was a systems man, who had come to the administration straight from running Ford Motors. He liked to know where he stood. On assuming office, he was horrified to discover that the Eisenhower administration had not developed a coherent escalation policy, or at least not one that gave an acceptable flexibility of response. Previous policy seemed as follows: basically, you fought with inadequate conventional forces until it looked like you would lose (which, because NATO's armies were no match for Soviet might, would probably be pretty soon), after which nuclear weapons would be unleashed, with terrible consequences for the world.

This policy, such as it was, was tailored to handling a situation like the North Korean invasion of South Korea; that is, a direct war between Eastern and Western client states. It fell into confusion when faced with Khrushchev's and Ulbricht's subtle and unpredictable tricks in Berlin. McNamara had already ordered a rethink. Escalation would be carefully calibrated in order to delay the use of nuclear weapons for as long as possible, thus giving time for a conflict resolution that might avoid nuclear war. Essential to this was an expansion of conventional American forces, so that the West would not be immediately overrun. It represented a partial reversal of the policy of 'nuclearisation' that had been generally accepted since 1945.

The Secretary of Defense's ideas had already got him into trouble with senior commanders, especially US Air Force General Lauris Norstad. Since 1956, Norstad had been both commander of American forces in Europe and Supreme Allied Commander Europe (SACEUR). The tall, chiselled-featured general, son of a Lutheran pastor from Red Wing, Minnesota, had been appointed as SACEUR by his wartime superior, Eisenhower. In 1961 he was fifty-three years old, an experienced soldier-diplomat. He believed that the Kennedy/McNamara axis was making a mistake by reasserting the importance of conventional weapons. Only, went the general's reasoning, if the enemy knew that nuclear weapons would be used, first tactically and then strategically, if necessary at an early stage, would he be reliably deterred.

Nevertheless, Norstad also tended to agree with those European members of NATO who saw the use of nuclear weapons as a joint responsibility – a view that met with little favour in Washington. No one said any of these calculations were easy.

For all these reasons, as Rostow had surmised, the solitary 'High Noon Stance' might well be the position that America was forced to take over Berlin in the days and weeks that followed.

Depending, of course, on what the Russians and their East German comrades did next.

The Communists' initial gambit, extreme and catastrophic as it appeared to the ordinary people of Berlin, was, in fact, carefully judged.

At least initially, West to East traffic remained free; or, to be precise, not specifically forbidden. It was stated that access to West Berlin from the East was available only to those who applied for permits. The fact that those permits would not be granted to all but a handful of East German *apparatchiks* was in international-legal terms a technicality. The important thing was, the West could not say that its rights had been fatally infringed; only those of East Germans attempting to enter West Berlin from the Soviet sector were affected.

This point was picked up immediately and gratefully by the Western governments, just as the Communists had calculated. Also important to the Western governments' perceptions were the observations made by their military missions operating in East Berlin and the wider GDR.

Staffed by trained intelligence officers, the military missions had been set up as liaison groups between the Allied military governments towards the end of the war. The missions' notional headquarters were housed in grand villas at Potsdam, just outside East Berlin, but most operatives attached to them lived in and operated out of West Berlin. Soviet missions were likewise attached to individual headquarters in the three Allied zones. The missions' chief role became to act as 'mobile on-site inspection teams'[14]. They neither 'ran' agents in the East nor conducted active subversion. They simply looked over the other side's territory, often in places where the other side would rather they didn't look, and reported back to their own superiors.

The missions' activities over the several decades of their existence included raiding Soviet and East German army waste-disposal areas, where careless army clerks might have left scrap documents, technicians broken equipment, and sanitary and medical staff (as the account delicately put it) 'medical waste'. All these could be taken back to West Berlin and analysed to gain clues as to the fitness and well-being or otherwise of the Cold War enemy.[15] Even unsurfaced roads and tracks used by military traffic could be examined to ascertain the weight of the vehicles that had passed over them and the nature of the tracks fitted, giving clues as to the extent and make-up of troop movements. The missions even kept an eye on the *Stasi*'s repressive activities, conducting regular forays into the 'forbidden area' in Hohenschönhausen.[16]

The military-mission officers and their drivers played a constant game of cat-and-mouse with the Soviet and East German military authorities, who tried, often illegally, to keep certain areas off limits and to intimidate mission representatives to keep away. It should be added that Soviet military missions attached to Allied military headquarters in the three Western zones of Germany played out a similar charade, and to the same purpose. East and West tolerated each other's official spies because each gained advantage from the agreement.

The three Western missions were very busy during the night of 12/13 and the day of 13 August, using their privileged access to the East to track movements of security forces and military units, to photograph units and military buildings and vehicles, and to subject these to a certain amount of preliminary analysis.

It was thanks in great part to these intrepid officers that, within hours of the commencement of 'Operation Rose', the Allied representatives in West Berlin knew two things: first, that East Berlin remained relatively peaceful; and second, that although Soviet units had moved into position in a ring around the capital, the emphasis of that ring seemed to be defensive rather than offensive. It was a curious, and often ignored, positive aspect of spying during the Cold War that it could calm fears as well as raise the alarm. In the days following the border closure, the West's officers and agents in East Germany made a powerful contribution to peace by their ability to discern and analyse the Soviets' intentions.

A cable from the British commander in Berlin, General Delacombe, during the evening of 13 August, informed London that two Soviet divisions had deployed defensively on the approaches to West Berlin, 'to prevent any attempt by dwellers in border areas to make a mass break for West Berlin'.[17]

Similar assessments came from Allan Lightner and his French counterpart.

Journalists, including Robert Lochner, the American-born and German-raised director of RIAS, had also found their way into East Berlin during the early hours and supplied eyewitness accounts of the tragic, sometimes chaotic scenes at the border crossings, especially the Frie-drichstrasse station. Media people were also, being extremely mobile, and usually with fluent language skills and good local contacts, better able than the diplomats to judge the mood in both East and West Berlin.

Such free-ranging observers certainly enjoyed a huge advantage over the administration's planners in Washington and at Hyannis Port. Dean Rusk, a farmer's son from Georgia, had studied briefly in Berlin before the war, but had gained his political and military experience in wartime South-East Asia. He neither liked nor pretended to understand the Germans. Rusk was not alone in this within the cabal of decision-makers, and at that time the State Department's European section, many of whose experts did understand (and even like) the Germans, was woefully understaffed.[18] This information shortage, which caused a sensitivity gap, had serious short-term and even long-term effects on relations between America and the people of West Berlin and West Germany.

For years, the Western governments and media had poured scorn on the bogus Communist regime in the East, promoted the legitimacy of German reunification, and emphasised West Berlin's integral importance to the German nation. And now? To the disgust of the West Berliners, the sealing of the border – an obvious first step towards the final division of Germany – was greeted by cowardly silence on the part of the Western Allies, especially the Americans.

Secretary Rusk was personally responsible for the failure of the Western commandants to issue a formal protest on Sunday 13 August.

After their meeting with Mayor Brandt, the three Allied commanders in Berlin weighed up their options, in the presence of their military and civilian advisers. They discussed the wording of a strong statement that might be sent to Marshal Konev's headquarters in Berlin-Karlshorst. The French commander, General Lacomme, then decided, to the exasperation of his colleagues, that he could not sign such a direct protest without consulting his government. With the French Foreign Ministry all but closed for August, like the rest of Paris, and the minister himself, the aristocratic M. Couve de Merville, absent on vacation, this promised to be a lengthy process.

By the afternoon, however, the commandants had agreed on a basic text that they felt could be issued in the form of a press release. This would represent an indirect protest only, without mention of counter-measures, but it would give an early signal of solidarity with the West Berliners, just hours after the East German action, and would therefore be better than nothing. Lacomme agreed that he could go this far without recourse to his ministerial boss. The drafting of the press release began.

At this point, Ambassador Foy Kohler, Special Assistant to Dean Rusk for European Affairs, rang up from Washington and asked to speak with Allan Lightner. Although the line was an open one, and the call was therefore assuredly the subject of a Soviet/East German wiretap operation, they discussed events. Lightner mentioned almost as an afterthought that the Allied commandants planned to release to the press a general statement criticising the Soviets' and East Germans' outrageous activities. The minimum they could decently do, pending instructions.

Kohler asked Lightner to read the statement out over the line. America's most powerful civilian representative in Berlin duly did so, for the benefit of Washington – and almost certainly the *Stasi* and the KGB. When he had finished, Kohler paused. 'The Secretary is right here,' he told Lightner in his gentle but insistent Ohioan tones. 'Let me tell him about it.'

Lightner waited out a long, 3,000-mile silence. Finally Kohler returned. 'I have strict instructions for you, Al, *not* to issue anything in Berlin,' he said. 'You can't go ahead on this thing. Anything that's going to be said on this issue has to come from the capitals. As a matter of fact, we'll get something out ourselves this afternoon.'[19]

That 'something' was the super-cautious State Department press release. After authorising this, Rusk left the State Department to attend a baseball game.[20]

It is difficult to see why, apart from a control-freakish desire for first expression, Rusk's more or less meaningless statement took precedence over an announcement by Allied representatives in Berlin. An informal protest on the part of the commandants, however non-binding and ultimately unthreatening, would have had the virtue of coming from officials who exercised military and political power on the spot, and might therefore have had a positive influence on West Berliners' morale.

The result of Washington's reluctance to commit would be a slow-burning outrage in both West Berlin and West Germany.

If the Western Allies swallowed this, the Germans' reasoning went, what would they not swallow? It was a genuinely concerned question, which demanded a genuine and straight answer.

How to supply that answer?

The Berliners were fortunate that during that weekend help was at hand, in the shape of a very distinguished American opinion-former, Edward R. Murrow.

Fifty-three-year-old Murrow was America's most famous broadcast reporter of the age, celebrated for his reports for CBS from beleaguered London in 1940 and for his war reporting from the European front after the D-Day landings. He had allowed himself to be poached by Kennedy earlier in 1961 for the directorship of the powerful United States Information Agency, spearhead of America's Cold War information and propaganda offensive. Since assuming office, Murrow had travelled extensively to outposts of his worldwide information empire. On Saturday 12 August, the great broadcaster happened to arrive at his latest stop, Berlin.

Conspiracy theorists have since claimed that Murrow's presence was no coincidence, that it 'proved' the West – or at least the United States – had been forewarned of the sealing-off of the border. Somehow, the theory goes, the whole project had its origins in a secret compact between the American administration and the Soviet dictatorship, to create stability in Central Europe at the Germans' expense. Why else would America's foremost propagandist arrive at exactly that time, except to mastermind a propaganda smokescreen that would conceal the truth about Washington's betrayal of Berlin?

The theory does not fit, as the actual events clearly show. Murrow's host was the director of the American-backed RIAS radio station, Robert H. Lochner. Lochner had spent the whole night of 12–13 August back in his old journalistic role, observing events in East and West Berlin. Arriving, exhausted, back at RIAS headquarters, he picked up Murrow. They debated whether to change their plans for the day. Lochner had planned to invite an East Berlin student of his acquaintance to lunch, to give Murrow an 'inside' view of things 'over there'. With the border closed, this was no longer possible. Moreover, a cocktail reception had been arranged for Sunday evening, at which the recently appointed USIA chief would get the chance to meet local broadcasters and media personalities, and military and civil officials. Should they proceed with what seemed like a mere social frippery?

It was decided that the reception should go ahead as planned. Any sense of 'fiddling while Rome burned' would be more than compensated for by the useful contacts Murrow would make. And in any case, why should Walter Ulbricht come between Americans and their cocktails?

Meanwhile, Lochner took Murrow first to see the border-sealing process from the Western side – and also the crowds of angry, frustrated West Berliners. Then they crossed into East Berlin:

> We went first to the Brandenburg Gate on the Western side and we went to the then still-existing rear wing of the famous Adlon Hotel, which is right next to the Brandenburg Gate and in there with the windows open we heard the noise of the hammers pressing the door, the street open, making a tremendous noise, and the angry shouts of the hundreds of West Berliners who were confronting them. And drinking warm, lousy East Berlin beer, Murrow reminisced a little about the many times before the war that he'd been in Berlin as a correspondent.[21]

For the two 'Americans on the spot', it was a busy afternoon. They later dropped by the home of the powerful German newspaper magnate, Axel Springer, a grand villa on the Bernadottestrasse in Wilmersdorf. Springer's tabloid *Bild* was the largest-selling newspaper in the country and a powerful mouthpiece for post-Nazi conservatism.

Springer was critical of America's passivity. 'You'll have to clear away the barricades,' he asserted. 'I'll guarantee that the Russians will accept it.' According to Lochner, the USIA director seemed shaken by Springer's words.[22]

Murrow was now convinced that he must alert America to the situation in Berlin. He called his deputy at USIA, Donald M. Wilson, in Washington and exhorted him to crank up the message on the border closure. The world should know how ugly this business was, and soon.

Wilson complied – Murrow was the boss, after all – though like many others he still guessed that the measures were temporary. He was, however, struck by the passion that crackled down the transatlantic line. Murrow was usually unflappably professional in his judgements and behaviour.

Lochner asserts that Murrow also contacted the White House. Slipping away from the party at the High Commission, Murrow spoke with Kennedy from the phone in Lightner's bedroom. He impressed on the President the seriousness of the situation. Not the danger of war so much, but the devastating impact that Western inactivity was having on West Berlin's morale. Perhaps Murrow's vivid, reporter's analysis helped Kennedy to understand that he had to take firmer, or at least more definite, measures than Rusk and the State Department people had so far countenanced.[23]

All this would have been early Sunday afternoon in Hyannis Port, just after Kennedy had finished his round of phone calls with other members of the administration and had approved the (to many in Berlin) feeble initial response to the sector-border closure.

Meanwhile, three and a half thousand miles away, the reception at the US High Commission in Berlin continued. More news kept pouring in all the time. More protests at the border. A major speech by Mayor Brandt. The hurried arrival from Bonn of a key political ally of Chancellor Adenauer, West German Parliamentary President Eugen Gerstenmaier. Lochner was approached by a senior West German intelligence official, with whom he was on friendly terms. The man was seriously upset. He drew Lochner into a corner. 'Isn't it incredible?' he wailed. 'Our secret services are so lousy that we had no inkling of this coming on!'

Mayor Brandt had spent the afternoon touring the sector border. At 6.30 p.m., he addressed the West Berlin city parliament. After reciting with great precision and in full detail all the ways in which the East Germans' action in sealing off East Berlin gratuitously transgressed against existing agreements, he called for urgent Western action to reverse these illegal acts. He referred to 'powers of darkness' and to 'the barrier fence of a concentration camp' that was being erected through the heart of the city. He requested Allied reinforcements for the beleaguered half-city he ruled. The mayor called, in effect, for moves that would show the East that America took what was happening seriously, and that the West meant business. None the less, Brandt also called for restraint from his own population. No provocations. No giving the enemy excuses to become even more blatant in their outrages.[24]

Brandt's speech was that of a passionate politician and a great leader-in-the-making. He expressed the Berliners' fury and pain, while at the same time channelling their feelings away from futile revenge. It was, however, also the speech of a man with very little actual power. As a mere mayor, words remained his only weapon.

Kennedy was said to have been irritated by the speech as it was summarised to him in his next 'check-list'. 'Look at this!' the President bristled, reading Brandt's demands. 'Who does he think he is?'[25]

Monday 14 August dawned. The Eastern side of the sector border still teemed with East German military might. The big anxiety, for the Ulbricht regime, was that large numbers of 'border-crossers' might attempt to flood across into the West. For whatever reason, they didn't. The numbers sneaking across the border through thinly guarded areas and as yet unblockaded features such as canals and lakes amounted, by comparison with what the Communists had feared, to a mere trickle.

Back in Washington from the Cape, Kennedy conferred with his aides. General Maxwell Taylor, the President's recently appointed liaison with the chiefs of staff, was opposed even to a reinforcement of the Berlin garrison. In strict military terms, he may have been right, but Berlin was not strictly or even mainly a military crisis. The morning wore on, but no practical measures were decided. There was vague talk of flag-showing activities, but the administration continued to veto statements by the American commandant. The President, although swayed by Murrow's dramatic report from Berlin, was still concerned that no one on the other side of the Atlantic should be allowed to force his hand.

In a way, this was understandable. As Egon Bahr, Brandt's press secretary, would later comment, the reality remained one of 'big Kennedy and little Brandt'.

And 'big Kennedy' was perfectly clear where he stood, despite Murrow's warnings and the 'Berlin Mafia's' pleas. Kenneth P. O'Donnell, a major figure in the Boston-Irish political establishment and now 'special assistant' to the President, heard the President's conclusions at the end of his first morning back in the Oval Office. Kennedy asked,

> 'Why would Khrushchev put up a wall if he really intended to seize Berlin? There wouldn't be a need of a wall if he occupied the whole city. This is his way out of his predicament. It's not a very nice solution, but a wall is a hell of a lot better than a war.'
>
> He leaned back in his chair and tapped his teeth with his fingers, the way he always did when he was reflecting. And then he said: 'This is the end of the Berlin crisis. The other side panicked – not we. We're going to do nothing now because there is no alternative except war. It's all over, they're not going to overrun Berlin.'[26]

The President's conclusion was pure, cold *realpolitik*.

The British were even less inclined to let the Germans dictate policy. On 14 August Sir Christopher Steel, Her Britannic Majesty's ambassador to West Germany, cabled London to cast doubt on the West Germans government's response to the sealing of the border. They had declared it a Soviet/East German plot to gobble up West Berlin, a view that was, Steel said, 'at variance with the obvious facts of the situation'. 'The Federal Government,' Steel wrote to his masters in London, 'are not really interested in reunification and their attitude is all politics.' He continued:

> I must say that I personally have always wondered that the East Germans have waited so long to seal this boundary. I think that hitherto it has been the fear of West German and Allied sanctions which stopped them doing so (as last winter) but the cumulative defections of the past month have forced them to action. I should think that in any settlement it would be almost impossible for us to re-establish a situation where East Germans are more or less free to leave the Communist world at will. We ought really, therefore, to get together with the Americans as soon as possible – albeit cautiously – to ensure that they, no more than we, regard this as the issue on which we break.[27]

The British ambassador's dry scepticism reflected the views of diplomats and politicians throughout the Western world. The East was not out to swallow Berlin. It was out to rearrange the situation there to its advantage, and in particular to secure East Berlin. As long as this was all the East did, the Allies would undertake no military counter-measures. The only exception, for the moment, was the French, who had their own fish to fry. Though Paris took an unenthusiastic, even hostile, view of German reunification, it was none the less keen to prise West Germany from the USA's embrace and bind it in a French alliance. Appearing to support a 'hard line' on Berlin was a cost-free way for de Gaulle to pile up brownie points in Bonn.

All the same, time was passing, and doing absolutely nothing was not an option. In Berlin itself, there was increasing popular outrage in the Western sectors. Demonstrations continued. The German popular press began to turn restless and critical.

Possibly with Murrow's encouragement,[28] Willy Brandt decided to make direct contact with the President of the United States. He must, he decided, make clear to the most powerful man in the Western world what was at stake. Brandt told Egon Bahr to draft a letter to Kennedy.

The problem with such a letter was twofold. First, there was the 'little Brandt and big Kennedy' dilemma. Then there was the perhaps even more important fact of the German election campaign. Brandt was running for chancellor, and a direct relationship with Kennedy would have indicated to some that the American administration favoured his candidacy.

The German hustings were, and remain, a pretty robust environment. Less than forty-eight hours after the border closure, Adenauer upped the stakes, for Brandt and by implication for Kennedy. At an election rally in Bavaria on 14 August, the old man brutally referred to the West Berlin Mayor as 'Brandt alias Frahm'.

This jibe constituted a double insult. First, it reminded his audience that Willy Brandt had been born with the name Herbert Frahm, in Lübeck, of a single mother. Second, it underlined the fact that his current name, by which the great Social Democrat leader would go down in history, was actually a *nom de guerre* acquired as a political exile in Norway. There he had worked with the local anti-Nazi resistance, returning to Germany only in the autumn of 1945, and even then wearing the uniform of a Norwegian officer. Adenauer was reminding his supporters (especially the nationalistically inclined ones) both that Brandt was born a bastard and that he was – by some interpretations – a 'traitor' who fought against Germany during the war.

The old man had decided to play hard ball. Brandt was deeply hurt, so much so that he felt constrained to abandon an evening sitting of the city parliament.[29]

Meanwhile, Bahr worked on, drafting the letter to Kennedy on behalf of his wounded and frustrated boss. With the continuing absence of any clear Allied action to oppose the 'security barriers' that the East Germans had erected, something needed to happen. At midnight on Monday, forty-eight hours after the first construction squads had moved in on the sector border, Berlin would enter its third full day as a divided city. Time was not on the side of those who wished to reverse that process.

Lochner, talking in an interview with the wisdom of hindsight, told the sad truth, both for Brandt and the 'Berlin Mafia':

At that time in our various post mortems of course we thought oh well, what could we have done? And one of the unrealistic scenarios was if we had immediately sent some tanks to remove the barbed wire – that's how the wall started out, they simply started putting barbed wire across the major thoroughfares – and immediately at the same time and publicly [we had] called the Russians and said, 'we realise that Saturday night till Sunday you had nobody on duty, so we took the liberty. Your East German henchmen are running wild here, they're clearly violating the free circulation of all of Berlin, so since we couldn't reach any of you we took the liberty on behalf of all four occupation powers to remove this silly effort to interfere with traffic.'

Well, that was theoretically possible, but no two star Generals could take such a decision. Any such decision required checking with Washington, London, Paris and Bonn – by that time, '61, you couldn't leave the Germans out. And that obviously was totally impossible within the span of a weekend. If any such measure had been taken later, that might have provoked a war or whatever, because only it could be done under this guise of actually coming to the help of the Soviets the very first night and within hours . . .[30]

Tuesday 15 August saw the working week advance. Every hour that passed without a challenge to the East German barrier spoke more loudly of its permanence.

There were more disturbances on the Western side of the border, more calls for action. Finally, there came the long-awaited note of protest from the Western commandants, delivered to their Soviet counterpart, Colonel Andrei I. Soloviev, at his headquarters by the three powers' liaison officers. It chided the East Germans for erecting an 'arbitrary barrier'. It complained that East Berlin had been turned into an 'armed camp', violating Berliners' right to free movement and employment. 'We must protest,' it concluded, 'against the illegal measures introduced on August 13 and hold you responsible for the carrying out of the relevant agreements'.

It would not have escaped Soloviev's notice that the one thing the protest did *not* contain was an ultimatum demanding the border barrier's removal.

In Washington, the Berlin Steering Group met at 10.45 EST (mid-afternoon in Germany) on 15 August. Present were the Secretaries of State, Defense, Commerce, and Agriculture, the Under-Secretary of the Treasury, the Attorney-General (Robert Kennedy) and the Director of the CIA, plus the Chairman of the Joint Chiefs of Staff, Wilson, Edward Murrow's deputy, and a clutch of the President's assistants, including Maxwell Taylor and McGeorge Bundy.

Short of an additional appearance from the President, this was about as heavyweight as a meeting got. So heavy that this one ended up muscle-bound. They discussed not how to reverse the closure of the sector border, but how to deal with the public-relations aspect. According to the minutes, Rusk was even more frank about the realities of the situation than Kennedy had been in talking to O'Donnell:

> The Secretary of State noted that while the border closing was a most serious matter, the probability was that in realistic terms it would make a Berlin settlement easier. Our immediate problem is the sense of outrage in Berlin and Germany which carries with it a feeling that we should do more than merely protest. It was not easy to know just what else we should do.[31]

'We must keep shooting issues and non-shooting issues separate,' Rusk declared.

Again, no sanctions against the Soviet Union and its allies were announced. True, at the BSG's meeting, the Secretary of Commerce had proposed that the US should publicly rule out sending subsidised food exports to Soviet-block countries (negotiations with Poland along these lines were already in progress). After discussion, however, such a statement was deemed unwise. Boycotting East Germany's great international trade window, the Leipzig Fair, was likewise ruled out. The same went for restrictions on the until now almost automatic issuing of Temporary Travel Documents (TTDs) for Easterners visiting West Berlin. The only suggested counter-measure that met with the approval of most present – though not of Secretary McNamara – was the idea of reinforcing the US garrison in Berlin. Plus a stepping-up of the propaganda offensive. Robert Kennedy in particular pressed for more forceful efforts in this area.

The world was still not even certain exactly what Ulbricht and Khrushchev were up to. At the meeting of the Berlin Steering Group the previous day, reference had been to a 'fence' rather than a wall. In the night, however, telephone contact between East and West was suddenly cut, and movement of mail restricted.

None the less, all that really occurred during the third day after the sealing-off of East Berlin was that Washington officials briefed energetically to the press. As the *New York Times* reported:

> The Kennedy administration set out today to portray East Germany's closing of the border between East and West Berlin as a dramatic confession of Communist failure.
>
> The highest officials here indicated that this would be the extent, for the time being, of the Allied response to Communist moves in Berlin. As long as Western rights of access to the divided city are respected, the officials said, protest and vigorous propaganda will be their primary form of retaliation.[32]

This was all perfectly rational. The first paragraph expressed the line originally proposed in the first, hasty cable to Pierre Salinger at Hyannis

Port the previous Sunday. The second paragraph, while engagingly frank and representing the reality of the matter, was the kind of thing that the West Germans and West Berliners were horrified to hear. Their anxiety all too easily led to a kind of prickly bewilderment that could easily tip into a peculiarly ambivalent anti-Americanism, a nervous biting of the protective hand.

Moreover, who could deny that the 'Berlin Mafia' and their German friends were in part right to be anxious? Was it not possible that the East was at heart concerned to do more than just defend itself? If one looked closely, even during these early days of Berlin's isolation, the Communists had already started to slice off some more juicy little morsels of the notorious salami.

In their original declaration of intent, issued during the small hours of Sunday, the East Germans assured the world that once the border had been 'protected', access to East Berlin would not be restricted, except for *provocateurs* and the like. None the less, within a day of 'Operation Rose', individuals had been forbidden access. On 15 August, Willy Kressmann, district mayor of Kreuzberg, attempted to drive into East Berlin and was denied entry as a potential troublemaker. This colourful Social Democrat – known as 'Texas-Willy' because during an American trip he had been made an honorary citizen of San Antonio – planned to distribute funds to 'border-crossers' who were resident in East Berlin but employed in Kreuzberg. These had been unable to collect their wages because of the border closure.[33]

There would soon be other cases. Sometimes unwelcome would-be visitors were only allowed into East Berlin on foot. The East could choose to interpret the word *provocateur* exactly as it wished.

Initially, in order to avert a violent Western response to the securing of the border, the Communists' impositions had been modest. Western chanceries had greeted this with relief and had drawn conclusions that profoundly influenced their crisis planning.

These first impressions, however, would indeed prove deceptive. There would be further challenges to West Berlin and the Allied presence. Were these steps in a ruthless, planned escalation that would see West Berlin swallowed by the GDR? Or were they merely attempts to keep the Allies permanently on the defensive in the inevitable negotiations, enabling Khrushchev to dictate from a position of strength? This was the uncertainty that began and would continue to plague decision-makers in the West for the duration of the crisis.

Willy Brandt's letter to President Kennedy arrived at the White House by cable (via Lightner at the US Mission) late on the afternoon of 16 August (Washington time). The Berlin mayor described its contents as 'personal and informal'.

Be that as it may, it was impossible for Kennedy to ignore Brandt's clear criticism of the West in general and the US government in particular.

'The illegal sovereignty of the East Berlin government,' the mayor told Kennedy, 'has been recognised by default, so far as the limitation in the number of crossing points and the restriction in access to the Eastern sector is concerned.' He wrote of 'inactivity and pure defensiveness' on the part of the Allies, which could lead to a crisis of confidence among West Berliners, and 'to an exaggerated self-confidence in the East Berlin regime, which already today is boasting in its newspapers of the success of its demonstration of military might'. The East had achieved the first part of its plan, to isolate and cut off West Berlin. Now the second step was only a matter of time, in which the island city would become an isolated 'ghetto'. If that happened, then instead of people fleeing to West Berlin, they could begin to flee from it. The Soviet Union should stand accused before the United Nations, on the West's initiative. Moreover, the three Western occupying powers should abandon the fiction of four-power rule and guarantee West Berlin's freedom and security formally without reference to the Russians.

Brandt's sharpest words came from the knowledge that, after refusing so long to talk to Khrushchev about his plans for a peace treaty, the West was suddenly eager to negotiate with the East, as a direct consequence of the sealing of the sector border.

> I . . . cannot think without bitterness of those declarations that rejected negotiations with the Soviet Union on the grounds that one could not deal under duress. We now have a situation of total blackmail, and already I hear that we shall not be able to refuse to negotiate.[34]

Brandt ended up with a pointed request for reinforcements to the American garrison in Berlin as a symbol of Western determination.

It would have been a frank communication even between equal heads of state. From a municipal leader in Central Europe, however prominent, to the President of the most powerful nation on earth, it was astonishing in its boldness. Or insolence.

Brandt went even further in putting Kennedy on the spot. Addressing an enormous mass rally in front of Schöneberg Town Hall that same evening, just a few hours after Washington had started its day's work, the mayor went public on his letter to Kennedy.

'We are not afraid,' Brandt told the huge crowd. 'Today I expressed my opinion to the President of the United States, John Kennedy, in all frankness. Berlin expects more than words. Berlin expects political action!'

The applause exploded, and went on in great waves for some minutes. It was what Berliners wanted to hear. And maybe the entire West German electorate, too.

However, Kennedy's instinctive reaction was to judge Brandt's speech and letter as facets of his bid to become chancellor of West Germany. Since he first drew breath, the President had lived and thrived in the ruthless atmosphere of Boston politics, where any event, however tragic, was fair political fuel. 'That bastard from Berlin', he declared, had decided to use the border tragedy as an electoral ploy.[35] At America's expense.

That Brandt was acting, in the broadest sense, as a politician, there can be no doubt. Running for the highest office in the land, he wanted to show he could stand up for Berlin and for Germany. As West Berlin mayor, he was also aware that bad feeling, potentially anti-Western and especially anti-American, was on the increase. He needed to head it off. It would not be the first time in the history of democracy that a politician harboured multiple motivations for a necessary act.

The Berlin press, moreover, was starting to turn nasty. Axel Springer had insisted to Murrow on the afternoon of 13 August that the East would back down if the West rolled back the barbed wire. The press magnate was obviously displeased that the Allies had ignored his advice. That morning, 16 August, Springer's *Bild* ran a banner headline attacking Western inaction. 'The West does nothing!' the front page bellowed. 'President Kennedy stays silent . . . Macmillan goes hunting . . . and Adenauer hurls abuse at Brandt.' Another paper claimed that Marshall Konev had warned the Allied commandants about the coming border restrictions before 13 August. This was immediately denied, but the rumour found plenty of credence among anxious, increasingly disillusioned West Berliners.

So, Brandt had to channel all this negativity and frustration, neutralise its effects. His speech must be seen as a high-wire performance that, at least so far as his immediate aims were concerned, succeeded triumphantly.

Whether Brandt also understood the effect that his letter and his speech might have on the White House is still not clear. He was encouraged to send the letter, not just by his German colleagues, but by Allen Lightner and Ed Murrow, the latter having acquired temporary membership of the 'Berlin Mafia'. The air had to be cleared, the city's plight presented in stark terms that would shake official Washington from its August torpor. He would probably have sent the letter anyway, even had he been able to predict the President's displeasure. Willy Brandt might occasionally have lacked judgement, but he was never short of courage.

Kennedy's reply to Brandt arrived a little less than forty-eight hours later. It was wrapped up in a much more dramatic exercise of power. The American leader's letter was hand-delivered to Brandt by Vice-President Lyndon Johnson, who by way of further reinforcement was in turn accompanied, on the President's order, by one of the great figures of the immediate post-war period: the former Governor of the American Zone of Germany, General Lucius Dubignon Clay.

The idea of yoking Johnson, the low-born Texas career politician, with the aristocratic army general from Georgia (son of a US senator), in a grand public gesture over Berlin, seems to have been floating around even before Brandt's letter arrived in Washington.

'LBJ', the renowned congressional horse-trader, and Clay, the renowned American war-horse, were personally and politically about as unlike as could be imagined. Clay, concealing his toughness beneath a low-key, polite façade, was also, politically, a lifelong Republican; Johnson was rough-mannered and extrovert, a combative New Deal Democrat from the first hour. Talk at the Steering Group meeting on 15 August of a military figure may have seemed vague, but in fact there is reason to believe that the 'drafting' of Clay was already under way. It may even have *preceded* the selection of Vice-President Johnson.

Eyewitness testimony from the time indicates that the 'Berlin Mafia' played a crucial role in engineering this move in the crisis. Influential journalists James O'Donnell and Marguerite Higgins, both fiercely anti-Communist old 'Berlin hands' now living in Washington, seem to have concocted the idea as early as Monday 14 August. Higgins lived near Clay and knew him well. Her husband, General William Hall, had served as General Clay's Air Intelligence Officer in the post-war period and they remained on friendly terms. Contacting each other shortly after the news of the border closure came through, O'Donnell and Higgins regretted that the State Department 'appeasers' seemed to have control of the situation.

How to provide a counterweight, someone who might turn the situation their way? Higgins had already discussed things on the telephone with Clay, and knew that he shared her distrust of the State Department. She suggested to O'Donnell that the general could be their man. After talking with O'Donnell, Higgins called Clay again; he agreed to volunteer for a mission to Berlin if the administration could be persuaded of its usefulness. Finally, Higgins spoke with Robert Kennedy. RFK accepted the idea in principal but was concerned that Clay represented a leftover from the Eisenhower era. This may have been when the idea of sending Johnson with him, to provide political balance, fell into place. Certainly by Wednesday, the teaming of these two powerful, charismatic men was being actively pursued.

The crucial session of the Berlin Steering Group, on the morning of 17 August, was attended by the President. It agreed on a combined trip to Berlin by Johnson and Clay. It also approved the almost inevitable strengthening of the American garrison in Berlin. This would involve withdrawing a battle group (1,500–1,800 men) from the Army's 8th Division, based near Frankfurt.[36] The detachment to go to Berlin would also include a battery of 105mm. Howitzers, the first artillery force – an essentially fighting rather than a mere occupation unit – to be sent through Soviet-controlled territory since 1945.[37]

Both the President's decisions were opposed from within the military-governmental apparatus by powerful voices. Senior officers – contrary to the cliché – showed themselves to be ultra-cautious in the sudden crisis, rather than warmongering. Generals Norstad and Maxwell Taylor continued to see any raising of the American military profile in response to the sector-border closure as potentially provocative and therefore dangerous. As for the plan to send Johnson, Norstad sounded just like a State Department 'dove'. He cabled the Chief of Staff, General Lemnitzer:

> The delivery of the President's reply to the Brandt letter by the hands of the hero of the Berlin crisis of an earlier day, General Lucius Clay, would appear to me to be a brilliant stroke; but to add to this the great stature of the Vice President would be overdoing it, and would run the risk of exciting great expectations in West Berlin and possibly also among the unhappy East Germans. This is a big gun which we may need and need badly in the weeks and months to come.[38]

But finally someone was present at a meeting who knew really Berlin and was aware of the fragility of the Berliners' morale. David E. Murphy was a senior CIA man who just weeks earlier had returned to the US after years as Deputy Director and then Director of Berlin Operations Base. He had been summoned to Washington from home leave in San Francisco.

Recognising a potential member of the 'Berlin Mafia' when he saw one, the President warned Murphy that he was interested exclusively in hearing about morale in West Berlin. 'Our writ does not run to East Berlin,' he told the CIA man. The border closure itself was not up for discussion. This must be accepted as *fait accompli*. Thirty years later, Murphy would recall his advice to Kennedy:

> The problem, I explained, was one of West Berliners' perceptions. Although they realized that since 1948 there was little the Allies could do to counter Soviet and East German actions in East Berlin, in essence Berlin remained for them one city. East Berliners could shop and attend

Victor and vanquished – Berlin, August 1945

The Blockade – coming in to land at Tempelhof, 1948

Stones against tanks, 17 June 1953

The Kurfürstendamm,
West Berlin, 1960

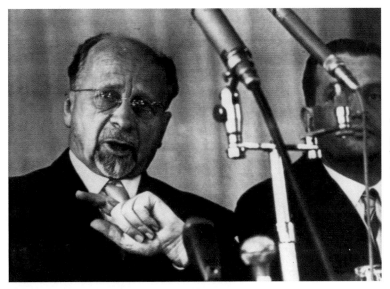

'No one intends to build a wall,' Walter Ulbricht, 15 June 1961

Exhausted refugees, Marienfelde reception camp, July 1961

The first hours – border troops on the Potsdamer Platz, 13 August 1961

Building the Wall, August 1961

East German Workers' Militiamen, 14 August 1961

Families divided,
August 1961

Families flee, Bernauer
Strasse, August 1961

Conrad Schumann
jumps the wire,
15 August 1961

A 77-year-old East Berliner
caught in a tug of war
between *Vopos* at the
window and West Berliners
below, Bernauer Strasse,
24 September 1961

General Clay (*left*), Vice-President Johnson (*centre*) and Mayor Brandt (*right*), 20 August 1961

Berliners welcome
US reinforcements,
20 August 1961

Götz Bergander, at the Reichstag, 1960

Bergander's fiancée, Regine, West Berlin, 1960

East German refugee
Joachim Trenkner in
his new 'Bubble Car',
summer 1961

US troops escort American officials into the East at Checkpoint Charlie, October 1961

A *Vopo* searches a tunnel, January 1962

High noon in the Friedrichstrasse, 28 October 1961

'Freedom Train' driver Harry Deterling and family, December 1961

Peter Fechter
dying at the Wall,
17 August 1962

President Kennedy (*fourth from left*) in Berlin, June 1963

Vopos patrol a cemetery by the Wall, 1963

Cracks in the Wall, 1966

Everyday terror – the Wall in the 1980s

Competitive building (West): Axel Springer's headquarters, right beside the Wall, with Peter Fechter memorial (*foreground*)

Competitive building (East): Karl-Marx-Allee (formerly Stalinallee) with television tower (*left background*) and Hotel Stadt Berlin under construction (*right background*)

'Little' Honecker and 'Big' Kohl,
Bonn, September 1987

The Brandenburg Gate, 1980s

The end of the Wall, November 1989

the theater in West Berlin while relatives and friends in both sectors exchanged regular visits. Whereas over the years there had been frequent crackdowns at border-crossing points, the actual closure of 13 August came as a deep emotional shock. This shock, plus the perception of Western inaction, caused many to fear that the Allies intended gradually to withdraw their protection from West Berlin. Thus, it seemed essential that steps be taken to restore confidence and rekindle the spirit of the West Berliners.[39]

This cool, measured contribution from Murphy seemed to crystallise resolve. The President's mind was made up. He would send Clay and Johnson to Berlin, and reinforce the garrison there without delay, sending this force along the road route through East Germany.

Kennedy's decision indicated that he had moved away from the passive, safety-first attitude promoted by some in both the State Department and the military, and shifted towards a measured show of determination, though still of a largely symbolic sort. To those who criticised the 'aggressive' tactic of reinforcing the garrison, Clay himself would retort that sending a force of 1,500 men, bringing the Allied garrison in West Berlin up to around 12,000, could not possibly indicate a plan to attack the Soviet/East German forces exceeding a quarter of a million that surrounded the city. Not even the most skilful Communist propagandist could make that accusation stick.

By late on 17 August the Johnson-Clay mission was a reality. Kennedy invited Marguerite Higgins into the White House for an informal briefing the next morning, and smilingly told her, 'I have good news for you. Not only have we decided to send General Clay to Berlin; we are sending the Vice-President too'.

Actually, the President's revelation came as no surprise to the formidably well-informed *Herald Tribune* columnist. She had been at dinner the previous evening with Clay, Vice-President Johnson, and Sam Rayburn, a Texan congressman and Johnson confidant, when LBJ was called to the phone to get his marching orders from the White House. Johnson was not pleased. Unfamiliar with foreign policy and no great traveller, he not only doubted the usefulness of his mission, but complained: 'There'll be a lot of shooting, and I'll be in the middle of it. Why me?'[40] After dinner resumed, all the persuasive powers of his companions, especially his old ally Rayburn, had been required before Johnson accepted the presidential command with something like good grace.[41]

On 18 August, Kennedy's note to Brandt was duly entrusted to General Clay, with instructions that it must not be made public.

This was understandable. The note would not have assuaged the populace of West Berlin or West Germany. The President's answer to the mayor's plea was polite and superficially positive, but Kennedy coolly refused every concrete action that Brandt asked for — except the reinforcement of the Berlin garrison, which had been already agreed in Washington. So, no three-power status for West Berlin, no appeal to the UN, no economic or military sanctions. And where Brandt had referred to the American as 'friends', in Kennedy's reply the West Berliners were 'partners':

Dear Mayor Brandt:

I have read with great care your personal informal letter of August 16th and I want to thank you for it. In these testing days it is important for us to be in close touch. For this reason I am sending my answer by the hand of Vice President Johnson. He comes with General Clay, who is well known to Berliners; and they have my authority to discuss our problems in full frankness with you.

The measures taken by the Soviet Government and its puppets in East Berlin have caused revulsion here in America. This demonstration of what the Soviet Government means by freedom for a city, and peace for a people, proves the hollowness of Soviet pretensions; and Americans understand that this action necessarily constitutes a special blow to the people of West Berlin, connected as they remain in a myriad of ways to their fellow Berliners in the eastern sector. So I understand entirely the deep concerns and sense of trouble which prompted your letter.

Grave as this matter is, however, there are, as you say, no steps available to us which can force a significant material change in this present situation. Since it represents a resounding confession of failure and of political weakness, this brutal border closing evidently represents a basic

Soviet decision which only war could reverse. Neither you nor we, nor any of our Allies, have ever supposed that we should go to war on this point.

Yet the Soviet action is too serious for inadequate responses. My own objection to most of the measures which have been proposed – even to most of the suggestions in your own letter – is that they are mere trifles compared to what has been done. Some of them, moreover, seem unlikely to be fruitful even in their own terms. This is our present judgment, for example, on the question of an immediate appeal to the United Nations, although we shall continue to keep this possibility under lively review.

On careful consideration I myself have decided that the best immediate response is a significant reinforcement of the Western garrisons. The importance of this reinforcement is symbolic – but not symbolic only. We know that the Soviet Union continues to emphasize its demand for the removal of Allied protection from West Berlin. We believe that even a modest reinforcement will underline our rejection of this concept.

At the same time, and of even greater basic importance, we shall continue and accelerate the broad build-up of the military strength of the West upon which we are decided, and which we view as the necessary answer to the long-range Soviet threat to Berlin and to us all.

Within Berlin, in the immediate affairs of the city, there may be other specific appropriate steps to take. These we shall review as rapidly and sympathetically as possible, and I hope you will be sure to express your own views on such measures clearly to Vice President Johnson and his party. Actions which effectively demonstrate our continued commitment to freedom in Berlin will have our support.

I have considered with special care your proposal of a three-power status for West Berlin. My judgment is that a formal proclamation of such a status would imply a weakening of the four-power relationship on which our opposition to the border-closing depends. Whatever may be the immediate prospects, I do not believe that we should now take so double-edged a step. I do agree that the guarantees which we have pledged to West Berlin should be continuously affirmed and reaffirmed, and this we are doing. Moreover, I support your proposal of an appropriate plebiscite demonstrating the continuing conviction of West Berlin that its destiny is freedom in connection with the West.

More broadly, let me urge it upon you that we must not be shaken by

Soviet actions which in themselves are a confession of weakness. West Berlin today is more important than ever, and its mission to stand for freedom has never been so important as now. The link of West Berlin to the Free World is not a matter of rhetoric. Important as the ties to the East have been, painful as is their violation, the life of the city, as I understand it, runs primarily to the West – its economic life, its moral basis, and its military security. You may wish to consider and to suggest concrete ways in which these ties might be expanded in a fashion that would make the citizens of West Berlin more actively conscious of their role, not merely as an outpost of freedom, but as a vital part of the Free World and all its enterprises. In this double mission we are partners, and it is my own confidence that we can continue to rely upon each other as firmly in the future as we have in the past.

With warm personal regards,
Sincerely

John F Kennedy

Meanwhile, at the interrogation prison in the 'forbidden district' of East Berlin, young Klaus Schulz-Ladegast had just spent his first night as a bewildered captive of the *Stasi*. If he or any other persecuted East German had expected that the West would take steps to reverse what happened on 13 August, then by this morning at the latest their disappointment would have been assured.

On 18 August, before Clay and Johnson boarded their plane for Germany, the East Germans quietly began to build a solid, breeze-block obstruction between the Brandenburg Gate and the Potsdamer Platz. Its aim was clearly to reinforce and replace the barbed wire they had set up in those first hours of 'Operation Rose'. An improvised 'border closure' was about to become a permanent, impassable physical barrier through the middle of a great city, a fortification without parallel in history.

Ulbricht's men had begun to build what the whole world would soon know as the 'Berlin Wall'.

CEMENT

12

WALL GAMES

TWO DAYS AFTER THE closure of the border, a young man reported for duty on the Eastern side of the divide. Just twenty-one, Private Hagen Koch was a fresh-faced, newly married soldier in the East German army, the NVA.

Koch, born in the historic Thuringian town of Zerbst, was at that time a true believer. He had joined the SED at the age of nineteen. After completing an apprenticeship in technical drawing, he succumbed to strong peer and employer pressure and volunteered for the East German military. Due to his perceived political reliability, he was selected for the élite so-called 'Felix Dzerzhyski Guard Regiment' in Berlin – the military arm of the *Stasi*. Because of his skills in draughtsmanship, he was assigned to its mapping department.[1]

Koch's service in Berlin brought him a wife, and increased his attachment to the Communist system. Even more, it increased his resentment against young people of his own age who lived in East Berlin but worked in West Berlin – sometimes part time and at weekends. They could earn 5 marks an hour in the West, which because of the unofficial 5:1 exchange rate, gave them 25 East German marks. So, for an afternoon's work, such a 'border-crosser' could earn 100 East marks, which happened to equal an army private's entire weekly salary. The 'border-crossers' flashed their money around, wore the latest Western fashions, and mocked those like young Koch, who existed on meagre Communist pittances.

So, when the border was closed on 13 August, Private Koch supported it with enthusiasm. 'The measures' would finally settle the hash of those kids who made, to his mind, a despicable profit out of living in a heavily subsidised socialist state while working in a dog-eat-dog capitalist one. Call it fair-mindedness or call it envy.

On 12/13 August 1961, Koch had been granted a rare weekend leave. He and his bride realised something was going on during Sunday morning, when they observed the first disturbances on the border. Koch was recalled to his unit, but it was not until 15 August that he was given a job. That job would make him rather famous. Or notorious. Again, depending on your point of view.

Around dawn on Tuesday, the young private was summoned to his commander and told to report to the East-West border. The staff responsible for the border closure was carrying out an initial inspection. Koch's task would be to accompany them and 'document the state of the extension of the border fortification works on topographical maps'.[2]

Koch got a new pair of boots, for this was going to be a long walk – most of the fifty or so kilometres from Pankow-Schönholz in the north to Alt-Glienicke in the far south-east. The hardest parts were places like the Bernauer Strasse, where only the buildings sat on GDR territory, while the pavements were already in the West. But Koch persevered, painstakingly drawing his maps on a folding portable table. The survey team made good progress, sometimes ferried short distances by jeep. They had covered twenty kilometres by early afternoon. Koch's senior companions changed from section to section; but the conscientious young private with his instruments, his drawing materials and his folding table remained a constant factor.

At around three p.m., the mapping party arrived in the old centre of Berlin.

There was now barbed wire all along the Zimmerstrasse leading to the crossing point known as 'Checkpoint Charlie', which since Sunday was reserved only for foreigners. Coming from the Potsdamer Platz, the party cut down the Mauerstrasse (literally 'Wall Street', named after the eighteenth-century customs wall) and arrived at the checkpoint in time to witness a large and noisy demonstration on the West Berlin side. Koch's superiors, superior *Stasi* men as they were, took offence at the Western 'provocation'. Something had to be done.

Soon Koch found himself with new orders. The 'aggressive forces of imperialism', he was told by an officer, had to be shown the limits of their malign power. The 21-year-old picked up a can of white paint and a brush and found the exact line of the border, which followed that between the boroughs of Mitte in the East and Kreuzberg in the West.

Starting at the pharmacy on the corner of Zimmerstrasse and Friedrichstrasse, and ignoring yells and catcalls from the Western side, Koch straddled the border. Bending to his work, he painted a precise white line to show the 'imperialists' where East Berlin began. Then he marched smartly back to join the mapping party.

By the end of that long summer's day, Private Hagen Koch's task would be complete, his feet thoroughly sore, and the 'white line' he had painted at Checkpoint Charlie on 15 August 1961 would be world-famous.

Just minutes later, a couple of kilometres to the north, another guardian of the GDR's borders was carrying out his duties. Corporal Conrad Schumann stood just inside East Berlin, on the corner of Bernauer Strasse and Ruppiner Strasse, facing a jeering group of West Berliners. In parts of Bernauer Strasse, concrete slabs had been positioned to block escape routes, but at this time nothing more formidable than a three-feet-high roll of barbed wire stood between this inexperienced, unhappy young child of the SED state and the Western 'enemy'.

Schumann, a nineteen-year-old Saxon fresh from NCO training school, had been drafted into the élite 'Readiness Police' and was one of 4,000 provincials who had volunteered for transfer to Berlin. When his unit first arrived just a few days earlier, he had been shocked to find that they were regarded with suspicion by East Berliners. Schumann remained in a confused and uneasy state, unsettled by the border closure and the ensuing events.

'The people were swearing at us,' Schumann explained later.

> We felt we were simply doing our duty but were getting scolded from all sides. The West Berliners yelled at us and the Eastern demonstrators yelled at us. We stood in the middle . . . For a young person, it was terrible.[3]

Schumann's discomfort was all too apparent. The young East German NCO was standing against a house wall, his machine-pistol slung over his shoulder. He chain-smoked, glancing occasionally in the direction of the Western protesters, mostly young men of his own age. They could read the doubt and indecision written on his face. Some stopped abusing him and started encouraging him to desert. 'Come over!' they called out. 'Come over!'

A rookie photojournalist from Hamburg, Peter Leibing – a year older than Schumann and in Berlin for less than twenty-four hours – was also watching.

'I had him in my sights for more than hour,' Leibing recalled. 'I had a feeling he was going to jump. It was kind of an instinct.'[4]

The urging from the Western side grew louder. A West Berlin police car drove up and stood with its rear door open and its engine racing. 'Come over! Come over!'

Schumann suddenly tossed away his cigarette and ran for the wire, casting aside his heavy weapon as he reached the barrier and jumped for the Western side.

Leibing's famous photograph – taken, ironically, with an East German Exacta camera – immortalises that extraordinary moment. The helmeted and jackbooted Schumann is captured in mid-leap atop the barbed wire, his young face immobile with concentration, symbolically overcoming this artificial and inhumane division and yet, for those of us who still look at the picture, frozen for ever between East and West.

'I had learned how to do it at the Jump Derby in Hamburg,' Leibing explained. 'You have to photograph the horse when it leaves the ground and catch it as it clears the barrier. And then he came. I pressed the shutter and it was all over.'

It is the picture of a lifetime, taken right at the beginning of a young photographer's career. All the more remarkable because his camera had no motor-drive. It was the only image Leibing had time to shoot.

Within hours the photograph appeared on the front of page of *Bild*. It found its way into scores of newspapers throughout the world and remains an iconic image.

Less famous – though in its way more revealing – is the photograph Leibing took of young Schumann once he got out of the police car in West Berlin. Bare-headed and with his collar loosened, Schumann looks suddenly like a bewildered small-town teenager, a little frightened and shocked at his own temerity and the attention it has suddenly brought him in a world he doesn't yet understand.

The two images gave the world two views of the GDR's youthful servants. One, the obedient Private Koch, 'drawing the line' of history; the other of the reluctant dissident, Corporal Schumann, who crossed it in one great, eternally remembered 'leap to freedom'.

All Schumann ever said, then or later, was that he hadn't wanted to shoot anyone. Going West was a way of avoiding a moral dilemma. Western interrogators were astonished at how poorly prepared the East German *Vopos* were from a psychological point of view. Schumann was the first 'deserter' but by no means the last. During these first thirty-six hours, nine more border guards would flee to the West, jumping the wire, crawling under it, or in one case scaling a factory wall.

Koch, by contrast, never had to worry about the kind of stuff that disturbed soldiers on the 'sharp end'. He was a privileged 'back-room' type, who spent the rest of that afternoon – while the bewildered Schumann was adjusting to a double-edged fame in the West – travelling onward, by boat and foot and jeep to the southernmost limit of the sector border. His main concern was resting his blistered feet, the result of taking that long, long hike in his smart (but tight) new boots.

The result of the inspection tour in which Koch took part was to define the border, and the result of that definition was the building of a more permanent structure, the so-called 'extension of the military engineering measures'.

At 1.30 a.m. in the morning of Friday 18 August, six crane trucks arrived on Potsdamer Platz, Berlin's Piccadilly Circus or Columbus Circle, south of the Brandenburg Gate. They unloaded dozens of concrete slabs of the kind hitherto used at checkpoints to control traffic. Some forty minutes later, a column of fire engines, concrete mixers, and a 'work brigade' of bricklayers arrived. Guarded by *Vopos*, they began to build a barrier across the entire square. Shortly after five, as dawn broke, they withdrew, leaving a concrete wall topped by two rows of cavity blocks, altogether just over five feet high, topped by metal staples suitable for the threading of barbed wire. At one point, this Wall (it feels legitimate to capitalise it from now on) ran inches from an entrance to the Potsdamer

Platz subway station, one of the few on the Western side. West Berlin
police and early commuters watched in astonishment.

Of course, the big station below the Potsdamer Platz was closed,
though subway trains still passed through without stopping on a line
that emerged from West Berlin, going north through East Berlin, and
then went back into the West again. Passengers noticed armed and
uniformed *Trapos* on the underground platforms. No civilians were to be
seen. The other former trans-sector subway line through Potsdamer Platz,
running West to East, was now truncated in the East and started at Otto-
Grotewohl-Strasse.[5] It ended on the Western side at Gleisdreieck, a few
hundred metres short of where it would once have crossed the sector
boundary or – before 1945 – crossed no meaningful boundary at all.

So the lifelines of old Berlin were cut. Hagen Koch's white line, a piece
of local defiance by a keen Communist officer, was like the indicator
mark for a surgical operation. It told the world that the nerve network of
a great city, which carried buses and trains, sewers and telephone lines,
was to be sliced, snipped and capped.

Berlin was a city of steel, stone, brick and wood. It was not alive in the
literal sense, so it could not bleed or feel pain. But its people lived, and
they felt intensely.

The day after a Wall first appeared across Potsdamer Platz, President
Kennedy's high-level representatives arrived in West Berlin.

Forty-eight hours before, Vice-President Johnson had been sitting in a
restaurant in Washington, bitterly bemoaning attempts to wrench him
from his familiar political habitat. Now the tough Texan was landing at
Tempelhof Airport in an airforce Lockheed Constellation on the afternoon of Saturday 19 August 1961, bracing himself to play a game in
which an extraordinary variety of roles was demanded of him: protector
and admonisher, idealist and realist, cheerleader and diplomat.

The Vice-President and General Clay had first flown across the
Atlantic in a Boeing 707. They were accompanied by a high-powered
State Department party that included Charles Bohlen and various high-
ups from the German Department (including Frank Cash and Karl
Mautner) plus Johnson's press assistant, George Reedy, and Jay Gildner
of the US Information Agency. There were also some young women,

inducted at Johnson's insistence for stenographic purposes, and a press party that included Marguerite Higgins. The 'Berlin Mafia' was strongly represented.[6]

The story went that the normally quite reticent Clay spent the trip telling stories about his experiences in 'beating' Stalin during the blockade and emphasising how tough they had to be with Russians now, just as they had been then. If Truman had allowed him to send an armoured column down the autobahn in '48, then the whole airlift wouldn't have been necessary. In fact, they could probably have avoided the Korean War into the bargain. If, Clay maintained, he were president, he would tear the Wall down right away. And, just as in 1948 'Chip' Bohlen had opposed fighting for Berlin, so now, in the cabin of the 707, he interjected that this sounded to him like a pretty good way to start World War Three. *Plus ça change* . . .

Unusually for Johnson, he did a lot of listening during that journey.[7]

They didn't fly directly to Berlin. Protocol considerations and 1960s technical limitations demanded a stopover at the Bonn/Cologne Airport. Here they were received by the American ambassador, Mr Dowling, and the West German Foreign Minister, Dr Heinrich von Brentano. This group accompanied them into Bonn, the modest university town where the West German government had been housed since 1949. There would be discussions and lunch with Chancellor Adenauer.[8]

The time since 13 August had not been Adenauer's finest hour. Far from leaping on a plane to Berlin, the Chancellor had merely carried on with his duties and his election speeches. Some of the public had started to ask why he hadn't visited Berlin in its hour of need. By way of contrast, since 13 August Brandt had achieved an uncomfortable amount of television and press exposure. Almost a week after the border was closed, Adenauer was finally persuaded by his aides that he had been a little lax on the Berlin issue, and that this might affect his poll numbers.

In the light of his recent realisation, what Adenauer really wanted was a lift in the Vice-President's plane to Berlin, a political coup that would enable him to score some points over the photogenic West Berlin Mayor. Adenauer was, naturally enough, too proud to ask outright for such a favour, and so chancellery aides had already been in touch with the US embassy about the lift-to-Berlin issue.

The possibility of such a request had been discussed in Washington, and the answer decided upon in advance. It was 'no'. To say 'yes' would risk appearing to take sides in the election. During the previous contest, Eisenhower's Republican administration had indeed expressed support for Adenauer's conservative CDU, souring relations with the SPD. President Kennedy had no intention of repeating such an elementary diplomatic mistake.

It was not until the very end of lunch that 'Chip' Bohlen was detailed to break the bad news, via Foreign Minister Brentano. Adenauer accepted the refusal in his habitual impassive manner. But he proved in no hurry to let Johnson depart. Clay had to muscle in on an 'unscheduled after-lunch conversation' between Adenauer and Johnson with the plea that 'there are a lot of Berliners waiting for us'.[9]

The Vice-President and General Clay must, it had been decided, land at Tempelhof Airport. This was in the American sector, close to the Mayor's headquarters at Schöneberg Town Hall, and had heroic associations with the airlift. However, the runway at Tempelhof was too short to receive the 707 in which they had crossed the Atlantic. The American party was therefore split up for the fairly short trip from Bonn to Berlin. The heavyweights flew to Tempelhof in a turbo-prop Constellation while the other ranks re-embarked on the 707, landing at Tegel, which lay in the French sector, an inconvenient distance north of the city centre.

Johnson and Clay's arrival proved impressive, moving, and, in the way of such things, also slightly comical. The two big names were greeted by a 21-gun salute and the playing of both country's national anthems. The reception committee consisted of Mayor Brandt and his leading aides. It also, to considerable surprise, came to include Adenauer's representative, Foreign Minister Brentano. At the chancellor's firm behest, he had also flown to Berlin, managing to arrive ahead of the Americans. Brentano then hurried over to the apron in time to join the party – and to ensure that Brandt and his SPD colleagues didn't have the entire vote-catching encounter entirely to themselves.

But the real surprise to everyone, most of all the American visitors, was the mass of Berliners who turned out to greet them on that August afternoon. The people of West Berlin turned away from their preoccupation with the barbed wire and the armed *Vopos* surrounding their half-city and flocked to the route that was to take the motorcade via the Potsdamer Platz to Schöneberg Town Hall.

Brandt and Johnson rode together in one of the American Mission's open Cadillac limousines, followed by Clay and then the others, with motorcycle outriders to clear the way. The trip to Potsdamer Platz, to see the atrocity of the new concrete Wall, which should have taken five or six minutes, stretched out to twenty. The convoy repeatedly came to a halt in the crush. There were at least 800,000 West Berliners in the streets, maybe a million. They cheered. They sang and chanted the American VIPs' names. They threw huge masses of flowers.

Clay, his aquiline profile known from airlift days, garnered special adulation. He, even more than Johnson, promised a successful resistance to the Communist threat. *'Der Clay ist hier! Der Clay ist hier!'* Berliners cried in awe. As it crawled through the streets, the general's limousine was bombarded with bouquets, including a bunch of red roses, tossed through the window with such violent enthusiasm that its thorns scratched his face. So many Berliners insisted on shaking Clay's outstretched hand that American commandant general Albert Watson, seated next to him, insisted he pull it back inside.

Johnson, though foreigners were not really his thing, decided that these were actually his kind of foreigners. Ignoring his security people's advice, he got out of his car — which in any case was moving painfully slowly — and worked the crowd like the professional he was, embracing, shaking hands, kissing available babies and even patting a dog. The veteran politician was in his element. And, of course, the Vice-President knew that everything was being filmed and that in a few hours, once the footage could be flown back to the States, everything would be on the morning TV news. 'Campaigning already', as Brandt press aide Egon Bahr noted wryly.

They never made it to Potsdamer Platz. Johnson ordered the visit to be abandoned. Everything was behind schedule, and maybe his instincts told him that a direct confrontation at the dividing line between the two hostile world-systems might not serve much purpose. It wouldn't calm things down the way the President wanted.

As it was, by the time the VIP motorcade got to the grey stucco Schöneberg Town Hall, with hundreds of thousands packed into the square in front and the surrounding streets, they were seriously late. Speeches were made, freedom invoked, and, although even Berliners who knew English sometimes found it hard to decipher the Vice-President's Texan drawl, they cheered him until they were hoarse.

Inside the town hall, Johnson addressed the West Berlin parliament. Like ordinary Berliners, the members of the city's assembly were over-joyed to have these two symbolically powerful Americans as their guests. They applauded incessantly throughout Johnson's speech. The Vice-President might be uttering jewelled phrases hand-crafted by Dr Walt Rostow, but to them all that mattered was his presence here, with the famous General Clay alongside. They showed America cared. Or perhaps, to be pernickety, that America didn't *not* care.

Heinrich von Brentano then spoke on behalf of the Bonn government. He sounded the only slightly sour (and exaggerated) note, claiming that the right of full self-determination was 'denied to no people in the world save the Germans'. But then, there was an election on. Willy Brandt delivered the final oration. Given his own anti-Nazi credentials, he could and did tell his guests that 'we will not bend our necks beneath the yoke of a new dictatorship, irrespective of the colour in which this dictatorship has decked itself out'.

A lavish banquet followed. Everyone got to bed late. They didn't necessarily get to bed where they thought they would. Ambassador Bohlen, aide to Roosevelt, Truman and Eisenhower, found himself, it is said, shifted out of the bedroom he had been assigned at Ambassador Dowling's residence in bosky Dahlem. This was now to be occupied by Vice-President Johnson's senior secretary.[10]

In the morning, Bohlen returned to Ambassador Dowling's house to rejoin the Vice-President, who had breakfasted on oatmeal and melon. Then Brandt arrived for a private meeting. Now real conversations could be had. Business could be got down to.

Johnson and Bohlen's first duty was to deliver President Kennedy's letter to the Mayor. It is clear that Johnson, a renowned political bruiser, used this occasion to give Brandt a severe dressing-down. Johnson's own report after his return to Washington merely indicates that the Mayor was 'chastened':

He was somewhat apologetic about his letter to the President and regretted that its contents had been given unauthorized publication in the Federal Republic, a disclosure for which he said he was not responsible. I said it did not add lustre to our cause to have our own allies writing critical letters to the President of the United States and putting him to the public question. I then remarked that I had not come to Berlin to debate the past but to reason together with him in quiet co-operation.

Mayor Brandt responded quickly to this approach and I got the clear impression that he was a chastened person, subject to one important exception; he seemed convinced that his letter, with all its faults, had at least moved American policy off dead centre.

I told Mayor Brandt that all the points in his letter had been most carefully and sympathetically considered in Washington, even when it had proved impossible to agree with them, and the American policy was set forth clearly and candidly in the President's reply. He appreciated this candour.[11]

Johnson's onslaught was perhaps even fiercer than indicated in his official report. The British ambassador to Washington sent a dispatch to London, following a dinner with Secretary Rusk. During the meal, the latter confirmed that

> the Vice President had spoken very severely to Willy Brandt, upbraiding him for reacting so impulsively to the East German move and for firing off in public impractical proposals and unwarranted criticisms of the Western Allies. Brandt was apparently very shamefaced, made no attempt to justify his behaviour . . .[12]

It was true that Brandt had not been responsible for the leaking of the text of his letter to the press. This indiscretion had most likely been a ploy by Adenauer.[13] Brandt was also right that the offending letter had helped to push Kennedy into a somewhat firmer commitment than the President would otherwise have wanted to make. From that standpoint alone, Brandt had probably been right to risk sending it – and to accept the consequences.

Later Brandt confessed that the effect of Kennedy's letter was to 'tear back the curtain and reveal an empty stage'.[14] Only many years later would Brandt also be able to express his understanding of America's problem. To Berliners and West Germans, the barrier that was now becoming a Wall meant everything. To the West's superpower, however, whose resources and risks extended throughout the world, it was, of course, important, but just one among several actual or potential flashpoints.

At the time, the hugely stressed West Berlin Mayor had an election to fight and a population to protect. There was no point in biting the hand that (in some ways quite literally) fed him and his city, and without whose protection West Berlin would be defenceless. Brandt had to grin and bear whatever the Allies thrust upon him, and if necessary show contrition to ward off their displeasure. And that was precisely what he did on that tense morning at the ambassador's residence in Dahlem.

Fortunately, there was better to come. The public naturally knew nothing of the tensions behind the scenes. Locals pinned a sign to the US guard post at Checkpoint Charlie that read touchingly if a little shakily: 'Kennedy – Johnsen (*sic*) – Clay / alle drei o.k.' (all three OK). The vice-presidential visit was an enormous propaganda success. Putting the second-most powerful man in America in harness with the legendary Clay was a stroke of genius. It also served to underline the fact that, whatever Clay's prestige and popularity, the civilians were ultimately in charge.

The Vice-President was, however, a restless man. At the end of the meeting with Brandt, he was eager to get on. Johnson had two things to do today in his official capacity: first, pressing some more Berlin flesh in trips to a housing project in Charlottenburg and to the refugee camp at Marienfelde; and second, receiving the American reinforcements that were supposed to be arriving via the 110-mile autobahn transit-route from West Germany later that morning. Their arrival time was unpredictable. In fact, there was even a small but unnerving suspicion that the force might not arrive at all, if the Soviets decided to block the access route.

All the same, as the Vice-President's motorcade set off once more at eleven on Sunday, heading towards Charlottenburg, everyone seemed cheerful enough. Vast crowds of Berliners packed the route into the centre of West Berlin. His six-feet-three-inch frame folded into an open-topped West Berlin municipal Mercedes, with a TV camera truck keeping just ahead to record his entire triumphal progress, Johnson was back in his element. He smiled and waved to the West Berliners like a man possessed, as his personality inclined him and his mission compelled him to do.

Again, the Vice-President repeatedly tested his anxious security people by stopping the car and striding among the crowd like a big friendly giant. Today he had an aide behind him with a bag. As Johnson pressed the warm, seething flesh with one spade-like hand, with the other he would reach behind to this bag and grab large fistfuls of goodies. Here a bundle of special ball-point pens, there a cascade of cards providing access to the visitors' area of the US Senate, complete with the vice-presidential seal and facsimile signature. They were snapped up by delighted fans.

That's what West Berliners wanted to see: a big, smiling Texan, units of whose big, serious army were heading up the autobahn towards their threatened city.[15]

The First Battle Group of the 8th Infantry Division, 1,500 men in all, had left base near Mannheim at just after four a.m. It was commanded by Colonel Glover Johns. He was, like the Vice-President, a Texan. The Soviets had been informed the previous day by General Bruce Clark, commander of the 7th Army, that the group was due to be transferred to Berlin. They had not replied. Some informal patrols of the transit-autobahn between Helmstedt and Berlin, including a sweep by Colonel von Pawel of the military mission, betrayed no special Soviet presence, but it was hard to know what the Russians would be holding up their sleeve.

It was a pretty conspicuous movement of military force. There had been TV crews filming as the group pulled out, and the long, strung-out column set off in the direction of the border with the Soviet Zone/GDR, more than two hours' travel to the north-east. The column included mess trailers and fuel and ammunition trucks, several rifle companies, and a 105mm. Howitzer battery, a clear signal that this was more than the simple reinforcement of a peacetime garrison. There were no problems except right at the beginning, when one of the mess vehicles got bogged down and held up the brigade's departure by five minutes.

They had lost another three minutes by the time they arrived at Helmstedt, meaning the column was eight minutes later than planned, but they had some time built in and were greeted, in the dawn light, by the peaceful sight of German civilian cars being checked through by a Soviet border unit. Again, no sign of the kind of large Red Army presence, armoured or otherwise, that might indicate a determination on the Communists' part to block the Berlin autobahn.[16]

Colonel Johns had never been to Berlin before. He was assigned a Military Police officer, Major Luce, who acted as guide and adviser. At 6.30 a.m., the first section of the American column rumbled forward into no man's land and stopped. It consisted of 276 men, and sixty trucks and trailers, some filled with high-explosive ammunition. Johns was astonished when the Soviets advanced on the trucks, to count the soldiers inside. He was not aware that this was normal procedure. Luce, who knew the routine, calmed him down.

In fact, the regulations said that Soviet border personnel were allowed to look into American military vehicles but not to climb on to them. And, once they had passed the Soviet barrier, American military personnel could not be made to dismount. This meant that if the American force was to be counted, it had to be done from a point outside the trucks. Colonel Johns rapidly realised that it would take, even at an average of one truckload per minute, an hour for the advance group to be counted, and three hours or so for the entire column of 200 vehicles.

Johns tried to help by getting his men to dismount so that they could be counted on the road outside their vehicles. The Soviets seemed puzzled, but eventually they agreed. The count then fell down on the fact that the figure arrived at failed to correspond to the US Army Movement Order in the Soviet's possession. It was far too few. This was, of course, because only part of the column was involved. The advance guard had to move several hundred yards into East Germany and allow the rest of the column to pass through the checkpoint and line up behind it on the autobahn. The counting began again . . .

An hour had passed. And yet again, the count did not fit the figures in the Soviets' possession. Johns tried to suggest that all the men simply be lined up in a single large column for easy counting, but the Soviets would not have it. Another count. Again no tally . . .

Johns, exhausted and infuriated, now wouldn't take 'no' for an answer. He insisted that all the men move away from their trucks and line up in single file, all 1,500 or so. Then, dragging the Soviet checkpoint officer with him, Johns strode along, counting them off with a touch in each man's chest and, after every ten or fifteen, turning to the Russian and saying, 'Right?' At which point, the Red Army man would confirm the running total in Russian.

They made it through and, miraculously, agreed on a figure. Less miraculously, this figure exceeded by one the number on the list the Russians had been given. The world's security – or at least the colonel's sanity – hung in the balance until someone gently pointed out that the name of Johns himself was not included in the paper total but stood in splendid isolation above it. But he had included himself this morning during the head count, as had his Russian counterpart.

John's battle group could now move off down the autobahn towards Berlin. There were no more hold-ups, though at various times during the hundred-mile trip, Soviet jets swooped down to take a look. One descended to about 500 feet, its bomb doors open to reveal a camera trained on the American column. East German *Vopos* were stationed everywhere, a pair for each highway bridge and access road. Others lurked in bushes by the verges, or stood in plain sight until, on the column's approach, they made for the woods or for the far side of the embankment. That shy creature, the *Vopo*, caught in one of its more unusual habitats.

There were not many civilians about, probably due to the *Vopo* patrols, but the few East German farmers in the fields and the oncoming motorists seemed, according to Johns, quite friendly. They waved, even smiled demonstratively at the Americans.

Bumbling Soviet border patrols, bashful *Vopos*, cheery collective farmers. Who could be thinking of a Third World War?

Nikita Khrushchev, for one. According to his son, Sergei, after he had been informed of the American reinforcements heading for Berlin, he became surprisingly nervous. Later, father and son were taking a walk when a bodyguard rushed up – an unusual occurrence when the Kremlin boss was taking his leisure – and for a moment Khrushchev seemed jittery. However, it was a false alarm. Khrushchev soon realised that Kennedy did not intend to undertake aggressive military action, and that the reinforcement of the Berlin garrison was a symbolic move.

In Berlin, there was a great surge in the popular mood when the Vice-President's and the mayor's triumphal progress towards the North Charlottenburg municipal housing project and Marienfelde was interrupted at around 12.30. Momentous news had been received. The battle group from West Germany was approaching the border between the GDR and Berlin. The VIPs must get ready to receive it. The limo turned south-west, weaving its way through back streets cleared by police cars with their sirens wailing and by skilful motorcycle outriders. The car was heading for the Avus highway, which would speed it down to the Dreilinden checkpoint. This was where the battle group would cross back into Western territory.

This moment, shortly after noon in Berlin on Sunday 20 August, was a potential turning-point in the West Berlin crisis. Nevertheless, by Brandt's account, as they roared towards Dreilinden in the open car, his Texan guest's mind seems to have wandered to other matters. To shopping, in fact.

Johnson chose this dramatic juncture make an enquiry of the mayor, not about Brandt's views on the crisis, or on the European scene, but about places where the Vice-President might be able to pick up some stuff to take home for the folks there. You know . . . what about the place where they did the wonderful china? Ah yes, Brandt responded helpfully. The former Prussian Royal Porcelain Manufactory, now the State Porcelain Factory. This was famous for its pale-blue chinaware, which had adorned the dinner table of Frederick the Great and was still produced for the international luxury market. They had an outlet, but of course, it being Sunday, the place was unfortunately closed. Johnson's reaction reflected his position as leader of a nation that lived to shop, forced to endure the privations of a nation that still, at that point in its history, shopped to live.

'Well, goddamnit!' he exploded. 'What if they are closed? You're the mayor, aren't you? It shouldn't be too difficult for you to make arrangements so I can get to see that porcelain. I've crossed an entire ocean to come here . . .'

Close to Dreilinden, the limo had to push its way through more crowds of jubilant Berliners. The American commandant, General Watson, took a secret-service detail and cleared a way through the final few yards to the reception podium by the side of the highway. There was a military band, plus the obligatory flock of news reporters and camera crews.[17]

Finally Colonel Johns was hauled up on to the saluting platform along with the Vice-President, who enthusiastically shook his hand and made an impromptu speech. Johnson's welcome was echoed by a few brief words in English from Mayor Brandt. Then Johns made his way back to his jeep. Preceded by a Military Police vehicle, the First Battle Group, with Johns at its head, rumbled forward, very slowly, through a vast throng of West Berliners, who threatened to bury the vehicles under a multicoloured torrent of flowers.

The battle group eventually struggled to its destination: the McNair Barracks in the south-western suburb of Lichterfelde. Formerly the AEG-Telefunken factory, since 1948 the buildings had housed the combat units of the American occupation forces in Berlin. The exhausted troops were there belatedly fed, then promptly formed up again and subjected to 'honest-to-goodness Deep South oratory' from the Vice-President.[18] In fact, all this welcoming was a little too prompt. Several of the newcomers collapsed in the August heat.

Nor were things over once the Vice-President had spoken. The troops were ordered back to their vehicles to prepare for a parade through West Berlin.

Meanwhile, Mayor Brandt had disappeared on city business back at Schöneberg Town Hall and the Vice-President was on his way to the nearby Marienfelde reception camp, one of the visits he had cancelled that morning. He was welcomed by a crowd of East German refugees. He was mobbed, in fact, almost to the point of suffocation. From Marienfelde the tireless visitor returned to Dahlem, to mount yet another saluting stand and start off the big – the really big – parade.

The subsequent drive-past of the battle group was even more memorable. Yet more bouquets hurled by joyful Berliners, yet more cheering and smiling and handshaking. Even the troops ended up grinning, leaning out and exchanging greetings with the crowd. A lot of them forgot altogether to salute the dignitaries as they passed the reviewing stand. It looked more like a welcome for a victorious football team than a military parade. They drove miles through the crowds, the length of the Ku'damm, every inch packed with humanity. Colonel Johns rode at the head in his open jeep, smiling until his face ached and waving until his shoulder all but came unhinged.

Afterwards, Johnson answered a few questions from the press back at Ambassador Dowling's residence and then, under pretence of a call of nature, handed over these tedious duties to Charles Bohlen.

Bohlen had avoided the parade and spent the afternoon with various State Department German specialists, plus General Clay and Allan Lightner, the civilian Head of Mission, driving around East Berlin. There they had unnerved the *Vopos* by making an innocent but unscheduled stop at the men's lavatories in Unter den Linden, just on the Eastern side of the Brandenburg Gate. So varied had been the diplomatic activities of the visitors to the flashpoint city, and so tense was the situation.[19]

Once Johnson had absented himself, Bohlen was determined to make clear beyond all doubt that America did not want war. 'We are not going to take any risks in Berlin,' he told the press.[20] Ulbricht and Khrushchev must have loved him.

After the press left, there followed a lively Sunday evening. Vice-President Johnson rapidly acquired a glass of whisky, and kicked back in his inimitable, expansive style. He soon decided that instead of the intimate private dinner at the residence that had been planned, he would invite everyone and their wives out to eat somewhere. The rooftop of the West Berlin Hilton? Great.

The landmark Hilton Hotel had been built in 1958, its black-white checkerboard architecture looming above the brashly rebuilt Budapester Strasse and the entire Kurfürstendamm area. As elsewhere, it represented, in Conrad Hilton's words, a 'little America', symbolising the USA's economic power and reinforcing a near-utopian vision of the super-power's lifestyle of freedom and plenty. Some other West Berlin politicians were invited. State Department specialists who thought they had the night off were summoned to perform translation duties.

So, everyone set off for the Hilton. But the bewildering blur of activity that was Lyndon Baines Johnson had not yet settled in one place. Just before they left for dinner at the Hilton, that other basic need – shopping – came up once more. After Brandt rejoined the party, Johnson noticed his loafers, and took a liking to them. Where did they come from? Leiser, the mayor replied, naming a well-known German manufacturer of quality shoes. Well, the Vice-President wanted to buy some . . . today. Brandt gave up resisting and put his chief of protocol on to the problem, asking him to also contact the porcelain factory as well. The American way had triumphed.

The Vice-President's renewed retail offensive proved successful. By the time they arrived at the rooftop restaurant of the Hilton, with its panorama of all Berlin, the manager of the State Porcelain Factory's showroom had agreed, given everyone's gratitude to the emissaries of freedom, to open up his store on the nearby Kurfürstendamm for the Vice-President alone. Everyone waited for dinner while Johnson was whisked along to investigate the precious wares on display. The manager, Herr Franke, agreed to supply his guest with a full dinner service for the LBJ ranch and also a set of rocaille plates bearing the vice-presidential seal.

At last, Johnson returned to the Hilton and dinner could begin. At the Vice-President's insistence, they all tucked into southern fried chicken, which to the Germans' mild alarm LBJ consumed as he would at home, in absolute hands-on fashion. He broke off only to receive a full inventory of purchases from the punctilious Herr Franke, who had stayed on in his showroom to do the paperwork.

Herr Franke refused the Vice-President's offer of a huge wad of dollar bills. He would, he explained with dignity, first ship the china to Texas, where the goods could be inspected and then, when found satisfactory, paid for. So impressive did Johnson find this reasonableness that he then ordered a host of ashtrays, likewise emblazoned with the vice-presidential seal, as a possible gift for honoured visitors in Washington. They agreed on the spot on a bulk-purchase price. As Johnson explained triumphantly to Brandt when the manager had left the room, 'They look like a dollar and cost me only twenty-five cents!'[21]

As the evening wore on and on, and the tireless Johnson insisted on going out to the edge of the terrace to take a thorough look over at East

Berlin, just a couple of kilometres distant, someone nervously asked one of the Secret Service detail if this was normal. Or . . . was the Vice-President 'on something'? 'Oh no,' the man answered, dead-pan, 'the Vice-President is just his usual bubbling self.'

After returning to the ambassador's residence, Johnson found samples of Leiser and Company's loafers waiting for him, Sunday or no Sunday. Before going to bed, he happily tried them all on, and ended up ordering half a dozen pairs.

The Vice-President left just after dawn for the return trip to the States, still unwearied, though his right hand was swollen from shaking. He had been in West Berlin for less than forty-eight hours.

The Johnson whirlwind was over, but the calm was yet to come.

Use of cement and brick had commenced the previous Friday, but records show that the leadership in East Berlin was still not necessarily committed to the massive, deadly engineering project that the border would later become. Although approval had been given for a cement wall, about the height of a human being, to be erected in the built-up areas of central Berlin (beginning with the Potsdamer Platz and extending over the next few days as far as the Brandenburg Gate and the Reichstag), the barrier would for the next few weeks still consist mainly of barbed wire, wood and cement slabs and bollards placed across traffic routes, closely patrolled by armed police. The cementing-up of the doors and windows of buildings bordering the West also proceeded apace within a few days of the formal border closure.

Meanwhile, the escape rate continued at a level that Ulbricht and the leadership found distressing, humiliating, and even – strange as this may seem – surprising. Around 417 East Germans would manage to reach the West during the month following 13 August.

Many of them were former 'border-crossers' who had jobs, friends and family in West Berlin. They had a motive, and they knew where they were going.

Just such a perfect escape candidate was Ursula Heinemann, seventeen years old and a waitress at the Plaza Hotel on the Kurfürstendamm in West Berlin. Every day since she left school, she had commuted with the S-Bahn from the family flat in the East Berlin suburb of Johannisthal, heading over the sector border – which lay just a little over a kilometre northwards – into the borough of Neukölln in the American sector, and from there to work.

Ursula had been shocked by what happened on 13 August, but with the courage of youth she had no intention of passively accepting her fate. She could see that the situation on the nearby Teltow Canal was frightening. Guards were stationed along the banks, motor boats patrolled the waters. She travelled with a girl friend the long route around the rim of Berlin in the middle of that week of enforced idleness, to see if things looked a little easier at Gross Glienicke, which sat on the border near Potsdam. They didn't. A day spent doing casual waitressing work at a beer garden frequented by border guards, some of whom affirmed their intention to shoot at escapers, convinced them that they were risking too much. Two days later, some close relatives, both disillusioned Communists, told her to 'Get out and over to the West as quickly as you can'. Once the East German state got around to dealing with her, as a known border-crosser, she would probably be shipped off to some collective farm in Mecklenburg or Thuringia.

It was on Saturday 19 August, the day of Johnson and Clay's arrival, that Ursula and her mother took a walk. They headed north-west, with a cemetery and crematorium on their right and woods to their left, crossing a bridge that took them to the far side of the branch canal, the Britzer Zweigkanal, that connected the main Teltow waterway with the river Spree.

Both sides of the canal were still in East Berlin, but just two or three hundred yards away lay the Sonnenallee crossing point. This was still open, though only to Westerners coming East. Mother and daughter did not approach the checkpoint head-on, but took a path leading through neglected vegetable allotments. At this point, Ursula quietly told her mother she was going to investigate the possibilities.

Ursula advanced alone into the deserted garden area, knowing that the border between the Soviet and the American sector lay a few score yards distant, over a grassy moat known as the Heidekampgraben. A small, apparently deserted dwelling stood near by and, immediately ahead, a newly erected barbed wire fence. Although she was dressed just in a sweater and slacks, and she knew her mother was waiting for her, Ursula decided to try to get through. It felt like now or never.

There was a gap beneath the lowest strand of barbed wire, just wide enough for her to squirm under. With agonising slowness she did so, forcing herself to ignore the barbs as they ripped the wool of her sweater. She had to use one hand to lift the wire to let her through. She winced with pain, ending up with a bleeding gash on her palm. All the same, she made it. Only to find a second fence, which had been added just recently. She repeated the procedure, acquiring further lacerations, tearing more pieces out of her sweater.

Ursula could see the sign indicating the sector border just ahead. Her heart leapt. If she could make it through this final barrier, surely she must be safe? Then Ursula noticed cigarette smoke drifting through the air towards her. Somewhere, within a matter of a few feet, was a border guard, maybe more than one. But it was too late to turn back. She eased her legs through the last of the wire, then crawled as quickly but as quietly as she could past the border sign.

Ursula had arrived in West Berlin, a fact confirmed by a man standing in the garden on the other side of the sign. Whether the border guard had seen or heard her, but had decided to let her go, she would never know.

So unprepared was Ursula for the huge step she had taken that she carried only her identity card and a handkerchief, but no money. Some kind soul lent her a couple of marks so that she could take a bus to the reception centre and register in the West.

Ursula's big advantage was that she had a job to go to. Within twenty-four hours of registering, she was back at the Plaza Hotel, where the management was eager to employ her again and provided her with accommodation.

The young woman even managed to set her mind to rest about her mother. Immediately after making it through to the West, Ursula was consumed by concern. After all, she had gone off to 'explore' and never come back. What would her mother think? But the Sonnenallee checkpoint was still open at this stage. The man she met in the garden willingly bicycled off, crossed into East Berlin, found her mother and reassured her that Ursula was safely in the West.

The situation of trouble-free access for West Berliners soon changed.

Having successfully pulled off the border closure without Western counter-measures, Ulbricht decided to turn the screw a little tighter. His government announced that from one a.m. on 23 August, the number of crossing points would be further reduced, from twelve to seven. Of these, only one would be open to foreigners and diplomats (Checkpoint Charlie on the Friedrichstrasse), two to West Germans, and four to West Berliners (including the Sonnenallee checkpoint near where Ursula had made her escape).

The restrictions on foreign visitors were worrying enough, and inspired the usual protests, as did the reduction of the West German crossing points to two. But there was a far worse sting in the tail for West Berliners. The designation of four crossing points for them was misleading. They had hitherto simply shown their identity card to go East. Now they must apply for visas from two yet-to-be-established branches of the 'Travel Agency of the GDR', which the Communists demanded be set up in West Berlin at Westkreuz and Zoo stations.

The answer from Brandt's city hall came back quickly. No deal. How could Brandt agree to such a thing? To allow East German visa offices in West Berlin would be to recognise the legitimacy of the regime, and to retroactively vindicate Ulbricht's illegal border-closure measures, thus effectively undermining the entire Allied position in the city. Moreover, what was to stop the East Germans using such offices, once established, as a means of political destabilisation and subversion? The East must have known that the West's agreement was extremely unlikely. The new visa order therefore, in reality, halted all access by West Berliners to East Berlin, dividing families, friends and lovers for the foreseeable future.

The next day came the first killing – the first death caused deliberately by those administering the alleged 'defensive' system.

Günter Litfin, twenty-four years old, was a qualified tailor at a fashion house in West Berlin, near Zoo station. Since he lived with his parents and brothers in the East Berlin suburb of Weissensee, he travelled daily to the West and was therefore a so-called 'border-crosser'.

Young Litfin was suspected not just for working in West Berlin, in a 'decadent' industry, but also for his politically untrustworthy family. His father, a master butcher, had been a post-war member of the East Berlin CDU. In 1948, when this party was robbed of its independence and its leaders forced to flee to the West, Litfin senior refused to join the leftover shell that was the Communist-controlled 'block' CDU. He remained loyal to the independent party. This survived in the underground and held meetings in West Berlin for its Eastern members, who until 13 August 1961 could cross the border to attend.

In that summer of 1961, Günter Litfin had planned to move to West Berlin. He had found a flat not far from the fashion house where he worked. On Saturday 12 August, he and his brother, Jürgen, took the S-Bahn over there and spent the whole day preparing the place for Günter to move in. They worked until late, catching an S-Bahn home at around one a.m. on Sunday 13 August. It must have been one of the last through trains to travel into East Berlin before the line was closed.

The young man's anger and despair at the border closure was understandable. He had worked hard, and now, at the very last moment, found himself robbed of the future he had planned. Instantly unemployed, like Ursula Heinemann he could also expect to be victimised by the East German state. Günter spent the days immediately after 13 August touring the border areas on his bicycle, seeing how the barriers were being strengthened and extended. Sections were being walled off. Litfin decided to take his chances on what looked like the weakest point of the new border: the waterways. He was a strong swimmer.

At around four in the afternoon on Thursday 24 August 1961, Günter made his way along Alexanderufer, a road running along the bank of the ship canal that connects Berlin's North Harbour with the river Spree. Here a bridge carried the S-Bahn between East and West, crossing what for eleven days now had been the heavily guarded border. The waterway was actually wider than elsewhere, about 150 yards across, forming a basin known as the 'Humboldt Harbour' (Humboldthafen). The advantage was that the far side, the Listufer, lay in the British sector of West Berlin. If Günter could just clamber ashore there he would be safe.

He continued to walk along the canal bank until he drew level with the railway bridge, under and around which were several mooring jetties. Suddenly Günter heard a guttural voice call out 'Stehenbleiben!' (Halt!) and froze.

There were transport police, *Trapos*, stationed atop the railway bridge, and they had spotted Litfin. But the young man was not going to just give up. He sprinted towards one of the jetties, from which he launched himself straight into the water of the Humboldt Harbour. Keeping the bridge to his left, he struck out strongly in the direction of the West. One of the *Trapos* stumbled after him along the bridge, and fired several shots in the direction of the swimmer, who was soon twenty-five yards or so from the eastern shore and moving fast towards his goal. Then one of the other guards locked his machine-pistol on to automatic and sprayed shots around the young escaper. After he let loose this 'targeted burst' (as the *Stasi* report would call it), Günter Litfin slumped in the water. A bullet had entered the back of his neck as he swam, emerging through his chin. It was, to all appearances, a deliberate kill-shot.

The sound of gunfire attracted a crowd on the Western side. Three hundred Westerners were forced to watch in helpless rage as, some hours later, East German police dragged Günter Liftin's lifeless body from the murky waters of the Humboldt Harbour. Like Ursula Heinemann, he was a 'border-crosser' who wanted to go back to his job and the life he was used to. Unlike her, he had been fatally unlucky.[22]

The shock on both sides of the border was tangible. In the first few days, shooting had been infrequent and confined to warning fire. The depths of the inhumanity involved in the new 'border regime' were now revealed for all to see. Within a few days, on 29 August, another young East Berliner, 27-year-old Roland Hoff, was also killed while swimming to West Berlin, this time across the Teltow Canal to the American sector.

A week later, a breathtakingly tasteless article appeared in the SED newspaper, *Neues Deutschland*, lumping together Litfin's and Hoff's deaths. Litfin's work for a fashion house sufficed for the paper to brand him a homosexual and to exploit this supposed lifestyle for their grubby purposes. Litfin, it was implied, had been seduced by the West Berlin *demi-monde* for who knows what disgusting ends.

The fiction was nevertheless maintained that it would have been possible for Litfin and Hoff to have applied for exit visas (which, though this was theoretically true, would never have been granted). The article says, with nauseating self-righteousness, that instead the two young men chose 'dark, forbidden routes':

. . . It is usual that soldiers or border policeman guard the borders of a state. All over the world, these border guards are armed, in order that they can prevent illegal movement across these borders. Our border guards did their duty, when they used their weapons against attempts to break through the border by force. Those who abused the border consciously and with aforethought put themselves in danger of their lives, and thereby died.

As for attempts to make heroes out of these ne'er-do-wells, we are familiar with this procedure. When the pimp Horst Wessel was killed in the pursuit of his not unrisky profession, he was turned into an object of Nazi hero-worship. Why then should not the homosexual with the nickname 'Doll', who jumped into the Humboldt Harbour, be turned into a hero of the Frontline City of West Berlin? Everyone should have the heroes they deserve. These attempts to create new heroes for the western world will subside into absurdity . . .[23]

This was a distortion worthy of Goebbels' lie factory. The truth was, of course, that most border guards throughout history and all over the world tended to be there to keep foreigners out, not their own citizens in. The East would always claim that escapes, successful or otherwise, were the work of 'agents' or 'criminals'. The developing Wall, and the armed border patrols, the fortifications and the death-traps, were thus purely 'defensive' in nature. The Communist authorities began to refer to the border as the 'anti-Fascist protection wall' (antifaschistischer Schutzwall).

Ulbricht himself was quite shameless in promoting this myth. On 28 August, in Neues Deutschland, his prose was more purple than ever:

Counter-revolutionary vermin, spies and saboteurs, profiteers and human traffickers, prostitutes, spoiled teenage hooligans and other enemies of the people's democratic order have been sucking on our Workers' and Peasants' Republic like leeches and bugs on a healthy body. Naturally, they would have liked to continue sucking the blood and life force from our people . . . but if one does not combat the weeds, they will smother the young seed . . . this is why we have sealed the cracks in the fabric of our house and closed the holes through which the worst enemies of the German people could creep . . .

Precisely how cynical was this distortion of the Wall's true purpose can be seen from secret documents of the time. Marshal Konev played the twinkling uncle to the Allied military-mission representatives a few weeks earlier to deceive them over the coming border closure, but his correspondence with the East German leadership from the weeks after 13 August tells a totally different story.

Konev was a man who had survived the hard school of the Stalinist purges, led a vast army from Stalingrad to Berlin through the hell of the Eastern Front, then crushed the Hungarian revolt of 1956. His task, once the border closure had been decided, was to make it tight. Saving East German civilians from the consequences, as he saw it, of their foolish, anti-Soviet actions, was not his business.

'The military engineering and technical extension of the border,' Konev wrote to East German Defence Minister Heinz Hoffmann, 'is to be undertaken in a direction calculated to deal with the main quarter from which border-violations can be expected'. Konev recommended that in the hundred-metre restricted zone on the *eastern* side of the border a 'military regime' should be instituted and 'firearms used against traitors and those who violate the border'. He could be referring only to people who, like the tragic victims of 24 and 29 August, committed 'border-violations' by trying to flee from East to West.[24]

Despite the shootings, there was continuing concern about the effectiveness of the new border controls. The question of what to do about the canals and lakes (which, given Berlin's geography, marked a substantial part of the border) or the so-called 'green border' areas that wound their way through woods, parks, and other open spaces, had still to be settled. This sense of unfinished business was increased when during September and October the escapes and escape attempts continued, growing more dramatic and ruthless in their methods as the border regime tightened.

On 20 September, a spectacular escape occurred, in which a truck was driven at speed through a concrete-post-and-wire barrier of exactly the kind that the experts had been concerned about. It happened between the boroughs of Treptow (East Berlin) and Neukölln (West Berlin) at a place where, by some vagary of pre-war local-government regulation, the sector border stopped following the Landwehr Canal, and a West Berlin salient therefore jutted out into the East.

The official report submitted to Ulbricht described the sequence of events:

On Sunday 17 September 1961 at around 18:25 a truck of the type H6, approaching from the direction of Graetzstrasse, travelled along the Bouchéstrasse (Treptow District) in the direction of West Berlin. Just before the Heidelberger Strasse, the vehicle signalled right. Presumably, this was to fake a right turn into the Heidelberger Strasse.

After it continued across the Heidelberger Strasse, the guard stationed at the top of the Schmollerstrasse observed that the vehicle increased its speed. After a slight turn to the right on the Bouchéstrasse, with the aim of aiming for a favourable breakthrough point the vehicle turned again in the direction of the pavement on the left side of the street, then drove through the barbed wire fence situated there (attached to posts) and reached the left section of the pavement. Here the anterior limit of the left pavement, which becomes a front garden, forms the state border with West Berlin.

As it turned in the direction of West Berlin, from his post at the top of Schmollerstrasse, the People's Police Guard fired a burst with his automatic weapon. It is thought that one of the occupants of the vehicle was injured as a result. The three occupants were able to escape to West Berlin.

The vehicle came to a halt . . . it stood on West Berlin territory, only the right-hand rear double-tyre extended out across the edge of the garden boundary (state border). The vehicle was later towed back.

The breakthrough point was then closed by a party of engineers.

We have sent in a responsible Party commission, which is checking all street crossing points independently of the staff of the Border Brigade to see to what extent the former transit routes to West Berlin have been made completely impassable. A report will be prepared for each of the streets concerned.[25]

Soon the Border Brigade reported that points along the border vulnerable to the methods used in the Bouchéstrasse escape were being worked on. Concrete slabs were cemented in like tank traps, and streets torn up and rendered impassable. Existing stretches of 'barrier wall' were improved by topping them with bent-steel uprights, to hold the barbed wire and deflect escapes from the Eastern side.[26]

More tightening of the border regime was, however, obviously required. On 14 September, on Ulbricht's personal order, the border-police brigades in Berlin – 38,000 men – were transferred from the Ministry of the Interior to the Ministry of Defence. What had been police units became soldiers, subject to military discipline. A new military post was created, city commandant of Berlin, a major-general in the NVA who reported to the Minister of Defence, Hoffmann.

There was another reason for imposing military discipline. Escape attempts were not confined to determined civilians. In less than a month after the barrier went up, 68 members of the special police units deserted to the West. Thirty-seven fled individually, like Conrad Schumann, while of the rest, a dozen cases were of two guards escaping together, with one group of three and another of four all deciding to go West.

These escapes represented a considerable achievement of planning on the part of the escapers. Superior officers, NCOs and *Stasi* were constantly probing what was being said and discussed in the guard posts, the barrack rooms and the canteens, with the aim of nipping such attempts in the bud. All but 3 of the police deserters were between 18 and 21, therefore likely to be single and without responsibilities or dependent family members who might suffer as a result of their actions. Most were not active anti-Communists. Three were SED members, 47 had belonged to its youth movement. The report on this problem blamed poor leadership, the fact that many of these units had been formed only a few weeks before 13 August, and – as usual when all else failed – 'insufficient political education'.[27]

At 8.30 a.m. on 20 September, there began a special meeting of the Central Staff, presided over by Honecker. Here the 'inadequacies in the border security system' were stated frankly on the agenda. Honecker sternly told the assembled ministers and officials that 'All attempts at breaking through must be rendered impossible'. They discussed the proposed new '18–20-km. border wall', plus the creation of anti-vehicle ditches to prevent escapes by truck or bus, an increase in the erection of upright concrete slabs and barriers, the sprinkling of sand on the border approaches to make detection easier, and the barring of the inter-sector sewer system, through which several spectacular escapes had already been made.[28]

Surprisingly, not all ministers supported the idea of a wall. *Stasi* Minister Mielke thought a barbed-wire barrier would be 'more durable and suitable for the prevention of border infringements', while Defence Minister Hoffmann was in favour of a system mostly composed of 'concrete blocks and ditches'. It was thought by these powerful and expert advocates of caution that in non-built-up areas a wall would throw shadows beneath which escapers could conceal themselves, thus negating the solid advantages of concrete.

Ulbricht's support for the 'border wall' none the less proved decisive. It was his contention that barbed wire 'tempted people and provoked them into more and more attempts to break through the border'.[29] There was soon confirmation of this. In the first week of October, a 260-yard stretch of post-and-barbed-wire fencing on the so-called 'green border' between Gross-Ziethen, in the East near Schönefeld Airport, and the district of Lichtenrade on the far-south-eastern rim of West Berlin, was actually torn down, leaving this part of the border wide open. To the *Stasi*'s alarm, border troops in the area did not even notice this was happening.

The barrier that would become the Wall was therefore taking shape, in large part simply in response to the continuing determination of East Germans to escape to the West, no matter the cost. The leadership was astonished and dismayed by the large number of escapes still being attempted. This was happening despite the obvious risk and despite the leadership's best efforts, as well as those of the tens of thousands of police, soldiers and work parties striving to make the border impassable.

For similar reasons, another threshold was quietly crossed. The instructions to GDR border troops of July 1960 had circumscribed the use of firearms, laying out a careful escalation of warning instructions and shots before guards could fire at the person of a would-be escaper – preferably aiming at the legs. But in fact, from the third week of August 1961, a *de facto* shoot-to-kill policy was in effect. The self-righteous gloating over the deaths of Günter Litfin and Roland Hoff indicated a clear change in the border regime to one of ultimate force.

At the 20 September meeting, a secret order declaring that 'firearms are to be used against traitors and violators of the border' made the situation quite clear.

On 6 October the Minister of Defence, under whose control the border forces now stood, issued an order in which he stipulated: 'A firearm may be used to the extent that is required for the purposes to be achieved.' The main 'purpose' was to stop the fleeing individual reaching Western soil at all costs.

A third fatal shooting took place on 12 October at a railway goods station bordering West Berlin, where two young Easterners were spotted in the small hours of the morning, trying to force a grille and escape across the border. When challenged they ran off back into the Soviet sector, but guards shot one of them, twenty-year-old Klaus-Peter Eich, anyway, inflicting a fatal wound. The other escaper, though pursued with dogs, managed to evade capture. So now even attempting to 'desert', and turning back, could be punished with death. It was another ominous development.

It came as no surprise that neither then nor later were any members of the GDR's armed forces tried for reckless use of firearms, manslaughter, or murder. The message was quite simple. All means necessary were to be used to hinder escape attempts, and if the authorities suspected that any border guards had deliberately allowed an escape, harsh disciplinary consequences would ensue. Ulbricht himself made his will brutally clear in a speech to Free German Youth officials: 'Whoever provokes us, we shall fire on them . . . Many say that Germans just can't shoot at Germans. (But) if we are dealing with Germans who represent imperialism, and they become insolent, then we shall shoot them . . .'[30]

The sole stipulation modifying border guards' freedom of action was simple: they must not under any circumstances open fire on West Berlin territory, so as to avoid international incidents. Otherwise, if an escape was foiled, by whatever means, promotions, medals and pay increases were the order of the day. It was hardly surprising, therefore, that members of the border-control forces tended to shoot at escapers in a way guaranteed to disable and likely to kill.[31]

So the knot began to tighten. October would bring the XXII. Congress of the Communist Party of the Soviet Union (CPSU) in Moscow, a huge international showcase for the international Communist movement.

Ulbricht hoped that Khrushchev would use the congress to formally announce the signing of a peace treaty with East Germany, and therefore the assumption by Ulbricht's government of all the powers in the Soviet Zone and the Soviet sector of Berlin exercised since 1945 by the Russian occupiers. Then Ulbricht would be free to squeeze West Berlin without restraint.

13

HIGH NOON IN
THE FRIEDRICHSTRASSE

AWAY FROM THE CAULDRON of Berlin, the world carried on. In West
Germany, of course, a rancorous election campaign was still in progress.

The day after Vice-President Johnson left, on 22 August, Adenauer
appeared in West Berlin. Naturally, as protocol demanded, the ruling
Chancellor was received by Mayor Brandt. Photographs of them together
show the men looking away from each other, their faces impassive. When
the old Rhinelander viewed the closed border at the Brandenburg Gate,
he was greeted with catcalls and boos – and that was just from the
Western side.

What happened on 13 August had presented Adenauer and his CDU
government with a serious problem. Their policy on German reunification, which the Chancellor had pursued throughout his dozen years in
office, was suddenly revealed as bankrupt. Through the so-called 'Hallstein Doctrine'[1], which stipulated that West Germany would not enter
into relations with any country that recognised East Germany (the USSR
being the only exception), Adenauer had tried to isolate the Communist
regime. Through insisting on the status of West Germany as the sole
legitimate German state, and Berlin as German capital-in-waiting, he
kept alive the idea of a unified country. And through the so-called
'magnet theory', according to which in the longer term East Germany
must be drawn into the orbit of the progressively richer, more dynamic
and more powerful West Germany, Adenauer had promised his people
the inevitable collapse of the Ulbricht regime.

After the primitive, brutally effective action of the Ulbricht/Khrush-
chev axis in Berlin – and the clear failure of the 'big three' Western
occupation powers to oppose it – Adenauer and his ministers stood naked

and helpless. Perhaps because of this, the Chancellor's trip to West Berlin was brief and fairly inglorious.

The election campaign continued. Adenauer grimly went on beating the increasingly hollow drum of conservative nationalism and blowing the rather more convincing trumpet of continuing economic success. His goal was to rally his hitherto reliable support among the vast middle class that had benefited from the post-war 'economic miracle' for which his government could claim credit. But the old fox no longer showed his habitual sureness of touch. The notorious and widely derided 'Brandt alias Frahm' speech was one example. In another bizarre outburst, this time in the Westphalian town of Hagen, Adenauer even characterised the Wall as 'deliberate electoral help on Khrushchev's part for the SPD'.[2]

In the elections on 17 September, Brandt failed to unseat Adenauer. The West Berlin Mayor and his supporters had hoped that the Wall crisis and his new status as a national figure above party politics would help the SPD out of the working-class electoral ghetto in which it had languished throughout the 1950s.

None the less, Brandt's party gained more than 4 per cent in the polls. Adenauer's CDU lost almost 5 per cent and its overall majority. The big winner was the business-orientated Free Democratic Party, which won over middle-class voters who saw the bankruptcy of the old Chancellor's policies but remained nervous of going all the way leftwards and voting for Brandt's 'Reds'. With almost 13 per cent of the vote, it held the balance. The problem was, the FDP had declared that it would not go into coalition with a government led by Adenauer.

After 17 September 1961, West Germany found itself in a situation of chaotic interregnum. Negotiations for a coalition government would last two months, eventually concluding only when 85-year-old Adenauer promised to step down midway through the government's four-year term, to make way for a younger man.

Ulbricht, watching the confusion in West Germany and in the Western Alliance from his perch in East Berlin, could be very satisfied. He had got most of what he wanted. The GDR was now locked firmly into the Soviet Bloc; the border situation had been stabilised at a stroke, and with it East Germany's demographic and economic situation. There could now be no possibility that the state he had struggled to build would suddenly collapse.

Nevertheless, being the practised and devious salami-slicer he was, Ulbricht was not about to sit on his hands and wait for Khrushchev to hand him the rest of what he wanted – a separate peace treaty, full control over the GDR as a sovereign state, and, last but not least, rights over access to and from beleaguered West Berlin.

In September, two British MPs visited the Leipzig Trade Fair in East Germany. They were treated to lunch with Ulbricht – and to a relentless tirade that showed how strong was the East German leader's lust to turn West Berliners into virtual prisoners of his border police. The MPs' report on their trip was passed on to the British Prime Minister's office:

> Ulbricht said that a Peace Treaty would be signed before the year was out and that it would be based on the Potsdam Agreement. Thereafter, no one could fly over or enter East German national territory without a visa from East Germany. Such visas would not be given to 'undesirables'. BEA [British European Airways] would not be allowed to overfly the East German territory without a special agreement. He did not think that Tempelhof would be a suitable aerodrome for Berlin, but if its use was continued there would have to be East German control there.[3]

It was this relentless inability of Ulbricht to leave well alone that led to a direct American-Soviet military confrontation on the streets of Berlin, and once more threatened to bring the world to the brink of war.

On Sunday 22 October 1961, ten weeks after the border closure, Deputy Leader of the American Mission Allan Lightner and Mrs Lightner approached the Friedrichstrasse checkpoint in a car bearing American occupation-force plates. They planned to attend the performance of a Czech theatre company in East Berlin. It was 7.15 p.m.

Military and civilian representatives of Western authorities in Berlin had been accustomed over the past sixteen years to come and go between East and West Berlin at will. The pragmatic British placated the East German officials with an airy wave of their ID cards (though they would not get out of their vehicles), but the Americans stubbornly refused to show any documents. This routine was about to be challenged. When the Lightners slowed down at the East German guard post, instead of waving them through, the *Grepos* stopped them and demanded proof of identity.

Something similar had happened a few days before to a less high-status group of American officials, so Lightner was forewarned. He refused to show any documents. If Lightner's status were to be questioned, it must be by a representative of the appropriate occupation power, not by an East German policeman whose authority he did not recognise. Lightner demanded a Soviet officer be summoned in order that the situation be resolved.

Thirty-five minutes passed, and still no Russian appeared. Lightner decided to drive on into East Berlin, steering his car around the crude barriers put in place to stop escape vehicles. He had driven forty yards into the Soviet sector when he was stopped by an East German patrol. He sat in his car, surrounded by armed border guards, and did not move.[4]

General Clay, the President's personal representative in Berlin, had by now been alerted. In the two months since his arrival as Kennedy's personal representative, Clay had bombarded Washington with calls for tougher action. He had also authorised 'Wall-busting' exercises involving American military vehicles, training troops for the possibility that the newly built sector border might need to be breached. However, he had remained primarily a figurehead, a rallying point. Many in Washington had expressed fears about Clay's gung-ho tendencies before he was dispatched to the beleaguered city. Their fears were about to be confirmed. Or so it seemed.

At nine p.m., an hour and three-quarters after Lightner first arrived at the border, eight American MPs, led by Lieutenant Claude L. Stults, were ordered by the US army provost-marshal in Berlin, Lt-Colonel Robert Sabolyk, to cross into East German territory.

With bayonets fixed, the escort party crossed the white line into East Berlin. They marched past the barriers and over to where Mr Lightner sat in his car. They escorted him on foot as he drove slowly past the speechless East German guards and a short way further into East Berlin. Then they returned to the Western side.

But the diplomat wasn't finished. Dropping Mrs Lightner off at the guard post, he drove back into the Eastern sector. He was stopped. Again the *Grepos* were forced to watch as Stults and his MPs marched with

Lightner as far as the Leipziger Strasse, a couple of hundred yards into the Soviet sector, and back again. A few minutes later, a Soviet officer finally appeared on the East German side of the border. It was to him that Lt-Colonel Sabolyk issued an official protest. At around 10.20, Lightner passed through again, unchallenged, and did his circuit to the Leipziger Strasse and back. He was followed by several other Allied civilian vehicles, which also went unmolested.

Mr Lightner never got to the theatre, but principle had been (somewhat theatrically) preserved. He considered himself entitled to enter East Berlin unchecked, and, with the aid of American military might, that is what he had done, albeit to take no more than a short evening constitutional or three. To reinforce the point, Clay also had four tanks appear on the American side of Checkpoint Charlie.[5]

The Soviets immediately declared through their spokesman that the whole business with Lightner had been a mistake on the part of the East Germans.

End of story? No. It was a worry – and perhaps a first indication of a certain dissonance between Soviet and East German priorities – when, the following day, the East German news agency ADN made an announcement on behalf of the GDR Ministry of the Interior. In future, all foreigners in civilian clothes would be required to show identity documents to East German officials when crossing the border.

Clay made no public statement about this, but privately fired off a sharp telegram to the Secretary of State, in which he emphasised the importance of not giving in to East German machinations.

I am convinced [he wrote] that the GDR will require identification at Friedrichstrasse for all US licensed cars not driven by soldiers in uniform as a first step in requiring identification for all allied personnel. This would of course eliminate any special allied rights in East Berlin as all foreigners have these rights.[6]

In other words, an American occupation official would have no more right of access to East Berlin than, say, a Belgian tourist, thus negating the entire notion of privileged four-power occupation rights in the former German capital.

Clay expressed 'serious doubts that Khrushchev really wants to leave to the GDR the full responsibility for control over access to Berlin with the risks of war which this involves' – a shrewd appraisal, as events would show. Unlike most officials in Washington, however, he saw this not as a lead to be followed in East/West discussions but as a reason for refusing to negotiate with the Russians 'under the present atmosphere'. Negotiations should only be resumed if the Soviet Union agreed to recognise the current status quo in Berlin as a basis. Only in this way, he suggested, would Khrushchev be 'forced to show his hand'.

Clay wanted this put to the Soviet ambassador in Washington immediately. Meanwhile, he said, he would not test the East Germans that same day (24 October) but felt that it was important to do so the next day (25 October).

So there was a 24-hour hiatus. The general was not starting from nothing on this issue. On 18 October, following the earlier incident where Americans were refused access to East Berlin, he had sought and been granted new instructions in case of possible Communist action to close the Friedrichstrasse checkpoint:

As approved by White House following course of action by USCOB [United States Commanding Officer Berlin] authorized in event Friedrichstrasse entry point closed either by unacceptable demands for documentation or erection physical barriers by GDR.

(1) Two or three tanks would be used to force barrier and demolish any obstacle barring entry;

(2) Tanks used for purpose would be withdrawn immediately after accomplishing mission and stationed nearby *inside* West Sector.

(3) Commandant in Chair for month, or alternatively, USCOB would then call Karlshorst immediately to protest GDR action and demand urgent meeting with Soviet Commandant, as well as assurance safe conduct through sector boundary for purposes of this meeting.

Press statement would be issued soonest Berlin, explaining Allied forces had destroyed barrier illegally erected by East Germans; matter was being protested to Soviet Commandant; Allies continue to hold Soviets responsible for assuring unrestricted Allied circulation in East Berlin.[7]

And if the Soviets refused to do anything about the East Germans' salami-slicing? The answer to that question was left unclear, probably deliberately. Clay, that rare creature – a gung-ho realist – would have been the first to realise this.

Meanwhile, however, it was not just the statesmen of the West from whom the Berlin situation was an unwelcome and dangerous distraction. Hundreds of miles to the east, the Communist world was splitting apart.

The XXII. Congress of the Communist Party of the Soviet Union began on 17 October 1961 in Moscow. More than 5,000 delegates from all over the USSR and representatives of four score international Communist parties attended to pay homage or, in one or two cases, make less flattering feelings clear.

The XXII. Congress appeared to represent the apogee of Khrushchev's power. It opened in a huge, new marble-and-glass building, the Palace of Congresses, that had been completed just days previously after a frantic race against time.

Since the defeat of the 'anti-party' group four years earlier, Khrushchev had consolidated his rule throughout the Soviet imperium. *Sputnik*, and the flights of the cosmonauts, had greatly increased Russian prestige. The Soviet Union itself was less repressive, and its citizens a little more well provided with consumer goods, than had been the case under Stalin. In the Third World, socialism seemed to be on the march. The Soviet Union's influence had even, thanks to its recently acquired protégé, Fidel Castro, arrived on the very doorstep of the United States. Just a few months earlier, in April 1961, the rookie US President's attempts to foment counter-revolution in Castro's Cuba had been a humiliating failure. In his introductory speech, Khrushchev proclaimed the ambitious plan of 'creating Communism' in the Soviet Union by 1980 and reasserted his support for 'national liberation' movements all over the world.

Russia's leader was therefore riding high. But he had problems. There was the growing rift with Mao's China, which disapproved of Khrushchev's denunciation of Stalin and was constantly pushing for a more aggressive policy against the West. Khrushchev held back from direct attacks on the Chinese, whose delegation was led by Foreign Minister

Chou En-lai; instead all the aggression was levelled against China's solitary ally in the European Communist movement, the Albanian party led by the tiny country's savagely eccentric dictator, Enver Hoxha. At the congress, Khrushchev all but called for Hoxha's overthrow. In the background, there also lurked questions about Khrushchev's wayward and highly personal agricultural policy, based on his attachment to maize-growing as a farming cure-all.

And then there was the continuing crisis in Germany.

The world had long assumed that the XXII. Congress would see a triumphant announcement on Germany. The construction of the border barrier in Berlin on 13 August had been achieved without conflict. It was now widely expected that the Soviet leader would give the German question another hefty, possibly conclusive shove in front of the assembled Communists from all over the world, and finally stymie the West by announcing a separate peace treaty with East Germany.

Those who believed this were wrong. And most wrong of all was Comrade First Secretary and Chairman of the Council of Ministers of the GDR Walter Ulbricht, who until now had been getting everything he wanted.

On 17 October, the opening day of the congress, Khrushchev announced matter-of-factly that he was rescinding his ultimatum to the West. He did not now envisage signing a separate peace treaty with East Germany before the end of 1961. He denied abandoning this goal altogether, and heaped fulsome praise and support on Ulbricht and his regime, but the message was clear.

Kvitsinsky, the Russian Foreign Ministry insider who had first informed Ulbricht of Khrushchev's assent to the Wall, explained the Soviet leader's logic:

> The Wall itself was the way with a lot of fuss and ceremony to bury the idea of a separate German peace treaty, in the sense of a separate treaty with the GDR. After the building of the Wall, the signing of a separate peace treaty with the GDR was not necessary. All issues that needed to be resolved were resolved. Ulbricht saw in a peace treaty a way to receive international recognition. For us, international recognition of the GDR was important, but not the most important [thing]. We saw that this

would happen no matter what; it was a question of time. After the borders were closed, there would be no other choice than for the West to recognise the GDR. And that is what happened.[8]

Ulbricht had got some of what he wanted. Khrushchev had got almost all of what he wanted, and with far less trouble than he had feared. The West had shown it could live with a divided Berlin and a closed-off East Germany. Any more ambitious demands, Khrushchev realised, would risk conflict with the West and possibly war. He would have been aware, through the comprehensive network of Soviet intelligence operatives in West Berlin, that Clay had set up a special training ground where his troops practised knocking down lengths of cement-block wall identical to parts of the recently erected border barrier. Why provoke the Americans further?

Moreover, although the Americans had continued talks with Moscow even after 13 August, they had not given substantial ground. President Kennedy had written to Khrushchev recently, precisely regarding the 'Ulbricht problem':

> This area would . . . be rendered less peaceful if the maintenance of the West's vital interests were to become dependent on the whims of the East German regime. Some of Mr Ulbricht's statements on this subject have not been consistent with your reassurances or even his own – and I do not believe that either of us wants a constant state of doubt, tension and emergency in this area, which would require an even larger military build-up on both sides.[9]

This may have resonated in the Kremlin. Another reason why Khrushchev had turned down the heat on the peace-treaty question (and was preparing to put it on the back burner) was that almost everything Ulbricht had done on his own initiative during the period between March and October seemed to underline the unwisdom of allowing the East German leader to determine questions of access to West Berlin. So long as the USSR retained a semblance of four-power involvement in Berlin, while at the same time supporting East German sovereignty in every other regard, it kept ultimate control. Otherwise

Moscow would be dependent on Walter Ulbricht's will, and would essentially allow him to make policy.

Ulbricht himself had been in Moscow for over a week when the 22 October border incident occurred. Whether he was personally responsible for Allan Lightner's avoidable detention at Checkpoint Charlie that evening, we do not know. However, whoever ordered the *Grepos* at the Friedrichstrasse crossing point to demand Lightner's ID and then refuse to call a Soviet officer when the American diplomat so requested, must have known they were unleashing a crisis. They must have assumed themselves to be acting in the spirit of the leader's desires.

There is absolutely no indication that Ulbricht, who was in constant contact with East Berlin from his Moscow residence, did anything to rescind that decision. The subsequent announcement by ADN that the East German authorities would continue to harass plain-clothes Allied personnel trying to cross into East Berlin must be seen as further evidence of a plan that had been authorised at the highest level.

On Wednesday 25 October, Clay decided to 'test' the East again. At 9.25 a.m. an American civilian official drove a car with US military number plates through the checkpoint. He refused, when challenged by the East Germans, to identify himself. Once more no Soviet officer appeared. An American officer then appeared and issued an ultimatum. If within an hour the East Germans did not allow the official through, a crossing would be achieved by force.[10]

At around ten a.m., American tanks appeared in the vicinity. Within a short time, ten had lumbered on to the Friedrichstrasse, where they sat with their engines running, fifty to sixty metres from the checkpoint. The two foremost tanks, as Soviet reports noted, were front-mounted with bulldozer blades. Also present were several jeeps and four armoured personnel carriers containing armed American soldiers.

At ten minutes to one, almost three and a half hours after the original incident, five jeeps, each containing four armed men, appeared. They escorted the civilian vehicle through into East Berlin, just as jeeps had accompanied Lightner the previous Sunday evening. Again, they turndled onward to a depth of about 200 yards before turning smartly and returning to the safety of the American sector. As they did so, two American air-force helicopters also flew over the area.

The tanks were withdrawn from Friedrichstrasse at two o'clock that afternoon, but all American forces in Berlin were placed on full alert. At the barracks in Lichterfelde, tanks were rolled out on to the parade ground. Armoured units were dispatched to the autobahn checkpoint at Dreilinden. Armoured personnel carriers were seen in the Tiergarten area, close to the border.

Within minutes, all this was known to Soviet Defence Minister Marshal Malinovsky and to Marshal Konev, who was also attending the XXII Congress in Moscow. Konev immediately ordered that a Soviet officer be stationed at the Friedrichstrasse crossing, opposite Checkpoint Charlie. The Soviet commandant, Colonel Soloviev, was instructed to receive his American counterpart.

The meeting between the commanders did little to defuse the situation. Soloviev could no longer simply dismiss things as a 'misunderstanding'. In this publicly escalating situation, the Soviets could not disown the East Germans without losing face. Soloviev therefore stonewalled, complaining of American stubbornness and pointing out that uniformed Allied personnel were not subjected to demands for proof of identity. The checkpoint incident on 22 October was described as 'an act of armed provocation that cries out to heaven'.[11]

During the afternoon of 25 October, several more American civilian vehicles were escorted on short tours of East Berlin. The East Germans did their best to make things awkward, in one case having a car drive at speed out of a side-street as an American vehicle and its armed escort – a jeep loaded with soldiers, plus two bayonet-wielding GIs on foot – were returning slowly to the checkpoint after their excursion. Only the swift reaction of one of the foot escort, who threatened to fire at the oncoming car's windscreen, averted a contrived traffic accident that would have given the East Germans an excuse for restricting American drivers in East Berlin.

After night fell, the East Germans directed powerful searchlights at the Western observers, making it difficult for them to see what was happening on the Communist side. The Americans retaliated by mounting a hugely powerful searchlight of their own on one of their tanks. The 100,000-candlepower beam was so dazzling that the *Grepos* were forced to turn their backs on it and withdraw into their guard hut. They turned off their own searchlights shortly after.[12]

That evening, a further escalation occurred. Unidentified tanks were spotted, moving in the direction of Unter den Linden. They parked in a bombed-out lot within what had once been the Prussian Crown Prince's palace. The next morning, a Russian-speaking CIA man with diplomatic cover was sent to check out the situation. He strolled up to one of the group of parked tanks. When a soldier popped up out of the turret, he asked him in German how to get to Karlshorst. The man stared at him in blank incomprehension. The American asked the same question in Russian. He was treated to a friendly grin and a stream of travel instructions.[13]

There was a total of thirty-three Soviet tanks parked a few hundred yards from Checkpoint Charlie. They stayed there all through 26 October.

This was the first time in years that Soviet armour had been seen inside East Berlin city limits. Even on 13 August, they had held back and allowed the East German NVA to man the potential front line within Berlin. Ten forty-ton American tanks and five armoured personnel carriers were now parked and at the ready in Friedrichstrasse. By now, the British had decided to show willing. According to Associated Press, they moved three anti-tank guns into position near the Brandenburg Gate, trained precisely on the area where the Soviet tanks were parked.

This was starting to look genuinely dangerous.

At three p.m., the Americans decided to test the border yet again.[14] The tanks moved towards the border, three of them stopping right on the line with their big guns trained on East Berlin. Then an American civilian in a blue German-made Ford Taunus threaded his way through the barriers the East Germans had placed there in order to slow down traffic. He progressed on to the Eastern side until he was stopped and asked for his documents. The man refused. He sat in his car for some time. Then American provost-marshal Colonel Sabolyk appeared on the scene again. He walked through the border post, past the East German border police, and got into the Ford.

'Let's get out of here,' Sabolyk told the driver. The man turned the car around but halted just before they got back to the border line. By now the area was filled with hundreds of civilian spectators – the theatre being played out here had become a kind of grim, high-stakes entertainment for the locals as well as the international press. Sabolyk leaned out of the car and asked for a Soviet officer to be summoned. He was told by a *Grepo* captain that such a decision was up to his superiors.

'That means no,' Sabolyk retorted. He indicated the American tanks, which were turning over their engines, and said: 'We're coming over. Tell that to your superiors.'

Three jeeploads of soldiers, wearing bullet-proof vests and with bayonets fixed, escorted the Ford Taunus into East Berlin. The jeeps peeled off once they reached the final barrier and the way was open. The car, containing the original driver and a Russian-speaking member of the provost-marshal's staff, cruised around East Berlin for five minutes or so, then drove back to the checkpoint. The East Germans again stopped it and demanded documents. The Americans again refused.

'This is the worst example of international impudence the world has known!' bellowed an East German officer.

'You seem to have forgotten,' said the man from the provost-marshal's staff, 'that we do not recognise you, and God forbid we ever should!'

The driver then flashed his lights in a pre-arranged signal. The jeeps roared forward and escorted the car back into West Berlin. Meanwhile, a carload of British personnel had also driven through from East Berlin. They had waved their IDs and been allowed through. This was starting to look like a farce, albeit a deadly one.

As an older Berliner said to the *New York Times*: 'If you could not act when they split the city on 13 August or when they cut you down to one crossing point, how are you going to make this stick?'

The Russians decided that they could not leave all the bullying to the Americans. The next morning, 27 October, after yet another American sally into East Berlin, they brought up ten tanks. Marshal Konev had spoken to Khrushchev. The leader had told his c.-in-c. to match the Americans exactly. But no shooting.

Once more, Khrushchev, with his strange and unnerving combination of impulsiveness and calculation, was engaged in both provocation and calibration. He was still involved in a major international congress, where he had launched another outspoken attack on Stalin – an attack that had led directly, while the congress was actually in progress, to the removal of

Stalin's body from the mausoleum it had shared with Lenin's since 1953.
Khrushchev's continuing denunciations of Stalin were unpopular with
the Chinese, the Albanians and various other unreconstructed organisations and individuals within the movement.

As a show of strength to foes in West and East, Khrushchev had
ordered the resumption of nuclear testing. A thirty-megaton device was
detonated on 23 October, during the first week of the congress, and an
even bigger test-bomb would be dropped from more than seven miles
above the island of Novaya Zemlya in the icy Barents Sea on 30 October,
just as the congress was winding down. The gigantic flash of the
explosion could be seen 700 miles away, and a swirling mushroom-like
pillar of smoke rose up to fifty miles into the atmosphere. Despite this
ruthless show of world-destroying power, and despite his ruthless coup in
dividing Berlin, Khrushchev's alleged failure to confront the West
remained a background issue. The Chinese delegation left before proceedings were over. The Sino-Soviet split – in which Beijing would
accuse Khrushchev of 'restoring capitalism' – would not become fully
public for another couple of years, but it was pretty much a reality by
October 1961.

While pursuing a reforming, anti-Stalinist line, Khrushchev could not
afford to show weakness on a key foreign-policy matter like Berlin. Hence
the tough stance, and his order to Konev to match power with power.
The two sides did indeed end up with ten tanks each, facing each other
across the border. The American tanks had their engines running, and
the ones with the bulldozer blades were prominently displayed. American helicopters continued to 'buzz' the checkpoint and carry out
observation flights over East Berlin, ignoring East German and Soviet
protests.

Once Clay was told that the tanks were definitely Russian, he was
quick to gain propaganda advantage. 'The fact that Soviet tanks appeared
on the scene,' he declared at a press conference in Dahlem, 'proves that
the harassments which were taking place on the Friedrichstrasse were not
those of the self-styled East German government but ordered by its Soviet
masters.'

At the time, and for years afterwards, Clay's view – that the Russians
unleashed the Checkpoint Charlie confrontation in order to humiliate

America – was generally accepted. However, what now seems more likely, with the hindsight afforded by several decades and the gradual unearthing of documentary evidence, is something different. Once more, Khrushchev had found himself forced by Ulbricht's aggressive anti-Western stance into going further than he wanted. Looked at this way, the decision to bring Soviet armour into East Berlin might be represented, not as an escalation, but as an attempt to claw back control of the crisis from the East Germans.

The stand-off lasted sixteen hours through a 'chilly, drizzly night'.[15] It was the first and only time during the Cold War that American and Russian forces faced each other at close proximity, fully armed and ready to fire if either side made a false move. Nor, as Defence Minister Malinovsky would carefully point out to the Central Committee, was the crisis necessarily localised. American and Western aircraft and warships were put on full alert throughout the world. During the Checkpoint Charlie confrontation, four missile-firing atomic submarines of the Polaris class were submerged in the North Sea, Malinovsky reminded his colleagues – each with sixteen warheads aimed at targets in the Soviet Union.[16]

Who would blink first?

Not Ulbricht. Still in Moscow, he fired off furious telegrams to the Politburo in East Berlin via his trusty supporter, SED organisation man Hermann Matern. On 27 October, as the tanks were moving into position, he told Matern to play down the actual confrontation between the three Western powers and the Russians for domestic consumption in the GDR. The protests of the American commandant, General Watson, and Colonel Soloviev's response were not to be reported in the East German press. The press was also to hold off attacking the West 'in exaggerated form' because other measures were being planned and at this point Ulbricht did not want unnecessary provocation. Nevertheless, 'previous instructions to the effect that civilian personnel of the three Western powers must show their identity documents are to be precisely carried out'. In other words, no giving-in to the Americans.

Mielke, the *Stasi* Minister, was commanded to ensure that within three days a steel barrier extending the whole width of the Friedrichstrasse had been constructed. This would be installed at a time to be advised.

Colonel Soloviev [Ulbricht concluded] has declared unambiguously to the Western powers that border controls are a matter for the German People's Police. He has protested at the act of provocative penetration into the GDR. He has announced counter-measures. Foreign Minister Gromyko has summoned the American ambassador, Thompson, to convey an identical declaration to him.[17]

In fact, although this may have been what was happening publicly, unknown to Ulbricht, in private something very different was already in train.

According to Clay, when he spoke with Kennedy that evening, the President asked him if he were nervous.

'Nervous? No, we're not nervous here,' Clay remembered answering. 'If anybody's nervous, Mr President, it will probably be people in Washington.'

This dig at the State Department faint-hearts and congressional liberals, who had opposed Clay's appointment to Berlin and continued to criticise his alleged brinkmanship on the matter of the Wall, failed to ruffle the President.

Kennedy conducted the entire call to Berlin with his feet up on his desk. 'Well,' he told Clay, 'there may be a lot of nervous people around here, but I'm not one of them.'[18]

The reason for the President's insouciance was simple. He almost certainly already knew that moves to defuse the situation were under way. Kennedy's brother Robert had been cultivating a relationship with Georgi Bolshakov, a personable press attaché at the Soviet embassy in Washington, and had already used the man as an alternative, unofficial channel to the top leadership in Moscow. In fact, Bolshakov was a colonel in the GRU (Soviet Military Intelligence) and his job at the embassy a cover, as the Americans well knew. RFK had contacted his friend Bolshakov soon after the 27 October tank confrontation brought things a little too close to the edge. Within hours, messages had passed back and forth between the President of the United States and the Secretary of the Communist Party of the Soviet Union.

Since this material remains classified, we do not know exactly what was said. What we do know is that at 10.30 the following morning,

Khrushchev spoke to Marshal Konev, who had hastily returned to Berlin. According to Khrushchev's memoirs, Konev told him that the situation at Checkpoint Charlie was unchanged. No one was moving, he told the Soviet leader, except for when the tank crewmen on both sides would climb out and walk around to warm up.

'Comrade Konev,' Khrushchev said, 'I think you'd better order our tanks to turn around and pull back from the border. Don't have them go very far. Just get them out of sight in the side streets again.' The Americans, he added, had got themselves into a very difficult situation. 'They're looking for a way out, I'm sure. So let's give them one. We'll remove our tanks, and they'll follow our example.'[19]

And that was exactly what happened. The Soviet tanks withdrew. Between twenty minutes and half an hour later — just enough time to confirm high-level instructions — the Americans also pulled back.

In his memoirs, Khrushchev makes it seem as if he had a sudden rush of common sense to the head. This led him to suggest a withdrawal, which his instincts told him the Americans would match. In fact, the suggestion had probably been put to him during the night of 27/8 October by President Kennedy via the RFK/Bolshakov connection, sweetened with a White House promise to ease up on the border-pass issue. So, Khrushchev had a little quid pro quo to save face, and knew that any unilateral Soviet withdrawal of tanks would be reciprocated by the other side.

During the confrontation on 27/8 October, London was wielding as much pressure as it could to avoid war over access to East Berlin.

British civilian personnel entering East Berlin had for some time now been showing ID if requested, and so London's sympathy for the American stance was limited. Moreover, the British managed, with evident satisfaction, to blame the French for the latest problem. 'The French,' a note from an aide to the British Prime Minister, Macmillan, asserted, 'have been caught bringing people across the border who were in fact not Allied personnel at all, although they were travelling in official cars.'

After reading a report from his embassy in Washington on the Friedrichstrasse crisis, the Prime Minister scribbled some marginal comments. 'What does the Foreign Office intend to do about this?' Macmillan asked. 'It's rather alarming' He wondered how long Britain could continue to 'be associated with this childish nonsense'.[20]

Few in London were of the hardline persuasion. The Foreign Secretary wrote on 27 October claiming that he was 'pretty close to an understanding with Rusk', who did not not want the question of showing passes to be made into a major show of strength. 'He has accepted our advice to try and reach a face saving compromise with Moscow.' Home considered Clay the chief problem. He advised Macmillan: 'The trouble is that the US soldiers do not yet seem to have been brought to heel on this point. I am sending an immediate telegram urging that specific instructions be sent. You might mention this to the President.'[21]

Whether British pragmatism (or weakness) actually played a role in taking the heat out of the crisis is uncertain. Downing Street tended to overestimate its influence on the White House.

The resolution of the Checkpoint Charlie stand-off showed the stark reality of superpower relations. Neither superpower leader was about to go to war over who showed what bit of paper to whom in the streets of Berlin. The only person to whom this was actually of vital importance was Walter Ulbricht, and at anxious times such as this a satellite leader like the East German strongman could be and was overruled. The Berlin Crisis was, arguably, over at the moment both sides withdrew their tanks on the morning of 28 October 1961.

The next day, Sunday, President Kennedy attended mass in Washington as usual and then flew to Fort Smith, Arkansas, for an official appearance.

Khrushchev continued with his congress, which had two days still to run.

Ulbricht continued to harangue his comrades in East Berlin by cable, chiding them for not having made the main flashpoints, such as the Brandenburg Gate and the Potsdamer Platz, tank-proof, and ordering them to begin immediate construction of tank traps at all crossing points, especially at Friedrichstrasse, to make it impossible for tanks of 'the occupation forces' to force an entry to East Berlin.

Before he left Moscow, Ulbricht complained to Khrushchev about his failure to announce a separate peace treaty. 'I do not agree that the more the conclusion of a peace treaty is postponed, the worse the GDR economy will be,' the Soviet leader responded irritably. 'We are having an old conversation with you.'[22]

To Polish Communist leader Wladyslaw Gomulka, Khrushchev made his true feelings plain:

> There will not be a war, but signing a peace treaty with the GDR might exacerbate the situation . . . Although there will be no war, we should not exacerbate the situation. We must continue our game. We are not afraid, but we do not want war.[23]

And although the time of truly perilous international confrontation was over, Khrushchev did continue his 'game'. Soviet forces in Germany stayed on their heightened state of alert for another two and a half months, until 11 January 1962. There were more minor provocations against American officials in December, but the West did not rise to the bait and the small storm blew over. In February there would ensue an elaborate game of aerial cat-and-mouse over the flight corridors into Berlin, but in general this was shadow-boxing.

Khrushchev wanted to show everyone, including Ulbricht and the Chinese, that, despite abandoning the East German peace treaty, he had not given in. It was easy to keep the Berlin issue 'live', and he continued to do so. He had, however, transferred his attention to the Third World, and specifically to Cuba. There, almost exactly a year after the Friedrichstrasse incident, another, even more perilous confrontation would again place humanity on the brink of nuclear Armageddon.

The British were hugely relieved that the Checkpoint Charlie incident went no further than it did. For some time they continued to worry that the supposedly aggressive attitude of the Americans in Berlin might lead to renewed confrontation.

A report to Macmillan on 1 November expressed fears that Kennedy, under pressure from the West Germans, the French, and a section of opinion at home in the USA, might 'be tempted to think that a prolongation of the present tension could be safely endured' and spoke of the risk of an 'accidental war' due to 'General Clay's game of chicken in Berlin'. P.F. de Zulueta, the Prime Minister's Personal Secretary, noted glumly: 'I am afraid that no one knows what the Americans may do.'[24]

In fact, for East as well as West, the near-simultaneous pull-back of American and Soviet tanks on 28 October represented a symbolic recognition of the status quo established on 13 August. After that day, the Americans no longer forced entry for their civilian personnel into East Berlin, and neither the East Germans nor Soviets made serious attempts to block access. The crisis was over.

New research is uncovering even more secrets of the Friedrichstrasse crisis. There is now a strong suspicion that, while Khrushchev's abandonment in October 1961 of pressure for a separate peace treaty meant a reduction in international tension, it also meant that Germany and Berlin were forced to swallow the bitter pill of a permanent, fortified Wall.

That does not mean that the East had 'won'. The persistence of Allied rule in West Berlin – including free air and land access – was implicitly recognised. The East Germans got their Wall in recompense. Until Khrushchev gave up his peace-treaty plan, both Moscow and East Berlin could continue to see the Wall as possibly a temporary measure, to be confined to barbed wire and in places a simple cement barrier. After all, once a peace treaty had been signed, would not the East Germans control travel between West Berlin and West Germany, and might a Wall therefore be no longer necessary? That had been Ulbricht's dream. And Khrushchev's too, because he knew the Wall would represent a defeat for the system he represented.

The Wall was in the long run a propaganda catastrophe for the East. Every day it existed, it screamed aloud one simple, damning statement: in Berlin we Communists stood in direct competition with capitalism, and we lost. Khrushchev and his successors had to live with this permanent mute accusation until a Soviet leader came along who just couldn't or wouldn't do it any more. But that miraculous moment lay almost half a lifetime in the future.

By this argument, the Wall originated not on 13 August 1961, when the wire went up, but on 17 October, when Khrushchev reluctantly abandoned his hope of a settlement that would nullify the Potsdam Agreement, force an Allied withdrawal from West Berlin, and give control of the entire city to his East German satellite.[25]

As a result, from early 1962 the East Germans began building a horribly ingenious system of fortifications, more ugly and more sinister still than simple breeze blocks and cement, a thing for which the term 'Wall' was wholly inadequate.

14

BREAK-OUTS

SOON AFTER ULBRICHT'S RETURN from the Moscow congress, work began on transforming the still-largely-improvised Berlin barrier into something durable and impregnable.

It had already been strengthened with anti-crash devices at points considered particularly vulnerable to heavy vehicles such as trucks and buses. Following the experts' report to Honecker's 'Central Staff' at the end of October 1961, military engineers began to 'extend' the existing arrangements. The aim was to make them both more secure and – at certain symbolic or notorious places, such as the Brandenburg Gate or Checkpoint Charlie – a little less brutally unattractive.

The need for further tightening of border security was made more urgent by disturbances that accompanied the 'Checkpoint Charlie' confrontation between 22 and 29 October. On the night of 27/8 October, in the French Sector, a sizeable force of West Berlin police was required to break up a crowd of 150 youths, who were attempting to cut down the barbed-wire border fence. According to the *New York Times*, twenty-two Easterners took their chance to flee during that single night, including a customs official in uniform.[1]

The propaganda barrage in East Germany continued, as did the arrests – though the wave of repression began to tail off towards the end of 1961. Superficial resignation was soon the dominant mood among the GDR's population.

None the less, the regime could not relax. In September it started rallying loyalist forces, especially the young enthusiasts of the Free German Youth, encouraging them to spy on and direct the thoughts of family and friends. The FDJ youngsters were organised in a campaign, 'Blitz against NATO broadcasts', meaning all Western television and radio stations. Kids would clamber on to roofs and redirect the aerials to stop them receiving signals from the West. Adults known to watch or listen to Western broadcasts were pilloried by youthful fanatics. In some cases, miscreants were reported to the authorities and radio or TV sets confiscated.

The regime's nerviness was to some extent justified. Western subversives of various kinds, particularly foreigners and West Germans, could still pass pretty freely between West and East Berlin so long as they didn't make their status too obvious.

Western intelligence services, which had been caught napping on 13 August, managed to rebuild skeleton agent networks within a fairly short time. The CIA's Berlin Operations Base (BOB) reported on 6 November 1961 that despite new border controls it had managed to keep or regain contact with twenty-five agents operating in East Berlin. Judging that access might be restricted at some point, canny BOB officials had already begun supplying agents with two-way radios or letter-drop arrangements, to replace the face-to-face debriefings that had been standard while the border remained open. However, there were still some who had to be contacted in person. It was true, as the 6 November report suggested, that despite the substantial numbers of Westerners still crossing back and forth since 13 August, this traffic was now coming under increasingly thorough physical and documentary control.[2]

Although the CIA's activities were curtailed by the Wall, BOB was none the less well aware of the mood in East Berlin, of the economic situation, and of the police actions being conducted by the Communist regime, and therefore able usefully to supplement the Allied military missions' reports. Within a year of 13 August, BOB had published 262 field reports based on two-way communication with thirty sources in the East, and carried out fifty missions in support of these agents without losing any operatives to the *Stasi* and KGB counter-espionage networks.

One thing was clear: the CIA could no longer actively build up any kind of 'resistance' network in the East. This had always been a slightly dubious concept, but with the Wall in place it became impossible. The best BOB could do was to maintain assets, and use the information those assets supplied in cleverer ways; for instance, to influence the propaganda war. A German-speaking BOB representative was added to the team that interviewed East German refugees, especially army and border-police deserters like Conrad Schumann. The BOB man's job was to quickly digest the material thrown up by the interviewers, detailing the escaper's reasons for leaving, disillusionment with the regime, and so on. Without having to wait for the full interrogation report, by which time the story might have gone 'cold', he would turn it all into punchy copy. This material would be rapidly fed to the press in West Berlin and the rest of the world, using the CIA's excellent journalistic connections.

But how much could and would West Berlin and the Allies do to help those imprisoned behind the recently built Wall?

The Allied and West Berlin authorities were in a quandary. No one wanted to provoke the East Germans or the Russians into cross-border interventions, so violent demonstrations by West Berlin civilians were discouraged. On the other hand, the West Berlin police could not resist becoming involved in escape attempts, helping refugees as far as they could, and even providing covering fire. They were, technically, forbidden to do such a thing, but the rules could be stretched. The West Berlin law-enforcers could plead that they had been shot at from the East, and so their weapons had been fired in self-defence. Since many escapes took place under cover of darkness, it was hard to prove otherwise.

Mayor Brandt himself was similarly torn between his heart and his head. At the beginning of December, he declared at a meeting:

> In the long run we cannot prohibit anyone, not just from saying what they feel about the Wall, but from giving a stronger expression to that feeling. Let no one believe it is easy for us to send in our police against young people when they demonstrate against inhumanity.

A few days later, he put it even more clearly: 'Our police force . . . is there to protect order in West Berlin, but not to protect the Wall.'[3]

The West Berlin Senator for the Interior, Joachim Lipschitz, had been forced to leave East Berlin in 1949 because of his commitment to the SPD. He had become passionately involved in training a new para-military police force to defend West Berlin from overt or covert attacks from the East. Lipschitz, a courageous leader of the socialist underground during the war years and a proven man of action, may even, if British official reports are to be believed, have been involved in a plan to blow up part of the Wall as a protest on New Year's Eve 1961/2. The senator's unexpected death, aged forty-three, on 11 December 1961, means we shall probably never be sure.

There were several such attacks on the Wall from the Western side, using high explosives, in the last weeks of 1961 and well into 1962. The largest was on the Potsdamer Platz in July 1962, after which the Western authorities were forced to take action for fear someone would get killed. These detonations were almost certainly staged by members of the 'Girrmann Group', a student escape-and-subversion organisation based in the Free University of West Berlin. None seems to have achieved much beyond a certain protest value. They did, however, cause a special kind of panic among the control-fiends who ran the GDR. Lengthy reports were sent to Ulbricht on such incidents. S-Bahn trains, which passed through West Berlin but were still operated by the Eastern authorities, were also favoured with several small bombs. These were a kind of violent complement to the boycott of the S-Bahn network by Westerners, which continued throughout the 1960s and into the 1970s.

But what really frightened the SED bosses, and encouraged Berliners and their sympathisers all over the world, were the escapers. The people who proved the Wall was not impregnable, who offered hope to the trapped millions of the GDR.

Heroism and tragedy were never far removed from each other in those early days. Hundreds escaped but hundreds more were arrested for trying and often sentenced to long prison terms. Thirteen human beings died trying to escape from East to West Berlin between 13 August 1961 and the end of the year.

Of the Wall's first martyrs, four fell to their deaths while trying to escape from windows and rooftops in the Bernauer Strasse, between August and October. After this time, the buildings skirting the West were purged of their tenants, and windows and doors systematically bricked up.

Six more people died trying to swim to the West, including two in the Teltow Canal, one across the Humboldthafen, two across the Spree river, and one across the Havel between Potsdam and West Berlin. The three killed by shooting – including Günther Litfin and Roland Hoff in August – were equalled by those who simply risked too much and drowned.

The victim who died in the Havel was a nineteen-year-old private in the 'Readiness Police' patrolling the border with Potsdam. He made a vain attempt to swim across the numbingly cold river to the Wannsee shore in West Berlin, but was retrieved from the water and placed under arrest. However, by this time he was barely alive, and died from exposure and waterlogged lungs on the way to hospital.

Udo Düllick, a 25-year-old engineer with the East German railways, was sacked after expressing anti-Communist sentiments during a political argument with colleagues. A few days later, on 5 October 1961, he tried to swim the Spree river between Treptow in the East and Kreuzberg. He came under fire from a border patrol, but was not hit. In the event, the exertion, the currents, and perhaps the terror were what killed him. His lifeless body was fished out of the water by West Berlin police.

Düllick carried no papers, and for days remained the 'unknown victim of the Wall'. Then his brother, who lived in Switzerland, arrived in West Berlin and identified his body. Only then were the worst fears of Udo's anxious parents in East Berlin confirmed. Their son was given a high-profile burial in West Berlin. The parents, pious Catholics, were permitted to hold a quiet memorial service at the chapel of rest in the Rehfelde cemetery, a few kilometres outside East Berlin. With typical cynicism, the *Stasi* imposed one condition: the priest who delivered the eulogy for Udo must not mention the cause of his death or any of the surrounding circumstances. Such enforced silence became the rule at services in the East for victims of the Wall.

The very last death of 1961 was one of the most heart-rending. The previous year, Ingo Krüger, twenty-one years old, had become engaged. His fiancée lived in West Berlin, and Ingo in the East. A mere inconvenience until 13 August, when they were caught on different sides of the border. Luckily, his fiancée had a West German passport, and could visit him in East Berlin, but the situation was unbearable.

Ingo Krüger's secret resource was his skill as a champion diver. He decided to don a wetsuit and breathing apparatus and swim under the water to the West. Several friends were let in on his plan, as was his fiancée. On 10 December 1961, a Sunday, she visited him before crossing back to the West. She would wait in the chill of the winter's night to receive him there. Everything had been arranged.

At eleven that evening, Ingo and three friends stepped on to the Schiffbauerdamm, which ran along the eastern side of the Spree below Friedrichstrasse station. They said their farewells. Ingo stripped off the coat that concealed his wetsuit and launched himself into the water. He did not plan to dart straight across from East to West. The point where Ingo dived under the surface was quite some way from the border itself. The idea was that Ingo would swim, helped by his wetsuit and breathing equipment, under the surface of the river for about 500 yards. He would negotiate an entire curve of the Spree, still in East Berlin, and pass under another bridge before finally reaching a point where he could move over to the Western bank and clamber ashore on to the Reichstagufer, hard by the old German national parliament and a few yards inside West Berlin. In this way he could avoid the attentions of border guards, who would be looking for escapers entering the water at the nearest point to the West.

It was a bold plan, but not foolhardy. Ingo was a sportsman, an excellent swimmer, with all the right equipment. So his fiancée, clothed to beat the December weather, waited anxiously but hopefully for him on the Reichstagufer.

At around 11.30 p.m., an East German customs launch found the body of a young male in the water by the Marschallbrücke, the last bridge before the border. Ingo Krüger's fiancée was forced to watch from 200 yards away in the West as, in the floodlit distance, a corpse was recovered from the river. Soon the launch disappeared again into the darkness.

The appalled young woman must have known the truth, but still she hoped. She wrote repeatedly to Ingo's mother, daring to believe that the body might be someone else's, that perhaps the man she loved had been arrested. He might be in prison, but he would be alive. No reply. Only in the early days of 1962 did she finally learn that her lover's mother had been prevented from writing to her. Frau Krüger had identified her son's remains on 12 December, less than two days after the escape attempt. His body bore no marks or signs of injury. Ingo had simply underestimated how icy the Spree could be in December, and overestimated his resistance to cold.

Of course, there were spectacular successes too. Several trucks managed to crash through into the West before the anti-vehicle barriers were strengthened in the late autumn of 1961 and 'no-go' areas extended.

On 5 December, an engine driver, 27-year-old Harry Deterling, drove a scheduled passenger train at full speed against the barriers that since August had blocked the line at the border station of Albrechtshof. He continued boldly on, travelling several hundred yards along the still-extant railway line and into the safety of Spandau, in West Berlin. Of the thirty-two people on board, twenty-four, including seven members of Deterling's own family and his fireman, Hartmut Lichy, were privy to the escape. Deterling had carefully recruited them for what he called the 'last train to freedom'. All cowered on the floor of the wagon as the train powered through the final border defences and a hail of bullets swept over them. Seven other passengers, including the train conductor, had known nothing of Deterling's plans, and dutifully returned to the East. One other unwittingly involved passenger, a seventeen-year-old girl separated from her parents by the Wall, spontaneously decided to stay in the West.

Such escapes were lucky or carefully planned, or both. Even before the Wall was fully fortified, to approach the border head-on and alone was a perilous business. Between 13 August and 31 December 1961, according to *Stasi* figures, a total of 3,041 people were arrested as a result of failed escapes to the West. The greatest number – 2,221 of these (73 per cent) – had tried to flee on foot. Another 335 (11 per cent) had made the attempt by rail, 244 (8 per cent) in motor vehicles, 114 by sea (the Baltic) (4 per cent), 96 by swimming rivers, canals or lakes (3 per cent), and crawling through the sewers 31 (1 per cent).

Was it surprising, therefore, that a need for expert help quickly arose, and that this help was in great demand?

Escape organisations came into being from the first hour. The early ones were built on idealistic foundations, as practical protests against the division of Berlin, and most originated among West Berlin's large student population. One such organisation was founded on the very evening after the border closure, on 13 August 1961, at the Eichkamp international student hostel of the Free University (FU) of West Berlin.

If there was one group peculiarly suited to the escape business, it was the student community. Young, usually fit, mostly without day jobs or family responsibilities, students enjoyed access to extensive, even worldwide networks of like-minded and often influential contacts. They were also, in many cases, possessed of valuable specialist knowledge, in languages, engineering, the law, and so on.

The original impulse of the three main founding members of the FU group – law students Detlef Girrmann and Dieter Thieme, and a little later theology student Dodo Köhler – was based on mutual student loyalty. Before 13 August, a substantial number of the FU's students – roughly 500 – commuted from the East. The three conspirators decided to get in touch with these 'Eastern' students and if desired to find ways for them to escape to the West and finish their studies.

Girrmann and Thieme were both in their early thirties – old for students, even in Germany. In fact, they worked for the university administration, specifically dealing with welfare issues affecting the Eastern 'ex-students'. This gave them access to the university's registry and thus to all necessary addresses, personal details and so on – as well as to photographs of the subjects.[4]

The founders were all West Berliners. After being effectively banned from the East after 23 August, they had to find students with West German or foreign passports to trace the 'ex-students'. These contact-makers became known as 'runners'.

The initial stage of contacting fellow students marooned in the East was a risky business. One of the 'runners', later intimately involved in many escapes, was Burkhart Veigel, a medical student with a West German passport. He described the normal method of approach once they had found their 'ex-student' ('Ex') targets:

It was of course not without danger for the runner, or for the potential escaper, for if the *Stasi* . . . got wind of it, then both would be arrested and tried, the one as escape organiser, the other for 'fleeing the Republic'. And so every runner visiting an 'ex-student' had to have a harmless story ready, a reason why he was visiting, e.g. to ask whether the 'ex' wanted to give him a final term paper, or whether the 'ex' could, despite everything, come to the West of the city for a meeting with their professor. The fake story had to be absolutely credible, but also sufficiently harmless, so that the runner looked at worst like a well-meaning idiot and never as a 'criminal' (in the East's jargon). Only when you were certain that no unwanted other was listening in, or the runner could be sure that the 'ex' was 'safe', e.g. not a spy or someone who had meanwhile been 'turned' by the *Stasi*, only then could you go very cautiously on to the next stage . . .[5]

Once it was decided that the contact was safe, then the possibilities for coming to the West could be explained and instructions given. This was done with an almost bureaucratic thoroughness. Forms were filled out, personal details put on file. Other important information could come from the official student database.

During initial contact with an 'Ex', a password and simple codes would be agreed, to keep contact time and incriminating conversation to a minimum. This was especially important when arranging an escape rendezvous. According to Veigel, the escaper would receive a phone call from, say, 'Uncle Josef', who would recommend a particular radio programme. This meant to meet exactly when that programme began. Or the caller would ask if the 'Ex' wanted a little 'fresh air', to which the right answer was 'Yes, but unfortunately I have a bit of a cold'.

Timing in these cases was very strict. Helpers were instructed not to wait more than a few minutes. In a totalitarian society such as the GDR had become, anyone seen loitering soon came under observation, particularly if dressed in Western clothes. If the delay seemed too long, the helper would leave and another rendezvous would be organised. If the problem occurred yet again, contact would be broken.

The actual methods used to effect escapes varied. Any escape project was known as a 'tour', whatever form it took.

The most popular way of getting people to the West was by providing them with forged documents. At least in the beginning, the so-called 'Girrmann Group'[6] could rely on the toleration, even the unofficial support, of the West Berlin and West German authorities. There was, all the same, no denying that these groups often operated at the limits of legality. The acts they undertook would have amounted, under normal circumstances, to fraud, forgery and criminal impersonation.

But in those weeks after the 13 August, West Berliners and democrats all over the world accepted that the situation was not 'normal'. The student group's foreign contacts were extensive. Foreign and West German passports could, of course, be 'borrowed', especially if the real bearer bore a physical similarity to the would-be escaper. Through sympathetic individuals in foreign diplomatic and official circles, they could also get hold of blank passports. Obtaining foreign documents became even more important after the end of September, when entry and exit visas were made compulsory for West German residents travelling to the East.

Veigel himself, supplied with the codename 'Schwarzer' (Black), did not just work as a 'runner' to East Berlin. He also visited foreign cities to collect batches of blank passports from contacts. One such trip was to Zurich. There Veigel met with Rolf Bracher, the son of a Swiss general, who used his position to obtain Swiss identity documents. Bracher had provided the same service to refugees from Soviet-controlled Hungary after the failure of the 1956 revolution.

Sometimes foreign sympathisers came to them. Veigel recalls a man arriving from Belgium with a suitcase full of passports and an official stamp from his home city, which could be used to certify the documents. In some cases – Veigel recounts with wonder – the people supplying these precious items had performed the selfsame service twenty years earlier, for refugees fleeing the Nazis.

Between two and three hundred blank passports were acquired in this way. The group preferred documents belonging to smaller European countries. To use British, American or French passports would risk embarrassing the occupation powers in their dealings with the East.

The group had quickly become adept at 'adapting' existing passports, but such gifts made their task much easier. Once documents had been delivered to East Berlin, the escapers had to acquire 'biographies' to fit their passport details. In the case of foreign passports, they were schooled in a few common phrases in their alleged languages. Finally they were taught to handle the exit formalities and to deal with any awkward questions from East German border officials.

For the first five months after 13 August, the 'passport' method worked very well, but it was not the only way to the West.

There were other routes. Via the sewers, for instance. Even before 13

August, these were often blocked with grilles. Many had been installed in the 1950s to block the movements of criminal gangs that smuggled cigarettes and other contraband goods between the Soviet and the Western sectors. The grilles were sturdy enough, but the Western students were determined. They came from the West Berlin side with hack-saws and cut holes in them.

The first escape organisers to use this route had been a group of senior high-school students, back at the beginning of September 1961. Like the FU conspirators, they were seeking ways of helping friends trapped in the East after 13 August, who wanted to get to West Berlin for the new school year. These teenagers – working on their own – learned by trial and error how to recognise sewer manholes. Then they sought a suitable sewer that ran directly from East to West.

Again, holders of West German passports had to do the research work in the East. They eventually found a manhole on the other side, 500 yards from the border. It was located in a factory area, so at night there was no one about. From here the sewer ran beneath the border into Kreuzberg. It lay 300 yards inside West Berlin in an abandoned lot. The entire run was therefore about half a mile. The sewer, following the street line, underwent a gentle thirty-degree bend after the border, so anyone climbing in or out on the Western side would not be spotted by sharp-eyed guards in the East. It was perfect. There was just one major problem: a grille some way into the East that had to be worked on without the *Vopos* noticing.

It took some days before the grille could be sawed through sufficiently for fugitives to wriggle through from the East. The biggest problem was that, having waded through a working sewer for half a mile or so, those who emerged on the Western side were covered in waste and reeked to high heaven. A laundry service had to be organised, since the last thing the high-school kids wanted was for their parents to find out. They might stop the operation.

Over some days, an unknown but substantial number of the boys from the East were brought through the sewer to safety by their classmates. It was an amazing achievement for a group of teenagers, operating without plans of the sewers or professional tools or other special know-how, and without the *Vopos* finding out. But – largely because of the odour problem – the operation could not, in fact, be kept totally secret. The 'Girrmann Group' had an efficient intelligence system.

Dieter Thieme, one of the FU students who had founded the organisation, decided to use the sewer route in a much more ambitious form. The passport method was excellent, but there were sometimes complications. For instance, it might be difficult to fit an existing passport to a would-be escaper. Or, if the escaper was from outside East Berlin, there might be no convenient flat in the city to use as a staging point, where the essential 'training' needed (including the tedious and problematic learning of the passport-holder's 'biography') could be carried out.

The sewer route had its own problems, naturally. The numbers Thieme and his colleagues hoped to bring through in this way were large. So, a correspondingly large number of runners had to be sent East.

With the increase in numbers, the danger of deliberate or accidental betrayal grew. The Westerners decided that escapers should be given as short a notice of their trip as possible. Best if they were told on the day they were leaving, rather than have them toss and turn through a last night in East Berlin, a night during which they might be tempted to share their fears with someone who turned out to be a *Stasi* agent.

This increased the safety margin, but the organisational burden was immense. In one case, a runner with several escapers to notify during a single busy day in East Berlin was forced to summon two female students out of a college lecture hall. Had he waited until they got home, the schedule would have been too tight.

Normally, one small group of escapers would begin to enter the sewer every half an hour during the hours of darkness, using the manhole first discovered by the high-school students the previous month. Everything was arranged in advance by the 'Girrmann Group'. Each escaper was assigned a group and a time, and informed accordingly. Precision and punctuality were all-important.

There was another crucial service required from the Western side. After the planned escapes were finished for that night, someone had to replace the heavy manhole cover on the East Berlin side. Since West Berliners were not allowed into the East, West Germans or foreigners had to cross the border to do this.

Two courageous students volunteered for this role in the sewer project. The first was a student from West Germany, codenamed 'Langer' (Tall) and the second an Austrian called Dieter Wohlfahrt. 'Langer' would ride through to East Berlin on a Vespa motor scooter, while Wohlfahrt would use a vehicle left in East Berlin by a previous escaper. This second vehicle played an important role quite apart from its value as transport. Wohlfahrt would drive it to the deserted area where the manhole was situated and meet 'Langer'. He would park the car right in front of the manhole so that the opening could no longer be observed. Then he and his colleague would laboriously lift the manhole cover, ready for the first party of escapers.

Wohlfahrt would conceal himself elsewhere in the factory yard. 'Langer' would stay in the open to greet this initial group, who were scheduled to arrive just after dark, around eight p.m. He would guide the first of the often terrified fugitives down into the sewer, telling them how to use the rough ladder and which direction to head in. Then, once he was confident the group could cope, he would jump on to his Vespa and ride the two blocks to the Heinrich-Heine-Strasse checkpoint. Within minutes, having shown his West German passport, he would be safely back in the West. There he would warn the organisers that their first customers were already wading slowly and gingerly through the stinking, darkness beneath the lethal border.

A small reception committee would advance as far as the hole in the grille, to assist the incoming escapers as necessary. The crossing was not as easy as it may sound. The tunnel started out about 160 cm. (a little over five feet) high at its eastern entrance, but slowly narrowed until, as they covered the final stretch to safety, the escapers were bent low above the muck-encrusted surface. However, so long as they kept going, within a few minutes they would breathe fresh air on the Western side. Those reception-committee members who kept vigil at the grille, on the other hand, were forced to wait for long periods between groups, knee-deep or worse in the muck. When Senator Lipschitz, the students' special friend in high places, was informed of this, he ensured that these noble volunteers were provided with the same high rubber wading boots used by the Berlin sanitation department's regular employees.

The last escaper of each group was obliged to wait behind, then greet and instruct the first of the next. Wohlfahrt, the Austrian helper, would observe the operation from his hideout, ready to intervene in case of serious problems, but otherwise not showing himself until the last escape group had left. This was almost always after midnight, which was why Wohlfahrt had been assigned this task – as a foreign national, he could stay in East Berlin until two a.m., whereas West Germans had to be back on the other side by twelve.

Once the last of the escapers entered the tunnel, Wohlfahrt would wait a few extra minutes, in case of latecomers. Then he would cross to the sewer entrance and drag the manhole cover back until it fell into position and everything looked normal. Afterwards he would drive the car to some out-of-the-way spot and park it ready for the next night. Finally he would return to West Berlin on foot via the checkpoint.

The first day of the operation began after dark on 8 October 1961. Dieter Thieme, the originator of the scheme, watched from the upper landing of an apartment block just on the Western side of the border, where he had a view of the East Berlin factory yard. Hour by hour, Thieme watched the groups enter the sewer. For four nights everything went perfectly. At least 134 escapers made it through, according to the highly informal lists kept by the student helpers. Veigel thinks it was actually considerably more, because accurate accounting was not a high priority, and proper lists were made only on the final two nights.

After they had made it through, the muck-encrusted refugees were piled into a Volkswagen bus and driven to one of the FU's student hostels. There they could finally strip and shower. Afterwards they were given fresh clothes. At a time of their choosing, they would report for registration as refugees at Marienfelde. They were told to use fictional cover stories to explain their escape, since it was known that the *Stasi* had agents in the camp administration.

It was on the fifth night of the operation, 12 October 1961, that something went wrong. Badly wrong.

Midnight had arrived. The last of the escapers were on their way through. Wohlfahrt had replaced the manhole cover and left. Another successful night's work, it seemed.

Then Thieme, watching from his lookout on the Western side, suddenly froze. The student leader saw an unfamiliar vehicle race into the factory yard and squeal to a halt. A squad of armed *Vopos* filed out and began flinging up all the manhole covers they could find. They then stood with their machine-pistols trained on the openings.

The *Vopos* made no immediate attempt to go down into the sewer tunnel. The horrified Thieme, of course, had no time to divine their ultimate intentions. He hurried down to the Western sewer entrance. He had to warn the members of the reception committee, who would still be crouching by the grille, ready to help through the last of the escapers. The grille lay on the Eastern side of the border. Anyone discovered there would be liable for immediate arrest or worse.

Fortunately, however, the last of the escapers was already safely through and the helpers were preparing to climb out on to the Western side. Reassured, Thieme returned to his lookout. The *Vopos* stayed there until six the following morning, still waiting by the open manholes. They never dared go down into the sewer.

So the most successful of the sewer escape routes was closed. Whether it was betrayed, or whether the *Vopos* simply observed suspicious activity and decided to take action, is still uncertain. Thieme found out from his contacts in West German intelligence that the East Germans installed a much sturdier, heavily reinforced grille in the sewer tunnel, one that no hack-saw could reduce.

This kind of reinforcement by the East Germans seems to have been general after mid-October. There were rumours that at least one more small group had made its way through a network of storm drains connecting Reinickendorf, in the French sector of West Berlin, with the East Berlin suburb of Pankow, but even so well informed an escape organiser as Veigel has no precise information on the matter. Like the 'Girrmann Group' organisation, such operators kept quiet about their routes, in order to foil *Stasi* agents operating in the Western welfare and registration agencies.

In these early days, the organisers also did not talk to the press. But some of their clients did. Once in the West, some of the East German escapers had a tendency to brag about their success. 'Yes, the press did wreck some of our escape routes,' Thieme would later tell an interviewer. 'But most of the damage was done by the refugees themselves. After us, the deluge, was the attitude. And there's always an urge to play the hero'.[7]

In the meantime, towards the end of September 1961 the 'Girrmann Group' had also completed its first tunnel. The sandy Berlin soil was fairly easily worked, but correspondingly loose. Because of this, tunnels also required proper support, props and roofs to protect those digging below.

This first tunnel was just over twenty-five yards long, starting from the basement of a shed on land adjoining the Schönholz goods station, just inside West Berlin. It ran directly under the border into the East Berlin district of Pankow, more precisely into the Pankow municipal cemetery. The Eastern entrance lay beneath the memorial slab of a conspicuously well-tended grave. That autumn, twenty-three East Berliners found their way through this slightly macabre portal into the West over a period of two weeks. Then the *Stasi* was tipped off by a double agent in West Berlin. The East Germans set up an observation post. When two young East Berlin women tried to enter the tunnel on 29 December, they were arrested and imprisoned.

But passports, not tunnels, were what the 'Girrmann Group' was famous for. Tunnels were exciting, dramatic, and caught the public imagination, but considering the effort, expense and risk involved, they were rarely as cost-effective as other escape methods – so long as those methods could be used.

In the months after 13 August 1961, the 'Girrmann Group' helped some 5,000 trapped East Germans to attain a new life in the West. Their efforts began as an informal attempt to enable FU students trapped behind the Wall to continue their studies in the West. By the beginning of 1962, the organisation had become something much bigger. Word had spread, and the 'Girrmann Group' now accepted any would-be escapers referred to them by their network of contacts in the East.

Forged or altered documents were the preferred method. They seemed to be almost foolproof, and until January the organisation lost not a single escaper or helper. Veigel recalls bringing through six refugees at a time in this way.

This first great phase ended quite abruptly on 6 January 1962. On that day, Burkhart Veigel went East yet again on his West German passport. In East Berlin he met up with an escaper couple, to whom he gave two foreign passports in the usual way. Then, as they waited in line at Friedrichstrasse station to undergo the border formalities, the couple were suddenly singled out and taken away by *Vopos*. The train they had been planning to catch left for the West. Veigel waited, hoping that his two escapers would return shortly. When they did not, he reluctantly obeyed the rules of the escape business and climbed aboard the next S-Bahn. Within minutes, he was safely on the other side of the Wall.

Later, Veigel heard that the escaper couple had immediately confessed everything to the *Stasi*. The train he took was the last to leave before the East German police shut down the S-Bahn and sealed off the station. Had Veigel waited just a few more minutes, he would have been caught like a rat in a trap.

The sudden disaster was simply explained. That same day, 6 January, the East Berlin authorities introduced a new measure for foreigners. Henceforth, all Westerners crossing the border into East Berlin had an entry permit inserted into their passports. This was given up when the visitor returned to the checkpoint before travelling back to West Berlin. So, anyone attempting to leave without such a permit in their passport could not have entered East Berlin earlier that day, and therefore must be an East German escaper. It was similar to the measure they had enforced for West German nationals back at the end of September.

Also in January 1962, the East Germans began to construct a road behind the border barrier, which gave a free run for guards, their vehicles and attack dogs, and also the beginnings of a 'free-fire zone'. To set foot in this area immediately criminalised the intruder, making them fair game for the heavily armed *Grepos*.

A gradual but inexorable tightening of the rules – West Germans were soon subjected to strict visa requirements when visiting East Berlin, making the passport route harder still – was followed by systematic physical reinforcement of the border.

In this complex and fast-moving game of cat-and-mouse, which would continue for years to come, the ingenuity and ruthlessness of both sides would be tested to the limit. And perhaps ultimately there could only be one winner.

The Ulbricht regime, after all, commanded the big battalions.

*

By the early spring of 1962, Veigel had become a known quantity to the East German security forces. *Stasi* documents show that on 24 March he was added to their list of key escape helpers. 'Active combating' of this prolific and daring facilitator was ordered, and a warrant issued for his arrest.

The business no longer even remotely resembled a student prank. The East launched a barrage of insults and atrocity accusations against the West and the tunnellers and escape facilitators alleged to be its agents. The reality was, of course, more complicated, and would rapidly become more complex yet, but Ulbricht's regime wasted no opportunity to label Veigel and his comrades as terroristic 'saboteurs' and heartless 'traders in human beings'.

A significant boost to the East German authorities' propaganda campaign against the Western escape organisations came on 23 May 1962. Private Peter Göring of the First East German Border Brigade, aged twenty-one, was on duty in the vicinity of the Invalidenfriedhof cemetery, hard by the Spandau Ship Canal. A figure was spotted scaling the border barrier. By the time the *Grepos* organised themselves, the escaper had crossed the last barrier and launched himself into the canal. On the far bank lay West Berlin. Despite warning cries and shots, he kept on swimming.

The fugitive was a young high-school student from the East German city of Erfurt named Walter Tews. He had come to Berlin specifically in order to escape, improvising his planned route from a tourist guide he bought at the station on arrival. He harboured an absolute, if perhaps naïve, determination to reach the West. Walter was also, though at 1.80 metres (5' 10″) very tall for his age, only fourteen years old.

When he had swum two-thirds of the way across, Walter was hit by automatic fire and seriously wounded. Despite this, he managed to pull himself out of the water on the far side and find some protection in an alcove in the canal wall. He was now inside the British sector of West Berlin. Several armed West Berlin policemen had arrived in the vicinity and made efforts to retrieve the boy from his hiding place.

East Germany's border forces were allowed to shoot at escapers, but with two provisos: no firing on women and children, or on to Western territory. Both rules were immediately broken. Despite his unusual height, Walter was a minor. He had also reached West Berlin soil. However, he continued to come under fire from the Eastern side. So did the West Berlin cops trying to rescue him. They accordingly fired back.

At last the shooting stopped. A civilian was able to dangle a rope for Walter to grab. They hauled the desperately injured teenager to safety and got him to hospital. By a miracle, young Walter Tews survived, but the crippling effects of the wounds he suffered during his swim to freedom remain with him decades later.[8]

Meanwhile, on the far side, the Border Brigade was about to gain its first martyr. Göring slumped down during the final exchange of fire and was found to have suffered three wounds: a superficial wound on his right hand, a bullet through his left shoulder, and a lethal ricochet that entered near his left kidney. He was dying. Another guard had been hit in the thigh, but was never in danger.

The East German regime seized its propaganda opportunity quickly and ruthlessly. Private Göring was granted a state funeral with full honours. Streets, military units and barracks, and schools were named after him all over the GDR, a process that continued until well into the 1980s. He was posthumously promoted to sergeant. He became part of the teaching in schools and at FDJ meetings.

The week after Göring's death, a poem authored by a 'First Lieutenant Grau' appeared in an East German weekly. Two verses give the tone:

> The foe's deceits you did despise,
> To us and to your oath stayed true,
> Saw right through his barefaced lies,
> So like a coward he murdered you.
> You gave your all, beyond persistence,
> You sacrificed for our good sake
> Your hope-filled, precious young existence,
> You fell for our proud republic.[9]

This doggerel would often be reprinted and anthologised in the years ahead.

The fourteen-year-old boy whom the martyr tried to kill is, of course, not mentioned either in the poem or in accounts published in the GDR.

The official version was that Göring and his comrades had been lured into a trap by 'terrorists' and treacherously attacked in a 'staged border provocation'. 'West Berlin troops . . . carried out an armed ambush with American weapons against border security forces of the German People's Police,' thundered the statement. The Easterners had fired not a single shot against Western territory. East Germany's Chief Prosecutor offered a reward of 10,000 marks (West) for the capture of those responsible.

In fact, both a secret report by the East Germans' own investigators and the enquiries of the Western police showed two things. First, the East Germans had fired off far more bullets than the Westerners – a total of 128 against 28. And second, against the specific orders of his superior, Göring had left cover, looking for a better position to deliver a kill-shot against the would-be escaper. He had thereby exposed himself to fire from the Western side. His own weapon was set to 'automatic fire'.

After Göring, the authorities created what were in essence shrines to 'murdered' border guards, often preserving the man's room in his barracks just as he had left it, complete with family photographs, possessions and so on. Groups of recruits, schoolchildren, and youth-group members would be given tours of such memorial sites. A guide would recite all the anti-Western catch-phrases, and rail against the 'provocations' of the West German and NATO warmongers, who had cut this young man down in his German democratic prime.

Peter Göring was the first of the Berlin border martyrs with whom the East German regime attempted to construct a myth of the 'noble defender of the border' and to establish a kind of macabre *esprit de corps* among the troops themselves.

This latter task was not necessarily easy. From documents recently uncovered, it is clear that Göring himself was among the keenest servants of the state, straining at the leash to do its bidding. Others were not so eager, their families even less so. The wife of a master sergeant from the First Border Brigade was reported as telling him, after she read the news of Göring's death: 'Under no circumstances should you sign up for another year's service'. The woman was summoned to the company commander for a 'clarifying conversation'.[10]

Of twenty-five soldiers of the East German border forces who died in Berlin during the Wall's existence, almost half – eleven – were actually killed by escaping colleagues (including, in one case, a fleeing Soviet soldier). Unlike most other fugitives, such escapers were fully armed and able to return fire.

Nineteen-year-old officer cadet Peter Böhme, in training at a camp in Potsdam, deserted on 16 April 1962 with a comrade. They took pistols and ammunition, and for two days succeeded in evading a sizeable manhunt. On 18 April the two young men tried to cross the fortified border into West Berlin, sneaking from the Potsdam suburban railway station of Griebnitzsee on to a small triangle of land belonging to the Western district of Wannsee. When challenged, they opened fire. A shoot-out ensued. Böhme died, while his companion, Cadet Gundel, was arrested.

The leader of the patrol that had challenged the fugitive deserters was shot and died soon after. Jörgen Schmidtchen, was killed by a bullet from the 'bandits' as an official East German report described the desperate young men trying to flee the workers' paradise.[11] Although this killing of a border guard in the course of his duties preceded that of Peter Göring, Schmidtchen was not hailed as a 'martyr' in the same way – perhaps because the circumstances of his death, involving the attempted escape by two disillusioned GDR soldiers, officer cadets into the bargain, would have raised too many uncomfortable questions.

In January 1962, the East German government finally introduced conscription. Until 13 August it had not dared to do so, for fear of unleashing a tidal wave of draft-dodgers, fleeing Westwards to avoid induction. Now there was nowhere else to go, compulsory military service could be imposed on the population. The law came into force in April 1962, and the first compulsory recruits were marched into their training barracks without delay.

Previously, recruitment was achieved by enormous social and emotional pressure. In schools and factories, staff and visiting recruiters did their best to get boys to sign up. FDJ organisers were given targets for sign-ups among their young people. There were financial incentives for volunteers, and the promise of preferential treatment in civilian life if a young man signed to 'do his bit'.

Once a youth had succumbed, he was the state's to do with as it wished. At eighteen, Hagen Koch, for instance, had applied to join the East German navy, but found himself, so he recounts, blackmailed instead into joining the *Stasi*'s military arm, the Felix Dzerzhynski Regiment. And so he ended up at Checkpoint Charlie with a pot of paint and a brush on that extraordinary day in August 1961.

Another young East German of approximately the same age refused to accede to the blandishments of the recruiters who came to his high school in Luckenwalde, around forty kilometres south of Berlin. The boy did more than just that, in fact. He stood up in school assembly and gave his reasons, then wrote a letter to his school principal in which he proclaimed: 'My mother did not bear us, her four sons, for war. We hate war and want peace.' The boy, a high-flying student and prize-winning athelete, found his marks automatically reduced. His ambition was to become a sports reporter. It was now made clear that without army service he would not gain entry to the course at Leipzig University that would enable him to follow his chosen career.

Instead, the boy enrolled as an external student at the Tempelhof High School in West Berlin. For two years he commuted between home and city, studying for his *Abitur*, the university qualifying examination he was denied in the East. On Friday 11 August 1961, at twenty-one now a young man, he set off again from Luckenwalde. His brother took him on his motor bike as far as Teltow, the beginning of the S-Bahn line. From there he travelled to West Berlin. Two days later, the border was sealed.

The young man's name was Rudi Dutschke. Marooned in West Berlin, he became not a sports reporter but a political scientist at the FU. He remained a Marxist, although not of the Ulbricht kind. Later, in the mid-1960s, Dutschke rose to international prominence as the most famous and charismatic leader of West Germany's radical student revolt.[12]

Before the Wall, there had been morale problems and desertions in the police and the army. It got no better after the border was sealed. Scores, and eventually hundreds, deserted to the West, often in pairs and small groups.

Some fled on the spur of the moment. One *Grepo* platoon commander, stationed on the suburban part of the border, who fled West with a comrade in December 1961, described the foxhole conversation that preceded the escape:

> As we were lying there, he suddenly said to me: 'What would you do if I were to clear off?' My answer was: 'Well, there's only one thing I'll say to you – as a Christian I can't shoot at another human being.' So straight away he said, 'I'm clearing off. Do you want to come with me?'

After some hesitation, the platoon commander went with him. They made their way over the fence and through the barbed wire, hurling themselves on to the soaking ground whenever a searchlight swept the area. They stumbled into a garden on West Berlin soil and introduced themselves to the surprised householder, who gave them each a cigarette and called the police to come and fetch them.[13]

Things got so bad that a report to the Politburo suggested that there were young men who joined the border police precisely so that they could get close to the Wall and have the opportunity to flee. Supposedly unreliable types were dismissed from the border units in December, on account of close family contacts in the West, or criminal records, or subversive utterances such as 'glorifying conditions in West Germany'. The mere fact of having visited West Berlin before 13 August was often enough, especially if it involved 'going to the cinema there and attending dances'.[14]

After every major desertion, anxious discussions went on, trying to discern why this individual or group had 'betrayed' their duty. 'West contacts' were often blamed, plus seductive offers from the West's 'traders in human beings'.

In one case, a guard's fifteen-year-old girlfriend, who lived in West Berlin, stood every day on her side of the border and pleaded with him to join her. Finally, he went 'over the wire'. Contrary to their indoctrination, which explicitly forbade conversation with people on the Western side, other guards from the lad's regiment had chatted to his girl across the border. They kept her informed about when and where he would be on duty. Among these young men, personal and group loyalty obviously took precedence over military duty. 'His comrades,' the investigation document concluded plaintively, 'had not identified, in this harmless young girl, the class enemy'.[15]

Searches of young deserters' rooms would reveal mind-warping audio-tapes of Western rock 'n' roll, letters from friends in West Berlin or West Germany, or in one case tell-tale photographs of Elvis Presley plastered all over the bedroom wall.[16]

Sometimes, however, the weak links just couldn't be predicted. Major Bruno Krajewsky was a senior officer of the East German Second Border Brigade. In fact, he was a very powerful man, whose signature could for years be found on disciplinary documents. A pre-war Communist and member of the SED, the major seemed the perfect, politically reliable People's Policeman. Officially entitled 'Sub-Departmental Leader for the Investigation of Special Occurrences' he basically acted as his regiment's troubleshooter and enforcer. It was Krajewsky they called in to investigate things that went wrong, including attempted desertions and successful escapes to the West. It was his job to write reports recommending disciplinary measures and proposing how further unfortunate incidents be prevented.

On 7 December 1962, however, the gamekeeper decided to turn poacher. In the small hours of a gloomy winter's morning, the man who had spent the past couple of years doing nothing but checking for flaws in the border defences, appeared quietly on the dark eastern shore of one of the border lakes (the exact location is not mentioned) along with his wife, three children, and another family group. They all clambered silently into a boat and launched themselves across the lake.

Krajewsky had chosen this night not just for its midwinter darkness but because the lake was covered in thick, drifting fog. As the incident report commented:

K. knew his way around the border area very well and knew that our patrol boats were stuck fast because of fog-formation. In contrast to the Western patrol boats, they are (as he also knew) not fitted out with radar . . .[17]

The major, his family and friends rowed quietly – very quietly – across the lake through the fog and made it to West Berlin, where they reported to the astonished police. The Westerners thought nobody could get past the Eastern patrol boats. And perhaps the supposedly ultra-loyal Major Krajewsky was one of the few who could.

The report on this expert escape was forwarded to Chairman Ulbricht himself. It blamed the influence of Major Krajewsky's wife, who had worked in the export department of a chemical works and got a bit too close to some Western clients.

Disappointingly, the big boss's reaction goes unrecorded.

With the relatively simple passport-substitution route closed off by new visa regulations, and barriers everywhere strengthened against all but the very heaviest of vehicles, the numbers of escapes dropped, but they became ever more professional.

One route was the so-called 'Scandinavian Tour'. This used rail connections that still ran from the Ostbahnhof in East Berlin to the Baltic ports of Warnemünde and Sanitz. From there ferries crossed to Denmark, which was NATO territory.

Couriers would supply escapers in East Berlin with non-German Western passports, plus tickets and travel documentation and even luggage, to make it look as if they were foreign travellers who had started out from Zoo station in West Berlin, then changed trains for Copenhagen. Escapers would mingle with the crowds on the platform at Ostbahnhof, exactly as if this were the case. Within a few hours they were safely in Denmark. From there they could easily travel to West Germany.

The 'Scandinavian Tour' ran successfully for a few months before being betrayed by a *Stasi* agent codenamed 'Franz Fischer' who had successfully gained the trust of the 'Girrmann Group', even operating successfully as a courier. Escapers and couriers arrested on that last 'tour' ended up with heavy jail sentences. The *Stasi* agent who sealed their fates was an affable Greek medical student at the FU named Georgis Raptis. This revelation, decades later, astonished all who knew him. For years afterwards, Girrmann had continued to describe the Greek as 'a terrific guy'.[18]

With all the relatively easy 'passport routes' now closed, the time between summer 1962 and summer 1964 was the era of the tunnellers. The underground routes were expensive, labour-intensive, and dangerous for other reasons apart from the usual ones. The Wall crossers risked being shot as they fled. The swimmers of lakes or canals ran the extra risk of drowning. The tunnellers, however, risked live burial. The sandy Berlin sub-soil was fairly easily workable, but liable to crumble. And if an inadequately supported tunnel collapsed or subsided, even if the tunnellers survived, there would be tell-tale sinkage and slippage on the surface that would mean instant discovery by vigilant border patrols.

There were two main kinds of tunnel. The short, shallow and narrow one, which could be dug in a few days, and the longer, larger, deeper, more durable one.

The first kind was favoured by Harry Seidel, a former East German champion cyclist who had left for the West after being forced to take performance-enhancing drugs. Seidel developed a passionate loathing of the regime he had abandoned. He was in the West when the border was sealed, but returned through the wire several times in the weeks after 13 August to get family and friends out. After being arrested on the border, and then escaping, Seidel decided to build tunnels instead.

A colourful and charismatic character, super-fit, strong and courageous, the then 22-year-old Seidel was a true working-class East Berliner. He enjoyed strong personal contacts with people on the other side of the border, which made finding would-be escapers easier and theoretically more secure. He quickly became famous for his exploits – and would pay a very heavy price.

On Monday 11 June 1962, Harry Seidel finished digging a tunnel from the Heidelberger Strasse in Neukölln (West) to the Elsenstrasse in Treptow (East). It was only 80 cm. (2′ 7″) across, just wide enough for an average human being to squirm through. The project was an act either of extreme courage or extreme foolhardiness.

Close by, on 27 March, Seidel and his team had dug another tunnel which was discovered by the *Vopos*. He and a helper, Heinz Jercha, emerged on the other side into a trap. The *Vopos* opened fire. Jercha got a bullet in his lung. Pushing the gasping Jercha ahead of him, Seidel frantically pushed earth into the tunnel entrance to block it. By the time the border police managed to find and reopen the tunnel, both men had made it back to the West. Sadly, attempts to staunch internal bleeding failed. Heinz Jercha died before expert medical help could arrive.

Undeterred, Seidel returned to the area in June. He set up his headquarters in the cellar of a pub on the Western side, and it was from here he began burrowing at a depth of two to three metres (six to ten feet), just above the water table, shovelling the sand into a bag crammed into the space beside him. When the bag was full, he would push it back to a helper, who ferried it back to the cellar for storage.

Seidel relied on the smallness and relative shortness of the tunnel (between twenty and thirty yards) for safety. He used no prop supports, nor was there any lighting. There was not enough oxygen down there to feed a lit candle. What fresh air existed in these cramped conditions was provided by the blast from a vacuum cleaner. To make sure the tunnel would hold, Seidel had a trailer loaded with coal run over the first part of its route to see if it showed any signs of collapse. It didn't – and according to Veigel, who worked with him on several projects, none ever did.

Once Seidel had broken through, into a private house on the Eastern side, the escapers could begin their journey. The conditions must have been unspeakably claustrophobic, the air foetid, but in the end fifty-four human beings made it through this single tunnel. Seidel's engineering proved remarkably sound – when, forty years later, building workers rediscovered the Neukölln–Treptow tunnel, journalists and other sensation seekers could still poke their heads in and see where it led.[19]

Seidel, in his short but spectacular career, brought at least two other groups out. Then, in November 1962, he was betrayed and arrested. The East German state decided to make an example of him. He was the athlete-hero, nurtured by the Communist system, who bit the hand that fed him. Or such was the regime's view. The notorious East German Justice Minister, Hilde Benjamin (known as 'Red Hilde'), originally proposed the death penalty for Seidel, but was overruled by colleagues nervous about international reaction. At his trial the state demanded 'only' life imprisonment. Seidel served four years before being freed as a result of a deal between East and West, but that was in the future.

The more elaborate tunnels, bigger and sturdier, took a lot longer and were more expensive. The 28 June 1962 tunnel between Sebastianstrasse (West) and Heinrich-Heine Strasse (East) took fifty days to dig. Many of the tunnellers were men who had wives and families in East Berlin and were desperate to get them to the West. This was a labour of love. They were betrayed by a *Stasi* double agent, a 24-year-old with the codename 'Pankow', who had insinuated himself into the scene by claiming he wanted to rescue his own wife, who lived in the East. This claim was literally true, except that rather than waiting anxiously for rescue she was enjoying the benefits of 'Pankow's' *Stasi* salary, paid in West marks.

The *Stasi* had known about the tunnel for three weeks before its builders broke through to the Eastern side. In an elaborate 'sting' operation, a number of escapers and three of the tunnellers were caught. One of them, 22-year-old Siegfried Noffke, who really had wanted to bring his wife to the West, was shot when a *Stasi* man panicked. Noffke was interrogated by the *Stasi* as he lay desperately wounded on the floor of the basement in East Berlin, and died on the way to hospital.

The Westerners soon decided to arm themselves on a routine basis. These young men, often with good reason to hate the Communist regime, saw no reason why they should just surrender or let themselves to be slaughtered. The trouble was, their weapons were usually illegally held, and while in the early days the West Berlin and even the Allied authorities turned a blind eye, they would be forced to disown the escape organisers if anything shocking occurred.

There followed a sort of arms race. Siegfried Noffke died because a *Stasi* operative, waiting at the exit of the betrayed 28 June tunnel, had panicked. The reason, in turn, why the *Stasi* man lost his nerve was probably because of an incident that had occurred ten days earlier, on 18 June 1962, not far from Checkpoint Charlie.

Border guards went on alert when they noticed unusual activity on the Western side. Cameras were being set up on the roof of an office complex belonging to Axel Springer, the Western media mogul, which was situated directly by the Wall. The *Vopos* consequently spotted a suspicious-looking group about to enter a building on the Eastern side. The suspects – a man, two women and a child, the report later claimed – ignored calls to present themselves for a document inspection. As the guards approached, the man pulled a gun from his coat and fired. He hit one of the East German patrolmen, twenty-year-old Private Reinhold Huhn. The fugitives then quickly disappeared into the building. Later the *Vopos* discovered the entrance to a tunnel, through which the gunman and his companions had escaped to the West.[20]

The successful escape group in fact consisted of a man, a woman, and two children. Rudolf Müller, who had shot Huhn, was the husband of the woman and the father of both children (one of whom the *Vopos* must have mistaken for an adult woman). Müller had dug the tunnel from within the grounds of the Springer building with the aid of his three brothers and other friends and family members. What the East German report also does not mention is that another group of escapers had been arrested at the time they first challenged Müller and his family. On the other hand, Huhn had not actively threatened or pointed a weapon at Müller. He had simply demanded he identify himself.

The unlucky Private Huhn was immediately transformed by East Berlin into another martyr. The Jerusalemer Strasse, where he had been killed, was renamed the Reinhold-Huhn-Strasse, and schools, factories and other institutions were also dubbed in his honour. He was buried with full state honours in his Thuringian home town.

The East German state's campaign was aided by the fact that the fiercely anti-Communist Springer, and possibly Western intelligence, may have been involved in Rudolf Müller's escape project. The media had been forewarned. Hence the cameras that appeared on the rooftop of the Springer building before the escape.

The case of Reinhold Huhn became a *cause célèbre* of the Cold War. It was claimed by the West Berlin authorities, and widely believed in West Germany, that Huhn had been killed by a bullet from one of his own comrades. Interviewed shortly after returning safely to the West, Müller none the less admitted having fired his pistol at least once.[21] Even those who – rightly in view of ballistic evidence that later came to light – acknowledged that Müller shot Huhn, argued a case for self-defence.

But again the question appeared: where did Müller get the gun? According to Allied occupation law, which remained valid in West Berlin, unauthorised possession of weapons by German civilians was a serious crime – technically, in fact, punishable by death. Was the serious offence of illegal gun ownership and use justified under such circumstances? At the height of the Cold War, most people on the Western side thought so, but this was not a morally straightforward case.[22]

As the summer of 1962 wore on, whatever scruples observers may fleetingly have harboured were effectively neutralised by the most clear-cut and cruel atrocity of the Wall's entire existence. The killing of Peter Fechter.

*

The East German regime anticipated the first anniversary of the Wall with deep misgiving. A state of 'heightened alert' was enforced among the border troops on 13/14 August 1962. On the day itself, there were a number of political meetings in West Berlin, accompanied by noisy and sometimes violent protests by mostly youthful crowds of up to 1,500 'hooligans' (as the East Germans always referred to Western demonstrators). The West Berlin police was ordered not to let such crowds within twenty yards of the border. None of the events got seriously out of hand.[23]

The real crisis came four days later, on 17 August.

Peter Fechter, eighteen years old, belonged to a circle of rebellious Eastern teenagers, who decided they would make a mass break-out to the West. As the planned day approached, predictably, most lost their nerve and dropped out, leaving just Fechter and a close friend.

Having dodged the guards who patrolled the restricted area behind the sector border, the two young men found themselves, early on the afternoon of 17 August, hiding in a disused building near the Wall. This was now a much more formidable barrier – or set of barriers – than it had been a year earlier. They were in sight of Checkpoint Charlie, the famous American border post.

Gathering their courage, they finally left cover and made their high-risk dash. As they mounted the first wire barrier on the Eastern side, his friend going first and Fechter following two or three yards behind, border guards opened up with automatic weapons from a distance of around fifty yards. They ran on. His friend reached the final eight-foot-high wall that marked the border with the American sector, managed to scale it, and vaulted over with bullets thudding into the cement inches from him. He made it safely to the West with some superficial injuries.[24]

Peter was not so lucky.

As he tried to follow his friend over the final barrier, Fechter was hit in the leg and slid back into no man's land. There he lay, moaning and crying for help, at first loudly, then in an increasingly weak and desperate voice.

The bullet in his leg had severed an artery. A heart-rending photograph shows the teenager sprawled, half dead, in his tight jeans and with his fashionable little quiff still intact, motionless and with blood – his life blood – seeping into the ground.

An angry crowd of West Berliners quickly gathered. No one arrived from East or West to save the wounded escaper. The Easterners would later claim that, with the deaths of Privates Göring and Huhn still fresh in their memories, they feared being shot by hotheads on the Western side. The Western police, meanwhile, were under strict orders not to trespass on to Eastern soil.

The GIs from Checkpoint Charlie also did nothing. One of them was reported to have shrugged and said: 'Not our problem'. His alleged remark would be endlessly quoted and become a source of increased anti-Americanism in West Berlin and West Germany.

Peter Fechter was unconscious and may have already died by the time a senior East German officer arrived and galvanised the guards into action. Fechter was manhandled from the scene. An unsuccessful attempt was made to obscure the operation from Western observers by means of a smokescreen. Another photograph, taken from the West, shows an East German soldier, part of the furtive little cortège, as he turns to glare into the Western photographer's lens, his face a strange combination of fear, shame and defiance. Peter Fechter was pronounced dead on arrival at the police hospital a few minutes later. Around an hour had passed since he was shot. The patrol commander and two of his men were granted bonuses for their achievement.

The Fechter tragedy was followed by the most violent demonstrations since 13 August 1961. Every morning, a Soviet bus entered West Berlin, carrying the soldiers who mounted guard at the Soviet War Memorial, a few hundred yards inside the British sector from the Brandenburg Gate. On 18 August, a large crowd blocked their way and began to stone the vehicle. The Soviets threatened to open fire on the rioters. The West Berlin police were forced to disperse the crowd with water cannon. After the demonstrations against the Soviet honour guard had continued for three successive days, the British provided a military escort.

Here were the makings of an international crisis. East German brutality, Russian pride, and West Berlin anger. In Washington, Kennedy discussed the situation with his National Security Adviser, McGeorge Bundy. They agreed to look into the possibility of providing first aid for cases such as Fechter, but there was the problem of encroaching on East German/Soviet territory in order to do so. The feeling was therefore that they 'just had to ride this one'. There was irritation, as usual, with the West Berliners, who were 'of course . . . not very generous . . . to us'. The priority was to stop it all blowing up into a confrontation.[25]

The East German authorities had rewarded those responsible for killing Fechter. None the less, they were appalled at the bad publicity, and steps were quickly taken to avoid such incidents in future. These steps did not stretch to a ban on shooting to kill, but they did include new standing orders for the patrols of the First Border Brigade, on whose patch the Fechter killing had occurred. Communications between individual patrols and brigade HQ were to be improved (so perhaps the fatal inaction after the Fechter shooting was in part due to failures in the chain of command), and above all measures were taken to ensure that the sighting, apprehension or shooting of any fugitives occurred in the parts of the border defences preceding the actual barrier Wall with the West.

The public and agonising nature of Fechter's death left the GDR authorities seriously rattled. It led within days to instructions that

> violators of the border who are wounded as a result of the use of firearms, are to be recovered *immediately and without delay* [emphasis in the original] and transported to the hinterland for first-aid treatment, so that this is not visible on the enemy side.

The number of paramedical teams on the border was to be increased and stretchers kept ready, one for each section of the Wall. Plans were drawn up so that any wounded escaper could be transported to hospital by the quickest and shortest route.[26]

In Peter Fechter, the Berlin Wall had found, not its first, but perhaps its greatest martyr. This was a shame from which the East German regime never quite recovered, despite its best, most cunning propaganda efforts.

If the Springer media empire had indeed become involved in helping with the costs of the 28 June tunnel (as well as providing a safe location for its entrance), its role was to be trumped a few months later by the American broadcasting giant NBC. The network agreed to actually finance an entire escape tunnel in exchange for the exclusive film rights. It paid DM 50,000 ($12,500 then or roughly $100,000 in today's purchasing power) to a group of tunnel builders including yet another colourful, complicated figure of the escape movement, Hasso Herschel.

Herschel, born in 1935 in Dresden, was a brawny, bearded adventurer and, like Harry Seidel, a champion athelete. In Herschel's case the sport was swimming, but his background was otherwise very different. Seidel's anti-Communism developed slowly, while Herschel had always been rebellious, running into problems with the East German authorities in his mid-teens. In 1953, he was arrested for participating in the June riots. Refused higher education because of his anti-Communist politics, like Rudi Dutschke he travelled to West Berlin to take his school-leaving examination. Back in the GDR, he was arrested in 1956 for possession of items such as a camera, a telescope and a typewriter purchased in West Berlin. He served four years in prison for breaking the 'law for the protection of inner-German trade'. Herschel would later admit to being active as a minor agent of West German intelligence.[27]

After his release in 1960, having persuaded the authorities that he was a changed man, Herschel became a trainee engineer for the East German railways. But in October 1961, he crossed into West Berlin with a forged Swiss passport.

Herschel enrolled at university in West Berlin, but his main priority was to get his sister and her baby daughter to the West. He decided not to shave until he had managed to help them escape, and in consequence sported a beard of Old Testament proportions. It made him an instantly recognisable figure on the escape scene.

In 1962, Herschel was introduced to two Italians also studying in West Berlin, Domenico ('Mimmo') Sesta and his friend Gigi. Mimmo and Gigi had known each other since high school in Italy. Both were now students at the FU – Mimmo, of construction engineering, and Gigi, of graphic art – and since the border closure had become marginally involved in escape projects. Mimmo had a German girlfriend, Ellen. Their closest student friend, Peter, married with a child, had been trapped in East Berlin by the Wall. They decided to get him out, and found a factory building in a side-street just off Bernauer Strasse that would suit the start of a tunnel. A similar search in East Berlin, aided by introductions from Peter's circle of friends and family, supplied a convenient basement a hundred yards or so on the Eastern side.

The Italians and a few friends began to dig 'Tunnel 29' in May 1962. At first the going was very tough, because just here the ground was mostly clay. They could only pray they would soon get through to easier sandy terrain. However, progress remained slow. They found themselves short of both of muscle and money.

The first problem, of finding labour for the project, was relatively easily remedied. University friends brought them into contact with Hanno Herschel, who, despite his rigorous anti-Communist opinions, at first sight reminded Mimmo of Fidel Castro. The Italians were impressed by Herschel's optimism and lack of self-pity, despite the four hard years he had spent in an East German jail.[28] Even more impressively, Herschel came with a circle of his own. They also recruited the members of a group who had attempted a tunnel further north at Wollankastrasse. It had suffered from subsidence, betraying their route and almost burying them alive.

Money was a more difficult issue. They needed materials for shoring up the tunnel, which was to be almost 150 yards long. It was also conceived as a substantial and fairly roomy route that might, with luck, be usable for more than one escape project. All of this did not come cheap.

The money problem was solved in June in spectacular fashion. Hearing that a local film company was making a drama about a tunnel between East and West, they approached them and suggested someone might want to film a real escape. From there, one thing led to another. After arguments and contractual problems – they needed a substantial sum 'up front' so that they could finish the actual dig – a deal was done with the American television network NBC. Apart from the production team in Berlin, only NBC's president in New York and his assistant knew the details. With an advance payment of DM 50,000, the tunnellers' problems were over. Their financial ones, at least.

A total of forty-one different tunnellers, mostly students, took part in the excavation. The organisers piped in air and provided tools and food – even an underground rest and dining area – for the tunnellers.

The work was interrupted by severe flooding and took until September 1962. Once they were through to the East and digging beneath territory where the *Vopos* and the *Stasi* were active, dangers increased. They faced 'an unpleasant surprise', especially if the East Germans put listening equipment in the basements of houses on the border. They tried to minimise the noise, but this was always a potential hazard.

So was the possibility of betrayal. With so many involved, there was always the danger that *Stasi* spies would infiltrate the operation. One day, two men appeared and introduced themselves as Rolf and Dieter. The pair both had partners in the East, they said, and wanted to bring them over. Dieter even had a child. They had borrowed money and tried to dig a tunnel of their own with hired help, beginning in a deserted bakery just up the street. However, the task had proved too much. Looking around, they had chanced on Mimmo and Gigi's tunnel.

The Italians and Herschel, who had now become joint project boss, decided there was something not quite right here. Rolf seemed OK, but they had doubts about Dieter. They agreed to let them join in, but under strictly controlled conditions.

Only after the Wall came down would they discover that it was, in fact, Rolf who had been the *Stasi* informer. His reason was quite straightforwardly emotional. He did in reality have a girlfriend in the East, whom he desperately wanted to help to escape. The *Stasi* picked him up when he was visiting her, put him in solitary confinement, and threatened him and the girl with long jail sentences if he did not agree to infiltrate and betray the escape movement.

The tunnellers had the wrong 'guilty man', but the effect was the same. In order to neutralise Dieter, they kept him and Rolf slightly apart from the others, and secretly changed the tunnel's destination.

They had discovered another suitable basement, closer to the Wall – so much closer that by this time the tunnel had already passed it. They left Dieter and Rolf in their belief that the tunnel was going on to its original destination, in the Rheinsberger Strasse, while making plans within their trusted inner circle to break into the alternative one in Schönholzer Strasse.

On the all-important day of the breakthrough, Rolf and Dieter were put under guard and confined to the antechamber. Escapers on the

Eastern side would be given the address in Schönholzer Strasse, but the *Stasi*, if they were being kept informed by a traitor, would continue to await a breakthrough in Rheinsberger Strasse.

The escape itself was a sophisticated operation. With the help of NBC, they obtained short-range radios to communicate with each other, including the helpers at the Eastern entrance. The escapers would come through in timed groups. Mimmo's West German girlfriend, Ellen, agreed to act as courier, appearing at various pre-arranged rendezvous in that part of East Berlin to alert the groups of escapers that the operation was 'on'. This she did by coded messages. She herself would know by a white sheet hanging from a window on the western side of the Bernauer Strasse, also visible from East Berlin side, whether there were any problems in the tunnel. Several very tense hours passed until everyone got through. Ellen herself returned to West Berlin via the Friedrichstrasse checkpoint, like any normal tourist.

In some of the most moving and dramatic film footage of the Cold War, the NBC team filmed helpers advancing through the tunnel and then bringing the escapers to the West. The tunnel had sprung a slow leak after the breakthrough into the Schönholzer Strasse basement, so that the floor of the escape route was wet and muddy. One young woman – determined to arrive in the West looking her best – crawled through the sludge in a Dior dress.

The escapers arrived covered in mud and sand, overwhelmed by a mix of happiness, relief and shock. They wept and they laughed. Rolf and Dieter were held until all the escapers – Peter and his family, Herschel's sister and niece, and the other fugitives, twenty-nine altogether – were safely through.

Then, and only then, was Rolf permitted to inform his girlfriend and Dieter's wife of the plan. Both women, along with Dieter's baby son, hurried to the Schönholzer Strasse and came through later that night. Rolf and Dieter disappeared almost immediately and the tunnellers never saw them again. Rolf knew all about the long reach of the *Stasi* and its unforgiving view of those who broke agreements.

There was just one disappointment. A water pipe had cracked during the breakthrough into the Schönholzer Strasse. The tunnel, which they had intended to keep using for some time, filled with water and had reluctantly to be abandoned.

DM 20,000 of NBC's money was spent on the actual tunnel. The rest was shared between the two Italians and Hasso Herschel. The sums of money involved, and the publicity provided by the NBC film, caused great controversy in the escape movement. The film accelerated the polarisation between idealistic volunteers and hard-headed, though not necessarily dishonest, professionals.

At the time, this split was not yet clear. While the Mimmo-Gigi-Herschel team were digging the final yards into East Berlin, a newspaper cutting of the dead Peter Fechter was fixed to the basement wall, just by the entrance, so that every digger beginning his shift would be reminded of why he was putting himself through this.[29]

For his part, for the next few years Herschel continued to organise escapes, and he took money from the escapers and their relatives in the West. He made a business out of it. But he delivered what he promised. And as for the money, when Burkhart Veigel decided to incorporate a compartment for refugee-smuggling into an American Cadillac, and he ran low on funds, it was Herschel who helped him out.

As 1962 became 1963 and then 1964, the tunnelling continued, but outside in the wider world things were changing. The crisis atmosphere that followed the building of the Wall slowly gave way to a kind of sullen acceptance.

After incidents such as the shooting of Private Huhn, the Allies began to put pressure on the West Berlin authorities to crack down on the rescue organisations. The final straw — and arguably the end of the 'heroic' period of escaping — came in the autumn of 1964 with the 'Tunnel 57' incident.

'Tunnel 57' was built by a man named Wolfgang Fuchs, who had himself escaped from the East with his wife and child shortly after 13 August. Fuchs, like many escaped Easterners a passionate anti-Communist, dedicated himself to helping others reach the West. For his big tunnel project, three years later, he made careful plans, raised money, and gathered a group of enthusiasts, mainly students from West Berlin, who were keen to help. He also hired a mining engineer to make sure the tunnel was properly shored up.

Fuchs's project seemed to be the consummation of all the technical and organisational developments since 13 August. Like the 'Tunnel 29' group, he solicited money from media organisations to help with up-front costs, including DM 15,000 from German journalists, $2,000 each from the French magazine *Paris Match* and the London *Daily Mail*, and a price of $370 per picture from the press agencies AP and UPI. Only recently has it also become known that Fuchs received DM 30,000 from a secret fund controlled by the Bonn 'Ministry for All-German Affairs'. The money was channelled through a student group connected with the ruling CDU party.[30]

Work began in the spring of 1964. Fuchs's team went under the Wall from a damp bakery cellar in the French sector, near the Bernauer Strasse, and dug 150 metres under the border to the bathroom of a flat in a block in the Strelitzer Strasse. The spacious tunnel was completed after seven months of back-breaking work. The metre-wide opening in the bath-room floor on the Eastern side was concealed by a packing-case, which could be pushed aside to enter the tunnel.

Many of the escapers were from provincial East Germany. The first of them were summoned by a telegram that informed them: 'Aunt Emma dead stop expecting you immediately stop Gisela'.

At Friedrichstrasse station they were met by a courier, with whom they exchanged a password. They were escorted to the Strelitzer Strasse. There the courier got in contact via walkie-talkie with an observer on the Western side, who was watching the guards' movements at the Wall. They waited anxiously for the moment when they could enter the building where the tunnel entrance was situated without being observed.

The route was known as 'Tunnel 57' because of the number of people who escaped through it. Like the September 1962 tunnel, it was supposed to provide a semi-permanent escape route that could be used over a long period of time.

However, its use came suddenly and disastrously to an end. Shortly after midnight on 5 October 1964, a party of helpers from the Western side surfaced in the courtyard of Strelitzer Strasse 55. They were confronted with two desperate-looking men who begged to be allowed to go West. When the helpers agreed, the men said they had to fetch a comrade who was waiting outside. No sooner had they left than a group of armed *Grepos* and soldiers appeared. 'Tunnel 57' had been betrayed.

The West Berliners retreated to the tunnel entrance. One of the armed tunnel guards, Christian Zobel, fired a number of shots to cover their flight, and the East Germans fired back. In the darkness and the confusion, one of the East Germans was hit and tumbled to the ground.

The *Vopos* pursued the West Berliners into the tunnel. Shots were again exchanged, but all the Westerners made it back to the French sector.

The man Zobel hit had died of his wounds. He was not a border guard but a regular soldier by the name of Egon Schultz, and he left behind a wife and children. Zobel himself was plagued by conscience about the death, and others shared his discomfort. Only after 1989, when the world gained access to East German government reports from the time, was it revealed that Schultz had, in fact, been killed by his own comrades. Zobel had indeed wounded him in the shoulder, and he fell to the ground, but it was East German bullets that actually killed Schultz – as he struggled back to his feet.

The East Germans nevertheless made Egon Schultz another 'martyr' to Western thuggery. They waged a long campaign to have his 'murderer' turned over to GDR justice.

Nineteen sixty-four was not 1961. The East German propaganda campaign achieved some success. The shooting led to widespread disquiet and to a campaign on the Western side against confrontational escape projects, where weapons might be used. There was suddenly talk of the money that had changed hands, of mercenary motives on the escape helpers' part, and of careless use of firearms. The newspaper and magazine articles were no longer so flattering. Fuchs, it was claimed, had made 'hundreds of thousands of marks'. The two Italians who had been paid by NBC for 'Tunnel 29' the year before had been able, one source claimed, to buy a hotel on the proceeds. Tunnel guards were portrayed as gun-toting toughs.

The tunnelling teams were no longer the darlings of the Western media. They learned – as one of them put it – 'for the first time . . . the meaning of character assassination'.[31]

It was also clear by this time that the escape organisations themselves were heavily infiltrated by the *Stasi*. The rate of betrayals and subsequent arrests of escapers and helpers was becoming too great to justify the benefit.

Indirect methods were called for, and they were found.

The reinforcement of the Wall was also a response to numerous spectacular escapes by individuals.

There was still room for individual enterprise. In 1962 Hans Meixner was a 21-year-old Austrian student in West Berlin. His foreign nationality enabled him to visit East Berlin much more freely than a West German or West Berliner.

Invited to a wedding in the East, Meixner met Margit, a young woman who worked as a clerk for the East Berlin city government. They fell for each other. Being optimistic young people, they applied for permission to marry and for Margit to join Hans in the West. The request was unsuccessful. As were successive, increasingly desperate pleas to various GDR authorities.

Luckily Hans was able to drive into East Berlin whenever he wanted. Returning from one such trip in the spring of 1963 via Checkpoint Charlie, he saw how a young woman in a sports car was given a hard time by the *Grepos*. Her vehicle was so low-slung that when she accidentally let go of the handbrake the sleek vehicle almost slipped under the heavy wooden barrier blocking the exit to West Berlin.

The incident set Meixner thinking. On his next trip, he managed to mark the exact height of that barrier. He then set about looking for a car that would go under it, if only by a couple of inches. Finally he found one – a British Austin Healey Sprite. As a bonus, it had a detachable windscreen.

Meixner rented the Sprite for a week, tested it on the East Berlin run and confirmed that without the windshield it could pass beneath the barrier pole. He practised for hours on an empty lot in West Berlin, swerving between oil drums and round piles of bricks, to simulate the four-feet-high walls placed at intervals across the road at Checkpoint Charlie, just before the crucial final barrier. Once through the border inspection on the Eastern side, cars still had to slow right down and weave in and out of these obstacles. Then, of necessity going slowly, they reached the horizontal barrier. Only once this was raised by the Eastern border guards and the car was actually in West Berlin proper could the driver accelerate away at normal speed.

When Meixner finally satisfied himself that he could perform this 'slalom' manoeuvre at speed, he drove over to East Berlin. He spent the daylight hours instructing Margit and her mother, who was coming with them, on what to do. After dark, he squeezed first his fiancée and then her mother into the space behind the seats. It was unnecessary that their presence withstand an inspection – only that they not be visible to the casual eye. Finally, he drove back to Checkpoint Charlie.

The little sports car was routinely waved into the inspection bay at the barrier. Meixner braced himself. He had already removed the detachable windscreen. He remained outwardly co-operative until the last moment – and then suddenly hit the accelerator. Instead of entering the bay, Meixner spun the wheel to the left and headed for the concrete obstacles.

Despite frantic shouts from the guards, Meixner swung his way among the barriers, left and right. Luckily both the car and its hidden cargo stayed in one piece and on course. He emerged safely – his worry had been that he might meet a car coming the other way – and accelerated towards the heavy barrier, which funnelled into a final, bus-width concrete-walled conduit leading into the West. It was the last test. He held the steering wheel steady, pointed the car at the barrier and pushed the accelerator to its limit, then ducked. The Austin Sprite passed beneath the barrier with just a crucial couple of inches' clearance.

Within seconds, Meixner was through into West Berlin. No time for the guards to open fire.

The astonishing break-out by the young Austrian and his two passengers was one of the most famous individual escapes of the time. And like most such feats, its very success ensured that no one could repeat it. Within days, the East Germans had placed double metal barriers across the Friedrichstrasse checkpoint so that no future escaper could pass through, no matter how low-slung their vehicle.

More common than such spectacular but idiosyncratic stunts was the building of secret compartments into trucks and regular cars, in which passengers could be smuggled to the West. Those driving back into

West Berlin from the East were automatically required to open up their car boots and bonnets. A compartment had to be fitted out so that only a thorough inspection, if necessary a dismantling of the entire vehicle, could be guaranteed to find the concealed fugitive. In Burkhart Veigel's converted Cadillac (which was painted a different colour and provided with different plates and licence documents for each trip) the secret compartment could be opened only by a complicated process involving button-pushing, lever-pulling, opening the front driver's door at an angle of thirty degrees – and tuning the radio to an exact, pre-programmed frequency. The area between the dashboard and the engine was a favourite, as was that behind or under the rear seat. In the end, the success of such methods brought on the use of X-ray devices.[32]

By autumn 1964, the border barrier that divided Berlin was generally known as 'the Wall'. This was not entirely accurate. There existed, in fact, a total of just fifteen kilometres (less than ten miles) of wall in Berlin, mostly consituting the city-centre sections.

There were 165 guard towers, in the early years constructed of wood, and 232 bunkers and firing/observation posts. The other 130 kilometres of barriers, including those bordering on the provincial GDR, consisted basically of barbed-wire fencing. The border strip was not yet comprehensively covered by searchlights, nor was the access road parallel to the strip continuous. The use of mines and self-triggering shooting devices, which killed and maimed many on the so-called 'inner-German border' between the Federal Republic and the GDR, was forbidden in Berlin for fear of international protests.

All the same, even before further major engineering work was undertaken in the mid to late 1960s, the 'Wall' (even if it was mostly still a fence) constituted a formidable barrier, one that even professionals found it hard enough to get the better of. And, as it got harder, so the price of going West went up.

The unhappy 'Tunnel 57' of October 1964 was probably the last 'not-for-profit' escape project in which refugees were not expected to pay. Thereafter, money was asked for and given.

Hasso Herschel, in his benign enough adventurer's way, was a symbol of the new, profit-based escape fraternity. Whether it was a matter of

digging a tunnel or converting a car to carry hidden passengers, escape
was becoming a time- and capital-intensive process.

Slowly, the student idealists and the passionate anti-Communists
started to charge an economic rate for their services, or they gradually
left the scene. Burkhart Veigel continued until 1967 and then returned
to his medical studies. After qualifying, he decided to put some distance
between himself and the *Stasi*, and left West Berlin for Stuttgart in West
Germany, where he built up an outstanding reputation as an orthopae-
dics specialist. Reinhard Furrer, another prominent escape helper who
had been involved in the 'Tunnel 57' incident, resumed his scientific
studies. He gained a physics Ph.D. and in 1985 enjoyed the distinction of
becoming West Germany's first astronaut, launched into space aboard
the US space shuttle *Challenger*.

Travelling between East and West Berlin with a fake Western
passport – a means by which thousands had come West during the
first months of the border closure – had within a couple of years become
very difficult indeed.

One solution was provided by the readiness of Third World (especially
Middle Eastern) diplomats based in East Berlin to bring escapers to the
West concealed in their cars. Diplomatic privilege meant that cars
bearing the 'CD' plates of countries the East Germans considered friendly
were rarely searched. But the services of such flexibly inclined envoys did
not come cheap. Another reason why during the 1960s the average escape
fee doubled to between DM 10,000 and DM 15,000.

Another solution – espoused by Burkhart Veigel once he had converted his Cadillac – was to bring escapers out, not through the Wall
inside Berlin, but via other 'socialist' states such as Hungary, Czechoslovakia and Yugoslavia. The borders between these countries and the
Western states adjoining them were well guarded, but with nothing like
the paranoid thoroughness of the borders between the two Germanys and
the two Berlins. West German tourists passed to and fro fairly freely. The
escaper would travel to Prague or Budapest, meet his or her escape helper,
be concealed inside a vehicle and transported across the border, usually
into Austria.

Klaus Schulz-Ladegast had been picked up by the *Stasi* four days after
13 August 1961 and imprisoned at the *Stasi* jail in Hohenschönhausen

and later the notorious Bautzen prison. He was released after four years, married, and found a job. But any romantic feelings he had once harboured for the East were long gone. He had now decided to go West and was simply awaiting his opportunity.

Unwilling to risk the Wall, Klaus entered into a contract with a professional escape organisation, which specialised in getting people out through 'the socialist abroad', as the other Communist countries were known. Klaus and his wife made their way to Czechoslovakia. At a village near the Austrian border, they met up with one of the organisation's representatives, a bluff, far-from-idealistic truck-driver type.

The deal was simple: the thousands of marks that this operation cost would be repaid by the escapers once they were in West Germany and earning hard currency. It was a very similar deal to that demanded by the 'traders in human beings' who operate between the Third World and Europe at the beginning of the twenty-first century. Then as now, such organisations had ways of ensuring that escapers held to the deal once they were safely in the West.

Klaus's wife went first, stuffed into a compartment inside an old Mercedes. The driver took her across the border to Austria, then returned for Klaus. Klaus was likewise pushed into this cramped space for what he hoped would be a short trip. His hopes seemed to be fulfilled, but just as Klaus thought they must be near the border, the driver turned off the main road. Klaus froze. Had he been betrayed? It was not unknown for escape organisers to sell their charges to the *Stasi*. The car stopped. Klaus heard the driver leave. When he returned, some while later, his sweating passenger heard several heavy objects being dumped into the boot of the car. Then the penny dropped. The objects were cases of beer. Booze was, of course, cheaper in 'socialist' Czechoslovakia than in capitalist Austria . . .

A little later, they passed safely over the border. Klaus was reunited with his wife. That evening, the young couple strolled through the Austrian border community where they would stay overnight before travelling to West Germany. They ate the first meal of their new life and took the chance to see their first Western film.

The movie being shown at the town's cinema that week was of John le Carré's *The Spy Who Came in from the Cold*.[33]

15

'ICH BIN EIN BERLINER'

THERE WERE SEVERAL REASONS for the decline of the escape-helper networks within a few years of the building of the Wall. The increasingly effective fortification of the Wall was one, but there were other, more subtle influences.

For almost two and a half years, West Berliners had been all but barred from the East. After lengthy and complex negotiations in the autumn of 1963, a 'crossing-permit agreement' (*Passierscheinabkommen*) was signed. Under it, West Berliners were granted temporary permits to visit close relatives in the East during the Christmas/New Year period. Over 700,000 took advantage of the concession in 1.2 million cross-border visits. Once the holiday season was over, the ban was resumed for all but the most serious family-hardship cases, but a precedent had been set – a hopeful one and yet at the same time subtly corrosive.

From August 1961 to December 1963, no East German could go to West Berlin (apart from a few loyalists, usually on the regime's business), and no West Berliner to the East. This was clear-cut. But once weeping, delighted families had been brought together again, if only for a short time, the hope of a more liberal visiting policy subsisted constantly in the background. It made the people of West Berlin suitable subjects for blackmail. The East Germans could threaten to snatch back the new 'concessions' if the West did not co-operate in, for instance, combating escapes.

Already while the first 'crossing-permit agreement' was being discussed, the West Berlin Senate had pressured escape groups to limit their activities, so as not to endanger the agreement. One of Wolfgang Fuchs's tunnels, which had been due to 'break through' and start getting people out at Christmas 1963, was reluctantly delayed until 5 January, the last day of the West-to-East visiting period. As soon as the postponed 'breakthrough' to the Eastern side was achieved, the organisers realised they had come out not in a basement, as planned, but in the neighbouring coal cellar. This would have been acceptable during the holiday period, but now the situation was much more risky. Sure enough, after a few escapers had been brought out on the first day, and despite efforts to camouflage the opening, the tunnel was discovered and reported to the Communist authorities – by coal-delivery men on their first day back at work after the seasonal break.[1]

In autumn 1964, negotiations began about another 'crossing-permit agreement' for the coming festive season. An agreement was arrived at, providing for two fourteen-day visit periods before the end of the year, including Christmas. Then came 'Tunnel 57' and the shooting of the East German soldier Egon Schultz.

After the 'Tunnel 57' tragedy, the East German negotiators began asking pointedly if the West Berliners wanted 'crossing permits and visits for relatives or a prolongation of the Cold War'. Short visit periods were also agreed for 1965 and 1966, but many in East Berlin were already doubtful. As early as 1964, a *Stasi* report frankly told the East German leadership that such concessions could not be justified if Western propaganda continued to celebrate the agreements as 'a successful penetration of the Wall'. Only if the 'enemy' agreed to respect totally the integrity of the GDR's borders should this concession be extended. After one final Christmas agreement (1966), the concession was not renewed. It would be years before West Berliners could once again visit the East – as part of a more general settlement which went a long way to granting the Communist regime the recognition it craved.[2]

During the Cuban Missile Crisis of October 1962, almost everyone had expected the Soviets to apply extra pressure via Berlin. The Americans had, after all, demanded the right to board and inspect Soviet missiles bound for Cuba. There had been anxiety that the Soviets would respond with a similar move against Allied traffic going into Berlin. This would have amounted to an effective blockade and put the West in a difficult position.[3]

The failure of Khrushchev to make such a move against Berlin, or anywhere else in the world where American interests were vulnerable, helped President Kennedy and his advisers to pull off a considerable victory over Cuba. After the failure of the West to prevent his imposition of a border wall in Berlin, Khrushchev thought he had Kennedy's measure. This led him to a foolhardy attempt to station missiles on Cuba. By facing down the Russians there, Kennedy finally proved that he was as tough and as smart as the Communist leader. If not smarter.

The humiliating outcome of yet another Khrushchev-engineered international crisis would help start other leaders in Moscow thinking that their brilliant but impulsive boss might be more of a liability than a benefit. Two years later, almost to the day, Khrushchev was stripped of all powers in a bloodless palace revolution.

As it happened, presidential adviser Walt Rostow visited Europe at the time of the Cuban Crisis and met Brandt. Despite the Fechter tragedy, which was still very much on everyone's minds, he thought West Berlin's morale was 'pretty good'. He expressed the basic situation regarding the Wall at the end of 1962 quite frankly:

> We should be aware that the impulse among students in West Berlin to take action to help refugees over and under the Wall is very strong. Brandt is aware of their activities and has decided that he cannot, in political safety, prevent them from carrying out such enterprises.[4]

Within a handful of years, the attitude towards the escape movement had changed radically. The inherently abnormal border situation had become, in effect, 'normal' – proof, if anyone needs it, that people will get used to just about anything over time. The kind of polarised anti-Communist attitudes that had been general in West Berlin at the beginning of the 1960s had given way, for much of the population – including the political and media élite – at best to a more nuanced view of the Cold War, at worst to a bite-the-hand-that-feeds anti-Americanism.

After the Cuban Missile Crisis, the main theatre of the Cold War did not switch back to Europe. Despite crablike progress towards a half-tolerable status quo in Berlin during the rest of the decade, and the usual East–West name-calling, at no point did the city become a potential flashpoint for the Third World War as it had been between 1948 and 1963.

President Kennedy's famous visit to Berlin in June 1963 represented a high-water mark in West Berlin's self-conscious status as a beacon of freedom. The visit was part of a wider European trip, which included an official visit to West Germany. This had been planned for some time, but only at the end of March 1963 did the President and his advisers finally decide to make a detour to Berlin.

The Adenauer government in Bonn had no interest in encouraging such a thing – as in 1961 during Vice-President Johnson's visit, they were aware that it might redound to the benefit of Mayor Willy Brandt, who would be seeking election as German chancellor once more in 1965. They would rather Kennedy stayed exclusively in West Germany proper. Important figures in Washington, including Information Agency chief Ed Murrow, also opposed a visit by Kennedy to the walled city. Kennedy's appearance there, Murrow felt, might imply that spirits needed lifting and would therefore would send a subtle message of weakness to the East.

But finally the majority, including especially the President's brother Robert, was persuaded that the trip could do no harm and that *not* to go would send a depressing message both to Berliners and West Germans. The Wall had now been in place for almost two years, but no leader of the Allied protecting powers – neither Macmillan of Britain, nor de Gaulle of France – had seen fit to visit Berlin. De Gaulle had, in fact, performed an entire state visit to West Germany in September 1962, touring in a wide arc from Hamburg to Munich, but had conspicuously ignored Berlin. For Kennedy, leader of the foremost and most passionately democratic of the protectors, to visit Germany and not go to West Berlin, would be to send an unmistakably dismal and discouraging message to its people and to the world.[5]

President Kennedy's arrival at Tegel Airport at 9.40 in the morning of 26 June 1963 brought him to the last stop on his four-day tour of Germany. There had been plenty of press interest during Kennedy's travels through the Rhine and Main valleys, but his visit to West Berlin was the high point for press and public alike. Some 1,500 journalists from all over the world flocked to West Berlin to cover the events.

Most people recall the four emotionally powerful (and grammatically dubious) words of German that Kennedy uttered during his address to almost half a million West Berliners from a temporary platform set up in front of the Schöneberg Town Hall: 'Ich bin ein Berliner'. Far from being a triumph, however, for his advisers and for the West Berlin administration the speech was altogether problematic.

Almost none of what now seems memorable about Kennedy's speech was in the text, typed on roughly A5-sized cards, that he carried up on to the platform with him. Prepared by White House and State Department experts, his address was supposed to be relatively low-key. The situation in Berlin was peaceful compared with two years earlier, and it was in everyone's interests to keep it that way. His main priority was to encourage the city and its people – without provoking the Soviets or the East Germans into new aggressive measures.

But Kennedy did not stick to the prepared version. Perhaps it was the emotional effect of the visit to the Wall earlier that morning – Kennedy had been visibly moved by his first on-the-spot view of the cement blocks, the barbed wire and the watch-towers – but the parts of his speech that he improvised were both more stirring to the audience and more aggressively anti-Communist than planned.

Apart from the 'Ich bin ein Berliner' improvisation (which he conceived during an informal talk in Brandt's office just before the speech, writing the phrase in his own phonetic code), Kennedy also departed drastically from the script by appearing, in a rhetorically powerful repetition, to preach not coexistence but a fundamental incompatibility between the Communist and capitalist systems. In these extemporised passages, Kennedy attacked those who saw no difference between the systems, who said democrats should 'work with the Communists', or who claimed that Communism was bad but produced beneficial economic results. After enumerating each of these sins, Kennedy – striking his lectern with an angry energy – declaimed: 'Let them come to Berlin!' And at the climactic end he repeated it in German: 'Lasst sie nach Berlin kommen!'[6]

Kennedy went on to attack the Wall, calling it 'the most obvious and vivid demonstration of the failures of the Communist system'. At the end of his speech he left the prepared text once more and uttered the famous words again, ending: 'All free men, wherever they may live, are citizens of Berlin. And, therefore, as a free man, I take pride in the words: "Ich bin ein Berliner."'

After the President finished, he stepped back quickly, almost abruptly. The vast crowd went wild. A chant went up, so ecstatic and powerful it could have been heard in every ministry and party bureau in East Berlin: 'Ken-Ne-Dy! Ken-Ne-Dy!'[7]

Brandt waited for the roar to die down, then began his own speech. The Mayor seemed tense and nervous. During Kennedy's attack on the Wall and Communism, instead of applauding he had stared stonily into the middle distance. During his speech, the excited crowd continued to chant Kennedy's name and to interrupt with shouted comments and cheers. Brandt's irritation was visible. It got worse when behind him the President and Adenauer responded to the interruptions with smiles and waves. At one point the crowd bellowed an Americanised version of Adenauer's first name, Konrad: 'Con-Ny! Con-Ny!' The Chancellor, delighted at this reception in a city where he was usually far from popular, stepped forward in acknowledgement, while his political foe, Brandt, was still speaking.

Brandt was worried by Kennedy's unexpectedly vehement anti-Communist tirade. There had been violent demonstrations by Western youths at the Wall the previous week, on the GDR's national day. He feared that this throng, roused by the President's fighting talk, could go out of control and turn Berlin back into a world flashpoint.

Above all, however, Brandt was surprised. Just two weeks previously, on 10 June, Kennedy had made an extremely important and well-publicised policy speech at American University in Washington, DC. On that day, Kennedy had talked openly of his hopes for détente with the Communists, and had referred to the common interest in peace that united an otherwise divided world.[8] Brandt himself was working with Egon Bahr and his other advisers on a new, more flexible approach to the Berlin question and the problem of the two German states. This did not fit in at all with an attitude which cast doubt on whether any kind of coexistence was really possible, as Kennedy's just-delivered speech seemed to do.

The truth seems to be that Kennedy just got carried away. In the immediate aftermath of his speech, he was thrilled with all the applause and the excitement. Then came discussions with his advisers. McGeorge Bundy, for one, threw a douche over the mood when he told Kennedy frankly: 'Mr President, I think you have gone too far.' Calming down, Kennedy seemed to agree. 'If I told them to go tear down the Berlin Wall, they would do it,' he ruefully told his military adviser, General McHugh.

Later, at the Free University's Henry Ford Building, symbol of American largess to West Berlin, the President gave another major speech. He stuck to the script. The talk was once more of peace and understanding, and of the part that Germany and Berlin could play in the relaxation of international tension. German reunification, the President was quite specific, could be approached only as a long-term project. While expressing full support for West Berlin's freedom, Kennedy made it clear, as the leader of a world power must, that the German question was part of, and not at the centre of, humanity's problems, and that like those other problems it would not be solved overnight.[9]

Kennedy's FU speech may have been a less emotionally moving address than the one at the Schöneberg Town Hall, but it was actually truer and more constructive. This too was something Berliners needed to hear.

At around 17.45, President Kennedy climbed back aboard *Air Force One*. He had been in Berlin for almost exactly eight hours, lead actor in a masterpiece of political and diplomatic theatre. The President flew off towards Ireland, there to revisit his family's Celtic roots and maybe garner a few extra Irish-American votes in the coming '64 election. On the plane, he told Theodore Sorensen, his Special Counsel that 'We'll never have another day like this one so long as we live'.[10]

Kennedy left behind an adoring city that still remembers him with gruff affection. He created at least one extra, lasting legend. The story of the 'jelly donut'.

For many years, a story has been entertaining the world, to the effect that when the President uttered those hastily included words 'Ich bin ein Berliner' outside the Schöneberg Town Hall, he was committing a laughable grammatical *faux pas*. By inserting the indefinite article ('ein'), he was calling himself not a citizen of Berlin, but a jelly donut (known throughout Germany – but not in the capital itself – as a 'Berliner'). This led, it is said, to great hilarity among the listening crowd.

Wonderful as this story is, it does not seem to be accurate. After all, when he was composing the phrase he had with him Rober Lochner and Theodore Sorensen, both of whom – especially Lochner – were fluent in German. The construction he used was an unusual one. Normally, a German simply describing where he comes from would say 'Ich bin Berliner' (or Dresdner or Münchner). But Kennedy was not actually from Berlin, as everyone knew full well. He was rather making a rhetorical flourish, including himself in the abstract club of being a Berliner in spirit. The insertion of 'ein' made this clear. One German author explains it so: an actor introducing himself at a party would simply announce, 'Ich bin Schauspieler'; but if he was making a big issue of being an actor, claiming that his calling was relevant to some important matter, he might say: 'Ich bin *ein* Schauspieler.' The alleged amusement among the crowd seems to have been added afterwards as the story got around. The general view at the time held that the audience felt profoundly moved.[11]

So the President left a legend behind and, thanks to his second speech, a somewhat reassured Brandt.

The West Berlin Mayor had spent the past two years originating a new policy that would take account of the new situation in divided Germany, and also of the obvious disinclination of any of the occupation powers to pull the German nation's irons out of the fire. The division of the country (mirrored in Berlin) was a fact. So what to do? Adenauer, now eighty-six years old and nearing the end of his long period in office, had been wrong-footed by the Wall. His government continued to loudly affirm the sole right of the Federal Republic to represent all Germans, and to complain about the illegitimacy of the East German regime and the barbarism of its border measures. However, neither the Chancellor nor anyone else had come up with a new policy that could offer hope of change or improvement in the situation.

By the end of 1963, Adenauer had been forced into retirement, Kennedy was dead from an assassin's bullet in Dallas, and Prime Minister Macmillan of Britain, wracked by scandal and exhaustion, had tendered his resignation to Queen Elizabeth II. Even Khrushchev would last only another ten months into 1964.

In the meantime, Willy Brandt had developed a policy which, controversial as it was to many nationalist and conservative Germans, represented a practical response to the facts on the ground in Germany. It would go under the name of 'Eastern Policy' (*Ostpolitik*).

Willy Brandt's most recent biographer sees the bloody events of August 1962 as the impulse to this new way of approaching the German problem. From this time, the Mayor started to move gradually, even furtively, towards a new, less uncompromising policy towards the East.

> If a crisis showed a cathartic effect [writes Peter Merseburger], then it was the one surrounding Peter Fechter. The Mayor toured factories and branches of the administration, trying to bring home to Berliners what was and was not possible. It was not possible to talk away, or curse away, or bomb away the Berlin Wall – but perhaps it was possible to create holes in it and make it transparent so that West Berlin could come to an arrangement with, learn to live with the hated monstrosity.[12]

So far, so logical. But could he take his people with him? Brandt gave his major policy speech three weeks after Kennedy's visit. His venue was the Evangelical Academy in Tutzing, on the idyllic Starnberger See lake, between Munich and the Alps. Here he found himself in the conservative south of Germany, hundreds of miles from Berlin, confirming that he should be reckoned a national figure.

The Mayor's speech was little more than a repeat of the address he had given earlier that year in English at Harvard University, and in many ways echoed Kennedy's words at the FU in Berlin the previous month. Despite this, it attracted huge attention. This was not really because of what Brandt said, but because of what his press assistant, Egon Bahr told that very same audience that same evening.

Once more, chance played a key role in events. Brandt was held up on his way to the meeting. In order to keep the audience occupied, Bahr delivered his own prepared remarks, not as an afternote to the Mayor's, as planned, but before.

Bahr's talk, entitled 'Change through Convergence' (*Wandel durch Annäherung*) had been calculated as a low-key illustration of how his chief's 'big-picture' policy of tension reduction might be realised on a practical level. Bahr declared that, so far as German reunification was concerned, the policy of 'all or nothing' had failed. So what could be done for Germans in East and West? The idea of reunification would not be abandoned, but instead of being a great dramatic act it might rather become 'a process with many small steps and stages'. In a world divided along ideological lines, the GDR was a reality, and so long as the Soviet Union continued to support it militarily and in other ways, the Communist German state, abhorrent as it might be, had to be lived with. The aim must be to make life easier for East Germans through mutual trade and contact. It the Communist regime survived for the moment, then that was just too bad.

Brandt had been gently creeping towards just such a public view – it reflected the private conversations that had taken place within his entourage and with the Americans over the previous months. However, Bahr's speech, especially since it now seemed to appear as the main item of the evening, aroused enormous attention, by no means all favourable. Bahr himself claimed to be astonished:

> When I dictated the 'Change through Convergence' speech I had no idea that I was being courageous or that I needed to be careful. I was just making concrete what was in Brandt's speech, weighing it up, thinking it through more precisely; the discussion was supposed just to be taken a little further.[13]

That evening in July 1963 none the less represented the beginning of a new era in relations between East and West Germany, and the beginning of what would become known as the *Ostpolitik*. This policy would recognise the facts of the post-war settlement, which had removed large areas of ancient German territory and awarded them to Poland, Czechoslovakia, and (in the case of the area around Königsberg – now Kaliningrad) the Soviet Union.

There was uproar in the press, especially in outlets owned by Springer. The CDU protested. But the fact remained that the conservatives did not actually have an alternative. Once the immediate brouhaha had settled down, this point seemed to percolate into the minds of the general population.

In West Berlin, as autumn drew on, the Mayor's representatives sat down and hammered out 'crossing-permit agreements' with East German representatives. The involvement of the West Berlin administration might have seemed like a major concession but, in fact, ever since the late 1940s, middle-ranking East and West German and West Berlin officials had quietly discussed mutual trade and transport concerns, with binding agreements arrived at. This was the reality on which Bahr planned to base his 'convergence'.

The West German conservatives might attack the 'convergence' idea as treachery, but the East was, in its paranoid way, more clear-seeing in this matter. The Communist regime was torn between its yearning for international recognition and a 'convergence' with West Germany which, as the GDR leadership realised, might lead to rather more intimacy than was strictly desirable.

In the September 1965 elections, the SPD made further gains. Brandt again failed to achieve victory, but the Social Democrats' share of the vote continued to edge upwards. The conservatives' share continued its decline, while the liberal Free Democrats lost quite heavily. But the conservative/liberal coalition, led by Adenauer's successor, Ludwig Erhard, hung on to power.

As Economics Minister, Professor Erhard had been the architect of the West German 'economic miracle' after 1949, but, like so many long-serving successful second-in-commands, once he finally heaved himself into the top position he swiftly confirmed why he had always been the deputy and not the chief. Erhard proved inept at both party-politicking and foreign policy. Moreover, for the first time since the end of the war, German industry went into recession and a 'black hole' appeared in the state finances. With half a million West Germans unemployed – paradisiacal, at just over 2 per cent of the work-force, as this may seem by twenty-first-century standards – in 1966 there was anxious talk of a return to the 1930s.

In the autumn of 1966, the political world turned upside-down. The SPD joined the government, and Brandt became Foreign Minister of West Germany. The free-market, middle-class liberals had walked out of the government after Erhard decided on tax increases to solve the budget problem.

A 'grand coalition' between SPD and CDU seemed the only solution. Brandt reluctantly agreed to leave West Berlin and go to Bonn as Foreign Minister. After Erhard resigned, Brandt and several other SPD ministers entered government with the old enemy, the CDU, under a new chancellor, Kurt Georg Kiesinger. A silver-haired, silver-tongued Swabian lawyer who looked the picture of a distinguished leader, Kiesinger laboured under the burden of having been a member for twelve years of the National Socialist Party and a prominent employee of Dr Josef Goebbels' Propaganda Ministry. The East German propagandists could scarcely believe their luck.

Brandt started cautiously with his policy of 'convergence', first dropping the 'Hallstein Doctrine' and taking up relations with East Bloc countries, even though they recognised the GDR. However, not until he became chancellor himself, three years later, would he make meaningful progress on the question of East Germany.

Meanwhile, there was no point in waiting for political or economic collapse in the GDR, as the West Germans had hoped until the rude awakening of 13 August 1961. By the mid-1960s, the East German regime had stabilised.

The day the Berlin Wall became a reality has often been characterised as the 'second birth' of the East German state, the moment at which it became truly viable. Ulbricht was right. Without the Wall, the state he and his Russian protectors had created would not have survived. With it, though horribly and permanently compromised in the court of international public opinion, at least the GDR had a chance.

After the Wall was built, the haemorrhaging of the GDR's working population from East to West Germany all but stopped. Robbed of the previous supply of new labour for its booming industries by the sealing-off of the East, in October 1961 West Germany took the radical and far-reaching step of signing a treaty with Muslim Turkey, allowing for Turkish 'guest workers' to fill vacant jobs.

The German population between the Oder and Elbe rivers was now trapped in the narrow confines of the GDR, and Ulbricht had achieved the total control he always yearned for. The wave of arrests that followed the building of the Wall ebbed by the autumn of 1962, but the underlying trend was still repressive. The number of *Stasi* officers increased from 17,500 in 1957 to three times that figure – 52,700 – in 1973, when Walter Ulbricht died, and this does not count the vast numbers of part-time informers 'Unofficial Co-Workers' (*Inoffizielle Mitarbeiter* = IM).

In the forty years of the GDR's existence, at least 600,000 individuals worked for the *Stasi*. Some experts claim it was as high as between one and two million.[14] This applied to a population that fell from around eighteen to sixteen million over the period concerned. Even if we take only the number of official, salaried *Stasi* officers, this gives a figure of roughly one secret policeman per 320 East Germans. By contrast, Hitler's instrument of covert police control, the Gestapo, numbered a mere 20,000 in 1939 out of a total Reich population (without Austria) of seventy million, amounting to about one per 3,500 of the population.[15] It is hard to escape the conclusion that the Gestapo's success in controlling dissent, with a mere tenth of the *Stasi*'s full-time strength, was helped by the fact that, for most of its existence, the Nazi regime remained relatively speaking as popular a dictatorship as the GDR was unloved.

The *Stasi* retained a partisan, narrow role that had been very precisely and chillingly defined a few years earlier: 'The Ministry of State Security is entrusted with the task of preventing or throttling at the earliest stages – using whatever means and methods may be necessary – all attempts to delay or hinder the victory of socialism.'[16]

Nevertheless, it was not enough just to keep arresting the country's awkward citizens and strengthening the already stiflingly efficient internal-security apparatus – though both these things occurred in the period after 13 August 1961. Ordinary East Germans had to be given reasons to say yes to the regime. Some steam had to be allowed to escape from the pressure cooker. There had to be carrot as well as stick.

In accord with this principle, that hitherto unrepentant Stalinist, Ulbricht, now found sufficient courage to start experimenting a little. He fell in line with Khrushchev's continuing anti-Stalin campaign at the XXII. Congress in October 1961. East Berlin's Stalinallee became Karl-Marx-Allee, and the great dictator's name vanished from other streets, factories, and other institutions too.

In economic matters, Ulbricht was surprisingly supportive of reform measures. There was more flexibility in pricing, an increased emphasis on the importance of technocratic expertise and R&D in industries, and the masses were also to be granted more consumer goods. This was a far cry from the triumphant attempt to overtake West Germany through rigorous 'command economics' in the late 1950s. It showed that Ulbricht was capable of learning a lesson if it revealed itself clearly enough.

While the so-called 'New Economic System' was being implemented, the government also brought in a whole new mass of social measures. These were intended to make the average East German more aware of the advantages of living in a closely knit, cradle-to-grave socialist system. Measures to improve the status and social involvement of youth (the young had always been a bit of a problem) while at the same time relaxing previously rigid political controls, an improved educational system, reformed family law, and so on – all impressively progressive and humane in their basic principles – were. intended to help the GDR's citizens, confined as they now were, not just to accept their lot but even to see some advantage in it.

The new youth code even allowed the kids some jazz and a little pop music, 'properly channelled' of course. There was a limited cultural thaw in which works were published such as Christa Wolf's novel, *Der Geteilte Himmel* (*The Divided Heaven*), which dealt with a family divided by the Berlin Wall, albeit in a way that on the whole favoured the regime. Satirical leftists like the young Wolf Biermann (an ideological immigrant from West Germany) were also tolerated for a while.

The new family law recognised marriage and children as the basic unit and encouraged men to help with those family responsibilities. The regime might still talk of creating the 'socialist personality', but for most East Germans their way of life was starting to more closely resemble that of the traditional lower middle class than of a proletarian-revolutionary vanguard.

The 'New Economic System' didn't work all that well, but it worked better than the previous model. With the haemorrhaging of the population staunched, and increased support from other East Bloc governments, the perception of most East Germans in the later 1960s and 1970s was of relative comfort and prosperity. Private consumption per household rose by almost a quarter between 1965 and 1970.

There remained problems with the supply of everyday items such as toothbrushes, potatoes, sanitary towels and toilet paper, but between 1960 and 1970, the percentage of households in possession of a TV set increased from 16.7 per cent to 69.1 per cent, of a refrigerator from 6.1 per cent to 56.4 per cent, and of a washing machine from 6.2 per cent to 53.6 per cent, 3.2 per cent of East Germans owned a car in 1960, 15.6 per cent in 1970 – though cars were expensive and waiting times for delivery years-long.[17] Some called it 'an East German economic miracle'. This was an exaggeration, but from a material point of view life was more tolerable than it had been in the 1950s.

The regime gradually gained from an obvious but key fact: the generation growing into adulthood within the decade after the Wall was built had no experience of any other kind of society. As one East German woman born around 1950 would say after 1989, she had not realised before the fall of the Wall that the place she lived in was so shabby, so grey, or its air so polluted. Compared with other Eastern European countries – the only foreign places East Germans could visit – the GDR seemed a quite advanced place that enjoyed a good standard of living.[18]

Apart from the élite – whose cosseted lifestyle at Wandlitz and elsewhere was hidden from the masses – almost no East Germans could be called rich. But there was free kindergarten provision, free medical care, subsidised rents and vacations (the latter usually organised through state-controlled trade unions and professional organisations), and free higher education for those of whom the state approved. If you conformed, and had no unusual ambitions or desires for an alternative lifestyle, and paid your dues literally and metaphorically to the SED or the 'block' parties, life could feel tranquil and secure.

And there were other things to be proud of in the 'other Germany'. In the early 1950s, the state began an enormously ambitious campaign of encouraging sport. What began as a measure to improve health and productivity turned into a headlong quest for national prestige. Promising young athletes were picked out at an early age and sent to special sports schools. There, apart from the usual school lessons, the children were subjected to intensive training under strict discipline and a background of uncompromising political indoctrination. As they approached adulthood, the most successful were directed into thirty or so extremely well-financed and equipped sports clubs in major towns and cities. These were often associated with the army and the *Stasi*, in which athletes were offered secure jobs that enabled them to retain a technical amateur status. At the Leipzig Researach Institute for Physical Culture and Sport (Forschungsinstitut für Körperkultur und Sport), high-grade sports instructors and coaches were trained to manage the sports offensive.

The rewards for successful coaches and athletes were high: foreign travel, privileged treatment when it came to homes and cars, bonuses in Western currency. Unfortunately, the price was often equally high. At the 1968 Mexico Olympics, the GDR's team achieved third place in the medals table, behind only the USA and the USSR. Many competitors were already on dangerous performance-enhancing drugs such as anabolic steroids and hormones.

Olympic success strengthened this trend. From 1969, a comprehensive doping programme was embarked on. The Leipzig Institute, the Academy of Sciences in East Berlin, and the Jenapharm drugs company all collaborated shamelessly to ensure that East German athletes kept their place at the top of the international rankings. Such world-beating achievements provided other countries with a positive image of the German Communist state, as well as a sorely needed focus for communal pride back in the GDR. For a state of only sixteen million to enjoy such success was indeed amazing. Only after 1989 would the extent of this ruthless state conspiracy become clear. Many children and young people were given these powerful and often damaging drugs without their parents' permission, and many, as they experience middle age, suffer from disastrous long-term effects.[19]

In his twilight years, Walter Ulbricht presided over a walled fiefdom that eerily resembled the autocratic Prussian state of two centuries previously. East Germany was likewise an obsessively micro-managed, paternalistic, militarised economy in which the market-place played second fiddle to necessities of state, and where freakishly pumped-up fighters (in this case from the sports arena rather than the battlefield) were paraded for its ruler's delectation. We do not know if the 'tall fellows' of the East German athletics team were marched through Ulbricht's bedroom, with the Communist leader in the voyeuristic role of the order-besotted 'soldier king' Frederick Wilhelm I. But since 13 August 1961 there was a wall around the city of Berlin once more – from which in the twentieth century 'deserters' would be shot while trying to escape, just as they had been in the eighteenth.

It would be for Ulbricht's successor to take the next logical step and re-introduce a cult of Prussia and Frederick the Great to provide some desperately needed historical backbone to the GDR. For East Germany's stubborn, squeaky-voiced creator, it was perhaps enough to have survived and fashioned, at whatever cost to its inhabitants, an entity that reflected what he had been dreaming of since his fevered, working-class adolescence back in imperial German Leipzig.

Ulbricht was removed from real power in the East German state at the age of seventy-seven, in May 1971. Leonid Brezhnev, Khrushchev's dour successor as leader of the Soviet Union, had decided that his German satellite needed new blood at the top.

Ulbricht lived on for a little more than two years, his health slowly failing, still left with the title of president of the Council of State, but bereft of the power he had once wielded. He was not even allowed to choose his own visitors, who were selected by the Politburo's protocol department.

A photograph of the celebrations for Ulbricht's last birthday, in June 1973, shows the visibly aged former strongman of German Communism at eighty. The venue is the banqueting hall of the Council of State building. He crouches in a chair from which he is unable to rise, due to infirmity. His gaze is levelled downwards. His successor, Erich Honecker, stands at a microphone reading from a commemorative album, while behind Honecker the members of the Politburo loom impassively in their ill-fitting, buttoned-up suits. This is a tedious duty call for them. So far as can be seen, there is no other audience to the event. The faint rictus playing on the prone former leader's face may express physical pain. Equally, it may express the frustration and anger of a decaying, once-mighty animal reduced to helpless dependency on creatures he once despised. If Ulbricht had the strength, perhaps he would tear all their throats out. But he does not and cannot.

Walter Ulbricht died five weeks later, on 1 August 1973, at his lakeside house on the Döllnsee. It was here, twelve years before, that he had invited his underlings to take tea with him and pay him obeisance, the day before the Berlin Wall was built.

MONEY

16

THE SURREAL CAGE

WEST BERLIN TOO HAD changed by the time Ulbricht died.

Joachim Trenkner had escaped the East in 1959, two years before the Wall was built. Although he had cheated the refugee system to stay in West Berlin, his initial time there was actually fairly short. A few months after 13 August, someone told him the Americans were offering scholarships to young West Berliners who wanted to study in the United States. These generous stipends were part of the cultural-exchange programme which the President's brother Robert Kennedy had promoted so keenly, seeing it as a way of inoculating Germans against Communism.

Joachim applied for a scholarship and got it. So in 1962, he went to study at De Pauw College, a small university in the American Midwest. There he met and married an American girl. Together they moved to New York, where he worked for some years at the magazine *Newsweek*, beginning a career as a writer and cross-media journalist that proved long and successful. The marriage eventually failed, and he decided to return to Berlin.

When Joachim (now often known as 'Jo') landed once again at Tegel Airport, he was thirty and the year was 1968. Money had poured into the beleaguered city since 1961 and the place was full of new building projects, like the modernistic Europa Center in the Budapester Strasse, which reminded him of a 'little Manhattan'. And the psychology of the place had changed too:

People seemed to be free of fear and less tense than earlier, the city had become more international, with countless Italian, Chinese or Turkish restaurants. Americans, Brits and the French looked after security, and the Berliners had grown accustomed to the Wall. And there was something else new in the late 1960s and early 1970s. Often, all too often, there were demonstrations taking place, demonstrations against the protecting power, America, which was pursuing a bloody war in far-off Vietnam.[1]

The late Hungarian composer, György Ligeti, who knew West Berlin well, called the half-city a 'surreal cage', a bizarre prison in which paradoxically only those locked up inside were free.[2]

In fact, in the late 1960s – and certainly by the 1970s – West Berlin came to resemble in significant ways the 'free city' that had been Khrushchev's brainwave back in 1958.

True, its population of just over two million survived because of huge subsidies from the half-city's rich 'big brother', the Federal Republic. But West Berlin was not West Germany. It operated under different laws and had – increasingly – a curious social and political flavour all of its own. Cut off from its economic and demographic hinterland, and from almost half its former urban area (and a third of its former population), West Berlin was truly an island in the Communist sea.

The majority of established Berliners were still pro-Allies and especially pro-American. They still cheered at Christmas, when the tanks of the 40th Armoured toured Steglitz and Zehlendorf with Santa Claus in full fig in the turret and toys for the local kids.[3] America was the guarantee that their freedoms would not go the same way as those of their friends and relatives in East Berlin.

But the established Berliners no longer entirely dictated the tone. During the 1960s, the balance of the city began to change. In the early days after the Wall was built, the city had feared a flight of financial and human capital. So-called *Zittergeld* (literally: tremble-money) was paid to families and individuals prepared to stay in or come to the city marooned among the Communists. Manufacturing industries, including electrical equipment, machine-tools and the garment business, suffered from the unreliability and expense of the transit routes that were now the only ways in and out of West Berlin. No armaments or equipment with military applications could be manufactured there. People of working age were leaking away to the West, along with major parts of the city's manufacturing industry.

By the 1970s, almost a quarter of all Berliners were over the age of sixty-five, twice the proportion in West Germany. By contrast, the percentage of children under the age of fifteen was 15 (in West Germany proper, around 23).[4] The West German government's extremely generous subsidies to West Berlin's infrastructure, plus a lower turnover tax for businesses there, compulsory relocation of production facilities and administrative offices of Federal government departments in West Berlin, and so on, helped keep the walled-in city alive.

West Berlin was nevertheless slowly depopulating. In the early 1960s, its birth rate was among the lowest of any city in the world. Most years, thousands fewer people came to West Berlin than left, a situation that continued until the late 1980s.

Significantly, in the 1960s, the newcomers were not the traditional immigrants looking for work, nor were they ambitious young professionals. West Berlin was not a place to go if you wanted advancement – that happened in thriving centres like Frankfurt (finance), Hamburg (the press), Düsseldorf (advertising and insurance) or Bavaria, where the new electronic industries were beginning to flourish.

No, those coming to Berlin in large enough numbers to make their presence felt were an interesting crowd, despite – or perhaps because – they were not mainstream. Here were people in search of alternative lifestyles, cheap rents, round-the-clock nightlife, and, last but not least, looking to avoid conscription into the West German armed forces, the *Bundeswehr*. Under Allied occupation law, a West Berlin residence card granted immunity to the West German call-up.

The students of 1961 had supported the escape-helper teams. The evil nature of Communism had been an item of faith. However, by the late 1960s, the student body had moved sharply to the left, fed by those escaping the cosy, conservative values of the West German 'economic miracle'. And with advent of the Vietnam War, the USA no longer symbolised freedom. On the contrary, when contrasted with 'imperialist' America, to these new rebels against capitalism East Germany, though stuffy and Stalinist in many of its external forms, didn't look so bad. Free to come and go in the East as they wished, Western radical tourists liked its lack of commercialism and advertising, the cheap food, the bookshop next to Friedrichstrasse station where you could buy very inexpensive copies of the Marxist classics. What could be so wrong with a state where you could buy a hardcover copy of Marx's *Eighteenth Brumaire* for the price of a cup of (terrible) coffee?

While enjoying the pleasures of a free and easy existence in West Berlin, many of the alternative crowd sneered at the existing population, mocking its consumerism, apparent social conservatism and continuing gratitude to the NATO forces who stood between their beleaguered part-city and its absorption into the surrounding 'Workers' and Peasants' State'.

Instead of spending the 1970s continuing to protest against the Wall, the radical activists who flocked to West Berlin spent their considerable free time protesting against imperialism in far-away countries and, closer to home, against the allegedly proto-Fascist nature of the post-war West German state created by Adenauer's conservatives. It was true that many more moderate observers had also been disappointed by the failure of the Federal Republic to make a really clean break with the past. West Germany kept many of the rigidly hierarchical structures and author-itarian attitudes of earlier eras. Konrad Adenauer may have disliked and despised the Nazis, but he had been a senior Prussian state employee before 1914, and Lord Mayor of Cologne under the last German Kaiser, and he espoused a pious Catholicism that accepted the absolute authority of the Pope.

As could be expected, the West Germany Adenauer and his political supporters created after 1945 was a parliamentary democracy that accepted the rule of law, but it was far from a natural home for radicalism and free thought. Berlin was historically more tolerant than provincial Germany, and this remained the case even though a robust anti-Com-munism became general in the Western sectors after 1945.

Gay and lesbian life had flourished in Berlin for at least a century, and had enjoyed almost total toleration in the 1920s, slightly but not completely modified by the existence of the so-called 'paragraph 175' which forbade homosexuality. In 1929, the last left-liberal coalition of the Weimar Republic actually passed a repeal of paragraph 175, but within months the Right took control, and the repeal was shelved. Three years later, Hitler seized power. The Nazis added 'paragraph 175a', which broadened the area of culpability to include activities not even involving mutual physical contact and also allowing castration for male homosexuals found 'guilty' of gay relationships. This resulted in a vast increase in the arrest and imprisonment of gay men, and to the deaths of many thousands in concentration camps.

After 1945, West Germany kept the Nazi ultra-restrictive '175a'. East Germany reverted to the old, less absolute, paragraph 175 and was reckoned in the immediate post-war years to be more tolerant, though there were crackdowns on public expression of gay sexuality, especially when East Berlin hosted 'world youth festivals' and suchlike. West Berlin, removed from strait-laced religious conservatism, remained in the area of sexuality, as in other matters, an island. Reinforcing the native community, gay men and women flocked there to live as they wished and needed to live, and by and large were able to do so. Both German states decriminalised homosexuality towards the end of the 1960s, but Berlin has remained a vibrant centre of gay culture into the twenty-first century.

So far as broader social and political attitudes were concerned, there had been some 'denazification' immediately after the war, but there is no question that in West Germany many who had made sordid, even brutal careers under Hitler seamlessly achieved the transition into the new post-war élite, in industry, the law, the state apparatus and the armed forces. The Allies, keen at first to purge the country of Nazis, quickly realised that to do so with any thoroughness would also purge Germany of the men (and they were overwhelmingly men) who knew how to run the place. And with the Cold War quickly dominating the international horizon, it was more important that the new Germany functioned, and joined the Western side, than that it was politically pure. A lot of investigations against useful men of a certain age and curriculum vitae were not pursued with due process or energy.

This was a point often made in East German propaganda, with some justice. On the other hand, the fact that 80 per cent of doctors in the East German province of Thuringia had been members of the Nazi Party before 1945 did not lead the Communist authorities to sack them all.[5] Exceptions were quietly made, and plenty of them. The same applied to other key areas of the administration and the economy. Neither Germany could really afford to start again with a completely clean slate.

The only area where the GDR did carry out an almost total purge was in the judiciary. By the 1950s, the old upper middle-class judges had been replaced by 'class-conscious' jurists, many of proletarian origins, who could be relied on to do the regime's bidding. The practice of deciding political offenders' sentences before the trial had been present under the Nazis, but in the GDR it became common practice. Klaus Schulz-Ladegast said that if one looked properly at the notes your *Stasi* interrogator was making, you could see him writing down recommended sentences according to the replies he was getting. His own, he recalls, was halved to four years as a result of adroit handling of one of his most vital interviews.[6]

But the purists of the radical Left in West Berlin during the late 1960s and the 1970s were not interested in such fine distinctions. They provoked the establishment and, when the establishment lashed out in response – angered by the contempt the radicals showed for the values that West Berlin had made such sacrifices to preserve – they proclaimed it as bad as the Nazis.

In June 1967, the ruler of Iran included West Berlin in his tour of Germany. As an authoritarian ruler and, so far as the Left was concerned, an American stooge, Shah Mohammed Reza Pahlevi was a fit subject for a big demonstration, and the demonstration turned violent. A student protester, Benno Ohnesorge, was shot dead during an encounter with police. Days of riots followed. Thereafter, many on the Left were convinced that in the Federal Republic they faced Hitler's heirs and therefore any methods were justified to defeat those who held power.

Symbols of America such as the US cultural centre near Zoo station, the so-called *Amerika-Haus*, were subjected to aggressive direct action. In fact, the *Amerika-Haus* remained more or less under siege for the whole period between the late 1960s and the late 1970s.

There were times when West Berlin seemed to teeter on the edge of violent anarchy. Rudi Dutschke, who ten years earlier had refused to join the East German army, was by this time a doctoral student at the FU – and the most prominent of all the student radical leaders. Serious-minded, fearsomely intelligent, a brilliant orator, he inspired equal measures of fear and respect, love and loathing among his fellow Germans. To the Springer press, he was the political devil incarnate – 'Red Rudi'.

On 11 April 1968, Dutschke was riding his bicycle in West Berlin when he encountered 24-year-old Josef Bachmann. Like Dutschke,

Bachmann had come West as a refugee from East Germany, but unlike Dutschke he was an ill-educated drifter. Having caused the student leader to stop, he pulled a gun and shot him in the head. Dutschke was all but given up for dead, but after a hazardous operation lasting many hours, his life was saved.

The result was more days of riots, in which there were assaults on all the symbols of the establishment, including an attempt by a mob to burn down the Springer headquarters, a tower block right by the Wall. The Springer press, especially the tabloid *Bild-Zeitung*, was blamed for whipping up feeling against the radical student leaders. *Bild* had written of 'intervening' against the 'ringleaders' of the Left. Bachmann was found to be strongly influenced not just by *Bild*, which was read by millions, but also by Nazi fantasies and the reading of much more extreme far-right publications. He committed suicide in jail in 1970.

Dutschke survived, and after many months of physical rehabilitation managed to regain his powers of speech and thought. None the less, although he continued to be active, he never quite resumed his dominant position on the radical Left. He was troubled by terrible headaches and epileptic fits for the rest of his short life. In the autumn of 1979, Dutschke travelled to Berlin from the Danish city of Århus, where he had taken a teaching job at the university, to participate in discussions about the formation of the German Green Party. By the end of the year he was dead. It is thought that he suffered a fit while taking a bath and drowned.

All the same, in the late 1960s and 1970s, West Berlin was a pleasant enough place to live. It had an intimate, piquant flavour, very relaxed and yet slightly dangerous, that you either liked or disliked, and if you liked it you probably loved it. You could avoid being confronted too much by the depressing fact of the Wall if you knew which routes to take. There was a lively party and cultural scene, plenty of interesting people. Little was forbidden, just about everything was tolerated.

The alternative lifestyle types could be seen, if you forgave their showy and sometimes violent excesses, as a kind of noisy, permanent street cabaret. It was in Berlin that several soon-to-be-notorious anarcho-radical figures, including student leaders such as Fritz Teufel and Dieter Kunzelmann, and the precocious Ulrich Enzensberger, younger brother of the famous German writer, Hans-Magnus Enzensberger, set up the so-called 'Commune One' (Kommune 1). Here sexualised politics and politicised sex became the order of the day. What most people understand as politics often receded into the background.

As Ulrich Enzensberger put it:

> We wanted to begin the revolution with ourselves. We wanted to revolutionise ourselves, the bourgeois individual, we did not want to become apparatchiks, gaga seminar-room Marxists in our wing-backed chairs with professorial bellies, wives, grandchildren and house-slippers, dead men walking, hands-in-pockets strategists, exhausted political cadres – and neither did we want to become dried-up organisation men or party functionaries, spinning the whole time on the eternal carousel of pay talks and discussion groups. The fact that life consists of cycles – biological and historical cycles – brought me, at least, into a state of white heat. Just get off the treadmill! But how? This was the deeper meaning of our motto: 'What's Vietnam to me? I have orgasm problems'. We wanted the great, the fantastic ecstasy, we did not want to sacrifice ourselves for something abstract, for a phantom, for literature or the world revolution. More honesty! We didn't want to hide anything. Our parents had hidden so much . . .[7]

Whether the people of Vietnam suffered from orgasm problems is not recorded by Herr Enzensberger or, preliminary enquiries seem to show, anyone else. Eastern Europeans who arrived in West Berlin were bemused by its leftist scene, this exotic political and social hothouse flower. They were appalled by the extent to which such far-left thought could be so widespread and dogmatically expressed, with the real-world results of Marxism-Leninism so painfully and cruelly apparent right on the rebels' doorstep, in the shape of the Wall.

Milos Foreman, the Czech film director, arrived in West Berlin in 1968, at the height of the Prague Spring (soon to be crushed by Soviet tanks) and joked: 'When we were trying to take the red flag down, they were trying to put it up!'[8]

While the pampered youth of West Berlin was testing how much punishment freedom could take while keeping some recognisable kind of shape, the East German regime had its own problems, but these did not stop it from tightening its hold on power.

In contrast with the West, where alternative lifestyles were by and large tolerated, in the GDR, between the sixties and the eighties, pressure on 'hooligan' or 'subversive' elements was intense. Hippies were bad enough, but probably the most serious conflict between the state and its young came in the late 1970s when punk culture spread to East Germany.

It wasn't just the clothes – the ripped garments, the fetish objects and chains – or the excessive drinking – drugs were almost impossible to get in East Berlin at this time – or the flaunting of evidence of self-harm. There was something else about punk that the authorities couldn't stand. Perhaps it was the key phrase of the movement, 'No Future!' In a society where the past was uncomfortable, the present seriously problematic, but the utopian 'socialist' future was *everything*, pessimism of the kind that punks luxuriated in was considered deeply anti-social.

As a matter of official policy, punk groups were refused service in cafés and bars, excluded from social occasions, sometimes thrown off trains and buses. For these young people, a great deal of each day was spent just trying to find a place where they could sit down and order a drink. *Vopos* subjected them to incessant ID checks, even if they were just walking in the park. It was bad enough in the suburbs, where most of these young people lived with uncomprehending or hostile parents, but once they came into the centre of the city they ran serious risks. The Alexander-platz, for instance, was known as a place where they could meet Western punks, usually in the self-service cafeteria by the television tower. This they very much wanted to do. To talk with such Westerners or even – highest honour of all – to be mistaken for a Western punk themselves, though their own S&M finery was generally home-made, remained a burning ambition.[9]

The punk groups were infiltrated by the *Stasi*, hounded, and often pulled in for interrogation sessions. Many were imprisoned, usually for short, sharp periods of a few weeks or months. They would be seized on charges of hooliganism, subversion or anti-social activity, or – if they got too close to Western punks – of 'state-endangering links' or even 'espionage'. The authorities had a varied bag of catch-all, small-print legal measures at their disposal. The fact that many punks were the children of loyal party officials did not necessarily protect them. Parents often seem to have 'turned them in', either from genuine outrage or fear for their own careers.[10]

From the 1960s onwards, wayward East German youth was subjected to the strictest, in fact downright brutal 're-education' in military-style so-called 'youth industrial schools' (*Jugendwerkhöfe*). These were attached to the Ministry of Popular Education (*Ministerium für Volksbildung*), which was presided over by Erich Honecker's formidable wife, Margot.

For a young person to be incarcerated in such a place, the crime need not be serious. In fact, there need have been no crime at all, in the usual sense of the word. Teenagers between fourteen and eighteen could be confined to these places without trial for minor crimes such as theft or fighting, but also for truancy or (in the opinion of the authorities) anti-social behaviour, such as having long hair, wearing unconventional clothes, or hanging out with the wrong crowd. Children of politically dissident parents, or of parents who had repeatedly requested permanent exit from the GDR, were also at risk.

The time in the institution began with the head being shaved and then several days of solitary confinement. The severe and minutely worked-out regulations, which covered every aspect of behaviour every hour of the day, had been developed in Stalin's Russia. Their aim was to turn troublesome young people into obedient members of the collective. The director of the most notorious of these youth prisons, at Torgau (a companion to the much-loathed adult prison there), stated that 'as a rule we need three days for the young people to come into accord with our demands'. Isolation cells, beatings (the teachers were allowed to 'defend themselves' and did so with relish), and collective punishments were the rule.[11]

In the early 1980s, East German punks found a refuge with the Protestant churches, whose pastors often offered them places to socialise and to practise and play punk music, sometimes as part of 'modernised' church services. The numbers of punks increased as in the 1980s discontent grew, along with the ranks of the skinheads, who represented an altogether more sinister trend towards racism and neo-Nazi nostalgia which the state, for all its power and rigour, seemed helpless to prevent.

*

The mid-seventies were a strange, tense time for the GDR and its rulers. Despite the apparent relaxation of the international situation, in Berlin the Wall was being repaired and extended to a degree that would bring it to its most lethal and secure condition.

What Western tourists called the 'Berlin Wall' was known to the Easterners as simply the 'border marker'. Most ordinary people from the East never even saw it. For them, the barrier existed between sixty and ninety yards back inside East Berlin, in the form of a concrete-slab barrier, the so-called 'hinterland' wall. This backed on to ordinary East Berlin streets or open ground and was festooned with stern warnings. Anyone who scaled this initial barrier was outlawing themselves; they were officially a criminal and could be fired upon.

Should anyone climb the hinterland wall without being observed and drop to the ground on the other side, they almost immediately faced the 'border signal fence', a structure of barbed wire and mesh stretched between concrete posts, with a sloping barbed-wire topping to discourage climbing. It was reinforced for a couple of feet at ground level to stop anyone crawling under it. Most importantly, it was wired to set off an alarm sound, and often a floodlight, when touched. If the border guards had not been alerted so far, they now knew an escape was in progress.

But for the escaper there was still a long way to go. Then came specifically anti-personnel devices, be they sharp metal tank-trap-like obstacles known as 'dragons' teeth' (*Höckersperren*) or even nastier arrangements, known in German as *Flächensperren* (literally, 'surface barriers'), which consisted of steel bars laid out on the ground and covered with metal spikes or teeth. Any would-be escaper leaping down unawares from the 'border signal fence' would find their feet or limbs lacerated by these instruments. If the escapers survived this, they would face being observed from one of the manned concrete observation towers that were now situated every hundred metres along the East Berlin/West Berlin border. The guards had orders to shoot. Then came the floodlit supply road that ran the entire length of the city border. And beyond that, the so-called *Kontrolstreife* (control strip) – more accurately known as the 'death-strip' – which consisted of a several-metre-wide expanse of carefully raked sand, on which footprints or other marks would be instantly noticeable. Often a dog-run would be set up along this part of the border.

German Shepherd dogs were supplied by the *Stasi*'s dog-training school at Lobetal, north-east of Berlin. Each animal would range along a hundred-metre-long wire. The wire, to which their leashes were attached, ran at around five feet above the ground. The animals would react exactly according to their training if they spotted an intruder, seeking and attacking. At night, during the 1970s, the dogs' lonely howls echoed eerily through the neighbouring areas of East and West Berlin.

Almost nobody got past that point in the 1970s or the 1980s, certainly not in the centre of Berlin. Then, and only then, would an escaper have reached the 'border marker' or 'foremost barrier element', the twelve-feet-high wall with its rounded, scramble-proof top. This was, for Westerners, the 'Wall'. The Western side was covered in colourful and wacky graffiti, subject of a million tourist photographs. It was actually all but insignificant from a security point of view.

There were four great reorganisations of the Wall. It was further extended and refined in the 1980s, but by the mid-1970s the defence had become all but impregnable. The guards knew their orders, and also the fact that if anyone did make it through to the West, they would be held responsible. One explained the dilemma:

> The responsibility was sloughed off on to the most junior man, the one who was the worst trained. I realised this problem when I myself came to stand guard. I thought to myself, what will you do if someone tries to escape here. We rehearsed that and asked ourselves, what shall we do if something happens at Lamp 35 – there was a numbered arc lamp every 35 metres – how shall we catch the border violator. If the visibility got a bit worse, we had to get down from the tower, so as to see better. It can take around fifteen seconds to leave the tower . . . everyone was happy if he could climb down from his tower with his duty over and with nothing having happened.[12]

This reluctance on the part of most border troops – who were after all largely conscripts – to fire on their fellow East Germans did not make much practical difference. The authorities were aware of such reservations and ensured that the guards would be too terrified to do anything other than obey orders and open fire. The squeamish guard could not even ignore the escaper and hope none of his colleagues noticed. Sooner or later, he could be sure that some expert investigator would pick out the telltale footmarks in the raked sand and realise that Soldier X, on duty in that section at that time, had let a 'border violator' make it through to the West. Soldier X would then be in very big trouble. Negligence was treated as equivalent to treachery, and penalties for treachery were draconian.

The only devices that were not installed on the Berlin border – though they existed on the border between East and West Germany, more than a hundred miles to the west – were anti-personnel mines and automatic shooting emplacements (*Selbstschussanlagen*), sets of self-firing guns that were triggered by trip wires or other contact indicators. The regime was concerned that international protests would follow the use of these unpleasant installations in an urban area frequented by tourists and foreign observers.

It was true that the East German Politburo was strangely sensitive. Its members wanted to keep their population shut up inside the GDR, but at the same time they wanted themselves and their state to be well thought of. Paradoxically, the maximum strengthening of the Wall occurred in the mid-1970s, after Walter Ulbricht's death, and also after agreements over West Berlin and the status of the two Germanys, which led to stability and to a regulation of routine travel between them.

Most of the travel was, as before, one-way, from West to East. Until the mid-1980s, only East Germans of retirement age could travel freely to the West. They were, of course, no longer productive. What did it matter if they chose not to return?

In 1969 Brandt became Chancellor of a 'social-liberal' coalition with the FDP and was free to pursue his 'Eastern Policy'. Under the 1971 Berlin Agreement between the Allies and the Soviet Union, West Berlin remained separate from West Germany but had its continued independence guaranteed by the Soviet Union as well as the Allies. The East agreed to ease transit traffic between West Berlin and West Germany. West Berlin would not be ruled from Bonn, but West Germany would represent the city in foreign affairs.

These agreements were conditional on a deal between East and West Germany on transit traffic, directly negotiated at a government level. In effect, this gave the Allies and the West Berliners stability at the price of *de facto* recognition of East Germany. Formal recognition followed two years later in the *Grundlagenvertrag* (Basic Treaty) between East and West Germany. After tortuous negotiations, this was signed just before Christmas 1972.

Various forms of words allowed West Germany to avoid completely sacrificing the notion of German unity (and its previous claim to be the sole representative of the German people). A formula was arrived at that stopped just short of the two countries' treating each other like foreign lands. East Germany set up a 'permanent representation' (*Ständige Vertretung*) in Bonn, and West Germany did the same in East Berlin. In practice, however, in the twenty-third year of its existence East Germany became a fully independent and accepted member of the international community and a member of the United Nations. No one in the world community seemed much to mind about the Wall.

The Brandt 'social-liberal' government's treaties with the USSR, Poland and Czechoslovakia, acknowledged the results of the Second World War and abandoned claims on territories lost by Germany in 1945. The agreement between the two Germanys represented the realisation of the 'Eastern Policy' that had caused such dissent ten years before when Egon Bahr and Brandt first presented it at the Tutzing conference.

So why did the 'spoiled old men' (*verdorbene alte Männer*) who ruled in East Berlin, remain so unhappy in many ways?

A clue is in the phrase. The description 'spoiled old men' to describe the GDR's leaders was coined by a figure with whom the élites in neither East nor West were entirely comfortable. His name was Wolf Biermann.

Born in Hamburg in 1936, son a of a half-Jewish Communist shipyard worker who died in Auschwitz, Biermann was an idealistic leftist by birth and conviction. At seventeen, he voluntarily emigrated from West Germany to the East, finishing his school education there and then studying in East Berlin. After working as an assistant at Brecht's famous Berliner Ensemble theatre after the great man's death, he founded his own theatre company and began to write political and satirical songs. In 1963, the youthful Biermann got into trouble by producing a play about two lovers separated by the newly built Berlin Wall. It was banned by the regime before its first performance. He was increasingly subjected to performance bans in the GDR but allowed to tour in West Germany, where he became very popular. For almost ten years, Wolf Biermann was in the bizarre situation of living in East Germany as a critical supporter of the Communist regime, while performance and publication of his work was banned. In the West, however, his records and books were massively popular and his concert tours sell-outs.

The one-man anomaly that was Wolf Biermann finally provided one of the great absurdist jokes of the Cold War. In November 1976, while touring in West Germany, he was stripped of his East German citizenship and banned from going home. A regime that had expended billions of marks and hundreds of lives to stop its people from leaving, now forbade one of its most famous citizens to come back.

At worst the regime's attitude towards those who refused to go along with its plans for a society composed of 'new human beings' veered into a murderous Stalinist security obsession. At best it resembled a puzzled adult trying to correct a child who keeps trying to go 'down' on an 'up' escalator. The 'up' escalator of History. Does this uninformed little person not see that such behaviour is not just wrong but dangerous?

All the same, the treaties brought a tidal wave of West German visitors to the GDR. Both West Germans and West Berliners could now travel at will, whether as simple tourists or to see families and friends long trapped behind the border.

At Friedrichstrasse station, where thousands now crossed between West and East every day, the GDR built a glass-and-steel bunker to process visitors in and out. Great queues would form at night there, when Western day-trippers (who had to be back on the train at midnight, Cinderella-fashion) entered and waited to go downstairs to the complex of underground processing halls, where he or she would shuffle their way to sections labelled 'Westberlin', 'BRD' (West Germany), or 'citizens of other states'.

The infamously ill-mannered and brusque border officials would check passports, ensure no one had abused the currency regulations (which forced compulsory amounts of East German marks to be taken into the country but none to be brought out) and – when finally he or she was satisfied that the security of the Workers' and Peasants' State had not been undermined in any major way – press a button that allowed the traveller to pass through. If they were entering the East, travellers would emerge into the Eastern part of the station, where taxis or further S- and U-Bahn trains would be waiting to take them where they wanted to go in East Berlin. If they were leaving for the West, they would end up on the westbound platform that would take they back over the Wall into West Berlin. Many heart-rendingly emotional scenes occurred outside, as East Germans greeted or bid farewell to their Western friends or relatives. Berliners dubbed this intimidating complex the 'Palace of Tears' (*Tränenpalast*).

Whether arriving directly at the border around the established checkpoints at Helmstedt or Hof, or taking advantage of the other frontier posts that were opened up in the 1970s, Volkswagens, Audis and Mercedes were now frequent sights on the pot-holed and cobbled roads of the GDR. The West German cousins were making full use of their visiting rights.

Claus Christian Malzahn, West Berlin resident but son of refugees from the Leipzig area of East Germany, recalls how in the 1970s, once the treaties were signed, they could suddenly cross the Iron Curtain and visit the rest of the family whenever they wanted. There would be scarce Western treats for the Eastern relations – Rolling Stones albums for the kids, fresh real coffee for the grown-ups. On the return trip home, the car would be loaded up with model railways (a speciality in the GDR), carved toys for which the Thuringian Forest was famous, and Christmas stollen.

Every summer without fail there would be a get-together of the entire clan. A great table would be laid out in the open, groaning with all the things the Eastern relations always complained they could never get, but which miraculously materialised on special occasions:

> The conversations at table would first centre on friends and relations: who's been sick, who got married, who bought a new car. Then the grown-ups would talk politics. First off, the spokesman for the East, my uncle by marriage from Keutschen, would complain about shortages of materials, the restrictive travel policy of the government, and the Soviet-style sloppiness in technical equipment. Then the spokesman for the

West, an uncle who had been born in the East but meanwhile lived in Schleswig-Holstein, would reply that things here were not so bad really. After all, a lot of stuff here was free, for instance places in kindergartens, and a lot was cheap, for example bread. And in the West everything wasn't perfect either, unemployment was a total scourge, especially among young people and so on and so on. The end of the song was that in the final analysis life could be tough in both countries, and everyone had his cross to bear. This had nothing to do with pretending that everything in the GDR was lovely. Rather, it was the basic condition for a family truce – and also a question of good manners.

Because among brothers no one should be better off than the others, and even if he is, for God's sake he should never admit it. Would it be right to paint the good life in the West in vivid colours for those stuck with living in the 'Dumb Remnant' [contemptuous Western slang for the GDR]? Would it be right to remind them that even a jobless guy in Bremen in the West could live better than a skilled worker in Eastern Bitterfeld? Of course, our relatives knew this perfectly well. So after an hour of political chat, we left it alone, drank another beer – and told jokes until dawn. As a child one thing really struck me: in my West/East family, there was a lot of laughter.[13]

But this 'normalisation' was only partial. The East still treated the West as 'the enemy'. Both sides had long spied on each other, but in the 1960s and 1970s the *Stasi*'s foreign-espionage department, the 'Main Administration for Reconnaissance' (HVA) was hugely expanded. Its head, Markus Wolf, had grown up in exile in the USSR as son of a well-known German Communist writer, Friedrich Wolf. Bilingual in Russian and German, highly intelligent and renowned for his charm, he rapidly climbed the hierarchy after 1945 and was put in charge of the HVA in 1957 at the astonishingly young age of thirty-four. He was both admired and feared in the West. John le Carré is said to have modelled his fictional KGB mastermind Karla, after Wolf.

With a strength totalling almost 4,000, lavishly funded and equipped, the HVA was especially adept at penetrating West Germany with 'sleepers'. One of these, specially trained and sent into the West in 1956 among many thousands of refugees from the GDR, was Günter

Guillaume. Guillaume's cover was that of a firmly anti-Communist Social Democrat, and so it was that over the years he rose through the ranks of the SPD to become a prominent aide to Willy Brandt and finally, in 1972, his personal assistant and constant companion.

Early on the morning of 24 April 1974, the doorbell rang at the villa in Bonn where Guillaume lived with his wife (also a *Stasi* agent) and his children (who knew nothing of their father's true identity). Guillaume answered the door in his dressing gown. His visitors identified themselves as officials of the Office for the Protection of the Constitution, West Germany's equivalent of the FBI or MI5.

'Are you Herr Günter Guillaume?' asked one of the officials. 'We have a warrant for your arrest.'

At this point, Guillaume made a fatal error. He drew himself up to his full height and announced: 'I am a citizen and officer of the GDR – respect that fact!'

Actually, they had no conclusive evidence against Guillaume until he incriminated himself.

Guillaume was the most prominent of a host of *Stasi* 'sleepers' or 'moles' in West Germany, including senior members of the West German intelligence service, government and business communities. His arrest changed the course of post-war German history. It spelled the abrupt end of Willy Brandt's career as chancellor. Brandt had survived a great deal, but he could not survive this. He took responsibility for the catastrophic failure of security and resigned, to be succeeded by a hard-headed SPD politician from Hamburg, Helmut Schmidt. Schmidt was a doer where Brandt could be a dreamer, tough where Brandt was instinctively conciliatory, a man who though never a Nazi had served like millions of other Germans in Hitler's *Wehrmacht*. Schmidt continued with the 'convergence' policy towards the East, but his most obvious achievements were those of the 'hard man' who handled the mid-1970s economic recession and the growth of leftist urban terrorism. A new era of pragmatism had arrived.

Few in either East or West thought that the GDR was doomed. To consider a case such as the Guillaume affair, which brought down a great political leader, was to feel regret and anxiety. It was, at the same time, hard to avoid a certain respect for an organisation like the *Stasi* that could achieve such a thing, and regard for the state that stood behind that organisation. And there was the Wall, stronger and more impregnable by the year. Above all, the GDR seemed to be enjoying a considerable amount of prosperity, not just compared with other Eastern countries, but also even when measured against much of the West.

If we were to believe the figures coming out of East Berlin, the GDR's own 'economic miracle' was almost comparable with West Germany's. Towards the end of the 1970s, it was even claimed (the figures were published by the World Bank) that the GDR had a higher standard of living, expressed as per-capita income in dollars, than Great Britain. This contradicted all other evidence, especially empirical observation, but was widely cited by the East and by friends of the Soviet system as a key indication that the GDR was turning into a rampant economic success story.[14]

In fact, the relatively sunny exterior of Honecker's East Germany belied permanent structural problems. Once the tourist got away from the showcase streets of East Berlin, Dresden, Leipzig or Halle, he or she would find decaying, shabby buildings (often beautiful old structures that in the West would have had materials and attention lavished upon them as a matter of course). By the same token, a combination of statistical sleight of hand, startlingly unconventional economic improvisation, and frankly brutal exploitation of human misery held sway behind the GDR's façade.

During the previous few years, like other Communist countries such as Poland and Hungary, East Germany had embarked on a policy of importing technology from the West in the hope of raising productivity.

To do this, the government in East Berlin had accepted Western credits, assuming it would be able to repay them from the economic improvements these imports would bring. But from 1973, when the first oil crisis hit, the GDR had serious energy and raw-materials problems. Cheap raw materials and oil from Russia made up for the truncated state's lack of natural resources, and favourable price agreements compensated for the lack of real productivity increases in the GDR's industry. In the mid-1970s, the Soviet Union raised its prices for vital supplies of fuel and raw materials. In 1979–80 came the second 'oil shock', and the Soviet

Union reduced its oil deliveries to the GDR. The country slid into a situation of massive indebtedness to both the USSR and the West.[15]

The GDR was in a state of crisis that continued for the rest of its existence. For Honecker, it had become an article of faith that the people must be kept happy with consumer goods and social benefits, or the regime would risk another 1953. There was a social-security and welfare system to pay for – the cradle-to-grave safety net that helped compensate East Germans for their lack of freedom to travel, express themselves fully, or enrich themselves. And an army and a security apparatus – after the USSR, the GDR had proportionately the second-highest military budget in the entire East Bloc (5.8 per cent of GDP), twice or even three times those of its allies.[16] The NVA, the *Stasi* at home and abroad, the cost of maintaining, extending, and manning the Wall, not just in Berlin but also along the entire length of the East/West German border, all these calls on the East German state finances were sky-high and, as the balance of payments situation deteriorated, crippling.

The state responded in a way unusual in a modern industrial country. It basically set up a completely alternative, secret economy that it didn't have to account for. The organisation that controlled this, a shadowy branch of the administration, highly secret and closely tied in with the *Stasi*, was known by the curious title of 'Commercial Co-ordination' (KoKo). Founded in 1966, KoKo was charged with earning hard currency outside the normal, planned economic system.

The advantage, as the GDR accumulated foreign debts, was that KoKo, this secret store of foreign currency, wasn't liable for payment of interest on foreign loans and could be used to plug gaps in the state's finances. Always allowed great independence, it was totally detached from the Foreign-Trade Ministry by a Politburo resolution in 1972, and thereafter its full activities (and the amount of hard-currency funds it controlled) were declared no longer subject to the usual banking super-vision. The full extent of KoKo's machinations was known only to a handful of figures in the leadership, especially Honecker.

Through KoKo, the élite at Wandlitz were supplied with Western goods and personal luxuries unavailable to the vast majority of East Germans. Once Honecker himself became leader in the early 1970s, he gained personal control of a hard-currency bank account, the so-called

'General Secretary's account', number 0628 at the Deutsche Handels-bank in East Berlin. By order, this had always to contain a minimum of a hundred million marks. Honecker used it for whatever purposes he saw fit. He might decide to donate forty million marks' worth of grain to Nicaragua, or make a grant of eighty million to Poland during the political difficulties there. He might, as he did one year, personally write a cheque for two million marks for the importation of apples in order to counteract a fruit shortage in the GDR.[17] The image of the General Secretary as absolutist ruler, dealing out largess at his gracious whim, grew year by year; back to the eighteenth century again.

KoKo in its most refined form was the creation of Alexander Schalck-Golodkowski. Born in Berlin in 1932 to stateless Russian immigrants, he was adopted at the age of eight by a German couple named Schalck, leading to his hyphenated name. He began work in a state-owned export company before rapidly switching to the GDR Ministry of Foreign Trade and Inner-German Relations. Clever, charming and politically reliable, with the face of a jolly medieval bishop and the mind of a highly efficient calculating machine, he scaled the ladder with extraordinary speed.

Schalck-Golodkowski rose to the key position of First Secretary of the SED party organisation in the Ministry of Foreign Trade, link man between the party and the export-orientated technocrats. In 1966, still not yet thirty-five years old, he was put in charge of KoKo, which even then was envisaged as a covert channel through which the state's financial solvency could be assured. In 1967, tellingly, he was given the rank of *Stasi* colonel and the title of 'Officer in Special Mission' (i.e. secret agent). To the outside world, he became Deputy Minister for Foreign Trade and later State Secretary in the Foreign-Trade Ministry.

By the mid-1970s, Schalck-Golodkowski was in charge of a personal empire unlike any other, East or West. He was certainly more powerful than the minister who was technically his superior, and operating on an equal level with Politburo members.

KoKo built up a labyrinthine network of more than 220 mailbox and front companies and more than a thousand bank accounts in East and West. It sold arms to the Third World – most successfully trading with both Iran and Iraq during the war that begin in 1980 – and through front companies secretly imported high-tech goods from the West that had been placed on the banned list by NATO. In some cases these illicit imports were put directly into service, in others the prototypes were simply copied in East German factories and manufactured in the required quantities. This particularly applied to sophisticated electronic equipment coveted by the *Stasi*.

KoKo also exported large quantities of valuable antiques and artworks to the West, where they were sold for hard currency. In many cases these treasures were confiscated from their owners, who had previously been presented with huge and mostly fictitious tax bills. In some cases, owners were imprisoned until they agreed to cede their possessions to the state.

A final, blatantly criminal source of foreign currency, whose proceeds were ultimately disposed of by KoKo, came from the GDR's sale of its political prisoners to the West. Political prisoners as 'export items'.

The trade in prisoners began in 1964, when Axel Springer cut a deal by which church and other oppositional figures were freed after payment of substantial sums of hard currency. This group included Klaus Schulz-Ladegast's father, though not Klaus himself. At least 200,000 East Germans were convicted of political crimes of some kind in the forty years of the GDR's existence. About 34,000 of those prisoners were released, usually to the West, on payment by the West German government. In the 1960s, the price per head was around DM 40,000, while by the 1980s the West Germans were paying almost DM 100,000 for each human being set free.

Prior to the 'sale', prisoners were transferred to a holding prison at Chemnitz (then Karl-Marx-Stadt). A West German bus contractor supplied specially modified buses, which were fitted with revolving number plates – East German ones for the trip from the border to the prison and back, and West German ones from the time they crossed into the West.

The official proceeds of prisoner-trading amounted to at least DM 3.4 billion; Schalck-Golodkowski more recently put the figure at around DM 8 billion.[18] There were cases when an individual lodged a (perfectly legal) visa application and was promptly arrested on a political charge, after which they could be 'sold on' to the West Germans. If they really wanted to leave, the East German authorities' reasoning went, the state might as well earn something from it.[19]

Add to this the agreements between East and West Germany on maintenance of the transit highways between Berlin and West Germany, blatantly exploitative visa and currency-exchange agreements, lucrative deals involving disposal of 'special waste' from West Germany in the East, and the manipulation of Western grants for the rebuilding and repair of Catholic and Protestant churches in East Germany, and the sums routinely transferred from West to East were enormous. They were thought to total between one and two billion per year in rock-solid West marks.

Honecker's regime always drove a hard bargain. And the West always paid up. No one believed that reunification was possible, but at least the Easterners' sufferings could be alleviated. For the quarter-century that followed the building of the Wall, this was the chief priority for the Easterners' richer, guilty Western cousins.

The final triumph – if that is what it was – of this ruthlessly hard-nosed begging-bowl diplomacy on the part of the East German regime came with the big West German credit agreement of the 1980s.

The spike in the oil price around 1980/1 caused a crisis, but soon found East Germany's economic bureaucrats playing a clever game, importing oil and gas products from the USSR at favoured-nation Eastern prices, then re-exporting these to the West, where they could be sold for much higher prices, with the GDR pocketing the difference in hard currency. To make this system work, expensive, ultra-sophisticated refining equipment had to be purchased from the West and Japan, but it was worth it. The sale of these mineral oil products made up about a third of the entire export earnings of the GDR in the early 1980s.

The problem was that these products had to be removed from the domestic market. Soon, with a shortage of oil-derived asphalt, East German roads began falling into disrepair. With East Germany unable to afford Polish black coal to replace oil, the country fell back on its own supplies of brown coal, also called lignite. The mining and burning of this dirty and inefficient fuel increased dramatically during the 1980s, as did the accompanying pollution. And, as part of a general export and foreign-currency drive, goods that normally supplied the domestic market were sold abroad, from eggs and butter to furniture and bicycles. In 1982, imports fell 30 per cent and exports rose by just over 9 per cent.

Honecker's bargain with his people, guaranteeing their standard of living in exchange for their compliance, was on the brink of collapse. Then the price of oil began to fall, which it would continue to do throughout the 1980s. Western lenders, who had seen East Germany as a reliable client, began to draw back from further lending.

The East German government was forced to make a drastic move. With the help of Schalck-Golodkowski and some surprising friends, the GDR enlisted a huge Western credit in order to keep going in the style to which it had become accustomed.

The particularly surprising friend was Franz-Josef Strauss, the bull-like, aggressively conservative Bavarian political boss who had been Defence Minister when the Berlin Wall was built. Strauss, twenty years previously vilified by East German propaganda as an ultra-reactionary warmonger who was trying to get his hands on a nuclear bomb for West Germany, now emerged as middleman. He arranged a deal between a consortium of West German banks and the East German government – or rather, a small group within the GDR leadership consisting of Honecker, chief planner Günter Mittag, and the ubiquitous Schalck-Golodkowski.

The GDR gained credit facilities on favourable terms, amounting to a billion in 1982 and almost as much in 1983. The East German government did not draw on the money, but used the fact of the credit's existence to restore faith in its own solvency. In return it had, for once, to pay a political price. In 1984, 35,000 East Germans were allowed to emigrate to the West.

Money talked. That had become a given in relations between Bonn and East Berlin. But the East-West situation was subjected to some seismic shifts in the 1970s and early 1980s, and it was not clear where they were leading. One moment there was a relaxation of tension, an intergovernmental visit or a credits deal, the next moment the great powers were stationing missiles aggressively close to each others' borders.

Out of this confusing scenario emerged, gradually, an endgame to the Cold War. The Western triumphalists claim it was the West's superior economic and military power that proved decisive. Others point to the inch-by-inch liberalisation that was quietly forced on the East by world opinion and changes in the desires and hopes of ordinary people in the Communist countries.

In other words, some point to the triumph of the Hawks, the others to the triumph of Helsinki.

Perhaps it was both.

17

ENDGAME

THE VERY FIRST AND very last victims of the Berlin Wall died by falling: the first in August 1961 after a desperate plunge from a window high on a block in the Bernauer Strasse; and the last in March 1989 when a home-made balloon crashed to the ground in the West Berlin suburbs, inflicting fatal injuries upon the man travelling in the basket beneath. The balloon's pilot and builder was a young East German who had planned to sail over the by now impregnable Wall. He actually succeeded, but almost immediately ran into bad luck, in the shape of a power line on the Western side. Had his wife not lost her nerve in the last moments before take-off, she and their small child would have perished with him.

It might be said that one died because at the beginning the jump to the West seemed fatally easy; the other because at the end of the Wall's life it seemed so terribly difficult.

And the Wall felt so permanent, to all but a few.

On 1 December 1978, *Stasi* observers at the border-crossing complex facing Checkpoint Charlie observed unusual activity on the Western side. An unknown man and a woman were being filmed by a TV crew outside the US army's checkpoint shack. When the filming finished, at 10.40, it was reported that they left the area. However, about four hours later they returned in a black Plymouth sedan with US Mission licence plates. An army sergeant drove them through the checkpoint and into East Berlin.

Only when they presented their passports were the couple in the back of the Plymouth identified as two Americans, a man of sixty-seven and a woman ten years younger. Their names were Ronald and Nancy Reagan.

The Reagans took an hour's drive around East Berlin, like any tourists, and then returned to the West. The East German authorities had for the first time laid eyes on the man who, many say, would prove to be the nemesis of their regime and all it represented. However, the *Stasi* observers do not, at that point, even seem to have realised who the man and his wife were.[1] This would change very soon.

The former governor of California and soon Republican candidate for the presidency would present a great challenge to the East. However, there was another challenge present that had already been there for several years but whose significance grew quietly, almost stealthily.

This one came in the form of a piece of paper, a document known as the Final Act of the Conference on Security and Co-operation in Europe, also known as the Helsinki Accord. The section dealing with human rights read in part:

> The participating States will respect fully human rights and fundamental freedoms, including the freedom of thought, conscience, religion or belief, for all without distinction as to race, sex, language or religion.
>
> They will promote and encourage the effective exercise of civil, political, economic, social, cultural and other rights and freedoms all of which derive from the inherent dignity of the human person and are essential for his free and full development.

Other clauses dealt specifically with promoting freedom of movement and of thought, and the reunification of families.

This ringing declaration was signed on 1 August 1975, after two years of negotiations, by the representatives of thirty-five nations from East and West, including the German Federal Republic and the German Democratic Republic. At the signing ceremony in the Finnish capital, Erich Honecker sat proudly between Chancellor Helmut Schmidt of West Germany and President Gerald Ford of the United States. Honecker was a legitimate, recognised international figure, and the GDR no longer a pariah regime.

There is a price for everything. The East German leadership, expert practitioners of *realpolitik*, none the less did not seem to suspect that what they had signed went against almost every practice of their regime, and most spectacularly against the atrocity that was their fortified Wall through the middle of Berlin.

Ordinary East Germans were, not for the first time, quicker on the uptake. On 10 July 1976, a 46-year-old doctor from the town of Riesa in Saxony, Karl-Heinz Nitschke, composed a 'Petition for the full attainment of human rights'. Referring to the Helsinki document, he and thirty-three other GDR citizens signed this petition with full names and addresses, demanding from the government that it comply with the treaty's guaranteed 'right to free choice of place of work and residence' and allow them to travel freely to the West. They delivered this petition to the State Council of the GDR, to the UN Human Rights Commission in Geneva and to the Western media.

Other citizens from the area around Riesa and Karl-Marx-Stadt (Chemnitz) soon gave their support to the document. Many were arrested by the *Stasi* and sentenced under the catch-all laws forbidding 'anti-state agitation' and 'anti-state connections'. Nitschke himself was imprisoned and interrogated over a period of two years until August 1977, when he was bought out by the West German authorities.

Far from discouraging the emigration movement, Nitschke's case acted as a spur. Collective applications for exit visas became more common, especially in the early 1980s. Western organisations such as 'Helsinki Watch' (which later changed its name to Human Rights Watch) publicised the persecution of such people. In 1984 East German citizens demanding the right to travel outside the GDR occupied Western embassies in East Berlin.

The regime responded by setting up special units of the *Stasi* whose purpose was to discourage citizens from applying to leave. Pressure was put on individuals at their places of work or study. Persistent appliers were pulled in for interrogation and on occasion charged with treasonable acts, which in East Germany were extremely broadly defined. Faced with more subtle forms of protest such as silent vigils, symbolic white ribbons on cars, and so on, the regime responded with subtle strategies of its own. The *Stasi* infiltrated dissident groups with agents whose job was to spread division and act as *provocateurs*, urging protesters into extreme actions that would give the state an excuse to intervene and inflict exemplary punishments.

This penetration exercise was particularly vigorous in the case of the churches in East Germany. Christian organisations had suffered considerably under Ulbricht, a lifelong anti-religious militant, but Honecker realised that the predominantly Protestant churches were becoming a refuge for dissidents, from punks to pacifists.

Something had to be done. Unwilling to crush the evangelical movement in the old, ruthless Stalinist style – Helsinki lingered uncomfortably in the background of the decision-making process – in March 1978 Honecker called a meeting with church leaders. He praised the churches' contribution to peace and their role as a 'positive social factor', and offered what amounted to a concordat. The state would tolerate free expression of religion in print and broadcast as well as in churches, and grant state aid to institutions such as senior citizens' homes and religious cemeteries. Priests would be permitted to make visits to prisoners in state jails. In return, the church leaders would be expected to exercise control over their flocks.

For a while, this seemed to succeed. But many young East Germans – the generation born since 1940, who were far more 'Ulbricht's children' than Hitler's – were attracted to the Protestant churches. Most had pleaded pacifism when called up for the NVA and been assigned as non-combatant 'construction soldiers' (*Bausoldaten*). This classification excused them from armed service but at the same time showed that they were not 'loyal', excluding them from careers in medicine, the law, or the universities once they returned to civilian life. To these young people, the church was a free, protected place, where modest careers could be made without kowtowing to the Communist state.

Rainer Eppelmann, a leading dissident, spoke for many who had grown up in the shadow of the Wall when he admitted that he joined the church from practical rather than merely religious considerations:

> I asked myself, what can you become, for a contented or even a happy life in this country? The only answer which occurred to me was: pastor . . . It was clear to me that only the study of theology was able to offer me a little mental freedom.[2]

A parallel 'alternative scene' arose in East Germany in the 1970s and 1980s. Intelligent, critically minded young people could not engage with society through the conventional channels, and so they founded their own subcultures and settled into niches within these groups. They made the best of things.

Matthias Neutzner, born in Saxony the year before the Wall was built, wanted to study aeronautical engineering, but because his elder brother had escaped to the West he was marked out as politically unreliable. This meant that Matthias was banned from working in the aeronautics industry – this would have given him access to aircraft, and aircraft can be flown over borders. As a consequence, he went into the fledgeling East German computer industry, which was being energetically promoted in the late 1970s and early 1980s as part of attempts to broaden the country's industrial base. Neutzner learned to program and to handle databases.

By the 1980s, Matthias he and his friends were in-demand experts, called on by hard-pressed state managers to solve logistical and supply problems by the magic of screen and keyboard. Their special niche was the GDR's cut-flower distribution network, a large part of which relied on their computer programming. This earned them decent money, made them largely independent of the state, and enabled them to take part in dissident activity. A strong pacifist, Neutzner could also find time to pursue his interest in recording the oral history of the Allied bombing of German cities through interviews with survivors. In the system of 'favours', of virtual barter, that pertained towards the end of the regime's life, his contacts often supplied him with, say, the use of a van or truck in exchange for computer work. East Germans made life a little more bearable through this unofficial 'black' economy. It enabled the exchange of goods and services away from the state's rigid, grasping hand. The fact was, even the government did the same. Think of KoKo.

Although Neutzner never applied to leave, there was a growing wave of exit-visa applications in the early 1980s. This motivated the regime's mass-issue of permits in the first months of 1984, a gesture supposed to please its Western political and banker friends while at the same time taking some of the pressure off the exit-visa movement. It may have succeeded in the former aim, but not the latter. The demand just kept growing. The *Stasi* could keep the dissident movement divided, and it could decapitate its leadership, but the exit-visa movement was something else, something close to a force of nature – a monster that the

Helsinki agreement had summoned from the depths of the East German people's unconsciousness.

And just a little more than two years after the *Stasi* had spotted him and his wife posing for the cameras in front of Checkpoint Charlie, on 20 January 1981 Ronald Wilson Reagan was sworn in as fortieth president of the United States.

President Reagan's incoming Republican administration offered little direct threat to the East German regime as such.

What it did represent was a kind of ruthless counter-revolutionary conviction that shocked and shook the Communist world. Backing the right-wing Contras against Marxist Sandinistas in Central America and the mujahidin against the Soviets and their client regime in Afghanistan, the Americans dared to mimic the kind of support for 'national liberation' movements that the Soviets had aggressively promoted since the 1950s. Twenty years before, the urbane Harold Macmillan saw himself as moderating America's alleged tendency towards extremes – Britain's classically educated Prime Minister liked to see his nation as wise, educated 'Greeks' to the primitive, power-orientated 'Romans' of the USA. Twenty years later, Reagan was backed to the hilt, and beyond, by his British counterpart, the no less uncompromisingly anti-Communist and pro-capitalist Margaret Thatcher.

If the Helsinki Accord amounted to the 'soft cop' working on the Eastern Bloc's contradictions – talking democracy while walking dictatorship was always a latent problem for Communist regimes – then the Reagan administration was the 'hard cop', confronting the Communist world on the most direct of levels.

In the late 1970s, the Russians introduced the SS-20 intermediate nuclear missile, with a range of about 2,700 miles. Though stationed on Soviet soil, it gave them the ability to hit targets as far away as Portugal in the west and Japan in the east. The Americans responded with the Pershing II missile, which had less than half the range but was much more accurate. Towards the end of his time in office, the Democratic President Carter had made preparations to bring Pershing into service, but at the same time, in the hope of keeping détente alive, he signed the complex and problematic SALT II arms-reduction treaty.

Then, on Christmas Day 1979, came the Soviet invasion of Afghanistan. Carter, who had begun his presidency as an apostle of détente, now put the SALT treaty on ice, asked for an expansion in the military budget, and introduced sanctions against the Eastern Bloc, involving curbs on grain and technology exports. America would also boycott the Moscow Olympic Games, due in the summer of 1980.

Reagan therefore became president in January 1981 at a time when the Cold War temperature had already dipped considerably. He continued Carter's plan to station a new generation of intermediate-range missiles in Western Europe, planned even bigger military-budget increases, and – last but not least – introduced a level of anti-Communist rhetoric not heard since the early 1960s. This gave his decisions (which may not have differed much from the ones that Carter would have made if re-elected) an extra 'bite' that was surprisingly significant on a world-historical scale.

Reagan told an audience at Notre Dame University, Indiana, on 17 May 1981, in a speech delivered with a president's gravity and an actor's flair: 'The West won't contain Communism, it will transcend Communism. It won't bother to dismiss or denounce it, it will dismiss it as some bizarre chapter in human history whose last pages are even now being written.'

The echo, conscious or otherwise, was of Khrushchev's notorious 'we shall bury you' speech from 1956. Khrushchev's remarks, though not so aggresively meant as some thought at the time, did indicate a new sense of self-confidence. A quarter of a century later, Reagan's words were intended to convey the same.

There followed a period of nervous stand-off. The Pershings and 'cruise' missiles were introduced into Western Europe, despite protests throughout the continent. Then in 1983 Reagan pulled what many still regard as a stroke of genius. He announced his intention to break the stalemate of 'mutually assured destruction' by developing a futuristic anti-missile system capable of preventing Soviet warheads from reaching American soil. This idea seemed to come straight from a Hollywood sci-fi epic (much talk of laser beams) and became known as the 'Star Wars' project.

In Moscow, Reagan's announcement caused something approaching panic and, as the conviction strengthened that perhaps the Americans could carry out their threat, a steady sense of demoralisation. Soviet air defences were placed on full alert. The atmosphere grew so jittery that when, in September, a South Korean civilian airliner strayed into Soviet airspace over the Far East region, it was shot down – on direct orders from Moscow.[3]

Leonid Brezhnev, Khrushchev's successor as Soviet leader, died a few weeks short of his seventy-sixth birthday in November 1982, after eighteen years in power. He was succeeded by KGB boss Yuri Andropov. Andropov lasted only sixteen months in office before succumbing to a kidney disease, aged sixty-nine, in February 1984, giving way to an older man in the shape of 72-year-old Konstantin Chernenko. Chernenko, a conservative figure already in poor health, lasted a mere thirteen months.

During his first term, Reagan – himself moving into his seventies – faced weak and ailing Soviet leaders. In 1982 his aggressive international stance was boosted by the collapse of the 'social-liberal' coalition in West Germany and the replacement of Social Democrat Helmut Schmidt with Helmut Kohl. Throughout the 1980s, three of the four major powers in NATO were ruled by right-wingers. And a conservative theologian from the Eastern Bloc, the Pole Andrei Karol Józef Wojtyła, was elected leader of the Roman Catholic Church as Pope John Paul II.

The strange thing was that during this period, when the hesitant détente of the late 1970s was abandoned and the Soviet Union and the USA reverted to a confrontational stance, relations between the two German states were not seriously affected. Rather the contrary.

True, the stationing of Pershing missiles on West German soil gave occasion for a vicious little propaganda skirmish. None the less, even after the conservative Kohl's election as chancellor in the West, Honecker enjoyed a standing invitation to visit Bonn. Only a Soviet veto prevented him from doing so in the autumn of 1984. The Moscow leadership summoned Honecker to the Kremlin in August and forced him to cancel his planned trip.[4] There was clear concern on the Soviets' part that East Germany was becoming too dependent on West German credits and payments. And what is more, in their unease the Soviets were absolutely right.

One younger member of the Soviet Politburo who had voted against allowing Honecker to visit West Germany was 54-year-old Mikhail Sergeyevich Gorbachev, Second Secretary of the CPSU. In 1985, after Chernenko died, he was elected First Secretary and *de facto* leader of the

USSR by colleagues tired of gerontocracy as a system of government. The first leader of Communist Russia to be born after the 1917 revolution, Gorbachev preached reform expressed through the principles of *glasnost* or 'openness', *perestroika* ('restructuring') and *uskoreniye* ('acceleration').

This amounted to an overdue admission in the heartland of Communism that something was very wrong with the system – and had been for a long time. In East Germany, however, the old men were still firmly in command. Despite the scramble for Western credits and the steady pressure from the exit-visa movement, the pretence remained that the GDR was the best of all Germanys in the best of all possible worlds.

In reality, East Germany was by now frighteningly uncompetitive outside the Soviet Bloc. Thuringia and Saxony especially had always been in the forefront of the industrial and technological revolution, from the early nineteenth century until the time of the Third Reich. Bomb damage, sequestering of plant and machinery by the Soviets for reparations, heavy-handed socialisation of industry, and the subsequent loss of expert management, capital, patents and skilled workers to the West, had weakened the country's economic fundamentals.

Before the First World War, Saxony, along with neighbouring Bohemia (now the Czech Republic), enjoyed the highest real net output in Europe. Chemnitz, with a population of 400,000, was known as the 'Manchester of Germany'. Until the collapse of the Third Reich, Dresden, with its camera and typewriter factories and electronics workshops, was the second-fastest-growing city after Berlin. Leipzig, Magdeburg, Halle and Jena were booming manufacturing centres

In 1939, industrial production per head in the region that would a decade later become the GDR amounted to 725 Reichsmarks per year. In the territories that would become West Germany, production per head was only 609 Reichsmarks.[5]

Take one example, the Saxon metropolis of Leipzig. After 1945, most of the publishing industry, the tobacco industry, the printing industry (including Gisecke & Devrient, the largest banknote printer in the world), all huge employers, left Leipzig for the West. The same went for the German bibliographical and copyright library, which transferred to Frankfurt-on-Main, as did the German Football Association.

The senior management at Zeiss emigrated from Jena and Dresden to the West in the aftermath of war. Although optics and camera works continued in operation in the GDR, and did quite well by comparison with other industries, the world-wide resurgence of the brand after the war was based on new, modern factories near Stuttgart. Wella, an international market leader in the hair-care, cosmetics and perfume business, founded in Rothenkirchen in Saxony in 1880, relocated to Darmstadt, in the American Zone of West Germany. The East Berlin brake-system manufacturer, Knorr-Bremse, moved to Munich. The examples go on and on.

In West Germany, the creativity and energy of an industrious, educated population, kick-started by the Marshall Plan and bolstered by rapid transfers of human and physical capital from the East, produced the famous 'economic miracle'. The East, which should have been even more advantaged, never really recovered under the bureaucratic, centrally directed command structure that remained, for all the talk of 'new courses' and so on, the basis of the GDR's economy.

'Never before in the two-hundred-year industrial history of Germany,' wrote an expert economist, 'probably never before in the industrial history of the entire world, has there been such a powerful transfer of technology, a transfer from the East to the West'.[6]

Despite this, with West Germany tapped successfully for credits, with relatively favourable terms of trade with the Eastern Bloc and parts of the Third World, and despite raw-materials and energy problems and mounting deficits, the GDR maintained a façade of success. As the East German state approached its fortieth anniversary, it appeared to many unsuspecting outsiders to represent a confident, progressive and egalitarian alternative to grasping, high-stress Western capitalism.

These people did not see – perhaps did not want to see – the polluted cities and shabby buildings, and nor did they experience the sudden, unexplained and often bizarre shortages, or the bureaucratic delays and petty restrictions that marred the life of the average East German citizen. They also did not get to compare the pampered lives of the ageing Communist *apparatchiks* in Wandlitz with those of their subjects.

Almost no one suspected that the GDR was approaching its doom. That the writing was, almost literally, on the Wall.

*

In September 1987, Erich Honecker achieved the ambition he had been harbouring for the past five years. He made a state visit to West Germany.

Finally, the GDR – and Honecker – could feel themselves on equal terms with their bigger, more prosperous neighbour.

The behind-the-scenes preparations for the visit had not been easy. The refugee organisations were outraged at such an invitation to the 'tyrant' and 'Soviet satrap' Honecker, and many on the respectable Right in West Germany also expressed doubts. There were attempts to avoid a reception by the West German President, and to keep Honecker away from Bonn, but finally the West Germans capitulated.

Honecker was received with dignity, politeness and even friendliness. None the less, in various subtle ways the West Germans managed to make it clear that to them he was still not quite a foreign dignitary and the GDR still not quite a foreign land. The trip was described officially not as a state visit but as a 'working visit'. Ex-Chancellor Willy Brandt described the curious refinements of protocol affecting Honecker's reception:

> Half amused, half amazed, I watched how the GDR's Chairman of the State Council was received in front of the Chancellery with a gently lowered level of ceremony: the honour guard was a bit smaller; it was led not by its commander but by his deputy; only anthems, not national anthems were played.[7]

Only seven motorcycle outriders escorted Honecker's limousine on the drive through Bonn, and the foreign diplomatic corps was not invited to the state dinner and to the receptions, to show that this was not an 'international' event.[8]

Nor did Chancellor Kohl mince his words on the principled question of reunification. At an occasion that was also beamed into East German homes, Kohl spoke of the right of the German people to 'complete the unity and freedom of Germany in free self-determination'. Honecker could only retort that the relations between East and West Germany were 'marked by the realities of this world', and – the old Communist showing his mettle – that 'socialism and capitalism can no more be united than fire and water'. It could not have failed to strike any viewer – and is clear from photographs of the encounter – that Honecker was a lot shorter and slighter than the enormous Chancellor Kohl, who at almost six feet four inches tall and weighing around 280 pounds, towered over him. To see in this juxtaposition a metaphor for 'big Germany' and 'little Germany' was inescapable.

In a way, it must have been a relief for Honecker to escape the treacherous hierarchies and invidious comparisons of Bonn and set off on his tour of the provinces. He was received in Düsseldorf, capital of the Ruhr industrial area that was the foundation of West Germany's industrial might. He visited Trier, where Karl Marx was born, and Wuppertal-Barmen, where the co-founder of Communism, Friedrich Engels, had been brought up in the first decades of the nineteenth century as the son of a wealthy textile manufacturer. Honecker was even fêted at the splendid Villa Hügel in Essen, former residence of the Krupp family. This was the symbol of German capitalism at its most successful – and politically corrupt.

But the moment that briefly provided a glimpse into Erich Honecker, the human being, was his short but intensely felt trip to his home town, Wiebelskirchen in the Saarland, so far west that the French border lay just a short drive away. On arrival, he visited his sister, who still lived in the family house, and paid respects to his parents' grave in the local cemetery. The powerful leader's eyes moistened as he heard the miners' choirs sing the songs of his youth. He chatted with pleasure in the distinctive dialect of his homeland. There were boos, and cries from the crowd of 'murderer', a handful of hostile or sarcastic placards, but on the whole the Saar greeted its long-lost son with a certain perverse approval. Its provincial premier, leftist SPD politician Oskar Lafontaine, told Honecker that 'people around here feel a certain satisfaction, even a certain pride, when they see a born Saarlander ruling over the Prussians and the Saxons'.[9]

So overcome with emotion was Honecker that in his final speech he for the first time strayed from his prepared text. The situation was, he said, that there were two Germanys, anchored in two power blocs, and that – here came the surprise – as a result, understandably, 'the borders are not as they should be'. One day, he added, it might be that 'the borders will no longer divide us, but unite us'.

The journalists went crazy. So did the Soviets. Honecker's speech was broadcast live in East Germany. Within minutes of the transmission, the Soviet ambassador was on the telephone to the Politburo's man in charge of security, Egon Krenz, who at fifty-two was reckoned Honecker's probable successor. Moscow was not pleased. It might be that if you looked at Honecker's speech carefully, it gave nothing away – but to use the word 'unity' in any context at all was very dangerous.

By the time Honecker arrived in Munich, for the last stop of his tour, he had recovered his composure. Bizarrely, the most powerful Communist in Germany was fêted in the capital of German conservatism by the Bavarian premier, Franz Josef Strauss, who had helped to arrange the vital credits five years before. As a mark of Bavaria's long tradition of autonomy, the band played three national anthems at the reception – the West German, the East German, and the Bavarian. And Honecker had a full compliment of motorcycle outriders.

Within days of his return to East Berlin, Erich Honecker delivered a lengthy and triumphal report for his Politburo colleagues. It stretched to 170 pages. The document boasted that his visit was 'of far-reaching effect and historical importance', clear proof of the independence and sovereignty of the GDR. The West Germans had been constrained to 'treat Comrade Erich Honecker as head of state of another sovereign state . . . documenting, for all the world to see, the independence and equality of the two German states . . .'[10]

Meanwhile, the *Stasi* carried out one of its surveys of popular opinion inside East Germany, with special reference to Honecker's visit to the West. 'Progressive citizens', it said, considered that the visit had proved the GDR's sovereign status. However, among young people, the view was that it 'signalled the obsolescence of the Berlin Wall and of the traditional negative image of West German imperialism'.[11]

Honecker had got off lightly in his visit to West Germany. Apart from Kohl's reference to German self-determination, and a few small demonstrations along the way, the East German leader could and did consider the trip a PR success.

Of course, it changed nothing. The GDR was still in bad financial trouble, and relations with Moscow under the new, reformist leadership were frosty. On the one hand, the GDR was too Stalinist for the Gorbachev clique, on the other Honecker and his supporters were too close to the West Germans (and their open-handed lending institutions) for the Soviets' comfort. If anything, the trip caused a further deterioration in relations with Moscow. Honecker had not consulted Gorbachev before announcing the visit, and it was a slight the Russian never forgot.

Honecker's trip to the West also changed nothing with regard to the Berlin Wall or the fortified border between East and West Germany. Though the automatic-fire installations had been removed from the interstate border in the early 1980s, as part of the Western credits deal, and in Berlin the notorious dog-runs had also been dismantled, the Wall was still there, as lethal as ever.

This subject had been raised while Honecker was in West Germany in September 1987. In an intimate meeting with Chancellor Kohl, the West German leader had almost casually questioned the 'shoot-to-kill' order. Before setting out from East Berlin, Honecker had prepared himself for just this eventuality. His assistants had ferreted out the wording of the regulations on the emergency use of firearms by the West German border police and included it in his briefing materials. Honecker now recited these back to Kohl and said, 'For our people, it's just the same as for yours'. Of course, in the West German case the firing of 'warning shots' was stipulated, but Honecker moved smoothly to assure Kohl: 'We don't want anyone to be killed. But you have to obey regulations in the restricted military area.'[12]

But the question would not go away. In the previous five years (1982–6 inclusive), a total of six deaths occurred on the Berlin Wall. The worst year was 1986, when three died, two of them in a single attempt to crash a truck through from East to West. The escapers perished in a hail of bullets when the truck came to a halt in no man's land. These killings could not be concealed – many had observed them from the Western side. In the case of the two following deaths, however, the East German authorities took successful measures to make the murders 'deniable'.

Michael Bittner, a 25-year-old bricklayer, had been born on 31 August 1961. He was just a few days younger than the Berlin Wall.

Bittner had applied several times to leave the GDR, without success. An hour or so after midnight on 24 November 1986 he approached the

Wall in the suburban area of Glienicke/Nordbahn, where it bordered on the French sector of West Berlin. He carried a ten-foot wooden ladder. With the aid of this, Bitter made it over the hinterland wall. Then he hit the signal fence and set off alarm sirens and automatic searchlights. This caught the attention of two guards who were patrolling about 200 metres distant. They advanced as he raced across the 'death-strip', and called upon him to stop. He did not do so. They fired warning shots. Still Bittner pressed on towards West Berlin. In fact, he actually reached the border wall with the West and managed to scramble on to it. He was now under heavy automatic fire from the two guards. He called out in despair, 'Let me over!' Those would be his last words. Michael Bittner was struck by several bullets and collapsed back into Eastern territory. He died half an hour later of a wound that had ruptured the heart wall.

The East Germans chose to overcome the embarrassment of this killing by pretending it hadn't happened. Within hours of Bittner's death, the *Stasi* moved to cover up the incident. The death certificate and autopsy report were destroyed. The East German authorities declared that he had made contact with a Western escape organisation (or 'trader in human beings') and had been successfully smuggled to the West. With breathtaking cynicism, they even issued a warrant for his arrest, which remained in force while the GDR still existed. Bittner's brother and mother were told he had escaped to West Berlin. For years, they hoped against all hope that this was true. Only in 1990, when East German government documents were accessed, did they learn of his death and the cover-up that had followed.[13]

Worse happened three months later. On 12 February 1987, 24-year-old Lutz Schmidt and his friend Peter Schulze tried to crash a truck through the Wall in the southern suburbs of Berlin, near East Berlin's Schönefeld Airport. The weather was foggy. In the confusion they almost collided with a border-police truck that was patrolling the border area. They careered off the road and their wheels got stuck in the soft ground. The two young men left the vehicle and headed off to cross the Wall on foot. Border guards opened fire. Schmidt was shot through the heart and died almost immediately. Remarkably, Schulze pressed on and made it over to the West Berlin district of Neukölln, perhaps saved by the poor visibility.

As in the case of Bittner, there was an imediate cover-up. Schmidt's wife was told that he had been shot, but at the same time was forced by the *Stasi* to corroborate the official story – that he had died in an unfortunate traffic accident. They never released his clothing to her or allowed anyone to view the body. The *Stasi* took over the organisation of Schmidt's funeral, at which his body was cremated. When neighbours continued to question the official story, his widow was forcibly resettled to another part of the city, where her tragic story would be unknown.[14]

After this, there were no more deaths on the Wall for almost two years. For the most part, East Germans had given up on this risky method of leaving the Workers' and Peasants' State. Instead, they were applying for exit permits.

Following the issuing of 30,000 such permits in 1984, applications rose to 27,000 in 1985 and 58,000 in 1986. In 1987, the year of Lutz Schmidt's death at the Wall and of Honecker's visit to West Germany, the number of applications reached 112,000.[15] For a complex of reasons, ordinary people were not as afraid of the East German state as they had once been. They wanted out, and they were prepared to say so.

In 1984, the *Stasi* registered less than forty 'extrusions' (*Ausschleusungen*), as it delicately referred to organised escapes from East Germany. Where in the 1960s these had been numbered in their thousands, and even in the 1970s in their hundreds, by the 1980s the escape business had become a tiny cottage industry, scarcely politically or statistically significant. Pressure was building up, but it was pressure of a different, less spectacular kind which would prove even more fateful for the GDR.

In West Germany there were few politicians of Left or Right who still made grand and angry speeches about the Wall, or who openly supported dissidents in the GDR. One of the few exceptions to the passivity of the Western politicians was the courageous Green Bundestag deputy Petra Kelly, who spoke her mind on official trips to East Germany far more frankly than her more right-wing colleagues. The notion of 'convergence' had originally, in the 1960s, been intended as a kind of slow and subtle route to self-determination for all Germans, but by the 1980s the means had become all, and the end had been largely forgotten.

The only major political figure to challenge this increasingly relaxed attitude towards the Wall was the same man who, in 1978, had attracted the attention of the *Stasi* observers at Checkpoint Charlie: Ronald Reagan. Now more than half-way through his second term as president of the United States, the 76-year-old had lost none of his fierce and occasionally undiplomatic anti-Communist drive. In June 1987 he arrived in West Berlin to join the city's 750th-anniversary celebrations.

'General Secretary Gorbachev,' Reagan thundered in front of the Brandenburg Gate, 'if you seek peace – if you seek prosperity for the Soviet Union and Eastern Europe – if you seek liberalisation, come here to this gate, Mr Gorbachev, open this gate. Mr Gorbachev, tear down this wall.'

All the same, three months later, Erich Honecker was received with honours in West Germany. No one was impolite enough to raise the matter of the Wall, or the deaths, or the continuing persecution of dissidents by the *Stasi*, or the fact that his people still had to put their hands in the fire before they wrote exit-visa applications. The attitude of most West German politicians was summed up by a prominent Social Democrat in 1987: 'Reunification is a big lie!' (*Die Wiedervereinigung ist eine Lebenslüge!*) he declared. His name was Gerhard Schröder, later to become Helmut Kohl's successor as chancellor of Germany.

East Germany seemed to be becoming a permanent and acceptable feature of the international landscape. In 1982 the SPD established a so-called 'Joint Commission for Fundamental Values', a kind of talking shop in which East German *apparatchiks* and SPD politicians could discuss issues of mutual interest amid lavish hospitality, for all the world as if the SED were a fellow democratic party competing in the same political market-place.

All this gave East Germany a new respectability. No wonder, then, that the East German leadership entered 1989 in a state of blissful self-confidence. No one seemed prepared to offer a serious challenge to their authority or legitimacy.

While Honecker and his supporters continued to promote a hard ideological line, there were indications that in certain areas East Germany was being allowed to liberalise. Honecker had become adept at uttering soothing bromides that would keep his benefactors in the West happy. In July 1987, the GDR officially abolished the death penalty. Just as Honecker had told Kohl in September 1987 that no one wanted to see deaths on the so-called German-German border, so he continued to deny that there was any 'shoot-to-kill' order.

Then, in February 1989, almost two years to the day after the Wall had claimed its previous victim, a young East Berliner decided to test the regime's new humanitarian claims.

Barman Chris Gueffroy was twenty years old and due to be conscripted into the East German army in May. He hated being made to defend a state that he loathed. Chris wanted to travel, especially to America. Then he and his friend Christian Gaudian heard from an acquaintance serving with the border police in Thuringia that the 'shoot-to-kill' order had secretly been abandoned. This was exciting news.

At around eleven on the evening of 5 February 1989, the two young men approached the border with West Berlin, which ran along the Britz district canal. It was a cold night, minus-three centigrade (27°F). They crept through a deserted 'weekend colony', a group of little allotments, each with their own hut, where Berliners came at the weekends and in the summer to relax. The friends had dismanted a clawed garden hoe and tied the spiked head to a length of strong rope. The plan was to toss this improvised grappling hook over the first barrier, a high barred fence, and haul themselves over. This part was a success. They got over the high fence undetected. Five metres further on stood a lower fence. They also managed to climb this without trouble. Perhaps it was true, and the whole Wall was now a harmless fake? But this last barrier turned out to be wired. Before they knew it, an alarm had been touched off and searchlights automatically flooded the area.

Reality bit, with a vengeance. Guards in a nearby watch-tower had been alerted to the intruders' presence. They fired warning shots. Trying to avoid their line of sight, the two young men ran in zigzag fashion parallel to the border, Chris to the fore, frantically seeking a way across the next lattice fence, the last before the canal.

Within moments they had tragic confirmation that the 'shoot-to-kill' order was no dead letter. They ran straight into two guards approaching from the opposite direction and were greeted with a hail of fire. Gueffroy caught ten bullets in the chest and died immediately. His companion, wounded in the foot, tumbled to the ground.

Christian Gaudian was arrested, recovered, and was put on trial. There was the by now habitual attempt to cover up the cause of Chris Gueffroy's death, but this time it failed. Western observers were alerted by a death notice in the East Berlin *Berliner Zeitung* which referred to the 'tragic accident' that had ended his young life.

Chris Gueffroy's mother was not allowed to see his body. Against his family's wishes, he was cremated, according to the *Stasi*'s standard practice. The world learned the truth about the killing from a reporter for the West German *Frankfurter Rundschau* who slipped through the *Stasi* security cordon to attend the funeral.

For the first time in years, a death at the Wall caused an international outcry. In April, Honecker lifted the 'shoot-to-kill' order. Too late for Chris Gueffroy.

Since the East Germans had never admitted that the order existed in the first place, Honecker's decision remained a state secret. It was indicative of the regime's growing guilt and unease that even in the official report of the killing, there is no mention made of shooting, or of the fatal wounds that Chris Gueffroy suffered. The document simply states in mealy-mouthed regime-speak that the border guards 'carried through border-tactical activities and placed both border violators under arrest'. By 1989, shooting people on the border was unacceptable, and even the cosseted old men at Wandlitz knew it.[16]

None the less, the Wall still stood proud and ugly, with its sturdy blocks, its spikes and fences and alarms and watch-towers, seemingly permanent and impregnable. Its fate would not be determined in Berlin. Mostly it would be decided hundreds of miles away, by people who had decided that a Communism which needed to be enforced by guns and barbed wire was not a Communism worth having.

The Maginot Line was another of the great walls of history. Running along the German frontier from Longwy in north-eastern France south to the Swiss border near Basel, the line was the brainchild of a French élite determined to prevent a repeat of the horrendous conflict that had devastated their country between 1914 and 1918. It would make another invasion impossible. Or so they believed.

The idea came from the supreme French commander, Marshal Joffre. It was supported by the legendary Marshal Pétain, whose defence of

Verdun, the greatest fortress on the Western Front, during World War One seemed to suggest that France could be successfully protected by a chain of similar strongpoints. The project was brought to fruition by André Maginot, French Minister of Defence during the late 1920s, and was built between 1930 and 1936 at a cost of three billion French francs (approx. $120 million in 1933 or around $2 billion at current values).

The Maginot Line had concrete walls thicker than in any fortress ever built. Its massive guns were placed on turntables in steel-plated cupolas. There were recreation areas, living quarters – many air-conditioned – and well-stocked subterranean storehouses. Underground railways connected various portions of the line so that troops could be moved swiftly to threatened points in the defences. The tunnels extended over 150 kilometres, with 39 military units, 70 bunkers, 500 artillery and infantry groups, and 500 casemates for guns, shelters, and observation towers.

There was one problem. As a pushy tank colonel named Charles de Gaulle had pointed out in the early 1930s, future wars were unlikely to be static. Mobile armour and air power would become increasingly decisive. Moreover, in 1936, Belgium, which had hitherto been France's ally and formed an integral part of a common defensive system, made a declaration of neutrality. This left the French northern flank embarrassingly exposed. The French built fairly desultory defences along the Belgian border and continued to proclaim the Maginot fortifications' impregnability to one and all. Many were impressed, above all the French public.

In May/June 1940, the German forces went into action. They were divided into three groups positioned in the shape of a huge 'sickle'. Their first army group sat tight on the Rhine border, where the Maginot Line was overwhelmingly strong, thus tying up large French forces. The second army group, however, swept in from the north to violate the neutrality of the Netherlands and Belgium. The third was the 'wild card'. Composed largely of mobile armour and mechanised troops, it sneaked through the Ardennes forest into Eastern Belgium and Luxembourg.

The Ardennes area was lightly defended because the dense woodland was thought impenetrable by large bodies of men. To prove them wrong, the German armoured spearheads pushed through into north-eastern France within a matter of days, cutting off the Maginot Line from the rear. France fell within the month, with scarcely a shot fired from the fortifications upon which France had bestowed so much treasure and so much trust.

So, the Germans in 1940 solved the problem of the Maginot Line by going round it. This was also a method often favoured by the 'barbarians' whom the Great Wall of China was supposed to keep out. The captive population of East Germany in 1989 was no different.

On 18 January, looking forward to the year that would see his seventy-seventh birthday and the fortieth birthday of the GDR, Erich Honecker allowed himself the confident boast that the Wall 'will still be standing in fifty or a hundred years, if the reasons for its existence have not been removed'. This despite the fact that three days earlier the GDR had signed yet another treaty in the Helsinki Process, clearly stating that any individual possessed 'the unrestricted right to leave . . . and return to his own country'. Afterwards, Honecker breezily explained to the Soviet ambassador that 'we gave instructions to sign it, but we won't carry it out'.[17]

There were also plans in hand to create this hundred-year Wall. It would, of course, be a 'high-tech' Wall, more advanced and more completely impregnable than any previous incarnations. Electronic sensors and cameras would enable the border authorities to detect and foil any would-be escapers well before they reached the actual fortifications, in this way reducing the unfortunate deaths that did so much to harm the regime's image.

As the commander of the border force expressed it, in a masterpiece of GDR jargon: 'Precedence will be given to the utilisation of physical mechanisms of action and technical methods such that, while maintaining high security, the enemy's ability to find excuses for defamation against the GDR will be reduced.'[18]

But, high-tech or low-tech, there were hints that the Wall was becoming superfluous. In the first week of January 1989, twenty East Germans who had unsuccessfully applied for exit visas sought refuge at the Permanent Representation of West Germany in East Berlin. They were allowed to leave on 11 January, without punishment and with the promise that within six months there would be a 'good end' to their endeavours. By the end of January, some had already arrived at the refugee camp in Giessen, West Germany.

But the real drama was not happening in East Germany, or not as yet. In January 1989, after years of uneasy manoeuvring, the non-Communist Polish trade-union movement, Solidarity, entered into negotiations with the Soviet-supported government in Warsaw. The subject of these discussions was the sharing of power, but their effect was to reawaken the ghosts of Stalinism. During the negotiations, the Soviets finally admitted responsibility for the wartime massacre of Polish officers at Katyn – which they had previously always blamed on the Germans. It was a hugely important admission.

Meanwhile, in the Baltic states, which had been carved up between Hitler and Stalin exactly fifty years ago, in 1939, a human chain of a million Latvians, Lithuanians and Estonians linked hands to protest against the infamous pact that had robbed them of their independence and led to death, oppression and deportation for many of their parents' generation.

Then came the act of physical liberation that would prove the ultimate doom of the Wall. On 2 May, the Hungarian government, now in the hands of pluralistically minded reform Communists, astonished the world by beginning to dismantle their hitherto fortified border with Austria. President George H.W. Bush, on a visit to West Germany, was presented with piece of barbed wire from Hungary's demolished border fence. 'Let Berlin be next,' Ronald Reagan's successor proclaimed.

The results of the Hungarians' action were sensational. It took a while for the significance of the change to sink in, but by 1 July more than 25,000 East Germans who had decided to 'vacation' in Hungary, somehow ended up in Austria. Erich Honecker's subjects had found a way around his Maginot Line.

Meanwhile, even in East Germany itself, the dissidents and the opposition were gaining confidence. A couple of weeks after the Hungarian border was demilitarised, local elections were held in the GDR.

As usual, government candidates received almost 99 per cent of the vote. But this time, church observers such as Pastor Eppelmann had been present when the votes were counted. They protested. The figures for 'no' votes published by the government were only a third of those actually declared in the presence of the church observers. The church openly announced that 'no' votes had made up at least 7 per cent of the poll, implicitly accusing the government of fraud. It was a breach of the 'concordat' with the regime that had kept an uneasy peace between God and Caesar for the past decade.

There were small demonstrations against the election results. Arrests were made, but they had little effect. In Leipzig, now becoming the largest opposition stronghold, special prayer meetings, held on Monday evenings, were attracting over 2,000 participants a week by the end of May 1989.

But the regime gave little or no ground. Although in practice more exit visas were being granted, the law was not changed. The government introduced an appeals process for refused exit visas, but the ability to leave East Germany remained a privilege, not a right.

In June, with discontent about the rigged local elections still simmering, Honecker made favourable remarks about the Chinese Communist government's violent suppression of pro-democracy demonstrations at Tiananmen Square in Beijing. The East German parliament passed a resolution applauding the 'suppression of a counter-revolution' in China. There was a continuing trickle of arrests. Many dissidents were immediately shunted off to West Germany, as had become the regime's habit over the past few years. However, plans had also been put in place by Mielke's State Security Ministry for the opening of secret concentration camps capable of holding up to 200,000 dissidents, should the regime decide it was necessary to bring the people to heel by force.[19]

The pressures from outside were becoming stronger. For the first time since 1945, semi-free elections were held in neighbouring Poland. In crass contrast to the shameless rigging of the May elections in East Germany, the non-Communist Solidarity movement won every seat it was permitted to contest in the *Sjem* (house of deputies), and 99 out of 100 seats in the Senate, where it could contest all.

Meanwhile, as summer approached, thousands still stood in line to meet the beady stare of the *Stasi*-trained border officials at Checkpoint Charlie or the underground cattle-pen of the 'Palace of Tears' in Friedrichstrasse. The action was not in Berlin. East Berlin was stifled under a blanket of security, and preoccupied with the grand celebrations planned for the fortieth anniversary of the GDR in October.

The signs of weakness behind the façade were all there, and easily spotted later with hindsight's wisdom. The prickly relationship between East

Berlin and Moscow was becoming all too apparent. When Gorbachev visited West Germany in June – and was ecstatically received by a nation weary of Cold War anxiety and nuclear confrontation – the reformist Soviet leader made no rejoinder to Chancellor Kohl's critical remarks about the Wall and the continuing lack of freedom in East Germany.

Gorbachev's reticence was viewed in East Berlin, quite correctly, as a change of tack and – in traditional Communist terms – a betrayal. Whatever their private feelings about the GDR, Khrushchev or Brezhnev would have felt duty-bound to strike back hard on their German satellite's behalf. Gorbachev said nothing.

In mid-July, Gorbachev went even further, publicly repudiating the so-called 'Brezhnev Doctrine'. This principle, formalised following the crushing of the Prague Spring in 1968, permitted the Soviet Union to intervene against any country within the Warsaw Pact that attempted to change its political or social system. Addressing the Council of Europe in Strasbourg, Gorbachev declared that all European countries were now free to choose their own social and political order and excluded the use of military force between East and West or 'within alliances'. One of his aides referred to this jokily as the 'Sinatra Doctrine', with a play on the singer's great hit 'My Way' – countries could now do things 'their way'.

The bizarre contrast between East Germany's continuing espousal of 'dinosaur' Marxism-Leninism and the new spirit of openness and risk in Moscow was shown by the Honecker regime's unheard-of decision, in 1989, to forbid the distribution of certain Soviet publications in East Germany. Especially singled out for a ban was the monthly German-language magazine *Sputnik*, which supplied a digest of the Soviet press. Such English-language delights as *Moscow News* and the newspaper of the British Communist Party, the *Daily Worker* – for many years the only British newspaper available in East Berlin – were also taken off the news-stands. Gorbachev's radical speeches were reported only partially, or not at all. However, criticisms of the Gorbachev reforms, by his internal opponents and by Mao's anxious heirs in Beijing, found their way into East German newspapers.

It was a feverish summer. And, in defiance of the natural order, as autumn approached the temperature rose even higher.

18

THE WALL CAME TUMBLING DOWN

FIRST TENS, THEN HUNDREDS of thousands of East Germans were on the move through July, August, and then September of 1989, in their Trabants and Wartburgs. They headed, by some tribal instinct, for Hungary and Czechoslovakia. Czechoslovakia, like the GDR, was still run by hardliners, but the trip to Prague was a short one for most East Germans. Hungary was further, but its reform-Communist government had declared itself ready to share power. And Budapest too had a West German embassy.

For East Germans reluctant to risk even the Hungarian-Austrian border, there was another solution. They packed their bags and took themselves to the capitals of neighbouring, still technically 'socialist' countries and headed for the West German embassy. There they sought asylum. Many were so eager that they simply abandoned their cars in nearby streets, often with keys still in the ignition. By mid-August, West German diplomats were in a desperate situation. On 13 August 1989, the twenty-eighth anniversary of the Wall, the West German embassy in Budapest was forced to close. Six days later, 600 East Germans forced their way through the border between Hungary and Austria. The Hungarian border guards simply watched.

Erich Honecker repeated in automatic fashion that the Wall would 'last one hundred years.' For the next six weeks, however, he was removed from the centre of power by an operation for a serious gall-bladder complaint, fully returning to his post only on 25 September. The 77-year-old leader had to be operated on twice, since at the first attempt he suffered from a circulatory collapse. During the second operation, they found not just an inflamed gall-bladder but a malignant tumour on the colon, which they removed. What the surgeons at East Berlin's famous

Charité Hospital did not know was that they had missed a second tumour in his right kidney, which would eventually kill him four years later. But meanwhile, it seemed, Honecker had been saved and made fit to take the helm for the fortieth anniversary.

The fact that the Politburo was more or less rudderless for that period may have contributed to the deterioration in the situation. Honecker had passed over Egon Krenz and appointed the compliant 63-year-old planning boss Günter Mittag as his caretaker. This he had done in a deliberately humiliating way. Told that Krenz had cancelled his vacation so as to be in East Berlin during the leader's health crisis, Honecker coldly instructed him to 'take a break' and said, 'Don't take yourself so seriously. You're not indispensable around here.'[1]

After obediently joining his family on the Baltic coast, Krenz received a visit from Eberhard Aurich, a friend and ally who now held the post of First Secretary of the party youth organisation, the FDJ. Aurich told Krenz the Politburo was floundering in the face of the refugee problem, and the old men were looking for scapegoats – especially anyone involved in the youth movement, who were blamed for failing to raise a new generation loyal to the regime. Aurich pleaded with Krenz to move against Honecker, but he refused. To undermine a sick man, and just before his big day at the fortieth anniversary . . . Aurich returned to East Berlin empty-handed.[2]

The problem of youth's growing disaffection was, it is true, especially serious. According to government polls, in 1985, 51 per cent of apprentices had identified 'strongly' with the GDR and 43 per cent 'with reservations', while 6 per cent 'hardly or not at all'; at the end of 1988 the figures had changed, catastrophically from the regime's point of view, to only 18 per cent 'strongly identifying', 54 per cent having reservations, and 28 per cent supporting the regime hardly or not at all. The figures for young workers were similar. Since 'unreliable' young people were not permitted to go into higher education, college students were in many ways the darlings of the regime, but even there support had deteriorated. Compared with impressive 1985 figures – 70 per cent of students strongly identifying, 28 per cent with reservations, and a mere 2 per cent withholding support – in less than four years the numbers had tumbled to 34 per cent, 51 per cent and 15 per cent respectively. Support had halved, reservations doubled, and outright opposition increased by a factor of seven.

The refugees in Prague, Budapest, Warsaw, and on the Hungarian/ Austrian border were overwhelmingly young, children of the Wall *par excellence*. They were those statistics expressed in mobile, resentful human form. And time was on their side.

On 10 September, Hungarian Foreign Minister Gyula Horn was asked on television what his border officials would do if, say, 60,000 East Germans arrived at the border between Hungary and Austria.

'They will,' said Horn matter-of-factly, 'allow them though without any further ado and I assume the Austrians will let them in.'

Twenty-two thousand East Germans promptly fled across that same border over just three days.[3]

At the same time, the West German embassy in Prague was full to overflowing. Many hundreds of East Germans, often entire families, had sought asylum there. A tent city mushroomed in the gardens of the historic Lobkovic Palace. Attempts to keep out newcomers failed. They simply clambered over the railings into the embassy grounds. By the end of September, the gardens housed 4,000 people. There was a real danger of disease in the overcrowded, unsanitary refuge, but the embassy's house guests refused to leave. They would not return to East Germany.

Throughout the month, the East German Politburo (average age sixty-seven) had tried to ignore the problem. Now, spurred by Honecker's recovery from his operation, it finally began to react. With America acting as broker, a deal was done between the Czechs, the Hungarians, and the GDR. On 30 September, the West German Foreign Minister flew to Prague. He announced to the masses waiting stubbornly in the grounds of the embassy that they would be allowed to leave.

Honecker had announced this decision to his Politburo colleagues after they had attended a gala performance at the State Opera in East Berlin in honour of the fortieth anniversary of the People's Republic of China. In fact, the Politburo meeting took place immediately afterwards, in the Apollo Room, the magnificent chamber-music and reception room of the Opera House. The very important comrades sat down at hastily supplied tables, by the light of glittering chandeliers, and Honecker regaled them with 'information regarding a matter of the highest urgency'.[4]

Honecker told them that he had agreed the refugees could go to West Germany via the GDR. They were to be placed in sealed trains for the journey through their homeland, and during the trip would have their East German identity documents confiscated and their citizenship withdrawn. This was intended to humiliate them and brand them as traitors. In an article in the SED organ *Neues Deutschland*, a bilious attack on the refugees declared that 'by their behaviour they have trampled on all moral values and excluded themselves from our society. Therefore no one should shed any tears for them'. The piece is said to have been dictated by Honecker personally.

The entire operation actually said far more about the true nature of the East German regime – Why sealed trains? Why treat your own people like some kind of dangerous bacillus? – than about the thousands of exhausted but exhilarated expellees who piled into the eight trains that left Prague on 2 October. There were by this time 12,000 of them.

Everything backfired for Honecker. His decision turned out to be a terrible misjudgement. On the route through East Germany, far from being shunned and humiliated, the refugees were greeted by thousands of ordinary East Germans, who lined roads and embankments beside the tracks and waved and cheered. At Dresden, the first major city across the border, the refugees were defiant. They did not reluctantly surrender their identity documents, as the authorities expected, but tore them up and tossed them out of the train windows, along with the worthless Eastern marks they would not be able to spend once they arrived in the West.

Meanwhile, 1,500 local people, mostly young, defied the authorities and assembled at Dresden's main station to greet the refugee trains. Demonstrators tried to climb aboard. The *Vopos* struggled to stop them. Fighting broke out. Substantial areas of the concourse were wrecked. One man slipped under the train and was so badly injured that he had to have his legs amputated. After the trains left, demonstrations continued. Many Dresdeners, including older citizens, gathered in a dignified demonstration outside the station. The crowd was ordered to disperse. It refused. There followed a stand-off with the armed police.

So much for Honecker's conviction that he could neutralise the bacillus by confining it to a sealed train. Matters got even worse when the trains bearing the refugees from Prague finally reached Hof, in northern Bavaria, and were received on to West German soil. The welcome celebrations were huge. Cheering West Germans. Smiling East Germans. Brothers and sisters welcoming brothers and sisters. The entire emotionally stirring scene was televised in West Germany, and almost all East Germans could pick up Western broadcasts. Those, that is, who were not already heading for the border in their trusty Trabants. Soon the embassy grounds in the Czech capital were filling up again with a new wave of would-be refugees.

In Dresden, the demonstrations outside the station were not forcibly dispersed. The *Volkspolizei* colonel commanding the forces of order had to decide whether to start shooting, and he decided not to. He became, and remains to this day, a hero in Dresden. Within hours the news spread, first to Leipzig and then to Berlin. People had defied the regime in Dresden, but the regime's policemen had not dared open fire.

On Monday 2 October, 10,000 citizens of Leipzig appeared on the streets. They chanted slogans about freedom, but above all they declared: 'We will stay HERE'. This message was, in its way, even more worrying for Honecker than that conveyed by the West Germany-bound hordes of refugees. The regime had got used to arresting its dissidents and dumping them in the West. Now they were determined to stay in the East, and there were too many to deport them all.

Despite everything, Erich Honecker pressed on with preparations to celebrate the fortieth anniversary of the regime he had fought and – it must be admitted – suffered to create. He was absolutely determined that this would be the greatest, most spectacular proof of the GDR's viability that anyone could possibly want.

The ageing, ailing General Secretary had obvious problems. First of all, the flood of refugees. The worst of this was stopped when on 3 October the right to visa-free travel to Czechoslovakia was 'temporarily' withdrawn. Then there were the demonstrations. These could be minimised by an increased police presence and more brutal intervention. But Honecker also had hidden problems, ones he never wanted to think about but which were now impossible to ignore. Such as the fact that the state he planned to celebrate with such pomp was actually on the verge of bankruptcy.

In the past few years the GDR had become reliant on West German largess. In the 1960s and 1970s East Germany had been relatively successful as an exporter. In the 1980s, when according to the economic plan the country was supposed to be turning into a high-tech, R&D-based modern powerhouse, the story had in fact been one of steady decline and increasing foreign indebtedness. The GDR could only imitate, not innovate. Between 1980 and 1988, the outlay required for a state enterprise to earn one West mark almost doubled, from 2.40 East marks to 4.40. Low productivity and high raw-materials prices meant that the actual trade deficit (without credits or other payments from West Germany) just kept ballooning. And worse was expected. The Soviet Union, with grave financial and economic problems of its own, had indicated that it would be scaling down deliveries of cheap oil to East Germany and raising foreign trade prices within the Eastern Bloc to world market levels.[5]

All the same, Honecker, who had grown used to ignoring uncomfortable economic realities, and who trusted the Marxist God of History to save him every bit as fervently as any fundamentalist trusts his deity, was determined to throw the biggest party imaginable for the GDR's big birthday.

Though Gorbachev had paid a triumphant visit to West Germany, for the past two years he had avoided the GDR. However, he could not ignore East Germany's fortieth. Nor, after his arrival in East Berlin, could he ignore the vast torch-lit parade of youth groups staged for his benefit, or the tanks and artillery pieces that rolled past the saluting dais where he stood with the GDR's leadership. As the long columns of FDJ members marched past in their blue shirts and red scarves, many called out over and over in honour of the Soviet reformer, 'Gorbi! Gorbi!' Some were heard to shout: 'Gorbi, help us!' The Polish Communist leader, Mieczyslaw Rakowski, asked Gorbachev if he understood what the young people were saying. The Russian nodded, but Rakowski translated for him anyway. 'They are demanding: "Gorbachev, save us!"' he explained incredulously. 'But these are the party activists! This is the end!'[6]

Later, there were talks between Gorbachev and Honecker, at which the East German leader refused to discuss Soviet-style reforms. Honecker asked instead, 'Has your population enough food, bread, and butter?'

And he compared the standard of life in the USSR unfavourably with that in the GDR.

The relationship between the two leaders deteriorated further during Saturday evening. At a meeting with the East German Politburo, Gorbachev made some more pointed remarks. 'When we fall behind, life punishes us immediately,' he observed with obvious reference to Honecker and his supporters. Honecker appeared oblivious, continuing to brag about the success of the GDR and its alleged status 'among the top ten economies in the world'. His words met with silence. Except from Gorbachev, who turned to his neighbour and let out a soft but clearly audible hiss of derision.[7]

Günter Schabowski, since 1985 First Secretary of the SED's key Berlin District, later remarked: 'We were assholes, we should have done the *coup d'état* right there, in front of his eyes!'[8]

That night over dinner, Krenz finally decided to wield the stiletto. By the end of the meal, he had pledges of support from Politburo members Schabowski, Siegfried Lorenz (SED boss in Karl-Marx-Stadt) and, most important of all, *Stasi* Minister Erich Mielke, eighty-one years old but still Moscow's man. The Soviets were discreetly informed, and the conspirators set to plotting Honecker's downfall. After eighteen years in power, the miner's son from Wiebelskirchen was a marked man.

In 1953, the SED regime had survived only because of Soviet troops. Rumours were already spreading that Gorbachev would not let the Red Army intervene if the same thing happened now. None the less, the government had no compunction in keeping 'order' in the streets during this crucial period by judicious use of force. This applied mainly to Leipzig and Dresden, where demonstrations were continuing and grow-ing. East Berlin was relatively quiet, in part due to sometimes brutal interventions by the *Stasi* and police to nip demonstrations in the bud.

Despite veiled threats and savage action against individual protesters during the fortieth-anniversary weekend, 70,000 of Leipzig's citizens flocked to the next Monday 'prayer meeting' at the Nikolaikirche, which had become the most important single focus for the opposition.

Informed of growing unrest in Saxony, on Sunday 8 October Mielke issued a 'code red' alert which, in effect, gave his forces a 'licence to kill' in the streets. 'There has,' the directive declared, 'been an aggravation of the nature and associated dangers of the illegal mass gatherings of hostile, oppositional, as well as further hostile-negative and rowdy-type forces aiming to disturb the security of the state . . .'

The order continued chillingly:

I hereby order:

1. A state of 'full alert' according to Directive No. 1/89, Para. II, for all units until further notice. Members of permanently armed forces are to carry their weapons with them constantly, according to the needs of the situation . . .

Sufficient reserve forces are to be held ready, capable of intervention at short notice even for offensive measures for the repression and breaking up of illegal demonstrations.[9]

The army had also been placed on alert. Orders were given for a regiment of paratroopers to be moved close to Leipzig in case of trouble. On the evening of 9 October, the security forces, armed with live ammunition, were stationed in the side-streets near the Nikolaikirche. Hospitals prepared for an influx of wounded.

In the end, the demonstration, though huge and clearly threatening to the regime, did not deteriorate into violence. The crowd responded to the admonishments of several prominent speakers, including the internationally known director of the Leipzig Gewandhaus Orchestra, Kurt Masur, with remarkable restraint. It has been said that Honecker ordered the security forces not to shoot, because he did not want to be blamed for possible civil war. Whatever the case, Gerhard Strassenberg, the police commander in the city, told his force to use weapons only in self-defence.

The ninth of October in Leipzig signalled a turning-point. The Russian occupation army failed to show itself, confirming that Gorbachev had confined it to barracks. The seventeenth of June 1953 had not been repeated in Leipzig – and neither had Tiananmen Square.

The fall of Honecker came just over a week later, by a simple vote in the Politburo. A defiant slogan had been taken up by the masses on 9 October: 'We are the People'. Even some of the police had joined in the chant. In the next few days, demonstrations spread through the GDR, to Magdeburg, Potsdam, Halle, Karl-Marx-Stadt and elsewhere.

Krenz and his fellow conspirators started to build the pressure on Honecker straight after Gorbachev's departure. They put together a document admitting the regime's problems and suggested corrective measures. Honecker attempted to block its discussion in the Politburo, but failed. He found himself supported only by Mittag, the guardian of economic orthodoxy, and by his old intimate and foreign-policy adviser, Hermann Axen. When challenged, however, Honecker insisted he would not resign. No one quite had the nerve to force the issue.

The conspirators paused to regroup. The phone lines ran hot. On 16 October 1989, most of the Politburo watched uneasily as a secret *Stasi* TV feed from Leipzig, filmed with cameras hidden on squares and street corners, showed a vast crowd – this time 120,000-strong – gathering peacefully for the Monday meeting. They were chanting not just 'Gorbi! Gorbi!' but 'The Wall must go!'. Honecker, appalled, exclaimed repeatedly, 'Now, surely, we have to do something!' but no one else in the room suggested using force. The army chief of staff, Colonel-General Fritz Streletz, specifically declined to unleash his men against the demonstrators. 'We can't do anything,' he said. 'We intend to let the whole thing take its course peacefully.'

The next day, 17 October, the Politburo was due to meet. Mielke, who despite his age still took a morning dip in his swimming-pool at Wandlitz, was up even earlier than usual. He phoned the security chief in the Central Committee building, who was, of course, a *Stasi* officer and Mielke's subordinate. The minister instructed him to ensure the meeting room was surrounded with reliable officers. Honecker must be prevented from summoning his own bodyguards when the moment of crisis arrived.

At ten the meeting began. Honecker seemed relaxed. He opened the meeting as if everything was quite normal and tranquil in the GDR, the best of all Germanys. Then he asked if anyone had any suggestions for the agenda.

There was a brief silence. Then 75-year-old Willi Stoph, chair of the Council of Ministers, indicated his desire to speak. Stoph had long been critical of Honecker in private letters to Gorbachev and had joined Krenz's clique. Like everything else that happened that morning, his remarks were pre-arranged with the other conspirators.

'Erich, allow me,' Stoph began in his bureaucratic monotone. 'I suggest: first item on the agenda, "The release of Comrade Erich Honecker from his duties as General Secretary and the election of Egon Krenz as General Secretary".'

Honecker froze and stared vacantly round the room. Then, after a few moments, he collected himself and said calmly, 'Good, then I open the discussion'.

They all betrayed him, one by one, in the three-hour session that followed. Even his long-time henchman, economic mastermind Günter Mittag, finally saw the way the wind was blowing and declared that Honecker had 'lost the trust of the party'. This was the man who had lied to everyone about the state of the East German economy, who more than any other was responsible for the country's plight. The other Politburo members could not suppress their mocking laughter.

At the end, they voted to get rid of Mittag too, as well as the chief press censor, Joachim Herrmann.

Honecker warned them, stiffly but calmly, that his resignation would not solve the GDR's problems. But if that was his colleagues' decision, then he must obey. The Politburo's vote to sack Honecker was unanimous. In accordance with 'democratic centralist' tradition, the General Secretary dutifully voted for his own dismissal.

Without another word, Honecker withdrew to his office. He dictated a letter, summoning the Central Committee for a meeting the next day at which his dismissal would be confirmed. Then he picked up the telephone and called his wife, Margot.

'It has happened,' is all Erich Honecker said to her.

Then he put down the receiver and started slowly and methodically to gather together his personal effects.[10]

The conspirators had succeeded in the first stage of the coup, but they still had concerns. First, they had to ensure that Honecker didn't manage some kind of counter-attack at the Central Committee meeting the next day, as Khrushchev had famously done in 1957. Khrushchev had found himself outvoted by the so-called 'anti-party group' in the Politburo, but had turned the tables on them at the subsequent plenum meeting, allowing him to reign in Moscow for seven more years. Second, they had to justify Honecker's dismissal – on grounds of, say, economic incompetence – without implicating themselves as co-decision-makers and therefore co-responsible individuals.

In the event, Honecker went without a fight. Vague health reasons were given. At the next day's Central Committee meeting, out of 216 delegates, only 16 voted against, including Honecker's own wife, who would immediately lose her job as Minister of Education, and Hanna Wolf, the octogenarian retired head of the SED Party School, a former wartime exile in Russia and stubborn opponent of all reform.

A tearful Honecker was given a standing ovation by the assembled comrades. Whether the tears were of sadness or impotent fury – Krenz in his memoirs plumps for the latter – we shall never know. Then the deposed First Secretary left the building, never to cross its threshold again. While Krenz was being acclaimed as new party leader, Honecker ordered his chauffeur to take him for one last woodland drive.

Krenz would rule for forty-six days. He immediately announced his intention to reform East Germany, and was astonished when the public jeered rather than cheered. Playing on his long features and prominent teeth, they called him 'horse face'. Posters carried at the ever-burgeoning demonstrations showed him wrapped up in a bonnet like the wolf in 'Little Red Riding Hood', with the caption: 'Why grandmother, what big teeth you have!' The public simply did not believe his sudden conversion to reform. A joke went: 'What is the difference between Egon Krenz and Erich Honecker? Answer: Krenz still has a gall-bladder.'

On 23 October 1989, 300,000 marched in Leipzig to call for Krenz's resignation. The following week there were demonstrations all over the GDR. On 30 October 20,000 gathered at the 'Red Town Hall' in East Berlin, where the chief spokesman of the new government, the articulate, in many ways likeable Berliner Günter Schabowski, attempted to explain its policies. The crowd heard him out, but still called for more than he was prepared to give.[11]

In any case, the movement towards reform came too late.

On that same day, 30 October, a highly secret 'Report on the Economic Situation of the GDR with Consequences' was submitted to the new Politburo. It made clear what had been hidden all those years, even from many members of the party leadership. The country was a wreck, and approaching bankruptcy like a horse galloping towards a cliff.

More than half of all industrial facilities were effectively classifiable as scrap. 53.8 per cent of all machines were write-offs, only reparable at a cost that could simply not be justified. Half the transport infrastructure was in a state of decay. Productivity was around 40 per cent behind the West's. State indebtedness had risen from 12 billion marks in 1970 to 123 billion in 1988. Direct debts to capitalist states and banks had increased during that period from 2 billion to 49 billion West marks.

The five-person team of planners who put together the report was led by Gerhard Schürer, Chairman of the State Planning Commission. Schürer had suggested relatively modest reforms to Honecker the previous year but had been knocked back. Now elected to the Politburo, he finally got someone to listen to him, but it was too late. As he admitted, a severe and thoroughgoing reform problem adopted in, say, 1985, might have relieved the situation, but now it had gone too far. The document declared grimly: 'Just to avoid further indebtedness would mean a lowering in 1990 of the standard of living by around 25%–30% and make the GDR ungovernable.'[12]

The GDR at the end of the Honecker era was, in effect, bankrupt.

Nor did all twenty-six members of the Politburo get to learn the full, awful truth. An even more searing three-page analysis (Geheime Kommandosache b5 – 1156/89) had also been prepared by Schürer, for the eyes only of General Secretary Krenz and veteran Premier Willi Stoph. It spelled out the bad news even more starkly, admitting that the GDR was already largely dependent on capitalist credit institutions, and that annual borrowing was running at 8–10 billion West marks. This was 'extraordinarily high for a country like the GDR'.

The country had embarked on an increasingly frantic game of financial manipulation, moving cash around the international money markets at speed, inflating the extent of its claimed assets and understating its true indebtedness in order to raise more credit, because if the international finance community knew the facts it would pull the plug. The GDR, like any over-indebted individual who knows there's a problem but can't stop the spending habit that's causing it, was covertly taking out short-term loans to make interest payments on long-term credit, and using this apparently creditworthy status to assume yet more debt. This was criminal deception, fraud on a vast scale.

What to do? Even the 'transit' payments due from the West to assure access to and from Berlin, guaranteed until 1995, had already been mortgaged and spent. To ensure solvency in 1991, it would be 'imperative' to start negotiations with the West German government for further credits amounting to 23 billion West marks, on top of existing credit sources. But what could the GDR offer in return?

Schürer's group had a quite simple but hair-raising proposal. They would put up the 'State Border West' as a bargaining counter. Or, as the report put it:

In order to make the Federal Republic conscious of the GDR's serious intention, it must be declared that . . . such conditions could be created, as early as this century, that will make the border that exists between the two German states superfluous.

Bluntly: you come up with the money and we'll bring down the Wall.

This was a logical if desperate conclusion to a thirty-year policy of making the West Germans pay for every tiny travel concession, every released political prisoner, every iota of access to and from the East by road, rail or air.

The trouble was, in order to perform this last trick, in order to save itself, the regime would have to saw away the branch on which it sat. And for that it was not yet ready.

On 1 November, Krenz flew to Moscow. There he held out the begging bowl one last time. Krenz, exaggerating his reformist credentials, engaged with Gorbachev in a wide-ranging discussion of the situation. Krenz knew that another big day of demonstrations was planned for Saturday 4 November. Venues would include Berlin, where until now there had been few problems compared with Leipzig and Dresden.

He shared his concern with the Soviet leader:

Measures must be taken to prevent any attempt at a mass breakthrough across the Wall. That would be awful, because then the police would have to intervene and certain elements of a state of emergency would have to be introduced.[13]

Gorbachev had his own preference for a new East German leader – the genuinely reformist Dresden Party Secretary, Hans Modrow – but was nevertheless prepared to hear Krenz out and offer him a little useful advice. He promised to ask his friends in the West not to destabilise the GDR. However, that was about all Krenz got. Gorbachev was no Khrushchev, who would always ultimately pay up to save the GDR. The Soviets refused to bail out the SED regime, either financially or militarily. The message was clear. *Sauve qui peut*. Every Communist for himself.

Egon Krenz returned to East Berlin empty-handed. The countdown to the end had begun.

The opposition had grown that autumn with bewildering speed. It had started out from relatively small collections of religious and pacifist-ecological groups, overtly non-political though clearly critical of the regime. By October, the SPD had unofficially re-formed in the East, and the various other citizens' action groups had developed into embryonic political movements.

Most prominent among the groups was 'New Forum'. New Forum had been founded in September after a call to action signed by a group of thirty oppositional intellectuals, scientists and religious figures. This declaration rapidly gathered hundreds and then thousands of further supporters. The aim of New Forum was to 'open up a democratic dialogue' between rulers and ruled in East Germany.

Despite being officially declared hostile to the state and 'unnecessary', New Forum grew quickly. Its aims were reformist within the existing framework of the GDR. It did not propose the reintroduction of capitalism or the reunification of Germany. All the more dangerous, so far as the state was concerned.

On 4 October, various organisations, including New Forum and the re-formed Social Democrats, combined to demand the release of political prisoners, abandonment of all political investigations, and free elections by secret ballot. They made reference to the United Nations Charter and the Helsinki Agreement, to both of which the GDR was officially a signatory. There was a new, confident tone to the dissidents' demands, though their support was still relatively small.

By the end of the month, it was obvious that something much bigger was happening. Tens, sometimes hundreds of thousands, of ordinary East Germans were turning out all over the country to demand democratic change.

The big demonstration in East Berlin on Saturday 4 November was the most threatening yet, because it would take place perilously close to the regime's seats of power. None the less, the leadership decided to allow it – in fact, it went even further.

Members of the SED leadership, most prominently the extrovert Schabowski, appeared on the podium alongside the dissidents. The Berlin Party Secretary defended the system and promised reform. He was greeted with boos and whistles. Others included the New Forum leaders and the writers Christa Wolf and Stefan Heym, the former a critical supporter of the regime, the latter an idealistic maverick who had spent the Nazi era in America and returned to Germany in a US army uniform, only to settle in the GDR of his own free will. Heym's works were banned in the East because of his support for Wolf Biermann, but the veteran writer refused to leave.

Another former exile who spoke at the rally was even odder case: Markus Wolf, raised in exile in Stalin's Russia, who had retired in 1986 as head of the *Stasi*'s foreign-intelligence department, the HVA, and Deputy Minister of State Security. The ever-plausible chameleon of the secret world had now transformed himself into a democrat. There were and are many who suspect the *Stasi*'s involvement in the entire transition process. Secret policemen are notoriously skilful survivors.

Wolf came from an artistic family – his father had been a well-known writer, his brother a film director. He always claimed to have favoured a more liberal line, but his own spectacularly disingenuous account of his participation on 4 November speaks for itself:

I tried to persuade the half million at the rally and the millions more watching on television not to resort to violence, but as I spoke, protesting the atmosphere of incrimination that made every member of the state security organisations scapegoats of the policies of the former leadership, I was dimly aware that parts of the crowd were hissing at me. They were in no mood to be lectured on reasonable behaviour by a former general of the Ministry of State Security.

So I learned painfully in those moments that I could not escape my past . . .[14]

As Schabowski's (and perhaps Wolf's) presence at the demonstration showed, the establishment was still hoping somehow to manage the changes, to ride the tiger of reform. It was putting forward its most 'people-friendly' faces. Two days later, the SED's propaganda department reported on the 4 November demonstrations and said that concessions should indeed be made, but only superficial ones:

> The demand for free elections can in principle be supported, since it corresponds to the basic principles of our socialist constitution, nevertheless this must not entail opening the door to bourgeois party pluralism . . . Demands for abolition of the leading role of the SED are totally unacceptable.[15]

In other words, free elections were perfectly OK if they were not actually free.

Precisely how they were to persuade the population with such bizarre authoritarian sophistries was not apparent. If half the population of East Berlin was prepared to attend a meeting calling for free elections and democracy, who was going to accept the 'leading role of the party', knowing this was merely a euphemism for its monopoly on power? The new ruling clique understood something of this. In the first week of November, seeing the need to impress the increasingly mutinous masses, Krenz carried out a purge of the old guard.

On 7 November, the members of the government headed by Willi Stoph handed in their resignations. On 8 November, the Politburo resigned *en masse*. It was replaced by younger and more reformist appointees, including Hans Modrow, who, although an important district secretary, had been excluded from the previous body.

Meanwhile, there were angry demonstrations outside government buildings, especially local offices of the *Stasi*. On 7 November, Mielke signed a lengthy and anxious report to the Politburo on the growth of the protest movement. There was little of the purse-lipped arrogance previously characteristic of *Stasi* documents. The report observed that the crowds outside *Stasi* buildings were shouting things like 'Burn the building down!', 'Out with the *Stasi* swine', 'Kill them', and 'The knives are sharpened, the nooses are prepared'.[16] Mielke promptly sent a secret directive to all *Stasi* districts and departments, ordering the destruction of sensitive documents, especially those that might incriminate the *Stasi*'s network of unofficial informers.

The air was thick with doubt and intrigue, a familiar, anxious reek in the corridors of power that conveyed one message only: *fin de régime*: end of the regime.

Proposals had already been published for more liberal travel and visa regulations, allowing up to thirty days of foreign travel per year. The application process would take around a month and 'normally not lead to a negative outcome'. No dates, however, were set for these suggestions to become law. An examination of the small print also showed that bureaucrats would remain able to grant or withhold permission pretty much at will. Besides, the maximum hard-currency allowance (fifteen West marks) would scarcely buy breakfast outside the GDR.

Meanwhile, Krenz, seemingly victorious in his battle for control of the SED, vowed to stay in office and called the Wall a 'bulwark' against Western subversion. The regime was threatening to drown in a torrent of mixed messages.

On the morning of 9 November, the sun shone fitfully in East Berlin. The thermometer crept slowly to ten degrees centigrade. That morning, an article appeared in *Neues Deutschland*, commenting on the continuing mass exodus from the GDR via other countries. It was not written by some party hack, but by a group of reformers. They pleaded with East Germans not to leave their country in its hour of need:

> We are all deeply uneasy. We see the thousands who are daily leaving our country. We know that a failed policy has reinforced your mistrust of any renewal of our community life until the last few days. We are aware of how helpless words are against mass movements, but we have no other means but our words. Those who leave diminish our hope. We beg you, stay in your homeland, stay with us!

On the first day of November, Krenz rescinded the ban on travel to Czechoslovakia, opening the floodgates once more. With Honecker gone and the new rulers clearly unwilling or unable to enforce their will in the traditionally forceful post-Stalinist fashion, more than 20,000 East German citizens had crossed from Czechoslovakia into Austria during the twenty-four hours preceding 9 November. Now it was the Czechs' own Communist government that was coming under pressure. They were threatening to close the border. The East German ambassador in Prague had been brusquely informed that the Czech government 'did not intend to build refugee camps for East German citizens'.

On 6 November, half a million citizens of what satirists were now calling the 'German Demonstrating Republic' attended the 'Monday Meeting' in Leipzig. Speakers pointed out the catches in the new 'thirty day' travel regulations and criticised the tiny foreign-currency allowance. They called not for a modification of the travel laws but for their abolition. 'In dreißig Tagen um die Welt – Ohne Geld!' (freely translated: 'Around the world in thirty days – but how to pay?') chanted the crowd.

At the Interior Ministry on the Mauerstrasse in East Berlin, a working party of four officials, including two *Stasi* officers, had been given the task of temporarily modifying existing laws to deal with the current crisis. On the morning of 9 November, they were due to draft at the Politburo's behest a resolution 'For the alteration of the situation regarding permanent exit of GDR citizens via the Czechoslovak Socialist Republic'. They had decided to entitle it 'Immediate Granting of Visas for permanent exit' but, one said later, as they laboured at the draft they felt less and less happy with the concept.

> We were charged [he explained] with coming up with a regulation for those citizens who want to leave the country permanently. But were we then supposed to *not* let out those who just wanted to go and visit their aunty? That would have been schizophrenic.[17]

The final draft stipulated that, so long as East German citizens were in possession of a passport and visa, no restrictions should be placed on either permanent emigration or private visits. People would be allowed to leave the GDR via any border crossing point between East Germany and either West Berlin or the Federal Republic. It added rather feebly that exits were to take place 'in an orderly manner'.

The material was couriered over to the Central Committee building, where the Politburo was in session. After presenting the document, Krenz reminded his colleagues of the pressure they were under from the Czech government, and assured them that the Soviets were in favour of the new measure. The Politburo members – most of them recently elected to replace hardliners and therefore unfamiliar with the details of previous regulations – nodded it through. The same went for the Council of Ministers, which rarely made changes to material approved by the Politburo.

A few minutes before six o'clock that evening, Günter Schabowski, the Central Committee's media spokesman, arrived at the International Press Centre in the Mohrenstrasse, where the government held its newly instituted live, daily press conferences.

The press centre was packed with print and television journalists, including – since East Germany had now entered the era of 'openness' – cameras from the GDR's own television news. Schabowski was tired and a little distracted. It had been a long day. He had not been at the meeting that approved the revised regulations, but half an hour earlier he had dropped by Krenz's office and asked the General Secretary about the day's proceedings. Were there any important announcements he needed to make? Krenz had passed him the document detailing the new temporary travel regulations, and Schabowski had hurried off to the press conference.

The conference, at which Schabowski was just one of the spokespeople, though the most senior, started at six exactly. However, there were other questions to be dealt with first. Things dragged on. The announcement of the new travel rules came as the final item on the agenda. Although technically it was a government and not a party matter, Krenz had personally given the document to Schabowski, and so it felt natural that, although he was actually the SED spokesman, he should convey its contents to the assembled journalists.

At 6.53 p.m., sweating slightly under the television lights and visibly exhausted, Schabowski peered down at the document Krenz had given him. It was still headed, a little gnomically, 'For the alteration of the situation regarding permanent exit of GDR citizens via the Czechoslovak Socialist Republic it is stipulated . . .' In a little preamble he told the press, rather wearily, that the document would 'make it possible for every citizen of the GDR to leave the country using border crossing points of the GDR'. Then he read out its somewhat dense bureaucratic formulations in mechanical fashion:

1. The decree from 30 November 1988 about travel abroad of GDR citizens will no longer be applied until the new travel law comes into force.

2. *Starting immediately*, the following temporary transition regulations for travel abroad and permanent exits from the GDR are in effect:

a) Applications by private individuals for travel abroad can now be made without the previously existing requirements (of demonstrating a need to travel or proving familial relationships). The travel authorisations will be issued within a short period of time. Grounds for denial will only be applied in particularly exceptional cases.

b) The responsible departments of passport and registration control in the People's Police district offices in the GDR are instructed to issue visas for permanent exit *without delay* and without presentation of the existing requirements for permanent exit. It is still possible to apply for permanent exit in the departments for internal affairs [of the local district or city councils].

c) Permanent exits are possible via all GDR border crossings to the FRG and (West) Berlin.

d) The temporary practice of issuing (travel) authorisations through GDR consulates and permanent exit with only a GDR personal identity card via third countries ceases.

3. The attached press release explaining the temporary transition regulation will be issued on 10 November.

Responsible: Government spokesman of the GDR Council of Ministers

[italics the author's own]

Then Schabowski leaned back in his chair, almost certainly not expecting any questions. The travel issue had been dragging on for some days, and this was yet another attempt to defuse it without giving the GDR's population more than the regime thought fit. After all, the measure was still tagged as 'temporary'. This saga would, it could be assumed, run and run, and there would be more episodes.

None the less, the journalists were intrigued. At 6.57, an Italian newspaperman asked Schabowski if this was some kind of mistake. Schabowski repeated that private travel and permanent exit from the GDR were now permitted and went on:

So, private travel to foreign countries can be applied for without presentation of existing requirements, or proving a need to travel or familial relationships. The travel authorisations will be issued within a short period of time.

The responsible departments for passport and registration control of the People's Police district authorities in the GDR are instructed to issue visas for permanent exit without delay, without the applicant's having to provide valid evidence of previous requirements regarding permanent exit.

There was murmuring among the press representatives. Someone – said to have been Tom Brokaw of the American NBC network – asked him exactly when this regulation came into effect. Schabowski seemed a little uncertain. He checked the wording of the document in front of him and then replied: 'So far as I know, that is, uh, immediate, without delay.' Schabowski had failed to see that the regulation did not come into effect until the next day, 10 November, and that until then there was supposed to be an embargo on the announcement.

There are a number of myths surrounding what proved to be a momentous event. The first is that Schabowski was forced to read from a hard-to-decipher note hastily scribbled by Krenz. He wasn't. Krenz had given him a copy of the actual announcement. This, however, Schabowski had hastily placed among a sheaf of his own notes, through which he later had to scrabble before finding the document and starting to read it to the assembled press. The second myth is that the news was an immediate sensation. It now seems that, in reality, the press hung around for a while after the press conference and that the atmosphere was one of considerable confusion. Some refuelled at the nearby coffee bar, still trying to work out the exact meaning of the document and to square it with what the SED spokesman had told them.[18]

The first reports from DPA and Reuters, which came over the wires at a couple of minutes after seven p.m., simply said that any GDR citizen would be entitled, from now on, to leave the country via the appropriate border crossing points. Low-key stuff. Then, at five past seven, Associated Press pulled ahead of the pack and spelled its interpretation out in a simple but sensational sentence: 'According to information supplied by SED Politburo member Günter Schabowski, the GDR is opening its borders.'

The storm broke. Within half an hour, all the other agencies had picked up the phrase. As did the news bulletins on the West German television stations. The generally trusted state-financed network, ARD, led its eight o'clock bulletin with those exact words: 'The GDR is opening its borders'.

By the time the news bulletin was over, a total of eighty East Berliners had already arrived at the Bornholmer Strasse, Heinrich-Heine-Strasse and Invalidenstrasse checkpoints and were requesting permission to cross into West Berlin. The border officials sought advice. They were instructed to tell would-be border-crossers to come back tomorrow.

The GDR's leadership had been caught completely off guard. The Central Committee plenum, which had been in progress for two days, did not end until 8.47 p.m. No one seems to have noticed the growing excitement over Schabowski's press conference. Krenz's main concern at this stage seems to have been his political position: to the General Secretary's disappointment, several of his reformist nominations for membership of the Politburo had been rejected by the Central Committee, in which the hardliners still formed a strong block. Immediately after the meeting was over, he retreated to his office and stayed there for some time.

Meanwhile, the news was spreading to the outside world. By 9.30 the Americans, the British, the French and the West German Chancellor Helmut Kohl had all realised that something remarkable was happening in Berlin. Kohl was on a visit to Warsaw (where there was now a government led by the non-Communist Solidarity movement). He heard the news while at a large formal banquet, and immediately realised he was 'dancing at the wrong wedding', as the German saying goes.

Some time after ten, Krenz received a phone call that would change everything. On the line was *Stasi* Minister Erich Mielke, who described the latest developments. Half an hour earlier, the crowd at the Bornholmer Strasse border checkpoint, between the north-central part of East Berlin and the French sector, had grown to between 500 and 1,000, all pressing to cross. On their own initiative, senior *Stasi* officers decided to let the most pushy through into West Berlin – though when they did, they stamped their passports 'no right of return', as they would an expellee. This so-called 'pressure-release solution' had little effect. The crowds continued to push forward, and more kept arriving by the minute.

Krenz quickly realised that attempts to hold back the tide were futile. He faced a stark choice. 'Either we shut the border so completely that it would impossible to storm it,' Krenz admitted later. 'That would have meant bringing up tanks. Or we let things run their course. There was no other decision possible.'[19] In the event, no order was issued.

Just before 10.30, the late bulletin of the East German state TV news, *Aktuelle Kamera* ('Topical Camera'), had made a final desperate attempt to halt the stampede.

At the request of many citizens [the announcer declared], we inform you once again about the new travel regulations from the ministerial council. First: Private trips can be applied for without having to first provide evidence of need to travel or familial relationships. So: Trips are subject to an application process!

Passport and registration offices would be open tomorrow at the usual time, the announcer added brightly, and, of course, permanent exit travel would also be possible *only* after application had been made and then granted by the appropriate authorities.

On that night in particular, most of the population of East Berlin was not, of course, tuned into the regime's stations to hear what time the passport and registration offices were opening, but was riveted to Western newscasts, eager to see what was actually going on in the real world. At around 10.40 p.m., ARD's late-night news discussion programme 'Themes of the Day' (*Tagesthemen*) began with the announcement: 'This ninth of November is a historic day: the GDR has announced that its borders are open to everyone, with immediate effect, and the gates of the Wall stand wide open.'

The strange thing was that when the programme went live to the Invalidenstrasse checkpoint to illustrate its claim, the border was clearly not open at all. The contradiction made no difference. It was at this point, largely in response to the ARD programme's sensational assertion, that the mass storming of the checkpoints began.

Within half an hour, the border situation was all but out of control. The 'pressure-release solution' had backfired spectacularly. At the Bornholmer Strasse, the huge crowds waiting behind a screen fence to go through the exit process were starting to push forward, and to threaten the handful of border guards trying to keep them in order. At around 11.30, a group of East Berliners pushed aside the screen fence in front of the border crossing and everyone swarmed into the checkpoint area *en masse*. Checkpoint commander Lieutenant-Colonel Harald Jäger decided that he was not prepared to risk the lives of himself and his soldiers. He ordered his men to stop checking passports, open up fully, and just let the crowd do what it wanted.

And the crowd knew what it wanted. Within moments, thousands began to pour through the checkpoint. They simply walked or, in most cases ran, into West Berlin. The sensation of running freely over the bridge, of crossing a border where such an action, just days or even hours before, would have courted near-certain death, brought a surge of exhilaration that, if we are to believe those who were there, all but changed the chemical composition of the air and turned it into champagne.

Large crowds had already gathered on the Western side. They greeted the Easterners with cries of joy and open arms. Many improvised toasts were drunk. By midnight, all the border checkpoints had been forced to open. At the Invalidenstrasse, masses 'invaded' from the West and met the approaching Easterners in the middle.

It was now twenty past midnight, and the entire East German army had been placed on a state of heightened alert. However, in the absence of orders from the leadership, the 12,000 men of the Berlin border regiments remained confined to barracks. The night passed, and the orders never arrived.

Between one and two a.m., human swarms from East and West push their way through the Wall at the Brandenburg Gate. Some are still in their sleepwear, ignoring the November cold. Thousands luxuriate in the sensation of walking around the nearby Pariser Platz – embassy row – an elegant city landmark closed for thirty years by barbed wire, concrete blocks and tank traps, turned by state decree into a deadly no man's land. People are clambering on top of the Wall to caper and dance and yell their hearts out in liberation and release and delight.

A mix of hype and hope has defeated bureaucratic obfuscation. A little over six hours after a fumbled press conference and a Western press campaign that took the fumbled ball of the temporary exit-visa regulation and ran with it, a revolution has occurred. One of the swiftest and least bloody in history. A revolution that has, whatever Gil Scott-Heron may have predicted to the contrary fifteen years before, most certainly been televised.

It will be followed by the biggest, wildest street party the world has ever seen.

And, perhaps inevitably, by one of the biggest hangovers, too. But that is another story.

AFTERWORD

THE THEFT OF HOPE

THE FALL OF THE Berlin Wall, like its construction, took place in a single night. Just as on 13 August 1961, a city and a people awoke to find themselves divided, so on the morning of 10 November 1989 that division was no more. Although how many people actually woke up to this revelation is debatable, since during that night in Berlin many had not slept a wink.

Joachim Trenkner, for instance. By then head of Current Affairs for the Berlin branch of the state-supported ARD television network Sender Freies Berlin (the Free Berlin Station), Trenker was in Warsaw, covering the West German Chancellor's historic visit, when he heard the news from the Wall. There were no flights to Berlin until the morning, and no trains. The whole press pack was going crazy, Trenkner included. Until it occurred to him, sometime around midnight, to call up the Polish taxi driver who had been chauffeuring him and his production people around Warsaw for the past two days while they organised the live coverage. He rang the man, asked him if he had a valid passport and was willing to drive to Berlin. The answer was, yes, and yes – in fact, he would be thrilled.

At one in the morning, they set off in a little Toyota and headed westwards through the night. For Trenkner, a man who might be considered a little jaded with travel, it was the most exciting trip of his life. Everyone struggled to stay awake, the driver included, but they crossed the GDR border at Frankfurt on the Oder around dawn. It was astonishing how easy and even friendly the usually curt East German *Grepos* had suddenly become. They drove on along the old Berlin autobahn. Everywhere, there were East Germans out in their Trabants and Wartburgs, honking and waving and smiling. Trenkner thought as they finally approached the city: 'This is German reunification'.[1]

The little Polish taxi rolled up outside the SFB studios at nine a.m. Once they reached Berlin itself, the sights and sensations had been even more amazing. The mood in the city was, *the Wall is gone, Berlin is once again Berlin*. By the time they arrived, Trenkner didn't just think he was seeing German unity, he *knew* it.

He was, of course, absolutely correct. For all the pussyfooting over the next year, there is little doubt that the moment the crowd had surged across the Bornholmer Strasse bridge, the end of the 'two Germanys' was just a matter of time.

There were a number of problems to be dealt with first. The idealists who had dared to oppose the regime during its last years were not, on the whole, full-blooded capitalists. They were of the Left, and Green, and aimed to build a collaborative rather than a competitive society; to transform the neo-Stalinist experiment that was the GDR into a laboratory for a 'third way' between capitalism and Communism.

The East German idealists were joined by leftists from West Germany, such as the Nobel Prize-winning novelist, Günter Grass. And the most powerful among the Social Democrats' leaders, Oskar Lafontaine, who just two years earlier had welcomed Erich Honecker home to the Saar. They opposed reunification for their own reasons, Grass because of concern that the sudden explosion into Europe of a united Germany might waken old, malevolent nationalist ghosts, and Lafontaine because of his fears for the generous social-welfare system of the West. Within days of the Wall's fall, Lafontaine was warning Easterners against coming West and proposing that they not be allowed to enjoy the same welfare benefits as their Western cousins. Even Walter Momper, SPD Mayor of West Berlin, swept up amid the celebrations of 9 November, had cautiously declared that this was not a question of 'reunification' (*Wiedervereinigung*) but of 'reunion' (*Wiedersehen*).

All these attempts to slow the process down met with utter failure. Willy Brandt, at seventy-five now the elder statesman and conscience of the SPD, had already seen the future. He said on the Friday that followed the dramatic night of 9/10 November: 'Now what belongs together will grow together.'

Brandt was right. But the growth did not prove to be slow or organic. It was more like a speeded-up nature film. By the end of that month, the momentum had become unstoppable. The call in October had been: 'We are the people!' By December it was, 'We are one people!' After decades of isolation, the people of the East had seen what the West enjoyed, and they wanted it too. But to pay for it they knew they must have hard currency. 'If the Deutsche Mark won't come to us,' the reawakened masses cried, 'we'll go to it!' They began to flood westward for a variety of reasons, some sentimental and some hard-headedly practical.

The GDR leadership had just about held on to its authority until 9 November. Almost immediately, its power began to dissolve. However, as usual, it was a somewhat more gradual and conflicted process than historical memory allows.

Even on Friday/Saturday 10/11 November, there were attempts at a quasi-reinstatement of the border. The dinosaurs were, after all, still in charge of the border troops and the *Stasi*. Generals Kessler and Hoffman, who had dedicated their lives to the Wall, could still issue orders, and during these next forty-eight hours they and their senior colleagues were in near-constant session. How to admit that the game was up?

Those who tried to leap over and enter the East that Friday night were politely but firmly sent back by border guards on their superiors' orders. None the less, alcohol consumption was considerable, and the boldness of would be Wall-jumpers increased in proportion. Eastern officials protested to the Western police to keep 'their' people under control. At one point, around midnight, dogs and water cannon were introduced at the Brandenburg Gate. A few intruders got a soaking, though the *Vopos* didn't turn on the power-jets. Someone rammed a jeep into the Wall from the Western side and took out a section several metres square. The Eastern guards carefully put it back.

The army and the *Stasi* remained on alert through most of the weekend. There were anxious consultations between the forces of order in East and West. Not until the afternoon of 11 November was all danger of bloodshed considered past. The East German army in the neighbourhood of Berlin was stood down, as were the *Stasi*'s forces. On the morning of Sunday 12 November, the mayors of West and East Berlin presided over the opening of a new crossing point on the Potsdamer Platz, 500 yards south of the Brandenburg Gate. The pressure now diminished.

Visitors could pass through with the mere wave of an identity card or passport, and a permission stamp was automatic.[2]

On 13 November there was another major reshuffle of the Politburo and the government in East Berlin. The former bosses of the GDR were rapidly being revealed as so many Wizards of Oz, cranking pathetic little wheels to maintain their huge, rumbling façade of power. And the most Oz-like of all was the *Stasi* Minister, 81-year-old Erich Mielke.

Appearing to give an account of himself before a newly emboldened East German parliament, the state's foremost secret policeman tried to present himself and the *Stasi* as diligent and humane guardians of the East German people. When heckled and booed by hitherto obedient parliamentary deputies, the old man seemed genuinely upset. 'But I love you all!' Mielke declared, on the verge of tears. 'I love all human beings!' Then he left the podium and never returned. If there was any truth in Mielke's bizarre outburst, it reflected an affection for humanity of the unhealthy variety, the kind so accurately expressed by the aptly named rock band, the Police, in their song about obsessive love: 'Every breath you take/Every move you make/I'll be watching you'.

On 3 December, Krenz announced his resignation as SED First Secretary. The party's members were now themselves leaving in their hundreds of thousands. In a vain attempt to show the the party's 'democratic' credentials, many of the old leadership, including Schabowski and Krenz, would soon be expelled.

Hans Modrow, Gorbachev's original candidate to succeed Honecker, had been made prime minister on 13 November. He stayed in office until the new year, when free elections were held. Although Modrow was respected as a genuine reformer, it was too late even for a respected SED leader to stay in control. To the vast majority of East Germans, the party was tainted goods. Even before the elections, Modrow was forced to accept non-Communist representatives into the government.

The first free vote in East Germany for almost sixty years was held on 18 March 1990. The SED received 16 per cent. This respectable outcome probably reflected its true support – time-serving *apparatchiks* combined with inveterate idealists – even throughout the long years of dictatorship. The CDU, whose Western leader Helmut Kohl had become a hero to the

East German masses for his promotion of reunification and promises of rapid prosperity, got 40 per cent. The SPD paid for its ambivalence on both these issues with a disappointing haul of around 22 per cent. Support for the 'third way' dissidents of 'New Forum', 'Democratic Awakening' and so on, who just months previously had seemed so influential, had dwindled quickly. Their votes amounted to no more than 6–7 per cent of the total. In April, a CDU-dominated government, led by Eastern CDU chairman Lothar de Mazière, took power. Reunification was inevitable. Only the terms remained a matter of speculation.

The wider world watched in surprise and some apprehension. 1989 brought the 'German problem' full circle. Just as in the summer of 1961, the building of the Wall had been greeted with covert relief by other Western powers, especially France and Britain, so its sudden demise in the autumn of 1989 brought into view all the hidden anxieties and rivalries that seethed behind the polite façade of Western Cold-War unity. For decades, the NATO powers had regularly protested at the undoubted brutality and ugliness of the German/German border. Now the full extent of the hypocrisy involved was mercilessly revealed.

After the Second World War, the Germans had been permitted, even encouraged, to revive their economy and military power, but their 'punishment' was, in fact, programmed to continue. As the most populous and efficient country in Europe, blamed for two bloody wars (three if you were French and remembered 1870/1), to many of its former enemies Germany looked altogether better divided than united. The deep-freeze of the Cold War had kept it in that condition quite effectively. Douglas Hurd, Mrs Thatcher's Foreign Secretary, remarked in December 1989 that the Cold War was 'a system . . . under which we've lived quite happily for forty years'.[3]

Hurd's boss, Mrs Thatcher, showed her feelings surprisingly openly. While anything that showed the weakness of Communism was manna from heaven to her, and the great night of the Wall's end contained undoubted delights, in the longer run she faced a dilemma. Thatcher had been and remained sceptical of the European project, and was frankly disturbed by the sudden collapse of the two-state Germany and its potential consequences, domestic and international. As someone who had been a teenage girl during the Second World War, she could not help but have (as her aide Sir Charles Powell recalled) 'memories that are very difficult to erase about what happens when Germany becomes too big and too powerful'. Furthermore there were concerns about how a sudden and dramatic, possibly even violent, collapse of Soviet control in East Germany might undermine Gorbachev rather as the Cuban failure in 1962 had fatally wounded Khrushchev, thus halting the progress towards a 'moderate, reforming Soviet Union'.

The situation for France was even more complex. President Mitterand was on intimate terms with Chancellor Kohl, and unlike Mrs Thatcher he felt no qualms about accelerating European integration. But instinctual French distrust of a powerful Germany, based on grim experience, came flooding back as the pictures from Berlin filled the television screen at the Elysée Palace in Paris, just as it did in tens of millions of other homes, humble and grand, throughout the world.

Thatcher recalled in her inimitable style a hasty meeting with Mitterand:

> I produced from my handbag a map showing the various configurations of Germany in the past, which were not entirely reassuring about the future . . . [Mitterand] said that at moments of great danger in the past France had always established special relations with Britain and he felt such a time had come again . . .

The Americans, especially President George H.W. Bush and Secretary of State James H. Baker, provided the heavyweight international support for German reunification. Washington saw great advantage in a strong, democratic and capitalist Germany, and virtually no down side.

It was Helmut Kohl, of course, who pushed it through with verve, determination and an invincible – some would say finally disastrous – capacity to suppress economic and social misgivings in the cause of the final political goal.

In the end, Mitterand decided against entering into a classic wartime-style alliance with Mrs Thatcher's dangerously Eurosceptic Britain. After thinking things over, the old fox in the Elysée seized the only other option, which also provided the chance of a permanent solution to the problem of overwheening German power. Mitterand's strategy involved drawing the newly enlarged Germany (and its physically no less considerable chancellor) into such a binding, permanent hug that the country's ability to divert that power into destructive channels would be severely limited. Mitterand promised Kohl his support for a reunited Germany, but at a high price. The price was closer European integration. In particular, it would mean the sacrifice of the mighty D-Mark and the introduction of a single European currency.

East Germany, with its inexperienced cabinet and parliament, plus a continuing and expanding financial deficit, was already beginning to fold over into its big brother, the Federal Republic. In Berlin, some controls remained in place until the spring, but public movement was largely unimpeded.

Already, official and unofficial demolition teams were at work on the Wall. The border-marker wall on the Western side, covered over the years in colourful graffiti, had become a tourist attraction and – for those who could lay their hands on hammers and chisels – an instant takeaway memento. In the central city areas, substantial stretches began to disappear. The financially embarrassed East German government was already debating what to do with the de-fortified but still largely intact structure. It decided, since the Wall seemed to be such an interesting commodity, to sell it as one might any other artefact: at auction.

The sale of the century – or least thirty years of it – took place at the Hotel Parc Pallas in Monte Carlo, Monaco, on 23 June 1990. The official who organised the transport of the Wall sections to the sale was, curiously, the same man who had first drawn up a map of what became the Wall and who, on Tuesday 15 August 1961, had painted the famous white line to show the border at Checkpoint Charlie: Hagen Koch.

There was an odd but compelling logic to it all. A private at the time of his first brush with fame, Koch had progressed to captain in the Dzerzhinsky Regiment before leaving the service of the *Stasi* in 1985, just before his forty-fifth birthday.[4] Never seen as a warrior type, and considered *schwatzhaft* (a loose talker), which was a distinct disadvantage for a *Stasi* man, his progress through the ranks had been slow. For fifteen years, he had pursued, if we are to believe his memoirs, a harmless existence as a 'cultural officer', bringing music and the arts to the troops – naturally, within the right ideological context. Not the area to be in if you wanted a high-flying career, and organising a 'talent show' without sufficient ideological content (but plenty of dirty jokes) did not help either. The job Koch got after his release was with the Department of Cultural Monuments, organising the transporting and setting-up of art and museum exhibitions. It was thus that, in the spring of 1990, he was instructed to organise the shipping of the Wall segments down to the Côte d'Azur.

Eighty-one sections, all certified as genuine, were put on the block, and all of them were sold, realising an average of DM 20,000 (£6,500) each, to international clients who wanted substantial chunks of the Wall in their businesses or homes. It was a quiet triumph for Koch. However, a West German television team was covering the auction, and they had done their homework. Koch kept out of the way while his department head gave the main interview, but when the report was aired, the camera zeroed in and froze on the hapless ex-*Stasi* captain. A stern voice-over identified him as a '*Stasi* operative' who had 'found a hiding place' at the innocent-sounding Department of Cultural Monuments. After all, was this not the fanatical creature who had drawn the notorious white line at Checkpoint Charlie so many years ago?

This marked the beginning of a fifteen-year battle for Koch, who found himself turned into a symbol of the Wall and its evils, a media scapegoat. He was soon fired from Cultural Monuments, and then hounded from a similar job working for a West German art-transportation firm. But Koch, overcoming considerable adversity, has since transformed himself into a respected Wall expert, writing and lecturing to anyone who will listen to or read what he has to say. That is how he now lives and finds his self-justification.

After 1989, the expiation of the Communist past and its simultaneous erasure became a curious twin-track process. At first, amnesia seemed the easy way out.

On 1 July 1990, the West mark became the official currency of both East and West Germany, as the two states remained for another few months yet. For the first 2,000–6,000 East marks, depending on various factors such as the age of the individual in possession of the money, the exchange rate was fixed at one West mark to one East. For all other sums held, it was 1:2. This was an astoundingly generous 'gift' to the East, since the open-market rate at that point from East into West marks stood at between 10:1 and 20:1.

The first of July was also the day that border controls between the two Germanys were abolished. On 23 June, the final structures at Checkpoint Charlie were removed in the presence of the Foreign Ministers of France, Britain, the USA, the USSR and of the two German states. The presence of the Soviet Foreign Minister, Eduard Shevardnadze, was a tacit admission by Moscow that unification was inevitable. Shevardnadze took the opportunity to make a surprising offer: that all foreign troops be withdrawn from German soil within six months of reunification. The timetable turned out longer – the last would leave in 1994 – but the principle proved true.

On 3 October 1990, German was formally reunited. All-German elections were set for 2 December.

Buoyed by a continuing wave of support from the East, Chancellor Kohl's Christian Democrats triumphed with 43.8 per cent, the SPD got 33.5 per cent, the FDP ('Liberal Party') 11 per cent. As in other post-Communist countries, the former ruling party had transformed itself into a democratic legacy outfit. The SED had changed its name to the 'Party of Democratic Socialism' (PDS) and proclaimed that it represented a reformed and reforming version of its former self. The PDS got only 2.6 per cent of the vote throughout Germany. Because of the so-called '5 per cent hurdle', this would normally have meant it was allocated no seats in the parliament. However, during the reunification negotiations it had been agreed that the East would not be subject to this rule. As a result, for the 1.1 million votes the PDS won in the East (10 per cent or so of the total), it was awarded seventeen seats in the first reunited Bundestag.

This was the Communists' low point and the high-water mark of the East German masses' enthusiasm for capitalism and its political representatives. For a while, due to the favourable transfer of savings and investments into West marks, the recently liberated population had hard currency burning a hole in its collective pocket. Trabis and Wartburgs were dumped in favour of Volkswagens and Toyotas. The 'new provinces' became a favoured dumping ground for old Western cars, many of which would have had trouble finding a buyer in the Federal Republic. Families from Saxony, Thuringia and East Berlin – so long trapped in Ulbricht's and Honecker's walled-in republic of virtue – launched themselves on to the European motorway network or jetted on bargain holidays to Majorca and Mykonos.

The backlash set in within a couple of years. The industries in which most of the citizens of the former GDR had worked and which, however their work-forces grumbled and chafed, had formed the social framework and economic basis of tightly knit community-based lives, were taken over and disposed of by an overwhelmingly West German public body known as the *Treuhandanstalt* (Trust Agency). Money from the West flooded into the so-called 'new provinces' of the former GDR, but much was spent by and on consultants and 'experts' who were seen, not unfairly, by the bewildered and increasingly angry East Germans as greedy carpet-baggers. The merciless 'Yuppie' culture of the 1980s West collided bruisingly with a society in the East that, behind the grisly but prophylactic barrier of the Wall, had kept many of those old-fashioned social values that had once been accepted all over the industrialised world but were now dismissed as wilfully eccentric, even contemptible.

There was an old joke about the social pact that made the Communist system half-way tolerable. It went: 'We pretend to work and they pretend to pay us.' By the mid-1990s, the joke was no longer funny. The polluting, rusted, often staggeringly inefficient industries of East Germany were deemed unviable and closed down. For wide swathes of the newly reunited population, especially the older people and the burghers of the smaller, more remote East German towns, and of uncompetitive heavy-industry centres such as Bitterfeld, the – admittedly relatively generous – welfare system taken over from West Germany became their only source of income. There was little realistic hope of long-term re-employment for such redundant workers. Perhaps a new motto might now have been more suitable: 'We pretend to look for work and they pretend to pay us.'

Many of the young and energetic went to the West. Ironically, after the Wall came down, a new wave of emigration soon rivalled in scale and socially undermining effect the exodus of 1949–61. For all its ideological and intellectual narrowness, East Germany had offered an efficient system of education and training to its young people. With severely limited opportunities in the East, there was only one direction for many of them to take their skills.

By the mid-1990s, East Germany's economy was largely kept alive by a busy reconstruction industry, which was hard at work restoring long-neglected towns and installing modern transport and communications systems. Real economic viability was confined to a few 'hot-spots'. The population was ageing dramatically. A political backlash benefited the PDS, which, after barely surviving the 'Turn' (*Wende*) as reunification became euphemistically known, climbed in the polls as the last decade of the second millennium CE progressed. The Communist successor party was helped by some appealing leaders, including the East Berlin lawyer and controversialist Gregor Gysi, a son of the old East German élite who became a standby on talk shows all over Germany. Perhaps more importantly, the PDS successfully asserted its rights as legal successor to the SED, and thus controlled a large number of bank accounts and properties that had belonged to the party when it was synonymous with the Communist regime. This made it perhaps the richest small political party in the world. Within a few years, the PDS's share of the vote had settled at around 20 per cent in most of former East Germany, including East Berlin.

But the PDS was largely a party of older people. Around 60 per cent of those who voted for it were themselves over sixty. The young of the former GDR – those who stayed behind – often expressed their disillusion, and the results of decades of intellectual isolation, in a tendency to swing not to the old far Left but to the new far Right. This was particularly true in smaller provincial centres, but there was also a strong presence in cities such as Magdeburg, Halle, and Chemnitz (which had changed its name back from Karl-Marx-Stadt). Racist skinhead gangs sought out the relatively few foreigners who lived in the East and often committed terrible acts of violence against them. Support for far-right parties such as the NPD and the DVU burgeoned. A fervent, if ultimately poisonous and stifling, 'national' subculture spread across the former East Germany, and remains a prominent and ugly feature of the 'new provinces' well into the twenty-first century. Transparently neo-Nazi parties are represented in the provincial parliaments of Saxony and Brandenburg, though they have as yet failed to make the same mark on the national political scene. A number of the major leaders of this movement in the East are, in fact, 'carpet-baggers' from the West. They saw an opportunity to break out of the electoral ghetto to which they had long been confined there, and consciously targeted the more fertile territory of the former GDR. In this they showed considerable astuteness.

As a substantial minority of East Germans swung back to the familiar tropes of the SED regime in reaction against the cold wind of capitalism, so at the same time a counter-trend saw a wave of accusations against those who had managed and served the state during the Ulbricht and Honecker years. Prosecutions followed.

Former conscripts, who had fired on and in many cases killed fellow East Germans attempting to cross the Wall, were hauled into court. The fresh-faced young *Grepos* of the 1960s and 1970s, now middle-aged, were forced to confront their actions. Decades later, the whole mess of fear, brainwashed enthusiasm, confusion and conformism that had dictated the world of the GDR's border guardians during those ugly years was the subject of well-publicised court cases.

It must have given some satisfaction to victims such as Walter Tews, crippled at the age of fourteen as he fled to the West, and to the families of such young martyrs as Peter Fechter, Günter Litfin and Chris Gueffroy, when they saw these men and the state they served held to account. But in these often bewildered and defensive men it is not usually possible to discern heartless killers whose actions should be treated as common murder. The courts have tended to find them guilty but hand out short or suspended prison sentences.

As for the SED leaders, the really big fish got away.

Ulbricht, the East German state's true begetter, died while his GDR still had a decade and a half of life in it. His successor and protégé, Erich Honecker, survived to be held responsible for the state he had helped create and the Wall whose construction he had overseen. He had fled to Moscow in the early spring of 1991, just as legal proceedings were being opened against him. After the Soviet Union itself collapsed, he was extradited back to Germany to answer accusations of having caused almost 200 deaths at the Berlin Wall and the border between the two Germanys.

However, Honecker escaped the worst because he faced the worst. By the time the former General Secretary came to court in 1992, now aged eighty, he was dying from a liver cancer that the surgeons had failed to find and remove during his hospital stay in the fateful summer of 1989. Sometimes, as he shuffled to and from the courtroom, he would bump into the likes of Mielke, Kessler, Hoffmann, all also arraigned for the Wall deaths. The elderly comrades would exchange gruff Marxist-Leninist phrases of encouragement, for all the world as if they were young, persecuted anti-Fascists again, with a future to fight for. Shortly after returning from Moscow, Honecker had joined the recently re-founded, 500-member German Communist Party. Though mortally ill, he admitted he could not bear to remain 'unorganised' – his Communist equivalent of a Catholic's horror of dying 'unshriven'.

The reunited German state took pity on the sick, tired old man in a way that his implacable apparatus of oppression would never have done under the same circumstances. Despite the fact that Erich Honecker defended the building of his Wall to the very last, he was released on health grounds on 12 January 1993. The court declared that Honecker's death was 'so imminent that the conduct of a criminal proceeding has lost its meaning'.[5]

The next day, 13 January 1993, the former East German leader climbed slowly aboard Flight RG 741 of the Brazilian airline, Varig, at Frankfurt Airport. The Boeing 747's destination was São Paulo. There Honecker would change flights and continue on to Santiago, the capital of Chile. In fact, right up to the moment the plane took off, those who wished him to be prosecuted, sick or not, continued efforts to prevent him from embarking on his journey into exile.

Honecker's choice of destination was based on personal circumstances. His daughter, Sonja, had married a Chilean exile who, like thousands of the country's other leftists, had sought and been granted refuge in the GDR during the bloody period of military dictatorship between 1973 and 1988. Margot Honecker had left Moscow after her husband's extradition to Germany the previous summer, and since then had been living in a comfortable villa outside Santiago. Honecker was welcomed enthusiastically by many Chileans. To them the GDR had been a friend. The *Stasi* had helped rescue endangered opponents of the military dictatorship and given them a safe haven. Looked at from their point of view, the East German secret police played the role, not of the 'Red Gestapo', but of the Scarlet Pimpernel.

The deposed SED leader died at his comfortable final refuge on 29 May 1994, in his eighty-second year. Homesick to the end – he spoke no Spanish – he none the less gave no sign of repentance or regret. Erich Honecker was buried in Santiago. The crucifix traditionally attached to a coffin in Catholic Chile was concealed, in the case of this lifelong atheist, by a black-red-and-gold GDR flag.

Honecker's defence of the Wall merits little consideration. All the same, the case for condemning it, while ultimately compelling, is no simple matter either. According to the German Federal Prosecutor's Office, between 13 August 1961 and 9 November 1989, 86 human beings died as a direct result of violence at the Berlin Wall. Other estimates run higher, largely depending on the criteria they use for classifying deaths as 'Wall-related'. The government-supported website www.chronik-der-mauer.de quotes a death toll totalling 125, including several East German border guards killed in exchanges of fire and a few unfortunate individuals whose death can be obliquely blamed on the Wall. One such was a gentleman in his sixties who had a heart attack while being searched at the Dreilinden control point in 1971. Another man died in 1983 while being interrogated at a border crossing. A five-year-old boy from West Berlin drowned in a canal on the border while trying to retrieve his football. And a baby from the East, concealed in a suitcase while its parents made a successful escape, was found on arrival in West Berlin to have died of asphyxiation. There was also a desperate young couple who committed suicide at East Berlin's Schönefeld Airfield after failing to steal an aircraft, which they had hoped to fly to a new life in the West.

The highest number of victims is cited by the Arbeitsgemeinschaft 13. August, an organisation associated with the late anti-Communist campaigner Rainer Hildebrandt's Haus am Checkpoint Charlie museum. This list encompasses individuals who died for any reason at all either at or because of the Wall. It includes those who were caught and secretly executed for escape attempts, those who escaped but were kidnapped back across the border and then killed, and even those successful escapers thought to have been 'liquidated' by *Stasi* agents while living in conditions of apparent safety in West Germany. The list's broad and changeable figure, contested by many experts, totals 227.[6]

It is not that these deaths were not tragic. They are terrible to see described, and appalling to record. But when we compare the experience of other countries that in the twentieth century were forced to survive on ideological or religious fault lines, we may find ourselves marvelling not at how *many* died in Berlin or at the border between East and West Germany, but *how few*. Compare the millions who died in similarly divided countries elsewhere – North and South Korea (another fortified border which still exists), North and South Vietnam, or Northern and Southern Ireland. Or in the collapsed remnants of Yugoslavia, or the disputed borders between India and Pakistan, or between Israel and Palestine, where once again the Wall solution, while embarked on for different reasons, embarrasses and troubles us . . .

But in the case of the Berlin Wall we can read the individual stories of violent death. In the cynical words of Stalin, who knew a thing or two about mass murder, 'a single death is a tragedy, a million deaths are a statistic'. And while every death, even when lost among millions, is a tragedy to someone, the Wall deaths are all obviously and unmistakably individual. None the less, altogether, even if we take the most pessimistic of the death tolls – 227 souls – then we are discussing a number equivalent to those killed in a commuter airliner coming down in a snowstorm. And if we accept the lower, more critically sifted figures, then we should add that the airliner was only half full.

That these deaths constituted a crime in principle and many score of crimes in practice, cannot possibly be denied.

But what, then, was the greater 'punishment' inflicted on the people of the East? Just three decades of ugliness, claustrophobia, shattered families, and a few score of violent, pointless deaths?

It was more subtle and long-lasting than any of those things. Within a few years after the end of the Second World War, the defeated Germans in the Western zones were permitted to establish parliamentary democracy and to launch what turned out to be one of the greatest economic recoveries in history.

Not so their Eastern brothers and sisters. Already held back by draconian Soviet reparation demands, and radical social and economic reorganisation in the Communist interest, by 1961 such formerly prosperous and advanced parts of Germany as Thuringia, Saxony and

Saxony-Anhalt, not forgetting East Berlin, had lost huge swathes of their productive capital, industrial know-how, patents and management skills to the dynamic, free-market Western zones.

After the Wall fell, two factors became shockingly clear. Firstly that the GDR's loudly trumpeted industries were almost entirely uncompetitive, both in the enlarged domestic and the wider international market. Secondly that those skills, manpower and productive capital resources lost to the West in the post-war period were not coming back – or at least not in the quantities that would have made possible a genuine revival of the region's fortunes to pre-GDR levels.

The true 'punishment' of the East – and the most insidious, lasting crime of its Communist masters – was this theft of hope.

Western German taxpayers poured billions upon billions into the East after 1989, but for little permanent gain. In the 1950s and 1960s, West Germany created its 'economic miracle', conquering the export markets in a post-war world crying out for the kind of quality goods that this energetic and skilled people could produce. Meanwhile, their brothers and sisters in the East stumbled along on a path which brought a modest revival, one that was almost considered another 'miracle' – until the so-called wonder turned out to be mostly statistical sleight of hand.

By the 1990s, when the East Germans finally got their chance to catch up, the world was a different place: an emerging global market-place. In the 1950s the West Germans had faced relatively little comparable competition, but in the 1990s there was Japan, Korea, Malaysia, a revived USA – and towards the end of the decade, China – all producing goods of a quality that could compete more than adequately in the world market.

In 1989, West Germany seemed so rich and successful that the general opinion was, the East Germans are the lucky ex-Communists. They had their big, powerful brother to help them, whereas the Czechs and Slovaks, the Hungarians, the Poles and the Baltic nations, would have to pull themselves up by their own bootstraps. In fact, the attachment to West Germany turned out in most ways to be a disadvantage. The unions representing East German workers demanded near parity between wages in the East and those in the West – while productivity lagged dramatically and would clearly take years to approach the West German level.

Result: millions of jobs lost or, instead of going to the East German provinces, exported to the low-wage, low-cost countries beyond the Oder river, with their aggressive tax breaks and eager, co-operative governments. At the time of writing (2006), it is reckoned that soon the highest proportion of automotive workers per head of the population in Europe will belong not to Germany or France or Italy (and certainly not Britain) but to Slovakia.[7]

There has been a lot of talk of the 'Wall in the head', as if East Germans were somehow dramatically different from West Germans. Statistics, spurious or otherwise, are regularly published in German newspapers or quoted on radio and TV to the effect that such-and-such a percentage of Germans in East or West 'wish the Wall could be rebuilt'. In truth, the situation between 'Ossis' and 'Wessis' is not that different to the feelings the Scots have about the English, and vice versa. It is rare to find a Scotsman with a good word to say about the larger country south of Hadrian's Wall (that wall thing again), but on the other hand they somehow never quite cut loose. As for East Germans, their history was certainly different to the West's for forty years or so, and largely worse. It will probably take a whole new generation, growing up since the end of the Wall, to begin properly integrating the 'two Germanys'. With a new woman chancellor, Angela Merkel, who grew up in the East and saw the fall of the Wall from the Eastern perspective, perhaps the process will accelerate. But maybe the problem is not the 'Wall in the head', but the simple fact of unemployment and hopelessness in one part of Germany versus prosperity in the other.

The 'Wall in the head' may represent a rationalisation of this hopelessness. Communities in crisis tend to blame others, and to fall back on the things and people they consider 'their own'. Hence the wave of so-called *Ostalgie* ('Eastalgia') in the ex-GDR, with its selective reminiscing about the 'good old days' of Ulbricht, Honecker, FDJ uniforms, guaranteed jobs and that shabby sense of belonging. It is to be found at its most harmless in hit films such as *Good Bye, Lenin!* (which has the advantage of being genuinely funny and charming) and *Sonnenallee*, and at its most toxic in votes for the PDS and resentment against caricatured West German 'yuppies'. We can hope that tougher, more realistic films such as the recent 'The Life of the Others' (*Das Leben der Anderen*), showing the grubby and life-destroying abuse of domestic surveillance for political purposes by the *Stasi*, will help redress the balance. This was a society where brother was encouraged to betray brother, husband betray wife. Life under the pitiless, probing gaze of the *Stasi* was composed of a hundred thousand tiny betrayals in the intimate sphere, between people who in any decent society should have been able to trust each other. To see life in the GDR any other way is to inhabit a rose-tinted fantasy world.

None of this means that, more than a decade and a half after the Wall tumbled, the former GDR does not have serious problems. The region's ancient and often beautiful small towns, though in many cases rebuilt and cleaned up with Western money since 1989, are decaying and losing their young people.

The population of the former GDR is ageing at a terrifying rate, and the birth rate is at a record low. In total the region has lost 8 per cent of its population since 1990, amounting to 1.3 million people (as of 2003). In 1949, 25 per cent of the population of Germany lived in the area that would become the GDR. Fifteen years after the GDR's demise, the figure was down to less than 18 per cent. It is predicted to fall to 13 per cent by 2050.[8] The tax base of the new provinces is still fragile, in some areas almost non-existent, and in a few years the rate of Western financial aid for the East is due to fall dramatically. Leipzig and Dresden show clear signs of life, as do Jena and Eisenach, where optics and automotive engineering respectively have revived, but the old manufacturing centre of Chemnitz, the 'German Manchester', has lost more than 15 per cent of its population since 1989 and has by some calculations the lowest birth rate *in the world*. Small cities such as Schwerin and Rostock have lost more than 20 per cent, and the population of the once-key chemicals centre of Halle, with more than one in five unemployed, has declined from 310,000 to 240,000, a loss of 22.6 per cent.[9] Recently (and expensively) renovated apartment buildings are now being torn down because the city authorities cannot afford their upkeep and there is no hope of finding tenants. In the Halle suburb of Silberhöhe, of 14,000 apartments, 3,500 stood empty before the recent wave of tear-downs started.[10]

The Easterners have reason to be disappointed and unhappy, and also – despite the generosity of the Westerners since 1989 – reason to be bitter.

The problem is that they often blame the wrong people – that is, the West, and not the SED bosses who kept them behind the Wall while the world changed around them, until it was all but too late to cope.

One dark, ambiguous footnote to all this is provided by the fate of Conrad Schumann, the young border guard who was so famously photographed as he leapt the wire from the Bernauer Strasse into West Berlin on 15 August 1961. At first sight, his was a success story. He integrated well into Western society, married a young West German woman and went to live in Ingolstadt, a prosperous town in northern Bavaria. He worked for almost twenty years in the Audi car factory, and brought up a family. Then the Wall came down. Schumann was finally able to visit his relations and friends, in a small Saxon town between Dresden and Leipzig. Cause for joy, it would seem. There, however, he found that he was not entirely welcome. He was the iconic Wall-jumper. Or, as he had been portrayed in the East, iconic traitor and tool of the imperialists. These were the accusations from which the Wall had protected him. Schumann could not reconnect with the friends and comrades of his youth, the ones he had left behind when he took that impulsive jump to the West all those years ago. With that 'desertion' he had excluded himself from being one of them, and never could be again.

Conrad Schumann hanged himself on 20 June 1998 in the orchard of his house near Ingolstadt. The family blamed his suicide on personal problems.

And Berlin? The Wall was not just, or not even, about Berlin. It was about imprisoning an entire country's population. Since reunification, surprisingly, Berlin's population has also declined, by around 45,000, despite the fact that it became the seat of government in 1991. And Berlin is broke. What used to be the Western sectors no longer receive the generous aid from the federal government that they enjoyed during the city's time as a protected capitalist island in the Communist sea. The same goes for East Berlin, which as capital of the GDR and the Workers' and Peasants' State's tourist showcase was also lavishly subsidised by East Bloc standards.

Berlin still mirrors the nation's differences.

The historic centre of the city, just inside what used to be East Berlin, has now been renovated and seems virtually indistinguishable from the West. However, in the areas east of the Alexanderplatz, where there are still tram services, the continuing difference becomes clear. The horizon is dominated by the looming, monotonous *Plattenbauten* (literally slab-building) apartment blocks that were built between the 1960s and the 1980s in the rush to house East Berliners in a manner that Ulbricht, Honecker and comrades thought fit. The clothes are cheaper and often drabber, the cars older. There's an old-fashioned clannish feeling here, a closeness and an often attractive lack of pretension. The east end of Berlin was always the working people's area, the place where a century or more ago the immigrants from the countryside and abroad tended to gather. So it's not just because of forty years of Communism that it looks and feels this way. All the same, as someone who got to know the East during the 1970s and 1980s when the GDR was in its deceptively solid heyday, when I'm there I don't need a street sign to know where I am.

But the city as a whole has survived, will survive, and will grow together, as Willy Brandt predicted back in 1989, because it belongs together. Individuals and companies are moving into the old East of Berlin because it is cheaper and, frankly, in many ways more interesting than the somewhat sedate and sanitised, often strongly middle-class, districts westwards of where the Wall used to be. The East is where most of the clubs are, the experimental theatres and venues, the funky restaurants and less expensive apartments. It has an edgy, unexplored feeling that for Westerners is attractive as well as slightly unnerving.

And strangest of all, the Communists now rule again in Berlin. Or rather, they co-rule. Since 2001, the PDS has been in coalition with the Social Democrats at city hall, to the shock and outrage of some and the wry amusement of others. PDS senators, many of them former SED members, run various departments of the united city administration. The comrades are back, in modernised form of course. At the last elections for city hall, they got a very respectable 23 per cent of the vote to the SPD's 29 per cent. The PDS fraction from the Berlin city assembly even dares to lay a wreath at the Berlin Wall monument in the Bernauer Strasse every 13 August, or at least it did so in 2005. On that occasion, the tribute disappeared in a matter of minutes. I never managed to find out exactly why, or where it went. The so-called 'Red-Red' coalition seems to work, but the wounds of the Wall have not yet closed. Maybe, even in an age of post-modern irony, it is still possible to take some things too far, too fast.

But Berlin has seen worse, a lot worse. It likes to party, and partying is what it does well, even when the city coffers are close to empty. Especially in the summer of the World Cup. The city has an openly gay mayor, Klaus Wowereit, who also has a high fun quotient and continues to enjoy high popularity. *Berlin bleibt Berlin*. Berlin remains Berlin. And with a little luck and hard work, perhaps Germany's time of punishment will soon be truly over.

For anyone who knew the city when the Wall cast its pall across Berlin, nothing can beat the pleasure of being able to stroll through the Brandenburg Gate and across the Pariser Platz, maybe heading for an espresso in one of the boulevard cafés on Unter den Linden. And nothing is sweeter than the awareness that, compared with twenty years ago, the greatest danger you run when taking these few unhurried paces is of being knocked into by an over-enthusiastic bicycle courier, not cut in half by a burst of automatic fire.

When we're doing this, and the sun is shining, sometimes we can believe that Hitler never happened, that Auschwitz was just the German name for an obscure village in Poland, and that the Berlin Wall was just a figment of somebody's mad imagination.

NOTES

1 Marsh Town

1 Entries in Clausewitz, *Berlinisches Stadtbuch*, cited in Alexandra Richie, *Faust's Metropolis: A History of Berlin* p. 29.
2 Giles Macdonogh, *Berlin* pp. 116f.
3 Richie, *Faust's Metropolis* p. 66.
4 Nancy Mitford, *Frederick the Great* p. 291.
5 Macdonogh, *Berlin* p. 117.

2 Reds

1 For a particularly interesting overview of this era, see *Wilhelminism and Its Legacies: German Modernities, Imperialism, and the Meanings of Reform, 1890–1930* ed. Geoff Eley and James Retallack.
2 Bebel's speech quoted in Jonathan Sternberg, *Yesterday's Deterrent: Tirpitz and the Birth of the German Battle Fleet* p. 195.
3 For this quote and details of Ulbricht's early life and political apprenticeship see Mario Frank, *Walter Ulbricht: Eine deutsche Biografie* pp. 64ff.
4 See Frank, *Walter Ulbricht* pp. 90ff.
5 Richie, *Faust's Metropolis* p. 401.
6 Quoted in Frank, *Walter Ulbricht* p. 105.

3 'It Must Look Democratic . . .'

1 Cf. Frank, *Walter Ulbricht* pp. 122f. Neumann, for instance, was shot in 1937. His wife, Margarete Buber-Neumann, was sentenced to five years hard labour in Siberia, but then handed over by the Russians to the Gestapo in 1940. She was imprisoned in the Ravensbrück women's concentration camp until April 1945. There she met and became close friends with Milena Jesenská, once the lover of Franz Kafka. Jesenská died of her privations in 1944. Miraculously, however, Buber-Neumann survived to write 'Between Two Dictators: Stalin and Hitler' after the war as well as many other works, including a biography of her friend Milena. She died in November 1989, in Frankfurt-on-Main, three days before the Berlin Wall was breached.
2 See interview with Wolfgang Leonhard, *Zurück in die Zukunft* in *Der Spiegel* 16/2005 8 April 2005.
3 David Clay Large, *Berlin: A Modern History* p. 371.

4 See Richie, *Faust's Metropolis* pp. 616ff. And in even more detail, with little horror spared, Anthony Beevor, *Berlin: The Downfall* pp. 406ff. (Chapter 27, *Vae Victis!*).

5 Quoted in Frank, *Walter Ulbricht* p. 193. And for the details of Ulbricht's work with Galadshev and Serov.

6 Figures in Mike Dennis, *The Rise and Fall of the German Democratic Republic* 1945–1990 p. 41.

7 Wolfgang Leonhard, *Child of the Revolution* p. 373.

8 Berzarin was made a posthumous honorary citizen of East Berlin in 1965. After 1989 he was not accepted as an honorary citizen of the united city, but after the 'Red-Red' coalition took power in Berlin a successful campaign was mounted to have the honour restored.

9 Clay Large, *Berlin: A Modern History*, as above pp. 379f.

10 Leonhard, *Child of the Revolution* pp. 396f.

11 Ulbricht's instructions taken from Leonhard, *Child of the Revolution* (German title: *Die Revolution entläßt ihre Kinder*) pp. 379f.

12 Cf. Tony Judt, *Post-War: A History of Europe since* 1945 p. 131 and again cited by Leonhard to his interviewer in *Der Spiegel* 16/2005 as above, where he also describes the early days of the Ulbricht Group.

13 Richie, *Faust's Metropolis* p. 626 and see also Ann and John Tusa, *The Berlin Blockade* p. 30.

14 Osip Mandelstam, 'We Live, Not Feeling' (1934) in Albert C. Todd and Max Hayward (eds.), *Twentieth Century Russian Poetry*.

15 General Lucius D. Clay, *Decision in Germany* p. 15.

16 Cited in Richie, *Faust's Metropolis* p. 632.

17 George Clare, *Berlin Days* 1946–47 p. 6.

18 Clare, *Berlin Days* p. 16.

19 Ibid. p. 21.

20 See the frank appraisal of this more or less obstructive position by a quasi-official French source in *Vive Berlin!/Ein Ort deutsch-französischer Geschichte* 1945–2003 /Un lieu d'histoire franco-allemande 1945–2003/A Focal Point of German-French History 1945–2003 (a Publication of the Allied Museum) pp. 49ff.

21 Frank, *Walter Ulbricht* pp. 212f. And for the 'block' plan.

22 Ibid. pp. 208f.

23 See Judt, *Postwar* p. 131. And, for the 'Austrian danger' (*Gefahr Österrreich*), Frank, *Walter Ulbricht* p. 213.

24 Douglas Botting, *In the Ruins of the Reich* p. 118.

25 Clay Large, *Berlin: A Modern History* p. 390.

26 Quoted in Richie, *Faust's Metropolis* p. 637.

27 Cf. Clay Large, *Berlin: A Modern History* pp. 391ff.

28 See Dennis, *The Rise and Fall of the German Democratic Republic* pp. 37f.

29 Richie, *Faust's Metropolis* p. 670.

30 Clare, *Berlin Days* p. 177.

4 Blockade

1 Claus Leggewie, *Die ehemalige Zukunft* in *Ein Land Genannt die DDR* ed. Ulrich Plenzdorf and Rüdiger Dammann p. 42.

2 Dennis, *The Rise and Fall of the German Democratic Republic* p. 45.

3 See Ann and John Tusa, *The Berlin Blockade* pp. 105ff.

4 Ibid. p. 144.

5 Richie, *Faust's Metropolis* p. 667 and, for an even more colourful description, Clare, *Berlin Days* p. 185.

6 Lt.-General William Tunner, *Over the Hump* p. 161.
7 Tusa, *The Berlin Blockade* p. 222. And for Reuter's speech.

5 'Dissolve the People and Elect Another'

1 Tusa, *The Berlin Blockade* pp. 360ff. and for the following.
2 Dennis, *Rise and Fall of the German Democratic Republic* p. 46 for Stalin's manoeuvres.
3 See Carolyn Eisenberg, *Drawing the Line* passim. But pp. 495ff. contain the bulk of Professor Eisenberg's argument that the Anglo-Americans were responsible for the division of Germany. Her book provides a fascinating document-based tour of the maze of betrayal, misunderstanding and power-political jiggery-pokery that was Germany between 1945 and 1949 and contains many valuable insights. It is clear that the Americans on the spot, including Governor Clay, were keen on creating a revived, capitalist Germany on the American model and willing from an uncomfortably early stage to push for it at all costs, including permanent division of the country. The problem lies in her narrowly focused, almost myopic portrayal of the Soviets as the justly aggrieved party. There is disturbingly little detailed reference to persistent Soviet bad faith. She does not pull back except in a rather perfunctory way to look at the brutal and repressive Soviet occupation policy in Germany itself and in newly 'liberated' Eastern and South-Eastern Europe as the other, equally important factor in influencing the Allies' move away from full implementation of the (in any case far from unambiguous) Potsdam Accords.
4 See Judt, *Postwar* p. 151.
5 For a summary of this see Peter Joachim Lapp, *Ulbrichts Helfer* pp. 1f.
6 Judt, *Postwar* pp. 152f.
7 See Claus Christian Malzahn, *Deutschland, Deutschland: Kurze Geschichte einer geteilten Nation* p. 83. And for the quote from the Adenauer letter from 1946.
8 Ibid. p. 85.
9 Vladislav Zubok and Constantine Pleshakov, *Inside the Kremlin's Cold War: From Stalin to Khrushchev* p. 159.
10 Diederich, *Die Grenzpolizei der SBZ/DDR* p. 203.
11 For this and the new leadership's back-flip after Stalin's death see Hope M. Harrison, *Driving the Soviets up the Wall* pp. 19ff.
12 Ibid. p. 34.
13 See Werner Koop, *Der 17. Juni 1953: Legende und Wirklichkeit* p. 41.
14 Ibid. p. 62.
15 Ibid. pp. 28f.
16 Ibid. p. 29. And for the following regarding the East German reaction.
17 Ibid. p. 34.
18 Malzahn, *Deutschland, Deutschland* p. 91.
19 See Koop, *Der 17. Juni 1953* pp. 145ff for a chronology of the East Berlin events. The saga of the government loudspeaker van appears in Malzahn, *Deutschland, Deutschland* p. 93.
20 Koop, *Der 17. Juni 1953* pp. 148f. And for the following, based on Koop's reading of *Stasi* and KVP reports for the day.
21 Dennis, *The Rise and Fall of the German Democratic Republic* pp. 66ff. For a detailed description of the Berlin part of the revolt and its suppression see also Richie, *Faust's Metropolis* pp. 684ff.
22 Dennis, *The Rise and Fall of the German Democratic Republic* pp. 67f.
23 Harrison, *Driving the Soviets up the Wall* pp. 35f.
24 'I've never seen such an idiot in my life': Beria quoted in Frank, *Walter Ulbricht* p. 251 (preceding section headed *Krisenjahre*).

25 Harrison, *Driving the Soviets up the Wall* pp. 39f. and Dennis, *The Rise and Fall of the German Democratic Republic* pp. 71f.
26 Harrison, *Driving the Soviets up the Wall* p. 42.

6 *The Crown Princes*

1   Pötzl, *Erich Honecker* pp. 43f.
2   Ibid. p. 40.
3   See Peter Merseburger, *Willy Brandt 1913–1992* pp. 18ff.
4   Ibid. pp. 122ff.
5   Quoted Ibid. p. 263.
6   See Dennis, *The Rise and Fall of the German Democratic Republic* p. 85.
7   See William Taubman, *Khrushchev: The Man and his Era* p. 331.
8   Taubman, *Khrushchev* p. 391. And for the press conference.
9   Cited ibid. p. 399.
10 Vladislav M. Zubok, *Khrushchev and the Berlin Crisis 1958–1962* Woodrow Wilson International Centre for Scholars Cold War International History Project, Working Paper no. 6 p. 13.
11 See Paul Bergner, *Die Waldsiedlung: Ein Sachbuch über 'Wandlitz'* pp. 16f. And for the following details of the surveying and acquisition of the building land.
12 Quoted in Bergner, *Die Waldsiedlung* p. 38 from Vera Oelschlegel's autobiography, *Wenn das meine Mutter wüßt*.
13 See Hans Halter, 'Ick fühl mir wie im Krankenhaus' in *Der Spiegel* 47/1999, 22 November 1999.
14 See Bergner, *Die Waldsiedlung* pp. 161ff.
15 For the details about the F-Club and the role of the settlement employees see Thomas Grimm, *Das Politbüro Privat: Ulbricht, Honecker, Mielke & Co. aus der Sicht ihrer Angestellten* p. 10. See also Halter, 'Ick fühl mir . . .' in *Der Spiegel* 47/1999 as above.
16 Ibid. p. 22.
17 Ibid. p. 11.
18 Ibid. p. 10.
19 Halter, 'Ick fühl mir . . .' in *Der Spiegel* 47/1999 as above.
20 See Bergner's remarks in *Die Waldsiedlung* p. 53: 'Despite an intensive search I found not a single statement from a former inhabitant of the forest settlement that he had liked living there or had moved there willingly or at least "without inner resistance". The terrible thing is that these depictions of the situation seem relatively believable.'
21 Grimm, *Das Politbüro Privat* p. 161 for the account by Ulbricht's cook, Helmut Bäuml.
22 Author's interview with Günter Schabowski, Berlin, 10 August 2005.
23 Bergner, *Die Waldsiedlung* p. 6.

7 *Wag the Dog*

1   Robert F. Dallek, *An Unfinished Life: John F. Kennedy* pp. 188ff.
2   For JFK's relative unpopularity among the Democratic Party's liberal establishment see ibid. p. 232.
3   Ibid. p. 177.
4   See SAPMO-BArch 4182/1.323 (Nachlass Ulbricht) MF 2 Memo 15.12.1960 from Gerhard Kegel, Ulbricht's senior foreign-policy adviser, on the influence of the Ford Motor Co., and the

lengthy report on the supposedly deteriorating US political and economic situation, including the influence of big business, 10.1.1961 from Deputy Foreign Minister Otto Winzer.

5　Dallek, *Kennedy* p. 309.

6　Ibid. p. 315.

7　Taubman, *Khrushchev* p. 485. And for the conversation with Ambassador Thompson. In fact, Khrushchev's eldest son, Leonid (b. 1917), who was killed in the Second World War, was a few months younger than Kennedy. Khrushchev's eldest child, however, a girl named Yulia Nikitichna, was indeed born two years before Kennedy, in 1915.

8　See Zubok and Pleshakov, *Inside the Kremlin's Cold War* pp. 192f.

9　Ibid. p. 190.

10　Harrison, *Driving the Soviets Up the Wall* pp. 194f.

11　Dennis, *The Rise and Fall of the German Democratic Republic* p. 88.

12　See André Steiner, 'Vom Überholen eingeholt: Zur Wirtschaftskrise 1960/61 in der DDR' in *Vor dem Mauerbau: Politik und Gesellschaft in der DDR der fünfziger Jahre (Schriftenreihe der Vierteljahrshefte für Zeitgeschichte Sondernummer* 2003) Herausgegeben von Dierk Hoffmann, Michael Schwarz und Hermann Wentkner, pp. 245ff.

13　Nikita S. Khrushchev, *Khrushchev Remembers: The Glasnost Tapes* p. 169.

14　Frank, *Walter Ulbricht* p. 357.

15　Harrison, *Driving the Soviets up the Wall* p. 128.

16　For the shortcomings of Soviet rocketry in the early 1960s see Taubmann, *Khrushchev* p. 537.

17　The illicit use of rocket fuel as a social lubricant quoted in Harrison, *Driving the Soviets up the Wall* p. 129.

18　For a detailed description of his campaign see Zubok and Pleshakov, *Inside the Kremlin's Cold War* pp. 255ff.

19　Ann Tusa, *The Last Division: Berlin and the Wall* p. 218.

20　For this, the Selianinov-König meetings, and Pervukhin's doleful end-of-year report see Harrison, *Driving the Soviets up the Wall* pp. 146ff.

21　Zubok, *Khrushchev and the Berlin Wall Crisis* as above p. 19.

22　Quoted in Frank, *Walter Ulbricht* p. 343.

23　Quotation from m/s of memoir *Coca Cola schmeckt nach Berlin* by Joachim Trenkner, with his permission. Further material from interview with Joachim Trenkner, Berlin, 17 December 2004.

24　Harrison, *Driving the Soviets up the Wall* pp. 169f.

25　Ibid. p. 169. Though it should be noted that defectors do tend to 'sing for their supper'. In the 1990s Senja also claimed in front of a Washington congressional committee that American MIAs from Korea and Vietnam were used in secret Eastern Bloc medical experiments. This assertion has been viewed with a great deal of scepticism in many circles.

26　See Matthias Uhl, 'Westberlin stellt also ein großes Loch innerhalb unserer Republik dar' in *Vor dem Mauerbau (Schriftenreihe der Vierteljahrshefte für Zeitgeschichte Sondernummer 2003)* as above pp. 315f.

27　Harrison, *Driving the Soviets up the Wall* p. 170. Pervukhin's report to Foreign Minister Gromyko of 19 May 1961.

28　Taubmann, *Khrushchev* p. 499. And for the comment on Khrushchev's repetition.

29　Cited ibid. p. 495.

30　Harold Macmillan, *Pointing the Way* 1959–1961 p. 356.

31　Uhl, 'Westberlin stellt also ein großes Loch . . .' as above p. 317.

8 Operation 'Rose'

1   Dallek, *Kennedy* p. 417.
2   Ibid. p. 423. And for the account of the situation in the Oval Office while Kennedy gave his speech.
3   Richie, *Faust's Metropolis* p. 715.
4   Taubman, *Khrushchev* p. 501. And for the McCloy encounter.
5   Quoted in Harrison, *Driving the Soviets up the Wall* p. 178.
6   'In der Argumentation muss ab sofort das Wort Republikflucht verschwinden und an dessen Stelle Abwerbung, Menschenhandel, Kopfjäger usw. gesetzt werden'. Circular dated 20 July 1961 from Abteiliung Agitation beim ZK der SED in BArch Berlin SAPMO DY/30/IVA/2/ 9.02.20 MF 3.
7   See Bernd Eisenfeld and Roger Engelmann, 13.8.1961: *Mauerbau Fluchtbewegung und Machtsicherung* p. 37.
8   Quoted in Harrison, *Driving the Soviets up the Wall* pp. 178f.
9   Norman Gelb, *The Berlin Wall: Kennedy, Khrushchev and a Showdown in the Heart of Europe* p. 97.
10 Harrison, *Driving the Soviets up the Wall* pp. 185f.
11 Kvitsinsky's account quoted in *Der Spiegel* 32/2001 6 August 2001, *Die Schandmauer*.
12 Ibid. and Harrison, *Driving the Soviets up the Wall* p. 187.
13 For which Mielke was finally tried and convicted in 1993. He served two years before being released on health grounds. He died in 2000, aged ninety-two.
14 See *Wer War Wer in der DDR?* pp. 579f., which accepts the French story. For a different version, which has Mielke in Russia between 1940 and 1945 see John O. Koehler, *Stasi: The Untold Story of the East German Secret Police* pp. 33ff.
15 See Herausgegeben und eingeleitet von Matthias Uhl und Arnim Wagner, *Ulbricht, Chruschtschow und die Mauer, Eine Dokumentation (Schriftenreihe der Vierteljahrshefte für Zeitgeschichte Band 86)* p. 43.
16 Pölzl, *Erich Honecker* p. 92.
17 Uhl, 'Westberlin stellt also ein großes Loch . . .' p. 323. And for the Soviet missile exercises and the appointment of Konev pp. 324f.
18 Zubok, *Khrushchev and the Berlin Crisis* p. 28 and n84.
19 Walt W. Rostow, *The Diffusion of Power* p. 231.
20 Uhl, 'Westberlin stellt also ein großes Loch. . .' p. 318.
21 '. . . der verstärkten pioniermäßigen Ausbau der Staatsgrenze . . .' ibid. p. 323.
22 See Harrison, *Driving the Soviets up the Wall* pp. 188f.
23 See ibid. p. 194 and Uhl, 'Westberlin stellt also ein großes Loch . . .' pp. 326f. For Ulbricht's handwritten notes on the meeting see BArch Berlin SAPMO Büro Walter Ulbricht IV 30/ 3682.
24 Introduction, translation and annotation by Douglas Selvage, 'The End of the Berlin Crisis: New Evidence on the Berlin Crisis 1958–1962' in *Cold War International History Project Bulletin* 11 (Winter 1998) p. 219.
25 Zubok, *Khrushchev and the Berlin Crisis* p. 24. Report of International Department 16 March 1962. According to Andropov, Soviet loans to the GDR amounted to 6.8 billion Deutschmarks (roughly DM 400 per head of the population).
26 See Selvage's remarks in Ibid. p. 222.
27 Uhl, 'Westberlin stellt also ein großes Loch . . .' p. 319.
28 Text of speech in BArch Berlin SAPMO Büro Walter Ulbricht IV 30/3682.

29 David E. Murphy, Sergei A..Kondrashev and George Bailey, *Battleground Berlin: CIA vs KGB in the Cold War* p. 366 and for Bob Harvey's objections.

30 Ibid. also p. 366.

31 Report on Paris conference reproduced in Foreign Relations of the United States, 1961–1963, Volume XIV, Berlin Crisis, 1961–1962 pp. 281–91.

32 See *Neues Deutschland* 4 August 1961 for text of *Anordnung zur Durchführung des Magistratsbeschlusses vom 4. August 1961 über Zahlungen im demokratischen Berlin durch Personen, die in Westberlin einer Beschäftigung nachgehen.*

33 *Protokoll Nr 39/61 der außerordentlichen Sitzung des Politbüros des Zentralkomitees der SED am Montag (7.8.1961)* in BArch Berlin SAPMO DY/30/J IV 2/2A/841.

34 Klaus Wiegrefe, 'Der Schandmauer' in *Der Spiegel* 32/2001 6 August 1961.

35 Merseburger, *Willy Brandt* pp. 393f.

36 Wiegrefe, 'Der Schandmauer' as above.

37 Manfred Rexin, 'Eine Mauer durch Berlin: Erinnerungen an den August 1961' in *Deutschland-Archiv* 34 (2001) 4 pp. 645 ff.

38 Quote from Mende's memoirs in Pölzl, *Erich Honecker* p. 71. From the autumn of 1961 Mende, a leader of the expellees from Eastern Germany (he was Silesian-born), would serve as vice-chancellor and Minister for All-German Questions under the coalition between the liberal FDP and the CDU that followed the 17 September elections. More conservative and nationalistic than most of his party membership, in 1970 he resigned from the FDP and crossed right over to the CDU.

39 Statement by refugee Gerhard Diekmann (twenty-five, single, worker in a state-owned factory), made in West Berlin on 14 August 1961. *Bundesministerium für Gesamtdeutsche Fragen (Hg., Die Flucht aus der Sowjetzone und die Sperrmaßnahmen des kommunistischen Regimes vom 13. August 1961 in Berlin* p. 76.

40 Honoré M. Catudal, *Kennedy in der Mauer-Krise: Eine Fallstudie zur Entscheidungsfindung in den USA* pp. 251ff. (English version: *Kennedy and the Berlin Crisis: A Study in US Decision-Making*).

41 See Uhl and Wagner, *Ulbricht, Chruschtschow und die Mauer* as above p. 34.

42 Von Pawel's account of the meeting with Konev in Peter Wyden, *The Wall: The Inside Story of Divided Berlin* pp. 127f.

43 Lengthy extracts from the protocol of Mielke's speech to the *Stasi* leadership, 11 August 1961, in Eisenfeld and Engelmann, *Mauerbau Fluchtbewegung und Machtsicherung* pp. 47f.

44 See 'Das Wetter in Berlin 1950–1961' by Paul Schraak of the Meteorological Institute of the Free University, Berlin in *Berlinische Monatsschrift* 3/2001 p. 193, also available on www.berlinische-monatsschrift.de. In common with many other historical events that happened to occur during the summer months, the building of the Berlin Wall is commonly and sincerely – though incorrectly – recollected as taking place on 'a glorious summer's day', with the proceedings 'bathed in bright sunshine' and so on and so on.

45 Interview with Joachim Trenkner as above.

46 Account of 'party' at the Grosser Döllnsee in Wiegrefe, 'Die Schandmauer' as above. Neumann's account in Siegfried Proskop, *Poltergeist im Politbüro: Siegfried Prokop im Gespräch mit Alfred Neumann* p. 176.

47 Testimony of Helmut Bäuml regarding the weekend of the border closure in Grimm, *Das Politbüro Privat* pp. 161f.

48 Pölzl, *Erich Honecker* p. 72.

49 Ibid. pp. 72f.

50 Ibid. p. 73.

51 Ibid. p. 74.

9 Barbed-Wire Sunday

1 Interview with Rober H. Löchner for the Cold War International History Project (WIHP) 1996, starting at http://www.gwu.edu/~nsarchiv/coldwar/interviews/episode-4/lochner1.html.
2 Interview by the author with Götz Bergander, Berlin, 1 October 2004. And for the following.
3 Interview by the author with Lothar Löwe, Berlin, 29 March 2005. And for the following.
4 Nuremberg speech quoted in Merseburger, *Willy Brandt* pp. 394f.
5 Merseburger, *Willy Brandt* p. 397.
6 Copy of telegram E. Alan Lightner in Berlin to Secretary of State 10.28 a.m. 13 August 1961 Kennedy Library Boston National Security Files Box 91a.
7 Ibid.
8 Account of meeting at the *Kommandatura* drawn from Merseburger, *Willy Brandt* pp. 397f. and author's interview with Egon Bahr as above.
9 Interview by the author with Wolfgang Baldin, Berlin, 11 August 2005.
10 *Abt. Parteiorgane, Kurzinformation Nr. 5 über die ersten Maßnahmen und Stimmen zur Durch-führung des Ministerratsbeschlusses vom 12.8.1961* in BArch Berlin SAPMO DY/30/IV/2.028 Bd 43 Bl.154.
11 *Kurzinformation Nr. 5* as above.
12 *Information über die Wirksamkeit der Arbeit des Gegners unter der Jugend* dated 22.8.1961 in BArch Berlin SAPMO DY/30/IV/2.028 Bd 43 Bl. 228–30.
13 Account here and following from the description by Till Meyer in his autobiography, *Staatsfeind* (Enemy of the State), reprinted in the newspaper *Junge Welt*, 11 August 2001 as '13. August 1961: Treptower Park, Endstation'. Meyer later became a violent left-wing extremist and was jailed for his involvement in the 'Movement of the 2nd June' armed terrorist group. Among other things, the group carried out the kidnap in 1975 of the West Berlin conservative politican Peter Lorenz, who was exchanged for several imprisoned leftists. Meyer was later exposed as having been an agent of the *Stasi* throughout most of the 1970s and 1980s. He is now a freelance journalist in Berlin.
14 Interview by the author with Klaus Schulz-Ladegast, Berlin, 16 August 2005.

10 Prisoners

1 The church itself was bricked up and used as a storage room and as a kennel for the trained guard dogs that patrolled the border zone. It was finally dynamited in 1985 and the area where it had stood levelled. The few remnants left – part of the altar, the bell, parts of the metal spire, etc. were incorporated into the 'chapel of reconciliation' built on the site and consecrated in 2000. This chapel is now used for the service that precedes the annual laying of wreaths at the Bernauer Strasse Wall Memorial each 13 August.
2 Johannes Wendland, 'Mit dem Feldstecher bei der Beerdigung der Oma' in *Das Parlament* Nr 29–30 12.07.2004.
3 Opfer-der-Mauer-Liste, Polizeipräsidium Berlin.
4 Ibid.
5 Werner Filmer/Herbert Schwan, *Opfer der Mauer* p. 86f.
6 See Curtis Cate, *The Ides of August: The Berlin Wall Crisis of* 1961 pp. 385f.
7 *Neues Deutschland, Organ des Zentralkomitees der SED*, 14 August 1961.
8 Interview by the author with Günter Schabowski, Berlin, 10 August 2005.
9 'Sie dürfen nicht an Schlusselfunktionen und besonders lebenswichtigen Anlagen in den

Betrieben beschaftigt werden.' Circular from Stoph among *Sicherheitsmaßnahmen der DDR vom 13.8.1961* in BArch SOPMA DC/20/4333.

10 MfS report 29 September 1961 in http://www.bstu.de/ddr/aigist61/seiten/agitations-well2.htm.

11 Circular from Stoph regarding 'West-Studenten' from BArch SOPMA dc/20/4333 as above. Also for the rules regarding school pupils.

12 Survey for Abteilung Agitation de ZK der SED *Argumente der Intelligenz – Stichtag* 20.9.61 and memorandum *Zu den Sicherungsmassnahmen der DDR* in report dated 8.9.61, both in BArch SAPMO DY30/1V 2/9.02 6.

13 Report to *Büro des Politbüros, Abteilung Parteiorgane* 21.8.1961 in BArch SAPMO DY/30/IV 2/2.01.

14 Ibid.

15 Dennis, *The Rise and Fall of the German Democratic Republic* 1945–1990 p. 102.

16 Information about the pre-GDR history of the industrial area from *Der verbotene Stadtteil: Stasi-Sperrbezirk Berlin-Hohenschönhausen* by Peter Erle and Hubertus Knabe pp. 22ff.

17 Klaus Schulz-Ladegast's experience in prison from interview by the author as above.

18 Erle and Knabe, *Der verbotene Stadtteil: Stasi-Sperrbezirk Berlin-Hohenschönhausen* p. 49ff.

19 Figures from *SED Bezirksleitung Groß-Berlin, Abteilung für Sicherheitsfragen* 10.10.1961 in BArch SAPMO DY30 IV 2/12 80.

20 Ibid. for reports on the clearing of apartment blocks close to the border.

11 'That Bastard from Berlin'

1 John C. Ausland, 'When They Split Berlin, Washington Was Asleep' in: *International Herald Tribune* 14 November 1989. Also Cate, *The Ides of August* pp. 305f.

2 Information on the poor state of President Kennedy's health in August 1961 from: Dallek, *Kennedy* pp. 471ff.

3 See Cate, *The Ides of August* pp. 330ff. Also for the details of Clifton's recall of Kennedy from the planned picnic cruise, based on Mr Cate's interview with Clifton.

4 Cable from the Situation Room to Mr Salinger, Hyannisport WH536–61 13 August 1961 in Kennedy Library Boston NSF Box 91a. Berlin Cables. Separate accompanying cable directly from Rostow from same archival source. The file also contains the original CIA report informing Washington of the sealing of the border.

5 Cited in Richard Reeves, *President Kennedy: Profile of Power* p. 325.

6 Cyril Buffet, 'De Gaulle, the Bomb and Berlin: How to use a Political Weapon' in: ed. John Gearson and Kori Schake, *The Berlin Wall Crisis: Perspectives on Cold War Alliances* p. 87.

7 Minute by Macmillan in response to Ministry of Defence memorandum 23 June 1961 in BNA Kew PREM 11/3348. 'Though,' he added, 'of course it would not be any comfort in being blown up to know one was bankrupt'.

8 Note by Harold Macmillan scribbled on estimates for potential Berlin airlift 13 July 1961 in BNA Kew PREM 11/3348.

9 Harold Watkinson to Harold Macmillan 12 September 1961 with handwritten annotation in BNA Kew PREM 11/3351.

10 Buffet, 'De Gaulle, the Bomb and Berlin' in *The Berlin Wall Crisis* as above p. 86.

11 See *Vive Berlin! Ein Ort deutsch-französischer Geschichte 1945–2003/Un lieu d'histoire franco-allemande 1945–2003/A Focal Point of German-French History 1945–2003*, a publication of the Allied Museum Commemorating the 40th Anniversary of the German-French Friendship Treaty 2003, p. 85.

12 Most frequently quoted original French version: 'J'aime tellement l'Allemagne que je préfère qu'il y en ait deux'. English attribution by the Conservative minister, John Biffen MP, in the House of Commons on 11 February 1989 in Hansard for that date, column 520.

13 Memorandum from WWR for the President: 'A *High Noon* Stance on Berlin' 22 July 1961 in Kennedy Library Boston NSF Box 82 Ger. As for the following.

14 See Christopher Winkler, 'Between Conflict and Gentleman's Agreement: the Military Liaison Missions of the Western Allies in Potsdam' in *Parallel History Project on NATO and the Warsaw Pact* at http://www.isn.ethz.ch/php/documents/collection_mlm/texts/intro_winkler_eng.htm.

15 Details from: *Mission erfüllt/Mission Accomplished/Mission Accompli: The Military Liaison Missions of the Western Forces in Potsdam from 1946 to 1990* (a publication of the Allied Museum, Berlin 2004) p. 27.

16 See Erler and Knabe *Der verbotene Stadtteil* as above pp. 41f., which includes a *Stasi* photograph of a British Military Mission (BRIXMIS) vehicle on the edge of the walled security area.

17 Cable No. 274 Berlin Situation Report August 13, 1800 hours. 'Situation is quiet . . .' in BNA Kew PREM 11/3349.

18 Cate, *the Ides of August* pp. 322f.

19 Ibid. p. 320.

20 Ausland, 'When They Split Berlin' in *International Herald Tribune* as above.

21 Interview with Robert H. Lochner for the Cold War History Project 1996 as above. And for his comments about Murrow's phone call to America.

22 Cited in: Peter Wyden, *Wall: The Story of Divided Berlin* p. 219. And for Murrow's call to Wilson.

23 We cannot know the precise content of this call. Dallek in *Kennedy* p. 426 has Murrow later cabling Washington to the effect that the star broadcaster's conversations with West Berlin's movers and shakers had indicated a degree of demoralisation that 'can and should be corrected'. Dallek continues: 'The absence of any "sharp and definite follow-up" had produced a "letdown" that amounted to a "crisis of confidence".'

24 Details of Brandt's speech to the West Berlin *Abgeordnetenhaus* of 13 August 1961 and comments in: Merseburger, *Willy Brandt* pp. 398f. For the entire text (in German) and protocols of the special session of the *Abgeordnetenhaus* see also the official government Berlin Wall website http://www.chronik-der- mauer.de/index.php/chronik/1961/August/13/.

25 Quote from Dallek in *Kennedy* p. 426.

26 Kenneth P. O'Donnell and David F. Powers with Joe McCarthy, *Johnny, We Hardly Knew Ye: Memories of John Fitzgerald Kennedy* p. 343.

27 Sir C. Steel to Foreign Office 5.00 p.m. 14 August 1961 in BNA Kew PREM 11/3349. And for the following opinion of Brentano's views.

28 Wyden, *Wall* p. 219. But Murrow's direct influence is not mentioned by any German sources.

29 Merseburger, *Willy Brandt* pp. 408f.

30 Interview with Robert H. Lochner for the Cold War History Project 1996 as above.

31 Minutes of the Steering Group on Berlin 15 August 1961 [document dated 16 August], in Kennedy Library Boston NSF Box 88. And for the following quotes.

32 Max Frankel in *New York Times* 16 August 1961, 'Reds Held Losing: Washington to Stress East German Move Confesses Failure'.

33 Cable from Lightner in Berlin to Secretary of State 15 August 1961 in Kennedy Library Boston NSF Box 91 a cables 8/61.

34 For Brandt's letter, his consequent speech at the *Rathaus*, and the consequences, see Merseburg, *Willy Brandt* pp. 400f. Full text (in German) available at the official website of the Wall Memorial Museum in Berlin: http://www.chronik-der- mauer.de/index.php/chronik/1961/August/16/.

35 Merseburger, *Willy Brandt* p. 402. And for the roles of Murrow and Lightner in the affair.

36 Account of Berlin Steering Group meeting 17 August 1961 in Kennedy Library Boston NSF Box 88. Present: the President; the Secretary of State and Mr Kohler; the Secretary of Defense, Mr Gilpatric (Deputy Secretary of Defense) and General Lemnitzer (Chairman, Joint Chiefs of Staff); the Attorney-General (R.F. Kennedy); Mr Dulles and Mr Murphy (CIA); Mr Wilson (USIA); General Taylor, Mr Bundy, and Mr Owen.

37 See the account 'Despatched to Defend: Welcomed by Citizens' in the US army's weekly Berlin newspaper *Berlin Observer* 25 August 1961.

38 Norstad to Lemnitzer 18 August 1961 in Foreign Relations, 1961–1963, Volume XIV, Berlin Crisis, 1961–1962 and online at http://www.state.gov/r/pa/ho/frus/kennedyjf/xiv/15862.htm Doc. 119.

39 Central Intelligence Agency, *Studies in Intelligence*, vol. 33, No. 4, Winter 1989 pp. 79f.

40 Dallek, *Kennedy* p. 427.

41 Cate, *The Ides of August* p. 402.

12 Wall Games

1   See Hagen Koch, *Meine Flucht nach Vorn* privately published on CD pp. 90ff. Herr Koch claims to have been blackmailed by a local *Stasi* officer into joining, having originally applied to join the East German navy. There is, however, no question but that he was a convinced and idealistic Communist at that time.

2   Ibid. pp. 132f.

3   Conrad Schumann, interview with CNN for Cold War series episode 9, see http://www.cnn.com/SPECIALS/cold.war/episodes/09/script.html.

4   Leibing cited in 'Ein Held, der keiner sein wollte' by Kai Guleikoff in *Junge Freiheit* 14 August 1998. See also the interview with Leibing in 'Na, springt der?' by Moritz Schwartz in *Junge Freiheit* 10 August 2001.

5   Now once more Mohrenstrasse.

6   Cate, *The Ides of August* p. 404 for the composition of the party.

7   Wyden, *The Wall* pp. 227f. Wyden also, however, cites Clay's later oral history depositions, in which the general admitted that almost a week after 13 August it was probably already too late for such a thing. And, in fact, if the East Germans had simply built their wall a few blocks back from the actual border, it would have been even harder to do anything about it without 'invading' East Berlin.

8   For the personal details of the Bonn meeting with Adenauer see Cate, *The Ides of August* pp. 407f. and Johnson's own account to the President on his return, available in *Foreign Affairs of the United States* Vol. XIV document 120, and also the Memorandum to McGeorge Bundy from Jay Gildner of the USIA 21 August 1961 in Kennedy Library, Boston NSF Box 74a Germany.

9   Memorandum from Jay Gildner for McGeorge Bundy as above.

10 Cate *The Ides of August* p. 412.

11 Johnson's report in *Foreign Affairs of the United States* Vol. XIV as above.

12 Sir Harold Caccia to Permanent Secretary Sir Evelyn Shuckburgh of the Foreign Office 21 August 1961 in BNA Kew PREM 11/3350.

13 Memorandum from Jay Gildner as above.

14 Quoted in Merseburger, *Willy Brandt* p. 205 and for the following.

15 Account of the day's activities with Johnson based on Willy Brandt's autobiographical sketches, *Begegnungen und Einsichten: Die Jahre* 1960–1975 pp. 31ff.

16 From Col. Johns' written account of the journey to Berlin, used in Cate, *The Ides of August* pp. 417–23.

17 See the above account and also the article in the Berlin US forces' newspaper *Berlin Observer* vol. 17 No. 34 25 August 1961, '8th Division Troops Dispatched by JFK to Beef Up Bastion'.

18 Cate, *The Ides of August* p. 427.

19 Memorandum from Jay Gildner as above.

20 Cate, *The Ides of August* p. 430. And for some of the detail on Johnson's dinner party at the Hilton (now the Hotel Intercontinental) not covered in Brandt's account.

21 Brandt, *Begegnungen und Einsichten* p. 33 (he quotes the Vice-President in English, clearly from fond memory). Cate in *The Ides of August* p. 435 cites thirty-three cents. Herr Franke was not available for consultation.

22 Account of Günter Litfin's life and death based on sources including *Stasi* files in Bernd Eisenfeld and Roger Engelmann, *13.8.1961: Mauerbau Fluchtbewegung und Machtsicherung* p. 95f.

23 'Mordhetze aus der Hauptstadt' in *Neues Deutschland* 2 September 1961.

24 See Uhl and Wagner, *Ulbricht, Chruschtschow und die Mauer* as above p. 49.

25 Paul Verner to Genosse Walter Ulbricht 18.9.61 Betrifft: *Grenzdurchbruch in der Bouchéstraße (Kreis Treptow)* in BArch SAPMO DY 30 3682 Büro Ulbricht Bl. 169.

26 Ministry of the Interior report of 22 September 1961 to Central Committee of the SED Betr: *Pioniermaßnahmen an der Grenze zu Westberlin* in BArch Berlin SAPMO DY 30 IV 2/12/72 Bl. 162f.

27 *Einschätzung der Fahnenfluchten im Einsatzraum Berlin in der Zeit vom* 13.8–10.9.1961 in BArch Berlin SAPMO DY 30 IV 2/12/72 Bl. 156f.

28 See Uhl and Wagner, *Ulbricht, Chruschtschow und die Mauer* as above p. 48

29 See Yuli Kvitsinsky's memoirs, published in German as *Vor dem Sturm* p. 187.

30 Frank, *Walter Ulbricht* p. 367.

31 Only in 1982 were these regulations to take legal form in the 'Border Statute' of that year. Hitherto it was a purely administrative measure, without legislative support.

13 High Noon in the Friedrichstrasse

1 Named after Dr Walter Hallstein, State Secretary at the West German Foreign Office during the 1950s, who originated the idea of isolating the GDR in this way. Hallstein was from 1958 the first president of the European Commission and a prime mover in the creation of the European Economic Community.

2 Merseburger, *Willy Brandt* p. 408.

3 Note from P.F. de Zulueta to Prime Minister Macmillan re. meeting with Barnaby Drayson MP and Robert Jenkins MP 13 September 1961 in BNA Kew PREM 11/3364.

4 Details of the Checkpoint Charlie events on 22 October from Gerd Wilcke, '9 American M.P.'s Cross Berlin Line to Free Official' in *New York Times* 23 October 1961.

5 For American commandant General Watson's letter of protest to the Soviet commandant, Colonel Soloviev, and description of the incident see Lightner's telegram to the State Department of 23 October 1961 in Kennedy Library, Boston POF/117 SF Ger. See also Eisenfeld and Engelmann, *Mauerbau Fluchtbewegung und Machtsicherung* p. 65.

6 Telegram from Clay in Berlin to Secretary of State 24 October 1961 in Kennedy Library, Boston POF/117 SF Ger.

7 Stamped 'Rusk', State Department to embassies and military including JCS 18 October 1961 in Kennedy Library, Boston POF SF Ger 62.

8 Harrison, *Driving the Soviets up the Wall* pp. 210f., from Professor Harrison's interview with Yuli Kvitsinsky in 1992.

9 Ibid. p. 217.

10 See the report on this from the Soviet point of view in Colonel General Ivanov's message to Defence Minister Malinovsky in Moscow 25 October 1961, reprinted in Uhl and Wagner, *Ulbricht, Chruschtschow und die Mauer* Dokument 36 pp. 158f.

11 Transcript of the meeting between Watson and Soloviev ibid. Dokument 37 pp. 160ff.

12 Cate, *The Ides of August* pp. 482f. And for the following.

13 Cate, writing in the early 1980s, was not aware that the affable emissary was a CIA man. See David E. Murphy, Sergei A. Kondrashev and George Bailey, *Battleground Berlin: CIA vs KGB in the Cold War* p. 391.

14 Details of this confrontation from Sydney Gruson, 'Soviet Advance: 33 Vehicles Are Mile From Crossing 'Point Used by Americans' in *New York Times* 27 October 1961.

15 Sydney Gruson, 'US and Russians Pull Back Tanks from Berlin Line' in *New York Times* 29 October 1961.

16 Reprinted in Uhl and Wagner, *Ulbricht, Chruschtschow und die Mauer* Dokument 38 pp. 164ff.

17 Reprinted ibid. Dokument 39 pp. 166f.

18 Cate, *The Ides of August* p. 486 based on Cate's interviews with Clay and with the President's secretary, Evelyn Lincoln.

19 *Khrushchev Remembers* as above p. 507.

20 P.F. de Zulueta to Prime Minister n.d. (probably 28 October) but annotated 29 October 1961 by Macmillan in BNA Kew PREM 11/3353.

21 Lord Home to Prime Minister 27 October 1961 in BNA Kew PREM 11/3353.

22 Harrison, *Driving the Soviets up the Wall* p. 215.

23 'Document No. 2. Rough notes from a Conversation (Gromyko, Khrushchev, and Gomulka) on the International Situation, n.d. [October 1961]' introduced, translated and annotated by Douglas Selvage, CWIHP Bulletin 11 (Winter 1998) pp. 223f.

24 P.F. de Zulueta to Prime Minister 1 November 1961 in BNA Kew PREM 11/3353.

25 See Gerhard Wettig, 'Chruščëvs Berlin-Krise, Ein Forschungsbericht' in *Mitteilungen der Gemeinsamen Kommission für die Erforschung der jüngeren Geschichte der deutsch-russischen Beziehungen* p. 143.

14 Break-outs

1 Sydney Gruson, 'US and Russians Pull Back Tanks . . .' from *New York Times* 29 October 1961.

2 From CIA Dispatch 6 November 1961, 'Berlin Since 13 August (MORI 14411)' published as part of *On the Front Lines of the Cold War: Documents on the Intelligence War in Berlin 1945–1961* available from the CIA website on http://www.cia.gov/csi/books/17240/art-9.html. And see David E. Murphy, Sergei A. Kondrashev and George Bailey, *Battleground Berlin: CIA vs KGB in the Cold War* p. 386.

3 Merseburger, *Willy Brandt* pp. 430f. And for the possible involvement of Senator Lipschitz in the bomb plan.

4 See Marion Detjen, *Ein Loch in der Mauer, Die Geschichte der Fluchthilfe im geteilten Deutschland 1961–1989* pp. 99ff.

5 Details of Burkhart Veigel's escape activities based on the article 'Interview mit Fluchthelfer Burkhart Veigel: Ein Koffer voller Blanko-Pässe' available at http://www.spiegel.de/sptv/

reportage/o,1518,149670,00.html and also Veigel's own account on his personal website at http://www.fluchthilfe.de in which he also writes in some detail about various other forms of escape, including through the sewers and through one tunnel.

6 The West German news magazine *Der Spiegel*, which interviewed some of the group's leaders for a 1962 article dubbed the organisation 'Operation Travel Agency' (*Unternehmen Reisebüro*), a romantic-thrillerish sort of title which also sought to conceal the identity of its founders, who did not wish to be identified. According to Marion Detjen in her comprehensive study of the escape movement *Ein Loch in der Mauer, Die Geschichte der Fluchthilfe im geteilten Deutschland 1961–1989* (2005), this student-based organisation was much looser and less coherent than such articles claim, and was known to the initiated as the 'Girrmann Group', which is the title that will be used here.

7 Detjen, *Ein Loch in der Mauer* as above p. 103.

8 'Die Augen feucht vor Wut: DDR-Heldenkult um 25 Soldaten und Polizisten' in *Der Spiegel* 28/1991 8 July 1991. The article erroneously states that Tews was 'lifeless' when retrieved. And for the circumstances of Göring's death and secular canonisation by the East German state. See also the account in Filmer/Schwan, *Opfer der Mauer* as above p. 287. Information on Walter Tews' appearance and injuries from reports of his appearance at the trial of three former East German border guards for his attempted murder in *Die Welt* 29 May, 31 May and 10 June 2002. The accused were eventually found not guilty on grounds that no intent to murder could be established, nor could the identity of the soldier who fired the shots that hit Tews.

9 Free translation by the author of the poem in *Der Kampfruf* (The Call to Battle), weekly newspaper of the Readiness Police 1 June 1961.

10 ZK der SED Abt. Sicherheitsfragen BArch Berlin SAPMO DY 30 IV 2/12 75 Bl.264.

11 Filmer/Schwan, *Opfer der Mauer* as above p. 281.

12 Malzahn, *Deutschland, Deutschland* as above pp. 129f.

13 Detjen, *Ein Loch in der Mauer* p. 91.

14 Cf. 'Anlage zur Abschlußbericht d. Ausb. Rgt.' in ZK der SED Abt. Sicherheitsfragen BArch Berlin SAPMO 30 IV 2/12 72 Bl. 278f.

15 Report of 3.1.1962 in ZK der SED Abt. Sicherheitsfragen BArch Berlin SAPMO DY 30 IV 2/12 75.

16 Report of investigators' search of a rented room belonging to a deserter in ZK der SED Abt. Sicherheitsfragen BArch Berlin SAPMO DY 30 IV 2/12 77 Bl. 60.

17 Report, 'Bericht über die Fahnenflucht des ehemaligen Oberoffiziers für Kommandanten-dienst der 2. Grenzbrigade, Major Krajewsky' in ZK der SED Abt. Sicherheitsfragen BArch Berlin SAPMO DY 30 IV 2/12 73 Bl. 106ff.

18 'Ein dufter Kerl', see Detjen, *Ein Loch in der Mauer* p. 117.

19 See 'Grabung ins Jahr 1962' in *Der Tagesspiegel* 27 October 2004.

20 See Filmer/Schwan, *Opfer der Mauer* as above pp. 288f.

21 'Das falsche Kaliber' in *Der Spiegel* 52/1998 21 Dezember 1998.

22 The legal consequences of this incident constitute one of the stranger controversies of the post-Cold War world. See the ruling of the German Federal Constitutional Court on 30 November 2000 rejecting Müller's appeal against conviction for murder at http://www.bverfg.de/entscheidungen/rk20001130_2bvr147300.html. Müller had first been convicted of the manslaughter of Private Huhn by a district court in 1999 and sentenced to one year's imprisonment (suspended), while the following year the German Supreme Court increased the charge to that of murder, though retaining the lenient sentence. Müller's arguments of necessity and/or self defence were rejected. The constitutional court also saw no reason to overturn this latter verdict whereby 'the federal court . . . considers the life of the border soldier of greater value . . . than the right of the plaintiff to protect

himself against the threat of illegal proceedings on the part of the GDR authorities'. The controversy continues. ·

23 See material in Abt. für Sicherheitsfragen, *Parteiinformation für die Zeit der erhöhten Einsatzbereitschaft von 13.08.1962, 08.00 Ihr bis 14.08.1962, 08.00 Uhr* in BArch Berlin SAPMO DY 30 IV 2/12 73.

24 Report of the commander of the First Border Brigade (B) 17 August 1962 reproduced in Filmer/Schwan, *Opfer der Mauer* as above pp. 104ff.

25 Transcripts of Oval Office tapes in ed. Timothy Naftali, *The Presidential Recordings: John F. Kennedy: The Great Crises* Volume 1: July 30–August 1962 pp. 534f.

26 Abt. Für Scherheitsfragen, *Befehl des Kommandeurs der 1. Grenzbrigade (B) Nr 56/62* 23 August 1962 in BArch Berlin SAPMO DY 30 IV 2/12 73 Bl. 311ff.

27 See 'Hasso Herschel – Fluchthelfer und Geschäftsmann' in *Spiegel Online* http://www.spiegel.de/sptv/special/0,1518,113392,00.html.

28 For their first meeting with Herschel see Ellen Sesta, *Der Tunnel in die Freiheit. Berlin. Bernauer Straße* pp. 57f.

29 Ibid. pp. 113f.

30 Detjen, *Ein Loch in der Mauer* p. 155.

31 Ibid. p. 158.

32 Ibid. p. 260.

33 Author's interview with Klaus Schulz-Ladegast as above.

15 'Ich Bin ein Berliner'

1 Detjen, *Ein Loch in der Mauer* p. 152.

2 Ibid. pp. 196f.

3 See report from Martin Hildebrandt of the German Section of the State Department (and of the Berlin Steering Group) 24 October 1962 in NARA Washington RG 59 150/68/80/01 Box 3 General Records of the Department of State: Records of Ambassador-at-Large Llewellyn E. Thompson.

4 Walt Rostow to William Tyler (Head of the European Section of the State Department) 22 October 1962 in NARA Washington RG 59 NND 98737 General Records of the Department of State, Records Relating to Berlin and Eastern Affairs.

5 Andreas W. Daum, *Kennedy in Berlin: Politik, Kultur and Emotionen im Kalten Krieg* pp. 72f.

6 'There are many people in the world who really don't understand, or say they don't, what is the great issue between the free world and the Communist world.
Let them come to Berlin.
There are some who say – There are some who say that Communism is the wave of the future.
Let them come to Berlin.
And there are some who say, in Europe and elsewhere, we can work with the Communists.
Let them come to Berlin.
And there are even a few who say that it is true that Communism is an evil system, but it permits us to make economic progress.
Lass' sie nach Berlin kommen. Let them come to Berlin.'

7 Ibid. pp. 124ff. and for Brandt's and the diplomats' nervous reaction to President Kennedy's rhetoric.

8 On the American University Commencement Address and its importance see Dallek, *Kennedy* pp. 619ff.

9 Daum, *Kennedy in Berlin* p. 141.

10 Dallek, *John F. Kennedy, An Unfinished Life* p. 625.

11 See the erudite discussion in Daum, *Kennedy in Berlin* pp. 131f.
12 Merseburger, *Willy Brandt* pp. 436f.
13 Egon Bahr, *Zu Meiner Zeit* p. 154.
14 Figures from Dennis, *The Rise and Fall of the German Democratic Republic* p. 214.
15 Figure for the Gestapo from Richard J. Evans, *The Third Reich in Power* p. 96.
16 1958 guidelines for the *Stasi* cited in Mary Fulbrook, *Anatomy of a Dictatorship, Inside the GDR 1949–1989* p. 47.
17 Dennis, *The Rise and Fall of the German Democratic Republic* p. 120.
18 Fulbrook, *Anatomy of a Dictatorship* as above p. 144.
19 Dennis, *The Rise and Fall of the German Democratic Republic* pp. 113ff. and for a more sensational but truly chilling glimpse of the long-term effects of the abuse of hormone treatments on young female athletes see Carolin Emcke and Udo Ludwig, 'Doping: Blaue Bohnen von Dr Mabuse' in *Der Spiegel* 9/2000 28 February 2000.

16 *The Surreal Cage*

1 Interview with Joachim Trenkner as above.
2 Quoted in Richie, *Faust's Metropolis* p. 770.
3 Recalled by Götz Bergander, Steglitz resident from 1963, in interview with the author as above.
4 See Richie, *Faust's Metropolis* pp. 776f.
5 Fulbrook, *Anatomy of a Dictatorship* as above p. 81.
6 Interview with Klaus Schulze-Ladegast as above.
7 Ulrich Enzensberger, *Die Jahre der Kommune I, Berlin* 1967–1969 p. 296.
8 Richie, *Faust's Metropolis* p. 779.
9 See in general Angela Kowalczyk 'China', *Megativ und Dekadent, Ostberliner Punk-Erinnerungen*. And in particular, for the ambition of looking like a West Berlin punk, the hilarious and touching account of pulling off just such a deception p. 48.
10 Ibid. p. 1.
11 For a case study see Maud Rescheleit and Stefan Krippendorf *Der Weg ins Leben, DDR-Strafvollzug im Jugendhaus Dessau* (published by Landesbeauftragte für die Unterlagen des Staatssicherheitsdienstes der ehemaligen DDR in Sachsen-Anhalt). Fascinating and chilling insights into this sinister aspect of the East German state are also to be found at the official historical website of the Torgau *Jugendhof* Association at http://jugendwerkhof-torgau.de/ ausstellung. Another website offers a forum, information, historical links and counselling for former inmates, many of whom are still in recovery from their experience. See http:// www.jugendwerk/info.
12 Oberst (Colonel) Klaus-Dieter Braun quoted in Thomas Flemming and Hagen Koch, *Die Berliner Mauer, Geschichte eines Politischen Bauwerks* p. 59.
13 Malzahn, *Deutschland, Deutschland* p. 150.
14 See David Childs, *The GDR: Moscow's German Ally* pp. 147f.
15 Dennis, *The Rise and Fall of the German Democratic Republic* pp. 161f.
16 Figures for 1978 reproduced ibid. p. 292.
17 Georg Bönisch, '21 Tonnen Gold im Keller. Alexander Schalck-Golodkowskis Geheimimperium KoKo: Äpfel für das Volk, Orchideen und Brillanten für die Funktionäre' in *Der Spiegel* 48/1999 29 November 1999.
18 See Sebastian Knauer, 'Vom Tigerkäfig in den Wunderbus' in *Der Spiegel* 51/1999 18 December 1999.
19 Malzahn, *Deutschland, Deutschland* p. 167.

17 Endgame

1 Koehler, *Stasi* p. 145.
2 Quote from Eppelmann's interview with *Der Spiegel* 1993 in Fulbrook, *Anatomy of a Dictatorship* p. 203n.
3 See John Lewis Gaddis, *The Cold War, A New History* p. 227.
4 Pötzl, *Erich Honecker* pp. 256f.
5 See the straightforward and concise statement of the problem, with figures, in Uwe Müller, *Supergau Deutsche Einheit* pp. 47ff. They include statistics gathered by the Allies in preparation for the Potsdam Conference of July 1945.
6 Hermann Golle, cited in Müller, *Supergau Deutsche Einheit* p. 48.
7 Willy Brandt, *Erinnerungen* p. 235.
8 Pötzl, *Erich Honecker* p. 263.
9 Ibid. p. 265.
10 Ibid. p. 268.
11 Dennis, *The Rise and Fall of the German Democratic Republic* pp. 180f.
12 Pötzl, *Erich Honecker* p. 262.
13 Filmer/Schwann, *Opfer der Mauer* pp. 50ff for the story as told by Bittner's mother.
14 Ibid. p. 148.
15 Detjen, *Ein Loch in der Mauer* p. 330.
16 Filmer/Schwann, *Opfer der Mauer* pp. 58ff., 148.
17 See the website of the German government agency Bundeszentrale für Politische Bildung/ Deutschland Radio/Zentrum für Zeithistorische Forschung Potsdam 'Chronik der Mauer' for January 1989 at http://www.chronik-der-mauer. de/index.php/chronik/1989/Januar/.
18 Flemming and Koch, *Die Berliner Mauer* p. 109.
19 Richie, *Faust's Metropolis* p. 823.

18 The Wall Came Tumbling Down

1 Pötzl, *Erich Honecker* p. 305.
2 Ibid. pp. 306f.
3 Richie, *Faust's Metropolis* p. 828.
4 Pötzl, *Erich Honecker* pp 310f. And for the article in *Neues Deutschland*.
5 Dennis, *The Rise and Fall of the German Democratic Republic* pp. 264f.
6 Pötzl, *Erich Honecker* p. 313.
7 Richie, *Faust's Metropolis* pp. 832f. And for the Krenz plot. According to Richie it was a snort, but a hiss was reported by others and seems more in character. See Cordt Schnibben, 'Makkaroni mit Schinken, bitte: Wie Erich Honecker und sein *Politbüro* die Konterrevolution erlebte' in *Der Spiegel* 17/1990 23 April 1990.
8 Cited in Schnibben, 'Makkaroni mit Schinken' as above.
9 For the entire several-page order MfS, ZAIG, Nr 451/89 see Herausg. Arnim Mitter and Stefan Wolle, *'Ich liebe euch doch alle!' Befehle und Lageberichte des MfS Januar–November 1989* pp. 208ff. Translation quoted as in Fulbrook, *Anatomy of a Dictatorship* p. 254.
10 Pötzl, *Erich Honecker* pp. 323–6.
11 Richie, *Faust's Metropolis* p. 833.
12 Müller, *Supergau Deutsche Einheit* pp. 60ff. And for the following.
13 Quoted in Fulbrook, *Anatomy of a Dictatorship* p. 260.

14 Markus Wolf, with Anne McElvoy, *Man Without a Face, The Memoirs of a Spymaster* p. 325.

15 Fulbrook, *Anatomy of a Dictatorship* p. 261.

16 MfS, ZAIG, Nr 496/89 reprinted in Mitter and Wolle, '*Ich liebe euch doch alle!*' as above p. 250.

17 Julie Lutteroth, 'Ein Satz, der Geschichte schreiben wird' in *Spiegel Online* 9 November 2004 at http://www.spiegel.de.

18 For this and the following, see the minute-by-minute account in Hans-Hermann Hertle, *Chronik des Mauerfalls, Die dramatischen Ereignisse um den 9. November 1989* pp. 149f.

19 Interview with Egon Krenz available online at http://www.chronik-der-mauer.de/index.php/chronik/1989/November/9/. Also for the *Tagesthemen* extract and the announcement on *Aktuelle Kamera*.

Afterword: The Theft of Hope

1 Trenkner, *Coca Cola schmeckt nach Berlin* as above.

2 Hertle, *Chronik des Mauerfalls* pp. 252ff.

3 Judt, *Postwar* p. 639 and for the quotation from Mrs Thatcher's memoirs.

4 See Koch, *Meine Flucht nach Vorne* as above p. 262.

5 Pötzl, *Erich Honecker* p. 363. And for the following.

6 See Margarete Raabe, 'Arbeitsgemeinschaft 13. August dokumentiert 57 weitere Todesopfer an der DDR-Grenze' in *Die Welt* 13 August 2004 and http://www.chronik-der-mauer.de/index.php/opfer.

7 See BBC web news report by Rob Cameron, 'Slovaks flock to Peugeot plant' at http://news.bbc.co.uk/2/hi/business/4932112.stm.

8 Figures from Müller, *Supergau Deutsche Einheit* p. 107.

9 Ibid. p. 109.

10 See Christoph Dieckmann: 'Die schwindende Stadt: Abriss und Aufbau, Menschenflucht und Gründertrotz – in Halle ballt sich die ostdeutsche Gegenwart' in *Die Zeit* 27/2001. See also, for the same phenomenon in Saxony, Götz Hamann: 'Wie schrumpft man eine Stadt? Sachsen erlebt, was westliche Bundesländer noch vor sich haben: Verlassene Wohnungen und verfallende Viertel in fast jeder Kommune. Stadtplaner, Politiker und Bürger lernen allmählich, mit der neuen Leere umzugehen' in *Die Zeit* 45/2004.

BIBLIOGRAPHY

Books and other full-length works referred to in the text

Allied Museum, Berlin, *Mission erfüllt/Mission Accomplished/Mission Accompli: The Military Liaison Missions of the Western Forces in Potsdam from 1946 to 1990*. Berlin, 2004.

Allied Museum, Berlin, *Vive Berlin!/Ein Ort deutsch–französischer Geschichte. 1945–2003/Un lieu d'histoire franco–allemande. 1945–2003/A Focal Point of German–French History. 1945–2003*. Berlin, 2003.

Bahr, Egon. *Zu Meiner Zeit*. Munich, 1996.

Beevor, Antony. *Berlin: The Downfall*. London, 2002.

Bergner, Paul. *Die Waldsiedlung: Ein Sachbuch über 'Wandlitz.'* Berlin, 2001.

Botting, Douglas. *In the Ruins of the Reich*. London, 2005.

Brandt, Willy. *Begegnungen und Einsichten: Die Jahre 1960–1975*. Hamburg, 1976.

Brandt, Willy. *Erinnerungen*. Hamburg, 1990.

Bundesministerium für Gesamtdeutsche Fragen (Hg.), *Die Flucht aus der Sowjetzone und die Sperrmaßnahmen des kommunistischen Regimes vom 13. August 1961 in Berlin*. Bonn & Berlin, 1961.

Cate, Curtis. *The Ides of August: The Berlin Wall Crisis of 1961*. London, 1978.

Catudal, Honoré M. *Kennedy and the Berlin Wall Crisis*. Berlin, 1980.

Childs, David. *The GDR: Moscow's German Ally*. London, 1983.

Clare, George. *Berlin Days 1946–47*. London, 1989.

Clay, General Lucius D. *Decision in Germany*, New York, 1950.

Dallek, Robert F. *John F. Kennedy, An Unfinished Life*. London, 2003.

Daum, Andreas W. *Kennedy in Berlin, Politik, Kultur und Emotionen im Kalten Krieg*. Paderborn, 2003.

Dennis, Mike. *The Rise and Fall of the German Democratic Republic 1945–1990*. Harlow, 2000.

Detjen, Marion. *Ein Loch in der Mauer, Die Geschichte der Fluchthilfe im geteilten Deutschland 1961–1989*. Munich, 2005.

Diederich, Torsten. Hans Ehlert and Rüdiger Wenzke, *Handbuch der bewaffneten Organe der DDR*. Berlin, 1998.

Eisenberg, Carolyn. *Drawing the Line*. New York, 1998.

Eisenfeld Bernd, and Roger Engelmann. *13.8.1961: Mauerbau Fluchtbewegung und Machtsicherung*. Bremen, 2001.

Enzensberger, Ulrich. *Die Jahre der Kommune I, Berlin 1967–1969*. Köln, 2004.

Eley, Geoff. and James Retallack (eds). *Wilhelminism and its Legacies: German Modernities, Imperialism, and the Meanings of Reform, 1890–1930*. New York & Oxford, 2003.

Erle, Peter, und Hubertus Knabe. *Der verbotene Stadtteil: Stasi-Sperrbezirk Berlin-Hohenschönhausen*. Berlin, 2005.

Evans, Richard J. *The Third Reich in Power*. London, 2005.

Filmer, Werner, and Heribert Schwan. *Opfer der Mauer, Protokolle des Todes*. Munich, 1991.

Flemming, Thomas, and Hagen Koch. *Die Berliner Mauer, Geschichte eines Politischen Bauwerks*. Berlin-Brandenburg, 2004.

Frank, Mario. *Walter Ulbricht: Eine deutsche Biografie*. Munich, 2003.

Fulbrook, Mary. *Anatomy of a Dictatorship, Inside the GDR 1949–1989*. Oxford, 1995.

Gaddis, John Lewis. *The Cold War, A New History*. New York, 2005.

Gearson, John, and Kori Schake (eds). *The Berlin Wall Crisis: Perspectives on Cold War Alliances*. Basingstoke & New York, 2002.

Gelb, Norman. *The Berlin Wall: Kennedy, Khrushchev and a Showdown in the Heart of Europe*. New York, 1988.

Grimm, Thomas. *Das Politbüro Privat: Ulbricht, Honecker, Mielke & Co. aus der Sicht ihrer Angestellten*. Berlin, 2004.

Harrison, Hope M. *Driving the Soviets up the Wall*. Princeton & Oxford, 2003.

HELP e. V. Hilfsorganisation für die Opfer politsicher Gewalt in Europa (Hrsg.) *Das gestohlene Leben: Dokumentarerzählungen über politische Halft und Verfolgung in der DDR*. Berlin, 2004.

Hertle, Hans-Hermann. *Chronik des Mauerfalls, Die dramatischen Ereignisse um den 9. November 1989*. Berlin, 1999.

Judt, Tony. *Postwar: A History of Europe since 1945*. London, 2005.

Khrushchev, Nikita S. *Khrushchev Remembers: The Glasnost Tapes*. New York, 1990.

Koehler, John O. *Stasi: The Untold Story of the East German Secret Police*. Boulder, 2000.

Koop, Werner. *Der 17. Juni 1953: Legende und Wirklichkeit*. Berlin, 2003.

Kowalczyk, Angela. 'China', *Megativ und Dekadent, Ostberliner Punk-Erinnerungen*. Berlin, 2003.

Kwizinskij, Julij A. *Vor dem Sturm. Erinnerungen eines Diplomaten*. Berlin, 1993.

Ladd, Brian. *Ghosts of Berlin: Confronting German History in the Urban Landscape*. Chicago & London, 1997.

Lapp, Peter Joachim. *Ulbrichts Helfer*. Bonn, 2000.

Large, David Clay. *Berlin: A Modern History*. London, 2001.

Leonhard, Wolfgang. *Child of the Revolution*. Chicago, 1958.

Macdonogh, Giles. *Berlin*. London, 1997.

Macmillan, Harold. *Pointing the Way 1959–1961*. London, 1972.

Malzahn, Claus Christian. *Deutschland, Deutschland; Kurze Geschichte einer geteilten Nation*. Munich, 2005.

Merseburger, Peter. *Willy Brandt, 1913–1992*. Munich, 2004.

Mitford, Nancy. *Frederick the Great*. London, 1970.

Mitter, Arnim, and Stefan Wolle. *'Ich liebe euch doch alle!' Befehle und Lageberichte des MfS Januar–November 1989*. Berlin, 1990.

Müller-Enbergs, Helmut, Jan Wielgohs und Dieter Hoffmann (eds). *Wer war wer in der DDR? Ein biographisches Lexikon*. Berlin, 2004 (CD edition).

Müller, Uwe. *Supergau Deutsche Einheit*. Berlin, 2005.

Murphy, David E. Sergei A. Kondrashev and George Bailey, *Battleground Berlin: CIA vs KGB in the Cold War*. New Haven & London, 1997.

Naftali, Timothy (ed). *The Presidential Recordings: John F. Kennedy: The Great Crises. Volume 1: July 30–August 1962*. New York, 2001 (transcripts of Kennedy tapes also available at http://www.whitehousetapes.org/pages/trans_jfkl.htm)

O'Donnell, Kenneth P., and David F. Powers with Joe McCarthy, *Johnny, We Hardly Knew Ye: Memories of John Fitzgerald Kennedy*. Boston & Toronto, 1972.

Plenzdorf, Ulrich, and Rüdiger Dammann. (eds) *Ein Land Genannt die DDR*. Claus Leggewie, 'Die ehemalige Zukunft'. Frankfurt, 2005.

Pötzl, Norbert. *Erich Honecker: Eine deutsche Biographie*. Stuttgart & Munich, 2003.

Prokop, Siegfried. *Poltergeist im Politbüro: Siegfried Prokop im Gespräch mit Alfred Neumann*, Frankfurt, 1996.

Richie, Alexandra. *Faust's Metropolis: A History of Berlin*. London, 1999.

Rostow, Walt W. *The Diffusion of Power*. New York, 1972.

Sesta, Ellen. *Der Tunnel in die Freiheit. Berlin. Bernauer Straße*. Munich, 2001.

Steinberg, Jonathan. *Yesterday's Deterrent: Tirpitz and the Birth of the German Battle Fleet*. New York, 1965.

Taubman, William. *Khrushchev: The Man and his Era*. London, 2003.

Thatcher, Margaret. *The Downing Street Years*. London, 1995.

Todd, Albert C., and Max Hayward (eds.), *Twentieth Century Russian Poetry*. London, 1993.

Tunner, William H. *Over the Hump*. New York, 1964.

Tusa, Ann and John. *The Berlin Blockade*. London, 1988.

Tusa, Ann. *The Last Division: Berlin and the Wall*. London, 1996.

Uhl, Matthias, and Armin Wagner (eds). *Ulbricht, Chruschtschow und die Mauer, Eine Dokumentation (Schriftenreihe der Vierteljahrshefte für Zeitgeschichte Band 86)*. Munich, 2003.

Wolf, Markus, with Anne McElvoy. *Man Without a Face, The Memoirs of a Spymaster*. London, 1997.

Wyden, Peter. *The Wall: The Inside Story of Divided Berlin*. New York, 1989.

Zubok, Vladislav, and Constantine Pleshakov. *Inside the Kremlin's Cold War: From Stalin to Khrushchev*. Cambridge, Mass. & London, 2003.

Other memoirs, articles and accounts referred to in the text

Koch, Hagen. *Meine Flucht nach Vorn* (self-published CD). Berlin, 2004.

Interviews with Robert H. Lochner at http://www.gwu.edu/~nsarchiv/coldwar/interviews/episode-4/lochner1.html

Rescheleit, Maud, and Stefan Krippendorf. 'Der Weg ins Leben', *DDR-Strafvollzug im Jugendhaus Dessau* (published by Landesbeauftragte für die Unterlagen des Staatssicherheitsdienstes der ehemaligen DDR in Sachsen-Anhalt). Magdeburg, 2004.

Rexin, Manfred. 'Eine Mauer durch Berlin: Erinnerungen an den August 1961', in *Deutschland-Archiv* 34 (2001).

Selvage, Douglas (introduction, translation and annotation). 'The End of the Berlin Crisis: New Evidence on the Berlin Crisis 1958–1962', in *Cold War International History Project*, Bulletin 11 (Winter 1998).

Trenkner, Joachim. *Coca Cola schmeckt nach Berlin*. Unpublished manuscript.

Uhl, Matthias. 'Westberlin stellt also ein großes Loch innerhalb unserer Republik dar', in *Vor dem Mauerbau (Schriftenreihe der Vierteljahrshefte für Zeitgeschichte Sondernummer)*, 2003.

Wendland, Johannes. 'Mit dem Feldstecher bei der Beerdigung der Oma', in *Das Parlament*, Nr 29–30, 12.07.2001.

Zubok, Vladislav M. *Khrushchev and the Berlin Crisis 1958–1962*. Woodrow Wilson International Centre for Scholars, Cold War International History Project, Working Paper no. 6.

Herausgegeben im Auftrag der Gemeinsamen Kommission von Horst Müller und Alexandr Tschubarjan, *Mitteilungen der Gemeinsamen Kommission für die Erforschung der jüngeren Geschichte der deutsch-russischen Beziehungen Bd. 2*. Munich, 2005.

Der Spiegel, Hamburg.

New York Times.

Die Welt, Berlin.

Online sources cited

Bundeszentrale für Politische Bildung/Deutschland Radio/Zentrum für Zeithistorische Forschung Potsdam, *Chronik der Mauer* at http://www.chronik-der-mauer.de/

Burkhart Veigel, web-published account of student escape activities at http://www.fluchthilfe.de/

Other books and publications consulted

Buckley Jr., William. *The Fall of the Berlin Wall*. Hoboken, 2004.

Childs, David. *The Fall of the GDR*. Harlow, 2001.

Dokumentationszentrum Berliner Mauer, *Die Berliner Mauer Ausstellungskatalog*. Dresden, 2002.

Funder, Anna. *Stasiland*. London, 2003.

Gaddis, John Lewis. *We Now Know: Rethinking Cold War History*. Oxford, 1997.

Garthoff, Raymond L. *A Journey through the Cold War: A Memoir of Containment and Coexistence*. Washington, 2001.

Glees, Anthony. *The Stasi Files*. London, 2003.

Hartewig, Karin. *Das Auge der Partei: Fotografie und Staatssicherheit*. Berlin, 2004.

Hauswald, Harald, and Lutz Rathenow. *Ost-Berlin: Leben vor dem Mauerfall*. Berlin, 2005.

Hilton, Christopher. *The Wall: The People's Story*. Stroud, 2001.

Klausmeier, Axel, and Leo Schmidt. *Mauerreste-Mauerspuren*. Berlin/Bonn, 2004.

Kleindienst, Jürgen (ed.). *Mauer-Passagen: Grenzgänge, Fluchten und Reisen 1961–1989*. Berlin, 2004.

McNamara, Robert S. *In Retrospect: The Tragedy and Lessons of Vietnam*. New York, 1996.

Schölgen, Gregor. *Willy Brandt, Die Biographie*. Munich, 2001.

Steingart, Andrea. with foreward by Klaus Hartung. *Schaupläze Berliner Geschichte*. Berlin, 2004.

Stützle, Walther. *Kennedy und Adenauer in der Berlin-Krise*. Bonn, 1973.

Tissier, Tony le. *Berlin Then and Now*. London, 1992.

Interviews

Professor Dr Egon Bahr, Berlin, 10 August 2005.

Wolfgang Baldin, Berlin, 11 August 2005.

Götz and Regine Bergander, Berlin, 12 December 2004 and 13 August 2005.

Reinhard von Bronewski, Berlin, 13 October 2005.

Hagen Koch, Berlin, 9 August 2005.

Lothar Löwe, Berlin, 11 August 2005.

Tony le Tissier, Salisbury, United Kingdom, 13 May 2005.

Robert S. McNamara, Washington DC, 5 September 2004.

Werner Mihan, Potsdam, 13 December 2004.

Mike Rayner, telephone interview Hong Kong/Cornwall, 5 July 2005.

Gerd Roth, Berlin, 10 August 2005.

Klaus Schulz-Ladegast, Berlin, 16 August 2005.

Stuart Money, Truro, United Kingdom, 22 July 2004.

Günter Schabowski, Berlin, 8 August 2005.

Peter Schultze, Berlin, 14 August 2005.

Emil and Anne Simmel, Berlin, 16 December 2004.

Joachim Trenkner, Berlin, 17 December 2004.

Archival research

National Archives (formerly Public Record Office), Kew, United Kingdom.

National Archives and Record Service, Washington DC.

Stiftung Archiv Parteien und Massenorganisationen der DDR (SAPMO) im Bundesarchiv, Berlin, Germany.

John F. Kennedy Presidential Library, Boston.

NB: In all cases sources of individual documents are as noted and identified in the text.

INDEX